DIEGO MARADONA

ONCE UPON A TIME IN NAPLES

(2018 New Edition)

JOHN LUDDEN

JOHN LUDDEN
ALL RIGHTS RESERVED

For Matthew
My treasure of San Gennaro

In a city where the devil would have needed bodyguards, Maradona became bigger than God himself. A perfect storm.

'Our Maradona
Who Takes the Field
We Have Hallowed Thy Name
Thy Kingdom is Napoli
Lead us Not Into Disappointment
But Deliver Unto Us the Title
Amen'
                      A Naples prayer

It's five o'clock in the morning and Diego Maradona and his entourage tumble drunkenly out of a restaurant. He's celebrating after leading Napoli to a memorable victory over Juventus. Diego is dancing and singing loud in the street as the others cheer him along. Nearby, in a tenement building an angry old woman who has been awoken by the noise opens her window, leans down and tells him in no uncertain terms to shut up. 'Who the hell do you think you are' she says. 'The king of Naples?' Maradona looks up at her and begins to sing his name like the most fanatical
tifosi on the San Paolo terraces. 'I'm Maradooooona!' The old woman suddenly recognises him. She claps her hands, smiles wide and blows Diego a big, long kiss….
Welcome to Naples!

Naples today and still Diego's city

Once Upon a Time in Naples is the basis for the Diego Maradona film directed by the Oscar winning Asif Kapadia and produced by Paul Martin and James Gay Rees.

CHAPTERS

THE STORY OF THE BOOK THAT REFUSED TO DIE

INTRODUCTION
VESUVIO ERUPTS

C1: IN THE DAYS BEFORE

C2: THE CORONATION

C3: LAVATEVI

C4: BADLANDS

C5: EL PIBE DE ORO

C6: IRREVERSIBLE SUNRISE

C7: CROWNS OF THORNS

C8: LOATHING SUPREME

C9: CRISTINA

C10: MEXICAN DAZE

C11: KING OF THE WORLD

C12: CAPTAIN

C13: TOUCHING HEAVEN

C14: BELLA GIORNATA

C15: MAGICA

C16: FATTACCIO

C17: ENDGAME

C18: STATE OF GRACE

C19: ENCORE

C20: NAPLES' LAST STAND

C21: REBELLION

C22: SNAKEBITE

C23: EPITAPH

C24: RETURN OF THE KING

C25: A LIFE TRULY LIVED

FIFTY QUOTES ON DIEGO ARMANDO MARADONA

THE STORY OF THE BOOK THAT REFUSED TO DIE:

Once Upon a Time in Naples was originally published 2005, by Parrswood Press in Manchester. It was a small outfit and they were based in a converted church with their office being in the original confessional box. Looking back now maybe there was someone from a high keeping an eye on this book, for it's been an extraordinary journey and one set to reach a pinnacle this summer when the Oscar winning Director Asif Kapadia, releases his film 'MARADONA'. Originally based on Once Upon a Time in Naples. Being a huge lover of Naples, football and gangster movies, then this heady concoction of a cocaine fuelled Diego Maradona and seven years in my favourite city making Neapolitan dreams come true, whilst partying with the Camorra. Throw in a moody volcano, match-fixing, drugs, murder, corruption and a patron saint San Gennaro that comes alive twice a year to bless this crazy, if beautiful place.

How could I possibly not enjoy penning such a tale? When originally writing I envisaged the imaginary canvas of a Sergio Leone movie landscape coming alive with my words. The music I listened to throughout was also vitally important to set the mood. Mostly, the wonderful Italian composer Ennio Morricone and the one of whom it was said, 'If God ever does return to earth then he will sing like this man'. Andrea Bocelli. For me the book needed a soundtrack to die for. Bocelli's, *Conte te Partiro*, as from a crystal blue Neapolitan sky, Maradona's helicopter first flies over a packed San Paolo stadium awaiting his arrival back on 5th July 1984. Whilst in the distance Mount Vesuvio loomed large...

Once Upon a Time in Naples was my second book published. The first, four years previously was Fields of Fire: The Greatest Football Matches Ever, by Mainstream Publishing in Edinburgh. The date it went in the shops, 11th September 2001. I remember signing copies in the Manchester Printworks when news broke and we spent the rest of the day in a pub huddled with people convinced this was the end of the world. In that initial book was a chapter on Maradona and Naples which basically became expanded from 3000 words into the now new re-released version of 130,000. Back then, it was a struggle to find stuff to go in, for so little was available, even online. Whilst this time around has been more a case of what to leave out. The latest edition has 35,000 extra words and a plethora of new information and stories. A labour of love. Hopefully, I've done it real justice.

In the beginning any pipe dreams I had of giving my day job up and writing full time on release of Once Upon a Time, due to "huge popular demand and massive sales" (I wished!), swiftly vanished. Within a month of it appearing on the bookshelves and online, the publisher went bust and my books with it. Sold off to pay his debts. Two thousand copies auctioned off. I sincerely never earned a penny off it back then. Luckily, I retained author's rights, but what good was that when the book I had the rights to had disappeared into thin air? There were highlights, amongst them being The Independent's 'sports' book of the week' for three weeks on the run and keeping Stephen Gerrard off top spot was nice. He got there in the end. Also, a certain review which compared the book to my all-time favourite film, Once Upon a Time in America.

…… ''Oh no! Not another book about Diego Maradona, this time about the seven incident-packed years he spent at Naples, during which he led them to the Serie A title? Ho, hum, you might think, as I did before embarking on the first chapter, but I was soon engrossed. John Ludden has created that rarity among the sporting genre: a genuine page-turner which rates among the best sports books I've read all year. The book maintains a cracking pace throughout, with Ludden frequently infusing his tale with religious imagery, a constant, if unsubtle, reminder of the diminutive midfielder's status among his newly-discovered Neapolitan family. From the moment he arrives in Naples by helicopter "like an angel descending from heaven", Maradona came as close to a footballing deity as any player ever has. Lovingly embraced at first by all quarters of a city "where the devil would have needed a bodyguard", once he casts out a pregnant Cristina Sinagra, the locals begin to cast doubt on his true character and his previously divine mask begins to slip. But this is not an elongated tabloid romp. From the outset, Ludden builds tension and excitement into each facet of Maradona's complicated Neapolitan foray, including Napoli's unlikely surge for the Scudetto, the Italian title. In the early 1980s, Napoli's president of fourteen years, Corrado Ferlaino, was under enormous pressure to inject style, a presence, into his club which would finally allow it to challenge Italian football's northern dominance. The author's description of Naples as a dirty, poor, corrupt, grudge-bearing metropolis where gangsters have ultimate control has presumably not been sanctioned by the city's tourist board. Yet this background is important to Ludden's tale as it was, he suggests, crucial in convincing Maradona, who hailed from a similar background, to leave the sophistication of Barcelona for the toe of Italy.

Barcelona had bought the Argentine for $7.3m, but his antics and cocaine-fuelled sessions with Spanish prostitutes hastened his departure from the Nou Camp. The enjoyable story of Maradona's transfer reads like a fifteenth century dispute between Europe's city states. A fee of $13m had been agreed between the two clubs when Barcelona's president issued a further decree to one of his emissaries, telling him "Bleed Naples dry" by asking for a further $600,000. Ferlaino didn't have the cash: the money was almost wholly collected from Naples' grateful poor in a day. Maradona was understandably keen to move to Italy. The $3m he earned at Barcelona had disappeared thanks to his extravagant lifestyle, gambling, drugs and several ridiculous commercial ventures. Signing for Naples guaranteed him a $6m signing-on fee, although throughout his stay, he was "a puppet dangling on a gangster's string." While at Napoli, Maradona played perhaps the most outstanding football of his blighted career, but a diet of unremitting debauchery is not recommended for a professional athlete. The drugs sustained Maradona for as long as he could 'do the business' on the pitch; urine samples were changed or officials were 'advised' by solid-looking men in long overcoats that Maradona should not be selected for post-match drugs testing. The end came when Naples' powerbrokers had had enough. Recognising that the club could save two years' astronomic wages, in 1991, Maradona was 'allowed' to finally fail a drugs test which resulted in his immediate suspension. The game was up; he was no more than "a lousy cokehead" and he knew it.

Ludden underpins the lurid tales with a magnificent (and plausible) conspiracy theory, one which, no doubt, contributed to the book's title, a take on Sergio Leone's 1984 film, One Upon a Time in America. On this occasion, however, the mobsters win''…...

Such kind words appearing helped a little to ease my mood at what occurred. However, as the months, years passed and I started to receive regular emails off people from across the planet who were enjoying it, I started to believe something rather strange was occurring. One message off a Palestinian police officer, reading it in Gaza, whilst being shelled by Israeli helicopters during an *Intifada* was one that stuck out. Happily, he's still around and we keep in contact. Cheers Fareed!
Another in 2008, off an English doctor working deep in the Congo, who read the book to keep him sane, whilst caught in the midst of a civil war. Glad you survived Charles and that myself and Diego could help! Just two of many, from the Falklands, to a guy who has become my favourite Australian-Italian. Ciao Marco!
Then, in 2011, one Saturday night, I received an email off a guy called Paul Martin, an English film producer. Paul had picked up Once Upon a Time in Naples in LA Airport. (Please don't ask me how it got there). Being a huge Maradona and gangsters movies' fan like myself. (Paul named his little boy Henry after Henry Hill in Goodfellas)! He was interested in doing a documentary on the book. After speaking to him on the phone it became clear his passion for the book matched mine and that took some doing, I simply told him go right ahead. Do whatever to make it happen. Anyway, armed with an original copy he did just. Paul's marvellous selling line of Maradona being

"Scarface in football boots" got him through many a famous door and this is the honest truth. Nobody ever turned it down, each was just bad timing. Finally, he approached the now Oscar winning Asif Kapadia and James Gay Rees whom had recently at that time just made the wonderful and record box breaking documentary, SENNA. They loved the idea and here we are today. MARADONA is set to open this summer with 500 hours of unseen footage, of which is a book itself on how that was unearthed. I'm certain that I, we, could not be in better hands, for in a way Once Upon a Time in Naples feels as much Paul's now as mine. All going back to the Sergio Leone landscape. I've provided the words and he, Asif and James will now produce the pictures. This book, with more lives than a cat, which refused like Diego to die goes on. The re-released version is truly epic in scope. I've thrown everything and more at this. It was emotional to return but also enjoyable for though Mancunian, a part of me will forever be Neapolitan after writing Once Upon a Time in Naples. Forza Napoli, viva Diego and Cheers!

Post Note: Once Upon a Time in Naples has also been published in Italian, (Ciao Adriana), Spanish, and I'm reliably informed there's an Arabic version doing the rounds in the Middle East. It has never been boring and something tells me that will never change….

John Ludden: 28th April: 2018

The original 2005

INTRODUCTION

VESUVIO ERUPTS

ONCE UPON A TIME:
One eye opened and the volcano rumbled. It's ancient slumber stirred. In 64 AD, the mad Roman Emperor Nero travelled deep into the South of Italy to bestow upon the troublesome citizens of Naples his royal presence. In any other part of the conquered empire such a visit from the esteemed, if lunatic emperor would have been the cause of huge festivities and great excitement, but not in Naples. They hated Nero for Neapolitans were no fools, they saw through this crazy clown from Rome who claimed nonsensically to be related to the Gods. They believed in the Gods, but not him.
Nero arrived uninvited in Naples to partake in their annual music festival. He was not as the legends relate just an atrocious fiddler, but also a truly abominable singer, whose screeching voice and idiotic lyrics reduced even his most fawning admirer to fervid stares of incredulity. Indeed horror, but you dare not laugh. One smirk or look of disdain, a sword to the throat awaited. As artists go he was of the genuinely temperamental variety, verging beyond psychotic. Nero's frightful renditions of the Roman classics had to be endured through gritted teeth, terrifying false smiles and then wildly applauded at their finish. Standing ovations, tears in your eyes.
Or else?
Praetorian guards blocked all exit's, no one was allowed to leave the auditorium whilst the emperor was performing and to do so risked instant death. Though really who would have dared chance the wrath of a man whose moods swung

on any given day from murderous to totally demented. With no choice but to indulge their master's every whim, Nero's huge all-obeying entourage arranged for him to make his first public performance in Naples and much to their great annoyance, a crowd of Neapolitans quietly going about daily business were roughly rounded up by soldiers and herded off to the theatre where the emperor was performing. Once shoved inside the doors were bolted and they were barred from leaving. All eyes on the stage as Nero appeared and the cheering, albeit false towards him was loud enough to have awoken a volcano.
Then, it happened.
Midway through Nero's ear screeching performance the building began to shake violently. For several seconds panic reigned as the Neapolitans feared their volcano had finally blown it's moody top and let loose in all hell, fire and lava down upon them. Astonishingly, through the ensuing chaos, Nero carried on singing appearing totally oblivious to any danger. Come the end of a soul-destroying encore, the entire room applauded wildly and with a fleeting wave of the royal hand a beaming Nero vacated the stage. The doors were finally opened and the Neapolitan trundled out. His huge ego satisfied, the emperor returned to Rome content in the knowledge Naples had been consummately enriched by his singing. When in fact only moments after the last person had left the theatre, the roof collapsed. Elsewhere, across the city the earthquake tremor was hardly felt. That was the only building destroyed. The superstitious Neapolitans wagged their finger North at the wailing lunatic. His voice was that of a howling jackal. Could it really have been Nero that caused Vesuvio to stir, for it was only ever a fitful sleep

and would not take much? Many were convinced so and they hated him even more for it.

The emperor's ultimate ambition was to enter the singing contest at the Olympic Games. Rome's finest fulfilled his crazed ambition for glory when he triumphed amidst stage-managed, mass scenes of adoration in Greece. Victory for the emperor appeared a certainty when Nero, with wonderfully typical self-interest invented a royal-decree barring other from taking part in the competition. He also triumphed spectacularly in the chariot race when despite falling many times off his, the other competitors kindly stopped and waited until Nero had got back on and gone past them before continuing. They dared not risk overtaking him. A man who had murdered his own mother and caused the great fire of Rome to make way for his planned palatial complex. Who then seized Christians as scapegoats and had them burned alive. Well, he would surely have had no qualms about putting a few measly Olympians to the sword.

As for the people of Naples, they fumed and cursed the mad emperor for the rousing of their 'Fire Mountain'. Neapolitans knew that once stirred it was feared only a matter of time before true disaster struck. So, they waited, watched and prayed. 'Stay sleeping old friend.' Fourteen years lapsed before finally hell in all it's fury came raining down upon their heads. Shortly after 1pm, on 18th August 79AD, Vesuvio erupted spewing death and destruction on all who dwelt in her foreboding shadow. A whole side of the mountain was torn away for a length of two kilometers, lashing tongues of red fire soared violently in all directions. Billowing clouds of black ash floated upwards, stealing the daylight and obscuring the afternoon sun. The surrounding cities of Pompeii and Herculaneum disappeared beneath a torrent of boiling rocks and poisonous gases. The death toll was horrific. Naples felt the deadly wrath of Vesuvio but survived the ghastly horrors that engulfed it's tragic neighbours. Five thousand people died in Pompeii alone. Many still stand, frozen in death masks; such was the ferocity and swiftness of the untimely end. Even today the sheer shock and horror so recognisable on their faces.

Meanwhile, back in Rome, Nero had by this time made the defining career decision of committing suicide to gain an entire new audience. After being informed that the Roman Senate had finally grown weary of his insane behaviour and issued an order that he be arrested and flogged to death, the emperor decided to vacate this mortal coil to torment the next world with his unbearable singing. His dying words, 'Qualis artifex pereo.' ('What an artist the world loses in me'). These were greeted with joy and great disdain in Naples. For the Neapolitans were left in no doubt who to blame for what had happened. The Roman despot had travelled to their city uninvited, unwanted and the carnage this evoked defied belief. From that moment on their lives became forever linked with the huge brooding menace soaring above them. Invested with the knowledge that hell may return at any waking hour the people of Naples began to live for the day. For the price of a song, an eternity of impending doom now hung over those who decided to chance all on the changing moods of Vesuvio. It fell back asleep, mostly silent, occasionally disturbed from an immortal slumber, but never fully opening it's eyes. The centuries passed and the fear she might erupt was only ever a moment away. At times Vesuvio did awake as if from a fearful nightmare and the southern Peninsula would shake violently and hold it's breath, before thankfully she would again go quiet and still. Though not even the mighty volcano could have stirred the city more than the arrival on 5th July 1984, of a one Diego Armando Maradona, to begin the story of once upon a time in Naples.

CHAPTER ONE

IN THE DAYS BEFORE

Quindi iniziamo. ('So, let's start') ....
Sunday 8th October 1983. The beleaguered President of SSC Napoli, fifty-two-year old Corrado Ferlaino, bore the haunted expression of a man being forced at gunpoint to witness his own funeral. Ferlaino hailed from a famous and wealthy Neapolitan family of Calabrian origin, but it was a stone-faced President watching on in dismay as a rampant AS Roma ventured South to inflict an embarrassing 3-1 defeat on his hapless Napoli side. After a horrendous start to the season, increasing pressure grew on the President from tifosi (supporters), to stand down. Even before the game began against Roma a small plane had flown low over the San Paolo stadium dropping thousands of leaflets, telling him in no uncertain fashion to go. FERLAINO VAFFANCULO! The blind loyalty of the Napoli following meant them capable of anything. Fires were lit on the terraces as mass brawling erupted between frustrated tifosi and police. Tear gas filled the air. Naples was on fire. Here was a city where, after family, football was life. One love, SSC Napoli mattered and any thought not giving their all for the cause were considered fair game. It was a fraught looking Ferlaino who tried in vain to ignore the insults hurled in his direction. All vile, vulgar and desperate and delivered by Neapolitans determined their President would not be allowed to ignore their calls for change anymore.

Two days later, whilst playing host to a fast dwindling band of loyal journalists and close friends, Ferlaino heard them clearly when a crude, homemade bomb was thrown into his garden villa and exploded as they were having dinner. With everyone hurling for cover, he glared through a smashed window and saw two young men sat on vespers smiling back at him. One even waved before they revved up and drove off. At the same time, another device went off at the San Paolo, injuring no one, but ripping through a wall of the ticket office. Elements of the tifosi had finally snapped and begun a sustained terror campaign of threats and intimidation. The message to President Ferlaino had reached deafening proportions and one he could no longer afford to ignore. Either step aside or prove your worth to the city of your birth. Ferlaino had been at the helm of this crazy runaway train of a football club for close on fourteen years, suffering constantly the wrath of a blood clan whom claimed he cared more about a personal bank balance than the well-being of their beloved team. Accusations raged that the President had abused club finances to fund other suspicious business activities. Neapolitan deception as money was spent, borrowed or cultivated deceitfully. True or not, in the past he was able to ride the storms, for there was always another season. Another dream. Not anymore, for the fanatical hardcore of Napoli had finally lost patience. The gloves came off and the balaclavas on. Time for Corrado Ferlaino had run out and he needed to act fast. In one of his many efforts to appease the many critics the President had brought back a former popular coach Rino Marchesi to steady the ship and he ultimately saved them, albeit, by a single point from being relegated. A minor victory. Corrado Ferlaino knew this was not enough to rescue him from the mob. In the distance, somewhere out there in the breath-takingly beautiful, but also so violent bay of Naples, a gallows were being built with his weight

taken into account. This in mind something truly special was needed to regain the trust of fellow Neapolitans. So, called blood brothers who wanted his head on a platter. No discussions or trial they had simply heard enough. 'Fuck you Ferlaino. 'Fuck you.' The President had one bullet left in his gun. A messiah in football boots.
His eyes drifted South, across the ocean to Spain and Catalonia. FC Barcelona. Whispers had reached him of an extraordinary, talented young footballer who for a tall price was willing to come and save his neck. Secret, if slow negotiations had been ongoing with Barcelona officials for a while, but time was now running out. The two sides could hardly stand each other. Catalan disdain and a Neapolitan natural mistrust of those whom believed themselves superior meant most comings together between them ended with a 'fuck you' from both. It desperately needed an explosion of new vigour. To reignite the talks. A fresh face and Ferlaino had one in mind. In a last throw of the dice the President made a phone call to an old trusted friend. The only one left he felt could break the impasse. 'I need you badly Antonio. Naples needs you. What do you say?' The man agreed and with great haste set off to Barcelona, vowing to himself to return home with the great Diego Armando Maradona.

Bought for a then world record fee of $7.3 million from Argentinian champions Boca Juniors, Maradona had struggled desperately to settle at Barca, in the chic, sophisticated surroundings of the Catalan capital. The kid from the Buenos Aires back-alleys slums of Villa Fiorito, was looked down upon as a *Sudaca*, an insulting term for a dark-skinned South American. During a troubled two-year spell at Barcelona, Diego Maradona shown only brief, if illuminating scraps of his true worth as illness and injuries dogged him endlessly. A severe bout of hepatitis brought on partly by his crazed antics off the pitch hardly helped his cause, sidelining him for three months. Maradona was also deep in debt to the type of people in Barcelona who didn't accept iou's. He was the go to bank for a posse of followers and hangers-on who lived off the back of his genius. Diego picked up every bill, whether it be for food, drink, hookers or cocaine. There, in the latter lay the curse. In it's infancy maybe but a constant companion. A perfect storm was rising. The well had run dry, time had arisen for the Maradona clan to leave town and fast.

As if cursed, there was also the infamous incident when Maradona fell victim to one of the most outrageous fouls ever witnessed in Spain. On 24th September 1983, at the Nou Camp, a horrific scything lunge from behind by the aptly nicknamed Athletico Bilbao's, 'Basque Butcher', Andoni Goicoechea, meant two screws having to be inserted into his left ankle. 'I just felt the impact, heard the sound, like a piece of wood cracking,' said Maradona later. For this heinous tackle the 'Butcher' received a mere eighteen-day ban, whilst his victim was ruled out for four months and career placed in serious jeopardy. This appalling injury sadly proved the most enduring memory of Diego Maradona's dismal stay in Catalonia. As for Goicoechea, he earned everlasting notoriety as the man who so nearly crippled Maradona and finished him. To this day he keeps the boot in a glass showcase at home as a sordid reminder of his moment in the Catalan sun.

Revenge showed itself the following season in the aftermath of a Spanish cup final defeat against Goicoechea's Athletico. Come full time, the football game had ended and then the real battle began. The ball was put away and hell in all it's fire and fury descended on the neutral venue of Real Madrid's Estadio Bernabeu. The outrageous events that occurred from the last whistle onwards are now forever immersed in the disgraced annals of Spanish football. Athletico player Elizade Miguel Sola made the mistake of celebrating victory by sticking a raised two fingers salute right into Diego Maradona's face. Only then paying a painful price as an outraged Diego, never the best of losers, let fly a punch that knocked Sola to the floor, and as the Basque lay cowering, Maradona quite shamefully set about finishing him off. Cue unadulterated madness as the entire Athletico team rushed to extract revenge on the Argentinian. Led by none other than the 'Butcher' himself, Andoni Goicoechea, who for the second time in his career, lashed out brutally with the sole intention of finishing off a job he started long ago in the Nou comp. The 'Butcher' caught Maradona around the midriff with an outrageous high kick that knocked him off his feet and was the signal for footballing Armageddon in the King's cup. In an eye blink, Maradona was joined by a blazing, wild-eyed wave of red/blue Barca team-mates charging into their Bilbao counterparts, with an astonishing array of karate kicks onto opponent's chests. Flying through the air came defender Migueli, as he landed feet first on a Basque stomach. Boots and punches flew as these two bitter adversaries quite literally went mad. It was carnage!

Sat looking on grimly in the VIP box was Barca President Josep Nunez. Ashen-faced, open-mouthed, and not knowing whether to scream in horror or burst into tears as an all punching and kicking Diego Maradona led the Catalans, on yet another death defying charge upon the Basque ranks. Alongside Nunez, King Juan Carlos watched the brawl below him unfold with incredulity etched upon his face. By this time baton-wielding riot police, with their shields had ringed off the pitch area where the assailants were battling, in what appeared a genuine ploy to keep the crowd safe from the players! Sporadic fights kept bursting out as private vendettas were settled in the glaring eye of public view. Ripped shirts, bloodied face, murderous glances and players knocked unconscious. Ever since the 'Butcher' first left his calling card on Maradona this had been a scenario waiting to blow. Finally, slightly calmer heads from both sides prevailed, and as officials and security staff successfully separated the warring parties the bedlam eventually subsided. Not before all involved had dragged their club's reputations through the mire. Athletico Bilbao went up to collect their trophy, a bedraggled lot, cut and bruised, their pride smarting but now determined to rub the Catalans noses even further in the dirt. Immediately, their players raced over to where their fans were and demanded they be allowed to join them on the terraces. Soon the King's cup was being joyfully passed around by thousands of joyful Basques. Waved in the direction of the depressed Barca fans whom stood dumbstruck after what they had just witnessed. Shamefaced and disgraced in this of all places, Madrid, their most hated rival. Where no doubt in the boardroom they would be roaring with laughter at the Catalan's humiliation. President Nunez knew he had to act in ridding his club of this pestilence. No more. Maradona had to go, blessed by angels they claimed. For Nunez he had become the devil's spawn and could not stomach no more this troublemaker dragging their proud name through the mud.

It went on.
Angry Catalans came to blows with members of Maradona and his entourage in a fashionable Barcelona nightclub and to show how far the player's star had fallen, it was he and his posse whom were shown the door. The tide had inevitably turned. When disturbing news reports reached the President confirming long-held rumours of him indulging in alleged cocaine-fuelled orgies with Barcelona prostitutes, the Catalan giants let it be known privately to the Neapolitans that for the right price Maradona was theirs'. Nunez had spies watching his most valuable asset. He knew all Diego's gripes and vices and had grown to despise this foreigner and peasant entourage, whose blatant disrespect and flouting disregard for his beloved club could not be tolerated no more. Barca's motto *'Mas que un club', ('More than just a club').*
No *Sudaca* from the backstreet slums of Buenos Aires would be allowed to stain Barcelona's colours, especially when not proving value for money.
It was ironic this all occurred as Diego Maradona starred in a Spanish television advertisement for an anti-drugs campaign. Set on a beach surrounded by a crowd of fresh-faced youngsters, a grinning Diego appeared the epitome of clean living as he declared to the camera, 'Enjoy life, drugs kill.'
The incoming Barca manager Terry Venables was asked his opinion of what should be done by Nunez. Much as Venables had looked forward to working with who he considered the best player in the world, after hearing lurid tales of Maradona's debauched lifestyle the Englishman realised he would be better off rid. 'Sell him,' he declared. Diego Maradona had outstayed his welcome amongst the Catalans, for even genius has a price and when it came

with such a curse even more so. Barca's Vice-President Juan Gaspart was ordered by Nunez to begin proceedings and oversee the transfer. 'Get this fucking sonofabitch out of my club.'

Antonio Juliano arrived in Barcelona on a wing and a prayer and with a suitcase of used bank notes. A swift deal was required. Napoli's legendary General Manager and most favourite son was the man entrusted by his President to bring Maradona home to Naples. Juliano was a living legend of the city who hailed from the tough backstreets of the notorious Forcella district. During a fifteen-year career he gave all for the club and earned the enduring respect of the Napoli tifosi, whom lovingly christened him 'Totonno'. Without Juliano, it's doubtful whether the transfer of Maradona would ever have happened. President Ferlaino's last instructions to his number two and close friend on departing for Barcelona bordered more a cry for help as he implored Juliano not to return without Maradona. His was a pivotal role in clearing the way of obstacles by massaging hugely inflated Catalan egos and ensuring with Neapolitan streetwise wisdom that those whose palms needed crossing with silver were taken care of. When tempers frayed and threats raged it was Juliano who calmed the waters. 'We can do business amigos,' he would declare with a smile that could melt ice and ladies' heart from a thousand yards. Respected by one side, adored by the another, 'Totonno' earned the eternal gratitude of all Neapolitans as his diplomatic skills paved the way for a deal to be brokered. Above all this was a man who recognised and appreciated genius. Antonio Juliano understood that footballers like Diego Maradona were worth their weight in gold. Priceless. His city for so

long the poor relations to the fat cats in the North had been handed a God-given opportunity to fight back with this kid. It could not afford to be wasted. Whatever the fee it would be cheap at twice the price. For Diego moved as if no one was ever in his way. Truly special.
Then, came the bombshell from the Nou Comp. With orders from Nunez, Juan Gaspart had suddenly placed a new world record of $13 million on the bargaining table. Take or leave it? There was a back-up plan for Juliano with a private plane on stand-by ready to take him to Madrid to try and entice Huge Sanchez off Real, if Maradona could not be had. Though this was hardly going to enthrall Napoli tifosi to the extent of Diego arriving. It was tense times. Their nerves were hardly helped by Gaspart, who with an obscene arrogance considered the Neapolitans nothing more than peasants. He enjoyed watching them squirm at the huge transfer fee. Juliano informed his President of the increased price and at first Ferlaino baulked at paying such an astronomical fee. He ordered Juliano home, it was not meant to be. Such a monumental sum was simply beyond them. However, 'Totonno' refused and argued endlessly for doing so. After being harassed, harangued and ultimately convinced by his fellow Neapolitan that they were actually getting a bargain, the under-pressure President agreed reluctantly to pay the king's ransom. Juliano found himself increasingly drawn to Maradona. Both hailed from similar backgrounds of hardened poverty. A friendship swiftly bloomed and the Italian told the Argentinian that in time he would become a living God in Naples. An idol to the Napoli tifosi. For if ever a player was born to galvanise the fanatical Southern hordes into action against the footballing aristocracy of Turin and Milan it was he.

The player himself was keen to push the transfer through for his finances lay in ruins. Maradona's long-time friend and appointed business manager, twenty-six-year-old Jorge Cyterszpiler had slipped up disastrously on the numbers. They were broke with no money left in the bank and a fortune owed. Gambling and losing heavily on a series of inept, commercial enterprises had left them all but bankrupt. The $3 million earned during a two-year spell in Spain had been frittered away. Cyterszpiler's pitiable attempts to make *Maradona Productions* a viable venture had proved calamitous. This, allied to Diego's extravagant lifestyle and huge entourage of family, friends and fixers constantly taking from the well? Indeed, it had plunged such depths that Maradona was forced to borrow cash off former Barca coach, his good friend and once Argentina national manager, Cesar Menotti, to bail him out. It was only Cyterszpiler's close relationship with his boss that saved him from getting the boot. The player would earn close to $6.5 million from the transfer to Naples. Maradona could hardly afford to let such a sum go begging. Signing for the Neapolitans was a financial necessity and could not be allowed to fall through. He spoke out.
'It's best for me to leave Barcelona and do so without creating any waves or saying anything critical. I must say though, it's only because we are all civilised people that at one of the meetings with the Barcelona directors, we didn't come to blows. I know that once everyone starts to look sensibly and seriously at the situation we will come to a satisfactory agreement. Now, all I want is to start playing football for Napoli.'
Juventus had also come calling contacting Barca and Jorge Cyterszpiler but were reluctant to pay the player more than

Napoli. Cyterszpiler reported this back to his best amigo and boss. 'If you go to Juventus you will win leagues like many others, but if you go to Naples, you will be in history forever. And,' he added. 'Earn more dollars.'

During the latter stages of the negotiations President Nunez appeared to be on the verge of a change of heart. Maybe he had been a little hasty in dumping his most prized asset? Despite all, here was the finest young player of his generation. This was leaked back to the Argentinians. Sensing trouble, Maradona moved fast and changed tact informing Barca officials that he had no intentions of ever kicking a ball again in the Nou Camp and would do all in his power to make life difficult as possible for them. Diego promised to become their worst nightmare raging at a press conference, 'Why are they holding me up? It makes no sense? Not even the fans want me to stay. But if I do, I'll always be injured and will never be able to play well. Never.' To the outrage of the Barca fans, Maradona even allowed himself to be photographed in a Napoli shirt. The pressure was unyielding from the player's camp. Finally, the Catalans reluctantly caved in and waived the rights to this jagged thorn in their side. It was adios Barcelona: Napoli had their man, or so it appeared.

Even before the ink was dry on the contract Naples was celebrating the signing of Maradona. Never ones to let a good business opportunity pass them by the Neapolitans cashed in. Traders dealt in bootleg tapes of songs extolling the beauty of all things Diego. The smiling face of their new boy was stitched onto banners and flags of SSC Napoli, sold on every street corner along the Spaccanapoli. A slashing, winding, ribbon road that stabs through the

heart of the city. Corrado Ferlaino could finally afford to smile again. Sadly, as ever with all things Naples there remained a last twist. With the entire Southern Peninsula ready to begin a carnival to celebrate Diego Maradona's 'imminent signing' the Barcelona supremo Nunez made his last spiteful move. With nothing to lose he sent a dramatic message to Gaspart. 'Bleed Napoli dry.'
Knowing well how desperate the Neapolitans were to have Maradona, the Catalans went for broke. In a blatant act of gamesmanship Gaspart made contact demanding a further $600,000, or the deal was off. On being informed Corrado Ferlaino had the look of a man facing a firing squad without a blindfold. After pledging to his birth city that Maradona's signature was theirs' he now faced up to the reality Nunez had signed his death warrant. Ferlaino had been made a fool of. The President exploded in rage for clearly the Catalans had no idea who they were dealing with? Ferlaino was a man that had made his fortunes in the murky world of the Neapolitan construction business. It was not wise to treat someone like he with such blatant disrespect. An open secret but whispered only across Naples was that the Napoli boss held alleged dark links with a criminal organisation that stretched it's poisonous hold over the South and deep into the heart of the region's capital.

Ferlaino had done a pact with the Devil, the Neapolitan version of the Sicilian Mafia, the Camorra. Many who knew of such things claimed they were even more ruthless in conducting matters than their more famous Sicilian cousins. Camorra activities ranged from corruption, bribery, drug trafficking, gun running, smuggling and murder. They also took an unhealthy interest in the exploits of their local football club, for amongst the vast legions of Napoli tifosi there were many who plied an illegal trade working for the city's Godfathers. With loyalty unquestionable and ruthlessness unnerving, they were Camorra foot soldiers that dealt in blood. Ferlaino understood only too well they would not take kindly to losing out on such a wonderful talent, for rumours were strong at the time it was mob money that made up a hefty slice of the transfer fee. If the Argentinian went elsewhere someone would pay a heavy price. The Camorra did not suffer such disappointments lightly. Membership to their ungodly world could only be earned by the committing of a murder for the cause. Unlike the Mafia, which was controlled by five leading families, this was an uneasy alliance of sixty bloodthirsty clans from the region of Campania. These tended to heed and fall in line with whoever was most ruthless at any given period. Since the seventeenth century, this sinister brotherhood of crime that originated in the city's prisons secretly ruled over the poverty-stricken heartlands of the Mezzogiorno, the Italian South, and nowhere were they more prevalent than in Naples itself. Their hold over the Southern capital was like an invisible cord that strangled the life out of anything or anyone who dared to defy them. A local shopkeeper would rather hand over ten per cent of his hard-earned money to a Camorra henchman, known as a guappo, than pay taxes to a state that neither respects or does anything for him. With the Camorra, you paid protection money and were allowed to do business. In Naples, they were the absolute law, whose rules and regulations differed from the norm but had to be strictly adhered to. Perversely, they called themselves the 'Friends of the poor' but there was no Robin Hood romanticism attached to the Camorra. If any dared to cross them the consequences would be brutal, deadly and swift.

The Catalans ruse of demanding more cash, apart from infuriating Ferlaino, shocked him to the core, for there was also the fearful notion of Maradona being stolen away at the last by other interested parties. Worrying rumours which were true, had swept Naples that representatives of the hated Juventus were in the city and ready to step in, if given the slightest hint of the deal collapsing. This sent cold shivers down Ferlaino's spine, for the world would not have been a big enough place to hide if he allowed Maradona to slide into Juve's grateful arms. 'La Vecchia Signora'. The 'Old Lady' of Italian football was the epitome of hell on earth for Napoli followers. Already in Turin, was the great French playmaker Michel Platini. With the Argentinian alongside him? It could not be allowed to happen. Losing Maradona at this late stage was not an option for such a huge loss of face against Gianni Agnelli's Fiat-bankrolled giants could never be lived down. A despairing Ferlaino was on the brink. There was no more money. He had bankrolled both his and Napoli's entire future on this one deal. The consequences of it collapsing around his ears could not be contemplated. There remained one card left to play, but it resembled neither an ace nor a joker, more a shot in the dark. In total desperation and in an act totally unprecedented elsewhere, Corrado Ferlaino went for broke and appealed directly to the citizens of Naples for the extra cash. It was a dangerous ploy and one that could easily have seen him hounded out of the city. The scenario of Ferlaino being frog-marched, burning torches and pitchforks, by a Neapolitan lynch mob to the summit of Mount Vesuvio and thrown into it's abyss was real and could not be ruled out.

Luckily, for him the response to his plea for help defied belief. The word spread quickly of the President's plight. In the crumbling tenements of the Quartieri Spagnoli (Spanish Quarter), that stretched from the legendary Via Santa Lucia to the over-hanging hills of Pizzofalcone, the collections began. This decaying, winding den of intrigue and blind alleys that spilt messily downwards to the seaport was home to the true hardcore of Napoli tifosi, and a place feared by strangers and Carabinieri alike. So, named after the invading Spanish army who billeted there in the seventeenth century, it remained forever sheltered from the sunlight by the endless sheets of flapping washing lines that lay festooned across the cobbled alleys.

A world in the shade and a law apart.

In the ravaged slums of the Forcella district, a Camorra stronghold of the fearsome Giuliano clan for two decades, people gave everything they could afford and more. Across the city long queues gathered outside the Bank of Naples offices, all desperate to help. For the thought of watching Maradona in the despised black and white Juve stripes would rip open their hearts. Neapolitans rallied round. Camorra guappos' helped collect the cash. No matter how small the donation people were determined to contribute. In a place plagued by crippling unemployment and wretched crime the sheer magnitude of this generosity shocked outsiders. Such was the craving to have Diego Maradona amongst them, families went without food, women pawned their best jewellery, children sold favourite toys. The more fanatical would have sold their soul to the Devil if it meant seeing the Argentinian playing for Napoli. It had to be seen to be believed. A modern-day miracle had occurred in Naples. The begging bowls were overflowing but it still was not enough. However, in a city where tricks and deception excelled unlike no other, there remained always one twist.

To set the scene, the deadline to register the Argentinian for the forthcoming season was almost upon them. Already, President Ferlaino had delivered by person to the Italian Football Association headquarters in Milan, a letter listing the names of players Napoli had signed up. Due to all the last-minute dramas Maradona's was not amongst them. Still, Ferlaino grasped onto lingering hope that something could be done. He had an idea. To try and raise the remaining sum required and demanded by Barca, the President, through mutual friends, a Neapolitan businessman and local politician Vincenzo Scotti, made contact with Professor Ferdinando Ventriglia, the head of the Bank of Naples. Discussion were had, it was made clear to Ventriglia that tickets sales would triple if Maradona was bought and emphasied by the businessman he would be doing him personally a great favour. After such a comment Ventriglia understood what was at stake both for Naples and more importantly himself. Finally, it was agreed Napoli would be allowed extra credit by the bank to possess the necessary cash to complete the deal. Now, time was running short. On the mid-morning of 30th June, the last day of the transfer market, Ferlaino phoned Nunez telling him he had a deal. Only one thing now remained to ensure Maradona became a Napoli player. That same, late afternoon, Ferlaino returned by private plane to the Italian Football Association headquarters in Milan and convinced the night watchman to let him enter the office, where he had deposited the original document with the player's names, saying he had accidentally left some personal letters inside also. Rumours to this day, say the guard, a Napoli supporter, waived him through and Ferlaino added Maradona's name to the others. With typical Neapolitan cunning Ferlaino had refused to let such a minor problem scupper his plans. So, come the moment of the document being opened, Diego Maradona's was miraculously amongst them. On seeing this, officials were astonished, after being informed by Napoli, Diego would not be signing?

They smelt a rat but nothing could be done. The night watchman simply shrugged his shoulders and swore he saw nothing untoward. This came as no shock to all those who understood how Neapolitans excelled in making such problems disappear, for in Naples there were those whose influence touched Prime Ministers and Presidents. They were hardly going to let the petty rules of a Northern bias FA prevent them signing Diego Maradona. Not exactly a miracle you may think but a darn fine trick nonetheless.

From around 8-30 that evening, Napoli tifosi had begun gathering at all their usual sacred meeting spots across the city awaiting confirmation. Many were nervous, refusing to dare and believe Maradona was truly on his way. Finally, around ten o'clock, news began to filter through from Italian journalists in Barcelona that the deal was done and Naples simply exploded! Thousands began an exuberant, spontaneous torch-light march through the Forcella back alleys, down to the coastal area of Mergellina, facing the Castel dell'Ovo. Singing songs of their beloved Napoli, San Gennaro and now Diego Maradona. Street vendors were swiftly on the streets carrying bags of T-shirts that had already been printed for weeks. On all local radio stations the crackling, extraordinary breaking news caused those listening Neapolitans hearts to soar. It had really happened. Grazie San Gennaro. Grazie!

Late on the evening of 30th June 1984, aboard President Ferlaino's luxurious yacht moored off the beautifully lit-up island of Capri, Diego Maradona soothed Neapolitan nerves by finally putting pen to paper. Celebrating alongside Jorge Cyterszpiler, Maradona must have thought all his money problems were over, but little did he know that because his debts were so great, despite entitled to fifteen per cent of the world record fee, Maradona would never see a single Lira of it. Corrado Ferlaino welcomed his new player in typical Italian tradition by kissing him on both cheeks. Their embrace appeared to those unknowing of a father embracing his long-lost son. But, in this city, such an act held a hidden meaning.
'Don't you ever try and fuck me.'
As the champagne corks popped, Napoli tifosi prepared for the biggest parties in their history, for Diego Maradona was coming to town. Fifty-two long arduous days and nights it had taken to negotiate. Christened Operation San Gennaro by Antonio Juliano it was finally over. They had got their boy. This very special boy. In the days before there had been nothing, but sadness and despair. Now, a new era dawned.
A sweet Neapolitan moon shone bright.
In Naples, life was about to become interesting.

CHAPTER TWO

THE CORONATION

It was truly a most wonderful day for the crowning of a king. Whoever said dreams don't come true could not have been in Naples at 6.30pm, on 5th July 1984. A day now etched into the rich tapestry of Neapolitan folklore.
'L'uomo della provvidenza' ('A gift from the Gods'). Like an angel descending from heaven the helicopter carrying Diego Maradona to his new kingdom soared high above Mount Vesuvio, before swooping low over the city. On board an excited but nervous Maradona gazed down at the sprawling, winding mess of Naples that seemed to stretch forever below him. Her poverty-stricken neighborhoods dominated by Camorra family clans and street gangs, but united on this historic day to pay homage to the greatest footballer in the world. The Southern rebels had long fought a losing war against the north but now came their Che Guevara. Ferlaino had delivered them a messiah in football boots.

Three hundred years after the crucifixion of Jesus Christ, Bishop Gennaro arrived in Naples to aid Christians against their cruel persecution by Rome. Gennaro hailed from the nearby town of Benevento and came armed only with a staff carved into the shape of a holy cross. His appearance outraged the Roman Governor Timotheus, who issued an immediate decree for the Bishop's arrest. Timotheus intended to make an example to the many troublesome Neapolitan Christians who chose to worship a long-dead criminal rather than the imperial emperor of Rome. Bishop Gennaro was seized by Roman legionnaires and taken to a molten furnace that blazed away eternally at the foot of Mount Vesuvio. The order had been received from Timotheus to kill him. Forced at sword point by the Centurion in command to walk to his death in the furnace, Gennaro did so only for the flames to die down before him and go out. The shocked Romans watched on aghast: feeling afraid the Centurion sent word back to his Governor of the strange event that had occurred. An incredulous Timotheus listened to the messenger and knew he had to act fast. Rome had suffered enough the antics of these Disciples claiming to follow in the shoes of the long-dead mystical shepherd from Galilee in troubled Palestine. Such a peaceful man the stories of old say, but who even three centuries after being nailed to a cross possessed the power to strike blind fear into the heart of the greatest empire the world had ever seen.

Word had already spread like wildfire across Naples of the strange happenings at Vesuvio. A second execution was ordered, this time at the gladiator arena in Pozzuoli on the edge of the city. Thousands rushed to watch as Roman soldiers began to form a wall of steel to keep out the vast throngs who came mainly out of curiosity to catch a glimpse of the ill-fated Bishop. On Timotheus's command, lions were released into the arena. A brave Bishop Gennaro stood waiting to face a savage end in the jaws of the roaring beasts, but, to the wonder of all, a miracle again took place, and as the Romans watched on open-mouthed the lions simply lay meekly down before him. The Neapolitans cheered loud and a red-faced Timotheus seethed with anger. This was not Jerusalem; Naples lay only a short distance from Rome. As the audience pleaded for the Bishop's life the Governor decided to end this nonsense. He called for the axeman. Gennaro would be beheaded on the guillotine. Suddenly, Timotheus cried in terror, as from a clear blue sky he was struck blind by a lightning bolt. The frightened masses screamed at this divine retribution. As the Governor fell to his knees in despair, the Bishop whispered a short prayer for this Roman to be granted his sight back. Immediately, Timotheus could see again. The crowd roared for a pardon, but in a fit of rage and embarrassment he ignored their pleas and ordered the axeman to end Gennaro's life. To gasps of horror amongst the watching hordes the ghastly sentence was carried out and the axe came down. An eerie silence settled over all. Finally, satisfied, the Governor gave instructions for the arena to be cleared and the body left to rot. Later that night a gang of Neapolitans sneaked back over the walls to remove the severed head of the Bishop. An old Lady dried Gennaro's blood and filled two small vials. Little did the Romans understand what their evil deeds had done, for in killing the man they succeeded only in giving birth to his eternal legend. For it was said San Gennaro never really died, his spirit remained to watch over the city of Naples in her many hours of need. Neapolitans have always claimed their patron has saved their necks on countless occasions. His has been an arduous and thankless task.

Many years later.
'Di Miracolo in Miracolo', ('The miracle of miracles'). Twice a year in Naples Cathedral a modern-day miracle occurs. The Archbishop raises high the clotted blood of San Gennaro and prays for it to liquefy live before a hushed congregation of hundreds and a television audience of millions across Italy. It's said that if the miracle fails to occur, impending disaster will strike the region. Examples

being in 1939, World War Two broke out and in 1980, there was an earthquake in nearby Irpinia that killed 3,000 people. It's well known in Naples that you do not fuck with San Gennaro. As the ceremony reaches it's climax, nearby on a stone in Pozzuoli, where San Gennaro was beheaded, a spot of blood is said to take on a brighter hue. At such a moment the miracle is deemed to have successfully taken place and the city of Naples gives thanks and breathes a heavy sigh of relief. In moments of dire need, and there have been many over the decades for the troubled football club of SSC Napoli, their tifosi, in a last throw took to praying en masse on the terraces to their patron saint. Cries of 'San Gennaro, aiutaci tu', ('San Gennaro please help us').

This has echoed countless times across the San Paolo stadium. On a memorable summer's day in 1984, their prayers were finally answered.

Let's begin the day before the official presentation when Diego Maradona was first introduced to his new theatre stage. After spending a few hours refreshing at the Hotel Excelsior on Naples seafront, in room 223, they headed through a back entrance to a waiting fast car and travelled the short distance to a deserted San Paolo stadium. He, Jorge Cyterszpiler and his personal cameraman Juan Carlos Laburu visited in great secrecy. The only other two present to greet him were club officials watching on with huge grins pinching themselves! Not being able to resist Maradona asked for a ball and from forty yards curled a ridiculous shot of perfection into the top corner. All applauded and he celebrated as if it was the winning goal against Juventus in a packed, seething San Paolo. The smile could not be wiped off the Argentinian's face. On returning to the changing room he exclaimed to Cyterszpiler, 'Cabezon, this place reminds me of Argentinos Juniors.' The passion for Napoli had already begun to take hold. On returning to the airport to board a private plane to Rome, Maradona gazed through the window at this vast Naples metropolis, this crumbling city. He watched and smiled wide on seeing some young boys all wearing Napoli shirts of one type or another, playing football on a small pitch with poles for goalposts. Maradona knew that in just a few short hours he would become these youngster's idol. Closing his eyes, he dreamed of the days to come....

At first, just a bright speck on the Southern blue horizon, the helicopter began it's descent and closed in on the San Paolo. A cauldron of rampant hysteria. 70,000 fanatical tifosi had converged on the Stadium to welcome and worship their new messiah. Each content to be charged a thousand Liras for the privilege of watching the Argentinian superstar set foot on their hallowed turf for the first time. Many Neapolitans from Italy and across the world had partaken in what was nothing short of a religious pilgrimage to be present on this fateful day for the city of their birth. They just had to see it with their own eyes.
'Maradona is a romantic. He plays well only when he feels loved, and he has come to the right place,' said one Naples historian.
A local newspaper wrote, *'Naples did not have a mayor, houses, schools, buses, employment or sanitation, but, none of this now matters, because we have Maradona!'*
It was utter hysteria. The stress of if had been replaced by the joy that the player was now theirs'. Such had been the

passion to ensure Maradona's signing during the lengthy negotiations, tifosi had gone on hunger strike to get him. One even chained himself to the railings of the San Paolo. Napoli had actually wanted Diego since 1979, when he was at Argentinos, though Maradona's teenage self knew little about his future destination. 'The name Napoli meant no more than something Italian,' he once wrote. 'Like pizza.'

Not anymore. So, as the bay basked in the warm glow of the late evening sunshine, Naples took a huge breath and prepared to give a most heartfelt 'Ciao' to one Diego Maradona. He entered the arena from deep within the bowels of the stadium. Dressed in white T-shirt and tracksuit pants, this twenty-four-year-old with the handsome fresh-faced good looks and thick mop of black hair appeared the epitome of Neapolitan cool. Maradona in appearance so like any other native of this fair city who roared down the alleys and streets of Naples on their Vespers at death-defying speed. He was handed a Napoli scarf and placed it with tender care around his neck. Then, taking a deep breath, Diego made the sign of the cross and headed up a small stone stairway that led onto the pitch into blinding sunlight and legend.

The beginning. 'My parents were humble working folk and so full of love for us,' recalled Maradona. The ten members of his family lived in three rooms with no real bathroom or running water, except the rain that fell through the roof and he remembers, 'You could get more wetter inside than out!' Young Diego once got lost in the dark and fell into a lavatory cesspit. It was an uncle who saved him shouting, 'Diego, Diego, keep your head above the shit boy!' Maradona's earliest memories are football,

football, football. He slept with a ball hugged to his chest. As a small boy, shirtless, barefooted, he ran errands playing keepie-uppie. If there was no ball then Maradona kicked an orange, apple or anything roughly round. At his first football trial aged nine-years-old, he was so good that the coach suspected this kid was actually a short adult. A dwarf!

The word got out. After making his debut for Cebollitas, the adopted youth club of first division side Argentinos Juniors, rumours spread of a magical boy who made the ball sing. Hundreds came to watch, bewitched by fantastic tales of young Diego in action. A scout for Argentinos, Francisco Cornejo, once claimed, 'Diego must have come from another planet, such was his ability to do whatever he wanted with a football.'

Soon the touchlines at every Cebollitas match brimmed full of football scouts and supporters unable to believe their own eyes at what they were witnessing. People came from all over Buenos Aires to catch a glimpse of this extraordinary talented youngster. Even at such a tender age the people of Argentina hailed Maradona with a true religious zeal. A dash of magic dust led to the birth of a kid who with the ball at his feet waltzed with angels. At ten, Maradona entertained a full house at an Argentinos Junior home match by juggling a ball for the entire interval. When the time arrived for the second half to recommence, the entire stadium rose to it's feet applauding and chanting loud

'Que se quede, que se quede', ('Let him stay on, let him stay on').

Unable to resist, the young Diego persisted on, and to the delight of the crowd and the utter astonishment of the two teams who waited to re-start the second half, continued to provide his adoring audience with an audacious encore. He would later say, 'It felt like I touched heaven with my hands that day.' This was not so much a rising star but a blazing comet. Maradona made his professional debut at just fifteen. After scoring over a hundred goals the time came to bid a tearful adios to Argentinos as the big clubs came calling. A $1 million deal saw him join his boyhood heroes, the famed Boca Juniors, where Maradona continued to forge an ever-growing reputation. Exceptional never did him justice. The genie was not so much out the lamp but careering around Buenos Aires on a magic carpet.

Boca: formed 1905, by Italian and Irish immigrants, Boca Juniors prided themselves in being the team of the working classes. The vast majority of their followers hailed from the poor downtrodden neighbourhoods of Buenos Aires docklands. Here, the similarities with Naples were many, indeed most of their supporters were only one or two generations removed from Southern Italy. Maradona's mother was of Italian descent, whose parents risked the dangers of an unknown continent to escape the despairing poverty of early 20th century Naples to find a better life. They, also like the Neapolitans, loved nothing more than putting one over those who considered themselves their superiors. The city's other major club, River Plate, were every Boca Juniors supporter's sworn enemy from birth. The murderous rivalry between the sets of fans made the Italian North/South divide appear like two nuns bickering over a sewing needle. River Plate was seen as the choice of the upper classes, the snobbish and the bourgeois. A national institution. When the two clashed either at the home of Boca's La Bombonera, or River's El Monumental stadium, all of Argentina anticipated fireworks. The Superclasico rarely disappointed as these giants went for each other's throat with a blazing ferocity dipped in the dangerous waters of tradition and class. It was during such blood-curdling contests that Diego Maradona experienced for the first time the immeasurable hatred that such a simple game generated amongst the masses. He would endure taunts from the River crowds regarding his father's Indian heritage and the childhood of pitiful poverty spent in the wastelands of Villa Fiorito. A breeding ground for assassins, pimps, priests and footballers. Maradona excelled in such hell-hole, intimidatory atmospheres and even though the Argentinian in his years at Naples was subjected to torrents of rabid abuse at most away grounds, it hardly compared to the tribal warfare on the bloodstained terraces whenever Boca and River Plate went head to head. A huge-money transfer to Europe proved inevitable as word reached across the globe of Argentina's finest. Barcelona jumped first and paid out a world record fee for this remarkable kid who was already being hailed as heir apparent to the great Brazilian Pelé. The journey beyond the stars had begun, but already there were whispers. Some told tales of Doctor's needles, others spoke of steroids for Diego Maradona appeared simply too good to be true…

Well aware of Maradona's imminent arrival in the Southern Peninsula, the day before saw the infamous Italian paparazzi start to lay siege to Naples airport. All exits appeared to have been covered but with typical Neapolitan ingenuity, an escape plan was hatched and Diego was smuggled through the press melee before being whisked off at breakneck pace to the harbour. It had been arranged for a speedboat to take him to the nearby Isle of Capri. Even there, photographers and camera crews lay in wait, desperate to be first to capture an image or a simple sound bite of conversations with the elusive Argentinian. To help evade the chasing pack Napoli employed Diego lookalikes to put journalists off the scent. There was no shortage of them! As news filtered back to Naples that the great man had been spotted on the island a great rush of journalists hurried over on the ferry or paid local fishermen to take them the short distance. With confusion reigning Maradona went the other way as he was then sneaked back to the mainland by hydrofoil and taken to a secret location in the city, enjoying the intrigue. The scenes back on the island as hard-bitten newsmen realized they had been duped were priceless. For the moment it was all a game, cat and mouse. Sadly, it would not always remain so.

To watch Maradona as he hurtled past opponents' challenges with alarming ease was to witness the ultimate craftsman at the peak of his powers. The tools, a bewildering low sense of gravity, a spellbinding sleight of foot, unnerving balance and a power unknown for someone so diminutive in size. Diego Maradona's upper body strength in his midriff and thigh muscles gave a fearsome advantage as defenders bounced off him. Lightning pace, speed of thought and dribbling ability allowed Maradona God's granted extra second to cause havoc in opponents' penalty boxes. In South America it was known as the *'Gambetta'*, a slalom-like dribble at top speed, a talent reserved for those only truly blessed. As a child this came naturally for here was a footballer without doubt heaven sent, his miracles clear to be seen on the pitch. When on form Maradona was impossible to handle;

whether by fair means or other, he could not be brought to earth. Previously, it had been widely regarded that the two best players ever to emerge from South America were Alfredo di Stefano and Pele. However, such was the genius of Maradona, even in his early twenties he was already being hailed as better than these two great icons. For Diego Maradona, the world was his, he simply had to go out and grab it.

Wild scenes of delirium broke out on the bouncing, dancing terraces as Maradona came into view. The *'Partenopei'* Napoli's nickname is said to derive from Partenope-the name of the siren from Greek mythology who tried to lure Odysseus onto the rocks during his travels back to Ithaca. When she failed, Partenope killed herself and was said to have washed ashore near Naples. Neapolitans loved their city dearly, a proud people, and this man would be a chariot of resistance against the hated Northern powers of Turin and Milan. For a second, he appeared to stagger, as if blinded by the thousands of camera flashes exploding in his face. Swiftly he recovered to make his way towards a centre-circle covered beneath a huge flag.
'Grazie Napoli, Grazie Ferlaino'.
 Stood waiting to greet him was the Kingmaker, a beaming Corrado Ferlaino who threw both arms around the Argentinian in an all-consuming bear hug. The President listened incredulously as the crowds chanted his name. How fickle the line between love and hate? Only a short time before they would have preferred him dead. Now, at least for a while they loved him again. Maradona blew a thousand kisses to his adoring audience. Rockets blasted high into the crystal blue heavens, crackers spluttered and

spat, homemade fireworks thundered with the ferocity of an awakened Vesuvio. A song rang out.
'All the city are celebrating, our sad seasons are over. Now that we have bought Maradona, the donkey is a lion. Maradona, Maradona, Ole'.
The San Paolo lay covered in a thick, hazy mist of smoke as a city trembled in expectation. The Neapolitans' inherited trait from their ancestors for a love of explosions shone through in an astonishing display of pyrotechnics. In the wide-reaching shadows of a fading sun, Maradona disappeared amidst a raging foray of photographers and pressmen. Madness reigned on the pitch as security guards and Carabinieri, surrounded the new arrival to shelter him from hordes of over-enthusiastic well-wishers. Across Naples, the winding steeped-alleyways that housed the rebel heart of the Neapolitan tifosi lay drenched blue and white. Paint-peeled doorways and balconies strewn with washing lines were anointed in Napoli colours. There, thousands gathered to watch on televisions. Banners flown high echoed the feelings of an entire city.
'Mo che arriva Diego Armando Tutto il Mondo Sta Tremando.' ('Now that Diego arrives here, all the world is shaking with fear').
Away in the distance the noise and furore rose high from the stadium and echoed joyfully across the bay. This city, whose great beauty drew a dark contrast to it's everyday reality hailed a young man whose arrival amongst them was being heralded as the second coming of San Gennaro. Thousands of balloons drifted high into the Neapolitan sky, off in the direction of the volcano. Maradona was handed a microphone in the centre-circle and he proceeded only to induce his adoring public to even further levels of hysteria. 'Buenos sera Napolitani. Sono molto felice di

esserscon voi.' ('Good afternoon Neapolitans, I am happy to be with you').

Smiling wide, he began to juggle a football thrown to him before lashing it far and high. A huddle of ball boys began a chase for the ultimate memento. The crowd went mad! Clutching hold of the Napoli scarf around his neck Maradona set off on a lap of honour. Finally, time arrived to leave the scene and he walked back down the stairs, his legs shaking. Waiting was childhood girlfriend Claudia Villafañe. He hugged her tight and they both wept. Maradona would later be quoted 'The whole day blew my mind.' The 5th of July 1984, was nothing less than a Coronation.

On arrival from Barcelona, Diego Maradona acted out his role as wide-eyed footballer to perfection on discovering that everything was not as it should be with his new-found Neapolitan friends. Maradona knew only too well his real paymasters stayed hidden in the shadows. The smell of the streets never left those who had experienced it's realities. During the press conference where he sat in front of a crammed auditorium alongside Cyterszpiler, Corrado Ferlaino and an interpreter, all appeared to be going to perfection.

An emotional Diego was speaking clearly from the heart when he declared, 'I want to become the idol of the poor children of Naples, because they are like I was when I lived in Buenos Aires.' Then, an explosion from the press ranks! The French journalist Alain Chaillou went for broke. 'Are you aware that a substantial amount of your transfer fee has been funded by the Camorra?' A shocked audience was reduced to a momentary silence when the foolhardy, brave or just plain stupid Chaillou handed Maradona this live grenade.

Suddenly, all hell let loose.
Before the Argentinian had a chance to answer through a worried-looking interpreter, bedlam erupted. Ferlaino hurled a pile of papers in the shocked Frenchman's direction and demanded an instant apology for the slur upon his city. As he suffered the outraged President's wrath, Chaillou suddenly found himself ripped from his seat and escorted out of the room by two burly Napoli security guards. They gently informed him that it would be wise to leave Naples; such was the disrespect his question had caused. The Frenchman did not need to be told twice and was soon on the way home to France.

Diego Maradona, this young man born and raised in a Buenos Aires slum, skills perfected on the ramshackle-dustbowl, Villa Fiorito football pitches. Who had been granted by God a gift so rare and wonderful, was offered the keys to a kingdom. That it's crown held pointed thorns seemed irrelevant on that day of wine and roses. Sadly, in time they would prick. For seven, memorable, crazy years, Neapolitans would indulge themselves in Maradona's sorcery as he led their quest for that elusive Scudetto and in doing so ignite a Southern revival and scare the living daylights out of the North.
So many moments of wonder, head down with the ball glued as if rigid to his left boot. Charging alone, frightened defences retreating, petrified, all to the delight of the masses as their hero roars down upon them. Then, the acceleration, the swift turn, lightning burst and whiplash drive. Goooaaaaal! Maradona wheels away in celebration over to the deepest throng of writhing Southern tifosi, all engulfed in ecstasy. He makes the Sign of the Cross and raises an arm in salute.

Milan, Juventus, Northerners all, the times they were changing.

A feverish bout of Maradona-mania had swept over the bay of Naples. A city was hooked, in this mad Neapolitan outpost where old men sit and gossip at traffic lights waiting eagerly for the next accident. Whose patron saint comes alive twice a year. Where the Devil and the ancient art of Voodoo are equally worshipped as Christ and the Holy Mother. A city closer to the shores of Africa than it's own far Northern borders. Maradona's time beneath the volcano would prove a wild, passionate love affair that reached the heights of footballing ecstasy, only to finish in dark, mortal despair.

San Gennaro watched from a high and prayed for a happy ending, but, alas, in the last city before Africa begins such things rarely came to pass. For when Maradona first dropped from the sky, it was not the politicians of Rome who ran the South, it lay instead in the ferocious murderous grip of the Camorra, as Napoli's new number ten would in time discover to his cost. However, that is for the future. For a while Maradona would be handed a crown and given king status, his every wish granted. Waltzing with the dark angels of the Neapolitan night, without ever knowing that all along he was dancing in the Devil's shade. Little more than a puppet dangling on a gangster's string.

Welcome to Naples.

CHAPTER THREE

LAVATEVI

Verona. The banner was draped for full effect over the advertising billboards on the bottom tier at the Curva Sud, (The South end). Painted blue and yellow, the battle-hardened colours of the Veronese, it read 'Lavatevi' ('Have a wash'). A poisoned arrow fired into the hearts of all Neapolitans. Simple, short and crude. Tinged with contempt, etched in disdain. The boys from Napoli unveiled their own. 'Juliet is a Tart'. Once a year the so-called Africans from the South went rampaging to Verona. Defiant and always in their thousands, the ragged hordes of SSC Napoli sang their war songs on the foreign terraces of the Stadio Comunale Bentegodi. Unloved, unwanted, pitied, and despised, to the Neapolitans it didn't matter anymore, for had these arrogant Northern bastards not heard? Maradona had come to Naples!

As Neapolitans clung on tight to the dying embers of their sweet summer of 1984, Diego Maradona set about making himself at home. In what was for him an extremely rare stroke of cute business acumen, Jorge Cyterszpiler scored great success with club President Ferlaino in agreeing for Napoli to foot the bill for his client's temporary accommodation in the city's finest hotel. Maradona and his tribe/ensemble of extended clan landed like a bad smell at the doors of the sea-front based Hotel Royal. Needless to say, that all chit's ran up by the indulging Argentinians found their way back to despairing Napoli officials. As the swirling clouds turned black over Mount Vesuvio, and darkness drew a veil over the Southern Peninsula, so the partying began. Sheltered from the prying eyes of outsiders and feeling safe and secure in a city only too willing to grant his every wish, the newly crowned King, Diego Maradona succumbed to temptation. He and his posse cruised Naples most notorious nightspots. Maradona partied with the *abbient, (Naples underworld),* and indulged in the more, much, willing excesses of Southern hospitality. Anything went, his every wish and vice catered for. He enjoyed the company of Naples' most beautiful women. They found the young Diego with the easy smile, sense of humour, dancing black eyes, coke and large wads of cash, irresistible. His long-standing girlfriend Claudia Villafane appeared for public consumption only as the Argentinian enjoyed the full hospitality of his adopted city. The public persona a charade, the reality was night and day.

The truth as ever lay hidden in the spicy gossip of downtown Naples. In the sidestreet café bars of the Forcella where Maradona's previous night-time antics were discussed, dissected, admired or frowned upon. 'This kid is no saint,' they laughed. More sinner, but messiahs come in all different guises. Even before a ball had been kicked in anger, Diego Maradona risked becoming the heady stuff of Neapolitan legend.

House rules. President Corrado Ferlaino had one unspoken rule for his young superstar. Fully aware of Maradona's outlandish lifestyle and certain habit's, Ferlaino was prepared to allow for a little dallying. However, he was adamant that from the Thursday onwards the player had to be clean of both drugs and drink. Extra precautions were taken just in case Diego ever broke these rules. Heaven forbid. It really felt for him that he was off the leash. After being forced to run a gauntlet of snobbery and antagonism

in Barcelona, the hot, alluring and sensual, atmosphere of Naples nightlife provided a perfect antidote for Maradona. His personal trainer/cheer leader, Victor Galindez, summed it up to perfection claiming, 'We escaped the hell of Barcelona and arrived in the heaven of Naples.' The Neapolitans' fascination with this young man who fell from the sky promising to make their wildest dreams come true knew no bounds and they quickly took him to their hearts. The painful memories of Catalonia were forgotten as Diego found kindred spirits who danced, sung, laughed and cavorted as if every night was their last.
'To Vesuvio,' went the toast. 'Fuck it. One day he will get us all.'
At Barcelona, Maradona used cocaine to block out obscene shooting pain from his crippling ankle injury and to help fight the boredom of many a bleak day spent recuperating. In Naples, the temptation to dabble once more proved overwhelming, only this time at the joy of being back amongst people like him. The sheer relief at being unshackled from Catalan chains made Maradona feel he was in paradise and for a while it would prove to be so.

The forty-seven-year-old Rino Marchesi was a very dignified man of much refined tastes. He enjoyed the finer things in life. A luxurious Cuban cigar, classical music, a civilized game of chess. All were a brief respite from his main purpose in life, which on and off since 1981, had been to manage the Neapolitan soap opera that was SSC Napoli. A short spell at Inter Milan was curtailed to see him lured back South. Though the pressures of such a job were enormous, Marchesi relished the dream that just maybe he could be the one to finally awake the slumbering giant and bring success to the football-mad Neapolitans.

Napoli was a club that did nothing by half and like the city she represented appeared eternally to be in a state of turmoil. The next disaster never more than a stone's throw-away. The signing of Maradona had upped the stakes dramatically. Sixty-seven-thousand season tickets had been sold and the President made it known both publicly and in private conversations with Marchesi that the under-achieving was over. The time had come for the Scudetto, the Serie A title, to come South. The city of Naples demanded an instant return on their huge investment. Both financially and in spirit the signing of Maradona was viewed as a last shot at glory. It was do or die. Sallustro, Altafini, Juliano, Sivori. These blue-shirted ghosts of the past still echoed in quiet moments across the playing surface of the San Paolo. Now, soon to be joined by a modern day great. Marchesi relished the rare opportunity of working with a talent such a Diego Maradona, though he was also a realist. Ferlaino's bold gamble in landing the much-lauded Argentinian meant expectations soar beyond the crystal blue Neapolitan heavens. For also coming to play under the volcano alongside him was the tenacious, classy, Italian midfielder from Inter Milan, Salvatore Bagni, and fellow Argentinian, the experienced winger Daniel Bertoni. Naples so very feared to dream, there had been too many false dawns. Too many broken hearts. The signing of Maradona may have roused the South, but the odds still appeared stacked heavily on the side of the Northern giants. In Turin, home of champions Juventus, and elsewhere in Milan and Rome they were hardly quaking in their boots. Rino Marchesi knew this and was not expecting to pick up his pension in Naples. Some things such as a Neapolitan Scudetto are simply not meant to happen.

Maradona did send hopes soaring for the forthcoming league campaign as he excelled in the early rounds of the Coppa Italia with a handful of goals and scintillating performances. These included a flashing free kick against Arezzo and an astonishing overhead strike against lowly Pescara, that he executed with stunning technique whilst lying flat on his back. Even an opposing defender couldn't help but applaud Maradona's moments of magic. This apart, the true test of his calibre would be amid the furore, passion and deep, dark intrigue of the Italian championship. At the San Paolo and in the rancidly, hostile, footballing arenas of the North, Diego Maradona would attempt to cement his reputation as the finest footballer in the world.

Let the games begin. It was on the eve of Sunday 16th September 1984, that the grand Northern city of Verona fell into a fitful sleep with one wary eye left half open. Verona was amongst the most elegant, prosperous cities in all Italy, especially famous for providing the setting for Shakespeare's Romeo and Juliet. In 1984, it again played host to pure theatre when Diego Maradona made his Serie A debut for SSC Napoli against Hellas Verona. Across the breath of Italy they came. The Neapolitans ventured into enemy territory in huge numbers to support their team. A pilgrimage to hell. By train, coach and car, their war songs resonating tales of bitterness and revenge. Their banners succinct and to the point. *'Fuck you Verona'*. The troubled residents of this noble city that sat proudly in the shadows of the majestic Dolomite Mountains dreaded the sight of these wretched Southerners descending like a herd of savages upon their precious, ancient, cobbled pathways. Not since Hannibal had they turned their noses up such.

Back then, whilst the legendary barbarian and his elephants were rampaging throughout the North, far South in Naples, Neapolitans would taunt their own Roman garrisons with the immortal line, 'Hannibal is at the gates!'

The coach of Hellas Verona was the wily tactician Osvaldo Bagnoli, who with meticulous care had created a formidable side set to take the Italian championship by storm. The heartbeat of Hellas was undoubtedly the man-monster German powerhouse Hans Peter Briegel. Bagnoli's master-plan based itself almost entirely on Briegel's immense physical presence and accurate long passing providing the bullets for a devastating forward partnership of lethal Danish hitman Preben Elkjaer and his Italian side-kick, Giuseppe Galderisi. Ready and primed to perfection, Verona were set to ignite. Napoli would never know what hit them. Like most Northern tifosi the Veronese loved to indulge themselves by heaping scorn on the heads of their despised visitors from the toe of Italy. Mockingly referred to in cities North of Rome as the 'Black South'. The Southerners sundrenched dark skin in comparison to the pale white faces of the damp North saw them subjected to monkey chants and incessant choruses of 'Seig Heil' throughout any match between the two. The hardcore of the Verona support came together under the sinister umbrella of a notorious ultra-right-wing mob of hooligans, the Brigate Gialloblu. The Neapolitans themselves were hardly shrinking violets and carried a fearsome reputation that came well deserved and battle-scarred. Treated with utter contempt wherever they travelled outside Naples, the Napoli tifosi chose to cock up their noses and swap punches, knives bats, curses, insults, anything they could get their hands on with their Northern foes.

All journeys up country saw the atmosphere inside stadiums simmer with an electrifying undercurrent of racism. The foul arid stench of pure hatred stalked the air. SSC Napoli was the scalp wanted by all on the Italian terraces. The most fanatical of Napoli tifosi was undoubtedly the CUCB, (Commando Ultra Curva B). Established in 1972, by the legendary Neapolitan figure of Gennaro Montuori, their numbers hailed from all corners of Naples. Petty insular squabbles were forgotten as the street gangs united under one sacred banner to take on all who dared to chance their arm against them. Montuori was amongst the first to organize large-scale away trips, safety in numbers being one of the CUCB's most important reasons for coming into being, for any trip outside Naples' borders, either to the battlegrounds of the North or equally embittered Southern rivals, carried more than a deadly dose of bad blood. It became essential that whatever their differences, once in enemy territory they stuck together, for in every town and city across Italy the local youths awaited with glee the arrival of the loathsome Neapolitans. Whilst a Carabinieri helicopter buzzed menacingly overhead, baton-waving local Polizia used heavy-handed tactics to shove the Southerners into the ground like a herd of cattle. Verona was amongst the worst.

Diego Maradona took to the pitch with his teammates for the pre-match warm up and looked visibly shaken at the hail of abuse hurled at him by the home supporters. So, this was Italy? The Argentinian applauded the end of the stadium draped in blue where his own adoring followers stood. Many still finding it hard to believe he was wearing their shirt. Finally, both teams made their entrance into the Comunale Bentegodi. To a deafening welcome the Verona Ultras took up their war anthem.

'Chi noi siamo?' ('Who are we')? 'Chi noi siamo, Brigate, Brigate Giaboblu!'

The Brigate had rolled a blue and yellow banner over the advertising hoarding on the bottom tier where they stood, grouped behind the goal in the Curva Sud proclaiming:

'Benvenuti in Italia' (Welcome to Italy).

Alongside it, the infamous *'Lavatevi.'* That cut deep. In time the Veronese would pay dear for such insults. The waving of 100,000 Lira notes at the Neapolitans was also a cause of great amusement amongst Verona's finest as the bowl-shaped Bentegodi roared in appreciation of such wit. The chants and songs swept down from the terraces. Amongst the hundreds of Hellas flags there lay sprinkled a sizeable number of Nazi Swastikas. A clash of cultures, the Mezzorgiorno badlands of the South versus the rich fat cats of the so-called White North. So much for Shakespeare's 'City of Gentleman'?

To the dismay of their supporters, the new Neapolitan empire appeared made from sand as they crumbled disastrously against a rampant Hellas Verona. In what was a torrid opening game Napoli were thrashed 3-1 and lucky not to be beaten by more. Both Maradona and Bertoni were isolated from the off as they found themselves roughed up by some brutal treatment dished out by the Verona defenders, who took turns and great delight in kicking them in the air. Up the other end of the field the Hellas forwards cut through with alarming ease. Inspired by the thundering runs of Hans Peter Briegel, the home side won convincingly. A first half goal from the German was doubled when Galderisi combined with Elkjaer to make it 2-0 on the hour. Matters went from bad to worse for Napoli when their veteran defender and longest-serving player Giuseppe Bruscolotti, was sent off in frustration as his team was overrun. This mean-faced son of Naples did not take kindly to seeing his beloved club humiliated and reacted so.

For a brief period in the second half with Diego Maradona showing some wonderfully incisive touches, the Neapolitans rallied. Maradona single-handedly took on the home defence, but amidst relentless attention from the Verona hatchet-men, whom felt nothing in scything him to the floor at every opportunity, his threat waned. Hopes were raised momentarily that a point could be salvaged when Daniel Bertoni lashed one back to halve the deficit, though any chance of a revival was dashed fifteen minutes from time. Hellas sealed a deserved victory with a third goal brilliantly finished by Italian international midfielder Antonio di Gennaro. A season in which the Veronese would surprise all and win their first ever Scudetto had begun in impressive manner. As for the Neapolitans? Different season, same old story.

The following week felt like an eternity for all connected with SSC Napoli as they ached to banish the nightmare of what befell them in Verona. Maradona got ready to tread the boards for the first time in his hometown theatre-house against Sampdoria. It was opening night at the San Paolo and expectations were higher than the infamous volcano that soared above them. You could not get a ticket for your life. The moment Neapolitans had prayed for arrived on the hour when in a fiercely fought encounter Napoli were awarded a penalty. Seventy thousand hushed as Diego Maradona stepped forward to take responsibility for the

kick. As Naples held it's breath Maradona coolly converted a cheeky chip-shot past Bordon in the Sampdoria goal.
The arena erupted!
Homemade firecrackers exploded, rockets crashed and roared impressively, if rather worryingly, high into the Naples sky. Thousands danced for joy on the packed terraces. Maradona raced away and fell to his knees near the corner flag, his teammates falling upon him as a mad melee ensued. Photographers and club officials rushed on the pitch in wild celebration. Sadly, for the Neapolitans the men from Genoa refused to lie down and on seventy-three minutes ruined the party when centre-forward Daniel Salsano shot past the Napoli keeper Luciano Castellini to take a point back North. 1-1. The final whistle saw the stadium empty swiftly. It had been an inauspicious start for Marchesi's team and they badly needed a win. The verdict amongst the Napoli tifosi regarding Maradona was mixed. In both opening matches he had found himself firmly shackled. Serie A bristled with top class defenders who though masters of their art, tended to err dangerously on the crueler side of brutality. The hatchet men across the land sharpened their studs and encircled his name on the team sheet. There would be no easy rides for Diego.
The following week disaster befell the Neapolitans with utter humiliation in Turin. Inspired by the incisive passing of Austrian midfield schemer Walter Schachner, and the attacking flair of the exuberant bushy-haired Brazilian fullback Junior, a 3-0 scoreline did Torino little justice for the quality of their play. The Stadio Comunale shared with hated city rivals Juventus erupted in the first minute when the electric-heeled, home forward, Italian international Aldo Serena caught the Neapolitans cold. A massacre

ensued as 'La Granata' ('The Clarets'), much to the delight of their supporters ran riot. At the final whistle Rino Marchesi's men appeared shell-shocked. Their supporters forlorn. What began as a season full of hope had quickly deteriorated into a shambles. President Ferlaino watched on in exasperated fashion as his expensively assembled team trooped sullenly off the pitch. Would this nightmare ever end? The disastrous events in Turin would prove simply to be one of many terrible Sundays for Neapolitans, as from that wretched afternoon up until the Christmas break, Napoli won only twice. They found themselves deeply entrenched in a horrible relegation dogfight alongside Lazio, Udinese, Ascoli and Cremonese. For a shocked and embarrassed Diego Maradona, it had been a shock to the system. Every game was a war. There had been few highlights: a first goal in open play at the San Paolo against Como, when in typical fashion he scythed through the middle to strike a tremendous shot that screamed high into the goal to electrify the terraces. A masterpiece of opportunistic skill in Rome against Lazio where he struck like a cobra to earn a vital point. Not enough, even though there had been tantalizing glimpses of genius that caused even the most rabid of Northern tifosi to gasp in admiration and whisper a silent prayer to the heavens that one day Maradona would wear their team's colours. A drop of the shoulders and three opposing defenders would be left in a bedraggled heap. Sadly, by far the disappointments outweighed such moments; precious as they were, the Neapolitans needed much more from their new boy.

A soul-destroying 2-0 defeat against the infernal Juventus in which they were totally outclassed caused dismay in Naples. The wonderfully artistic Frenchman Michel Platini sealed the win to raise the roof off the Comunale by stroking home a decisive second goal. A banner by the Juve tifosi taunted the despised visitors. *'Vesuvio we are counting on you'.*

This only rubbed salt in the wounds of the disgruntled Neapolitans whom travelled home feeling their title dream was further away than ever. The gloom continued when they lost to Internazionale of Milan at the venomously hostile San Siro. Inter's winner was a last-gasp effort by striker Allesandro Altobelli to leave the despondent Napoli players at the mercy of a gloating Milan crowd rejoicing at their misfortune. The banner reading, *'Maradona, suck on a banana',* displaying a lesser-known side of a city normally citied for class and style.

The shutdown at Christmas handed the club a chance to regroup. Neapolitans were under no illusions, they knew unless performances drastically improved Napoli was in grave danger of being relegated. There was only one Christmas wish in Naples that year, survival. To escape the rising tension Diego Maradona packed his bags for a short vacation and headed home to Buenos Aires. He felt a sense of shame in how things had gone. The depth of feeling and goodwill shown Maradona in Naples had overwhelmed him and it showed no signs of easing up even during the struggling campaign. Even the most torrid of love affairs needed time to cool and come back down to earth. Maradona truly appreciated the attentions lavished upon him but to repay such generosity and loyalty he had to recharge his batteries and get away. For despite rumours to the contrary in Naples, he was only human. Napoli would take only a sad total of nine points into the New Year. The normally festive, joyful Christmas period would instead be an anxious time for the city as it pondered the coming months. As ever, that most illustrious of prizes, the Scudetto appeared an impossible dream, indeed relegation to Serie B was more likely. The jury was out: the time had come for the king of Naples to dig Napoli out of it's self-made hole at the bottom of the table and prove to his subjects he was worthy of the crown bestowed upon him. Maradona returned early in the New Year refreshed and in dogged frame of mind to prove his many doubters wrong. The Neapolitans' league campaign restarted on 6th January, with a match at the San Paolo against fellow strugglers Udinese. The visitors had enjoyed a fine season the previous year when against all expectations they finished sixth. Blessed with a potent striking duo of Brazilians, Edinho and the man nicknamed the 'White Pelé,' Zico, Udinese arrived in the Southern capital determined to beat Napoli in their own backyard and place Marchesi's side under intolerable pressure by dumping them into the bottom three. Level with the Neapolitans on points but lagging behind on goal difference, it was billed as a clash neither side could afford to lose. Udinese entered into the seething atmosphere of the San Paolo wearing their traditional black and white stripes. This served only to irritate the hell out of the already fraught Napoli tifosi, the ghosts of the bastards Juve forever in their faces. Played in driving rain, sleet and a cold bitter wind that cut deep into the bones of everyone present, a classic game of football ensued. On this holy day of the blessed feast of the Epiphany, the under-pressure Rino Marchesi raged towards the heavens when in the twelfth minute his team conceded a penalty that Edinho converted. The rain-soaked Napoli coach must have heard the sound of knives being sharpened all around him as the small, but enthusiastic band of Udinese followers celebrated loudly. The

Neapolitans rallied and to the delight of the home supporters Diego Maradona equalised ten minutes later, also from the penalty spot. With both teams going hell for leather Daniel Bertoni shot Napoli in front, only for Udinese to hit back once more a minute before the break. At 2-2, Maradona was seemingly playing the visitors on his own. Time and again he bore down on the Udinese rearguard. As Naples shivered in the midst of a January blizzard, he warmed his adopted people's hearts with a bravura performance. Fifteen minutes from the end Maradona scored again from the spot and when Bertoni grabbed his second moments later the game appeared won. With the massed blue-clad hordes of the CUCB indulging in their victory songs, Udinese lashed back one final time when Billini crashed home to create a grandstand finish. To the joy of President Ferlaino, a stressed-out Marchesi and hordes of whistling Neapolitans, the referee finally ended the match and the city of Naples sighed a collective gasp. A jubilant and much relieved Diego Maradona leapt across the advertising billboards that surrounded the pitch and went across to acknowledge the Neapolitans for their ferocious backing in what had been an enthralling encounter. Maradona had given a wonderful display and on this form worth every penny of the king's ransom paid to Barca for his services.

From that day on Napoli lost only two games in the league. The blessed feast of the Epiphany celebrated Jesus Christ rising from the dead. On Sunday 6th January 1985, Diego Maradona lit the flames to spark the fires that ignited a football revolution. The badlands of the South were once more ablaze. The charge for the Scudetto was on. As the blizzard increased in blind fury across the Southern

Peninsula and snow fell heavily onto the steep slopes of Mount Vesuvio, a city paid homage to it's king.
When offstage and away from the San Paolo, Maradona's behaviour in the nightclubs and seedy fleshpots of Naples was so shocking as to even disturb Neapolitan streetwise morals. A steamy affair with a local television presenter while Claudia was visiting family in Argentina became public knowledge. Much to Jorge Cyterszpiler's concern it was leaked to the press and all hell let loose in Naples. It was a leggy Californian born blond called Heather Parisi who kept him warm during that January. One of the coldest months ever recorded in Italy. True to form Heather surprised no one by later kissing and telling her story to the infamous Italian gossip magazine Oggi for a sizeable fee. Despite all, it would be his God-given genius with a ball that made Maradona invulnerable to criticism. Diego was having the time of his young life and while he cast magic spells on the football field no one would be allowed to ruin his fun, no one. Maradona danced between the raindrops.
He was untouchable.

CHAPTER FOUR

BADLANDS

Alas, for Neapolitans, their bedraggled, much put upon, but always beloved football SSC Napoli, had struggled miserably through the years against the mighty Northern powers. In what felt like an eternal procession of funeral marches the teams of Juventus and Milan turned up each season in Naples to beat them with soul-destroying ease. In doing so they laid down the law, for a football pitch was good a place as any to keep the Southern Terroni (lowlifes) in their place. 'Do as you're fucking told.' Despite the endless bouts of heartache and failure the Neapolitans refused to give up on their boys. The worse they were beaten and treated, the more they yearned and ached for success. It was a relationship that bore all the hallmarks of an eternally doomed love affair. Love, hate and love again. Amore: it has always been so.

The grand old tale of SSC Napoli begins in the early years of the last century. The flourishing seaport of Naples was enjoying a boom, attracting huge foreign investment. Amongst them Cunard Liners, whom in 1903, transferred one of their top mechanics to the Southern Peninsula. The Englishman James Poths arrived in Naples, carrying a suitcase in one hand and a football under the arm. This man had been an avid, amateur footballer, who made up for what he lacked in skill with sheer enthusiasm. Poths was simply mad about the game and wasted little time extolling his passion to all who would listen. However, in Southern Italy, football remained at that time still practically unknown. Nobody played; it was only in the far

North of Turin, Milan and Genoa that the game mattered. Poths was a determined character who viewed himself as a footballing missionary. He, along with his newfound, friend, a Neapolitan engineer called Emilio Anatra, managed to scrape together a side to play the crews of visiting ships. Poths and Anatra very grandly christened their team Naples Cricket and Football Club, and a show of hands saw them vote to play in strips of light and dark blue striped shirts. So, from such small acorns began a long enduring love affair between a city and it's football team. That they consisted only of English sailor would soon become highly problematic. Their first match took place against eleven crew members of the visiting British liner, Arabik, and proved a great success with Naples winning 3-2. The victory was shown to be even more impressive considering the crew of the Arabik had only recently beaten Genoa, whom were considered by far the best club side in Italy. News of this shock result spread like wildfire and to Poth's utter amazement, a most unlikely invitation dropped on his desk from the Sicilian royal family. The King himself wished for them to partake in a prestigious tournament on his island. Delighted to accept, off went Poths and his band of merry Englishmen abroad to Sicily, where they beat the hosts 2-1 and returned triumphantly to Naples with the impressive-looking trophy. However, there would be no welcoming reception put on by the locals whom due to the insistence of James Poth picking only Englishmen for his team, had simply disowned them. The Neapolitans were outraged at the arrogance of this foreigner who took the name of their city and yet refused to play any of it's citizens. How could Poth's men possibly represent Naples when the players were constantly sailing off elsewhere and he was replacing them with more of his countrymen? It wasn't right, there was only one option. Another team was born, US Internazionale came into being. They, of course, to prove a point built their side around Neapolitans and a great rivalry, bitter and fierce, swiftly developed between the two. Neither took prisoners when the two clashed. Many an English sailor departed the port of Naples nursing a black eye or a broken bone.

Finally, in 1920, both clubs came to their senses, shook hands and merged to become Internaples. It was not until 23rd August 1926, in a famous meeting at the restaurant D'Angelo in Naples, that they became Associazone Calcio Napoli, enrolling in the Italian Southern division. A prominent local businessman Giorgio Ascarelli was nominated as club President and they were up and running. Chosen as club emblem was a proud galloping black horse. Their first season turned swiftly into humiliating failure with only a single point earned in a lone draw against Genoa. Altogether, a shambolic tally of 69 goals conceded to 7 scored had all Naples shamefaced with embarrassment. Indeed, the Neapolitans themselves changed the symbol of their club to a sad, downtrodden, if somewhat loveable donkey christened *'O Ciuccio'*. An enduring image that returned many times, even to this day in haunting them.

All was not doom and gloom, for in it's midst Napoli possessed a treasured gem of a footballer. A Neapolitan legend long before Diego Maradona fell from the sky making dreams come true. The child prodigy Attila Sallustro, made his debut at the unbelievably tender age of twelve. Born, the son of Paraguayan immigrants, but raised in the poverty-stricken backstreets of Naples, the attractions of this unique youngster saw Napoli performing to packed houses both home and away. Sallustro's talents were such that even though the Neapolitans were thrashed by all in their fledgling opening year, relegation was avoided due to the Italian Football Association realizing they could ill afford to lose such valuable income. Instead they voted in an incredulous ruling preventing Napoli from going down, thus keeping Atilla Sallustro and his pulling power within their grasp. To Naples' great relief the same decision was repeated the following year when again they found themselves beaten out of sight on most weeks. Amazingly, such was Sallustro's love of the game he declined wages to play. Being a true gentleman, he saw the game as merely a hobby and refused point blank a salary. However, after one particularly impressive season, a determined President Ascarelli insisted Sallustro accept his offer of a luxurious new car on behalf of the club. Grudgingly, he accepted. With his strutting manner and film star good looks, the player was also a popular figure amongst the ladies of Naples, who would giggle with delight and clap politely whenever their hero received the ball. This remarkable character went on to have a glittering career with SSC Napoli, with 137 goals in 259 games. Even in the city today his name is spoken in hushed tones of awe. Atilla Sallustro, a true legend of Naples.

Napoli's finest moments in those early formative years came under the much-travelled hand of another Englishman, Willy Garbutt. In 1933 and 34 the former Arsenal player led the football-mad Neapolitans to two consecutive fourth-place spots, behind Inter, Milan and Juventus. A little pride but this apart Napoli's trophy cabinet remained bare. The title (championship shield) remained North in Turin, for they had the money, best players and, it appeared, most disturbingly when the need arose, the referees also. There were many times when supposedly impartial referees caused outrage in the South with highly controversial decisions against Napoli that defied belief. Some things don't change. This also caused great unrest amongst the supporters, constantly spilling over into disturbing scenes of crowd violence and unrest. Against such unmatchable odds the hopes of Neapolitans wrestling the title away from such formidable foes appeared astronomical. However, on 15th March 1936, hopes soared in Naples when shipping tycoon Achille Lauro became club President. Lauro vowed to end their barren run and bring success to the passionate followers of SSC Napoli. Born, neighbouring Sorrento, Achille Lauro inherited his first ships in 1912. In time he built up a sizeable fleet of freighters and cruise liners that were to make him rich beyond his dreams. Lauro was also a man of huge ego and political ambition and though undoubtedly using the role of Napoli supremo as a stepping stone to becoming Naples' Mayor, he did possess a burning desire to bring South for the first time the Holy Grail of the championship trophy. Sadly, all became scuppered by the cataclysmic outbreak of World War Two. As the Southern Peninsula became drenched in blood, thoughts turned to matters other than football. Living and dying.

Naples 1941: Benito Mussolini, Il Duce, believed he had a splendid idea. The pompous despot had grown increasingly annoyed at the Neapolitans' total lack of regard for him and his rabid Fascist black shirts. Their annoying habit of drawing Charlie Chaplin moustaches on his wonderful self on the many posters that adorned the city walls caused the great one to lose his temper. Hardly known for his sense of humour the mad dictator decided they must be taught a painful lesson. He issued a decree for the city's air raid sirens to be randomly switched on even when there was no threat of bombs falling. Finally, on 4th December 1942, the ominous drone of American B-24 liberators flying from their base in Egypt was heard over Naples as they came in low over the Tyrrhenian Sea to hit the city. As the sirens wailed many Neapolitans were confused as to whether the alarm was genuine and did not go to the underground shelters, thus sealing their fate. On hearing of this a smug Mussolini smiled declaring, 'A good dose of terror will turn the people of Naples into true Italians.' Such cruel acts of folly caused blind panic and fury amongst a people whom had already suffered terribly from relentless allied air attacks. It was also rumoured, crazy as it sounds that American intention was to bomb the crater of Vesuvio triggering an eruption that would devastate the region. Also, Mussolini's infamous comments that 'It gratified him when Naples was bombed,' hardly endeared him to the citizens of this much put-upon city. As his pipe dream of a new Roman empire crumbled into dust the allies landed at Salerno and headed up to Naples. The Americans and British forces found themselves aided by Camorra fugitives who played an integral role in the Neapolitan uprising of 1944, Quattro Giornate. In a ferocious four-day battle they helped to organize resistance, handing out guns and ammunition as the city rose in fury to kick out the last remaining German forces. As the Nazis retreated Northwards the chasing American and British forces entered the Southern capital. On 1st October 1944, Allied forces liberated Naples to find nothing short of hell on earth. The burnt smell of charred wood forever lingering in the air, starvation and disease rife, as a once proud city and it's people appeared broken.

Ravaged by incessant Allied bombing and Nazi revenge, Naples lay dying. Dirty, hungry children begged and pleaded with Allied troops. The cries of 'biscotti' and 'sigarette' were everywhere as soldiers found dreadful scenes of starvation, horror and neglect. No other city in Italy suffered the wanton devastation than that which was wrought on Naples.

The war did end and in 1952, Achille Lauro's lifetime ambition of becoming Mayor was finally realized. Now, one of the most powerful figures in all Italy, 'Il Commandante', as he had become known, set about winning his electorate over by announcing plans for a spectacular new home for SSC Napoli. In such a moment the San Paolo stadium was born, and on 19th November 1959, it became a reality. A fond, if rather overdue arrivederci was said to the rundown, though still highly, evocative arena of their former ground in the city region of Vomero. Surprisingly, it was arch enemies Juventus whom were invited South by Lauro to provide the opposition for the stadium's grand inauguration. In front of a full house a goalless draw saw honour served on both sides, as just for a day the two adversaries declared a ceasefire.

Finally, on 21st June 1962, SSC Napoli could boast of silverware when the Coppa d'Italia was won in Rome. Thousands had travelled up from the South to celebrate this historic 2-1 victory for their club over little Spal in the Eternal city. For the first time Europe beckoned with a place in the European Cup Winners' Cup secured. On being handed an opening tie against lowly Welsh non-league side Bangor City in the preliminary rounds, Neapolitans gleefully rubbed their hands. For most had never even heard of Wales, never mind Bangor and their football team? That soon changed, for on 5th September 1962, on an unforgettable evening at Farror Road with a capacity 8,000 crowd roaring their team on, Napoli slid shame-faced to defeat. Unbelievably, a side of part-timers, lying sixth in the Cheshire League, inflicted upon their supposed vastly superior and highly illustrious opponents, a 2-0 loss. A Bangor team playing a typically British long-ball style totally overwhelmed the Italians, who simply collapsed under the incessant pressure. Two goals were scant reward for the rampaging men from Gwynedd who also twice hit the bar and created numerous other opportunities to score. Led by their manager, ex-Everton and Wales star Tommy Jones, Bangor became the first Welsh side ever to win in Europe. Back in Naples, this result was greeted with a mixture of incredulity and anger. These much lauded, highly-paid superstars were left in no doubt by their fanatical support that nothing more than a massacre in the return would save their necks.

Three weeks later Bangor City's first ever flight to the continent so nearly ended in tragedy when lightning struck the plane, forcing it to make an emergency landing in Switzerland. After such a harrowing experience, the rotten fruit and urine bags hurled at them from the San Paolo terraces simply paled into insignificance. So, the game began. Inspired by 80,000 rabid tifosi screaming for Welsh blood, Bangor ignored the abuse and in bravura fashion took the game to Napoli on their own patch. Tommy Jones's brave side crashed into tackles and gave everything in a gallant effort to attempt the impossible. As the game wore on class finally began to tell and on thirty minutes 'Azzurri' international Mariani struck a slow shot from the edge of the penalty area that beat City goalkeeper

Len Davies. Suddenly, Welsh fire waned and Neapolitan passions erupted. Bristling with newfound confidence, Napoli's pass and move game mesmerized the Bangor defenders. A terrible error by the normally reliable Davies let in the electrifying forward Ronzon to level the tie and delight an enraptured San Paolo. A second half promised only further carnage for a home team seeking revenge, but yet again Bangor showed wonderful spirit as they found hidden depths of courage to take on the Neapolitans. A heart-stopping display by this remarkable ensemble of factory workers, electricians and plumbers pinned back the shell-shocked Italians and ten minutes from time they received their just reward. A long throw-in from Bangor defender Ken Birch caused confusion in the penalty area. Waiting to pounce was City winger Jimmy McAllister who fired past a despairing Pontel in the Napoli goal, silencing the stadium. Knowing full well they faced a real prospect of being lynched on the pitch, Napoli tried one last time to save themselves. With the City defence wilting a dramatic lifeline was grabbed when their speedy winger Pornella kept his cool to make it 3-3 on aggregate. Naples heaved a heavy sigh of relief, for it had been a close call.

Unlike today, away goals never counted for double, and the tie went to a play-off match. The venue chosen, much to Neapolitan chagrin was the home of Arsenal Football Club, Highbury. Napoli officials argued vehemently, but with a woeful lack of British geography, that London was practically a home game for Bangor City! They demanded to play elsewhere in either France or Spain. Meanwhile, as the argument raged, the Welsh were equally irritated at being regarded as English by their opponents. Despite fierce Italian objections the footballing authorities decided to over-rule and the game went ahead. On Wednesday 10th

October 1962, fifteen coach loads of Bangor supporters added their own particular brand of passion to the 21,895 present at Highbury. Finally, third time around, the Napoli players showed their true style and though the Welshmen fought tenaciously, the gulf between the sides became apparent. On thirty-six minutes, after many close shaves, the sublime Argentinian Rosa, let fly a wonderful twenty-yard shot that screamed past a helpless Len Davies. He had little need to feel guilty though, for if not for Davies it would have resembled a rout. That Bangor remained just one down at half-time was itself a minor miracle, and due solely to their heroic keeper. The second period saw little respite for the Welsh minnows as the Italians swarmed all over them. Opportunities arrived only to be wasted, some through sheer bad finishing, other foiled by the magnificent Davies. With time running down and the Neapolitans settling for 1-0, it just had to happen. Bangor centre-half Brian Ellis headed down for the darting Jimmy McAllister to fire his second goal in three games against Napoli. This famous old ground, sensing a most unlikely upset, exploded. Sadly, for Tommy Jones, his wonderfully courageous team were utterly spent of energy and seven minutes from time, Rosa struck to score his second of the night and win the tie. The Neapolitans were through, but only after the most frightful scare. Bangor City returned to European anonymity, but with their place in Welsh footballing folklore secure. It had been an epic journey and a truly monumental effort.

As for SSC Napoli, their short-lived adventures in the Cup Winners' Cup ended in the next round when OFK Belgrade knocked them out. That same season the Neapolitans also suffered the ignominy of relegation. In Naples, the song remained forever the same.

Come 1965, and Napoli supremo Achille Lauro had grown increasingly frustrated at his clubs' constant under-achieving. Armed with his own money Lauro went for broke and signed two of the great players from the North. This self-styled original 'King of Naples' drew a line in the sand, a gesture of defiance. He offered two of Napoli's sworn enemies, AC Milan and Juventus, a king's ransom to part with their star South American wizards, the Brazilian centre forward Jose Altafini and Argentinian winger Omar Enrique Sivori. Altafini had performed only a cameo role in Brazil's legendary 1958 World Cup-winning side in Sweden, but his talent had already been noted. Jose Altafini proved a marvellous signing, scoring freely and never more so than during AC Milan's 1963 victorious European Cup campaign, hitting a record fourteen goals. Included amongst these were two special strikes at Wembley stadium in a 3-1 victory over Eusebio's famed Benfica. As for the sublime, if temperamental Omar Sivori? He went to Naples after falling foul of Juve's Paraguayan disciplinarian coach, Heriberto Herrera. The hard-nosed Herrera was not for Sivori, who saw himself as a free spirit. He was labeled 'El Cabezon' 'Bighead,' by Italians for a tendency to enjoy making opposing defenders appear ridiculous with his magical ball skills. Sivori would run past opponents exclaiming, 'Congratulations, you have just been beaten by the best player in the world!' Never one to hide his true feelings, the fiery Argentinian hardly helped his cause when on one memorable occasion he beat a full-back, noticed Herrera on the touchline, and smashed the ball into his midriff making him cry! As Herrera screamed abuse back the smiling Sivori milked the moment, for he knew his glittering career with Juventus was at an end. It was time for a new challenge. A worthy 150 goals in eight seasons in which he shared a magnificent partnership with the great John Charles and being voted the 1961 European Player of the Year, meant Omar Sivori would be forever remembered as a true Juve legend. The price for both players was incredibly high and Lauro helped subsidise the transfers by handing Gianni Agnelli a lucrative contract to fit out his fleet of ships. Despite a close friendship with Agnelli, he knew well that the intense feelings in Naples against Juventus meant he had to appear that any dealings with Turin's royal family were akin to a pact with the devil. There also was an agreement with AC Milan not to sell Jose Altafini to any of their rivals for a period of at least three years. Lauro shook hands with the Milan hierarchy on this but was severely tested when Juve immediately proposed a double your money offer to buy the Brazilian. However, not wishing to cause a civil war, and hardly relishing the idea of being hung from the highest tree by irate Neapolitans, the Napoli supremo declined. The bold capture of these exceptional footballers electrified the Southern tifosi. It was seen as a wonderful coup by all of Naples. Both men were born entertainers who quickly became idols on the terraces of the San Paolo. More so Omar Sivori, who with socks rolled down to the ankles enchanted the Neapolitan crowds with his alluring wizardry and theatrical gestures. Sivori mirrored in style and attitude another Argentinian who followed in his exalted footsteps many years later. Although Sivori's time in the blue of Naples would be haunted with endless injuries, he still earned a place in Neapolitan folklore, such was his artistry and showmanship.

Also, arriving in the Southern capital to aid Neapolitans in their championship quest was the highly regarded goalkeeper Dino Zoff. Signed from lowly Mantova, the young Zoff was destined in time to become the greatest number one in Italy's history, culminating in 1982, when at the grand old age of forty he lifted the World Cup. These days he now stands alongside Gianluigi Buffon to share that honour.

Zoff proved a formidable barrier at the back for Napoli before his eventual departure to Juventus.

Sadly, the title continued to elude and frustrations spilled over onto the terraces. Outbreaks of violence became increasingly common and there were many incidents at the San Paolo and elsewhere that shamed the club. One of the worse took place at home against Palermo when an incensed Napoli tifosi had to be restrained by water cannons from lynching a referee who had particularly annoyed them. The poor official was only rescued when a helicopter landed on the pitch and lifted him to safety. The Napoli crowds greeted his great escape with mocking applause.

A close shave.

Trouble also flared in matches against Genoa and Bologna where full-scale riots broke out on the stands. Pitch invasions and scenes of mass brawling forced the authorities to act and the Southerners were fined extraordinary heavy sums and ordered to play home matches away from Naples. SSC Napoli's extraordinary gift for self-destruction meant there appeared not a single chink of light in what had been a long, dark tunnel stretching back decades. Neapolitans prayed for a miracle.

…Far away in a dustbowl, ramshackle slum of Argentina's capital Buenos Aires, a young boy played alone. He was entertaining himself by juggling a small orange from left to right foot, before flicking it upon a shoulder, then onto his head, before starting all over again! All was achieved with a snake charmer's ease. Dreaming of great adventures, a five-year-old Diego Maradona played on and on, and …

In 1967, the Neapolitans were drawn against another unfancied British side Burnley in the Fairs Cup. Even today, in this rural Lancashire town the occasion is recalled with a shudder and infamously referred to as 'The Battle of Naples'. With a confidence bordering towards cockiness Napoli journeyed to England for the first leg minus many of their star players. The Napoli hierarchy appeared to have learned little from their nightmarish experience against Bangor City, for many in Naples scoffed that they had never heard of the Lancastrians. The South American contingent of Altafini and Sivori were notable absences, although their omissions were said to have been down to injuries. Both had succeeded setting Naples ablaze with their talents, and Argentinian maestro Sivori had just recently been awarded an engraved gold medal by his grateful adopted city for scoring the winning goal against fierce rivals Roma. The Romans being one of many clubs that the Neapolitan tifosi tended to have problems with. Napoli coach Enrico Zuppardi raised eyebrows amongst the English press when asked what he knew of his opponents. Zuppardi's reply entered Burnley footballing folklore when he declared in all seriousness. 'Harris, Lochhead, Irvine and Turf Moor are all new names to me, but I am sure they are all first-rate players.'

The Napoli head-man watched on quizzically as hard-bitten newspapermen fell to the floor in fits of laughter. The Italians abandoned their usual free-flowing style and switched to the dreary, defensive system of Catencaccio. Still fuming from his embarrassing 'Turf Moor' line, Zuppardi had the sole intention of securing a 0-0 draw and finishing off the English in Naples. He reckoned without a Burnley team that had been dangerously under-estimated. With the home ground packed to the rafters and the blurry haze of the floodlights illuminating the black Lancashire sky, Burnley thrashed the cocky Neapolitans 3-0 in a tempestuous contest. The bloodcurdling Napoli centre half Dino Panzanato, was sent off for sticking the boot into centre-forward Andy Lochhead, as he lay injured on the ground. Revenge was mercilessly swift by the Burnley players as they sought out Panzanato seeking retribution. Anarchy reigned: chaos ensued on the pitch as bodies from both sides became involved in pushing and slanging matches. Punches were thrown as infamously short Neapolitan tempers snapped. Finally, with officials, policemen and managers on the field, order was temporarily restored. The two Captains were hailed towards the beleaguered referee and warned the game would be abandoned if the melee continued. To make matters worse Dino Panzanato then refused to leave the field. It was only through the intervention of his coach Zuppardi, who coaxed him off that the game was allowed to resume. Lochhead had the last laugh when he drove home a late third to ignite Turf Moor and set up a firecracker of a second-leg. The embarrassed Napoli players went home vowing that under the all-watchful eye of Mount Vesuvio revenge would be had.

On 8th February 1967, Burnley entered into the bear pit of the San Paolo. A fiercely partisan crowd of sixty-thousand Neapolitans greeted them in inimitable style by hurling abuse and anything else they could get their hands on from behind a six-foot perimeter moat that encircled this huge gladiatorial arena. Napoli brought back the big guns. Omar Sivori and Jose Altafini returned from injury to help bury the English. Also, back in the starting line-up was local hero and wonderfully talented midfielder Antonio Juliano. Another name in the team was Ottavio Bianchi. Later as manager, Bianchi was destined for great deeds with Napoli. Left with no choice, Enrico Zuppardi had decided to throw caution to the wind. From the first minute to the last it would be all-out attack. Neapolitans gathered in their hordes expecting the three-goal deficit to be washed away in a blue tidal wave. Woe betide if they were left disappointed. In what proved to be the game of his life Burnley goalkeeper Harry Thompson produced a heroic display to keep the Italians at bay. In the first minute Jose Altafini showed his class by letting fly from fully thirty-yards, only to see his blinding shot crash loud against the crossbar. A massacre appeared likely as the wizardry, pace and movement of the Napoli forwards had their opponents constantly on the back-foot, but still refusing to yield. Sivori led the frantic onslaught as he weaved his magic, but time and again the magnificent Thompson was at hand to foil them. Fantastic last-gasp saves from Altafini, Bianchi and Juliano caused Neapolitans to shake their heads and ponder if they would ever beat him? Five minutes before half-time Naples erupted when they were awarded a penalty. As Jose Altafini struck it towards the left-hand corner, Thompson leapt miraculously across his goal line to push the ball away. Altafini pounded the floor in disgust, for he never missed. Remarkably, only four days previous he had scored a sensational hat-trick of spot-kicks in the league. The game wore on and still Burnley held out. As the locals grew increasingly restless fires started on the San Paolo terraces. Twenty minutes remained when Jose Altafini was forced to leave the battle after a clash of heads. With blood seeping from a forehead wound, the home supporters showed little mercy and the Brazilian's unfortunate exit was met with a hail of coins and cushions hurled in his direction. In Naples, even heroes had to dive for cover when all went awry. As the clock ticked down and the home side realised the cause was lost, tempers erupted. Omar Sivori got away with murder when he elbowed the Burnley player Dave Merrington in full view of the referee, only then for the official to prefer not to see it.

Come the final whistle and though jubilant, the intimidating atmosphere meant English celebrations were sober and subdued. It was no time to gloat when only a surrounding moat and a vastly outnumbered, half-hearted handful of policemen and soldiers stood between them and a possible murky fate. The Italian players prowled around, menacing, eager to pick a fight. They were in no mood to accept defeat and go quiet. Burnley's finest Harry Thompson went to shake Napoli's Alberto Orlando's hand, only to be spat at in the face and floored by an Orlando right hook. As the unfortunate goalkeeper lay distraught, other home players took out their frustrations on the felled Thompson. The Burnley reserve keeper Adam Blacklaw charged across the turf and immediately laid into his team-mate's assailants. Blacklaw was a rugged, tough Scot who could handle himself. In a fury he grabbed one Neapolitan and hurled him down a set of stone steps. In no time he was surrounded by a herd of irate Italians howling for blood. Not fancying the overwhelming odds, Blacklaw ran off and fortunately survived to tell the tale.

Outside the stadium, a Neapolitan lynch mob had gathered to vent their anger at the Burnley coach. It was only when police fired shots above their heads that the crowds dispersed into the night, going home glumly to their beds. Even then no chances were taken as the embarrassed authorities attempted to make amends to their visitors. To the utter astonishment of the English, a military convoy armed with enough firepower to kickstart a revolution roared up outside the San Paolo. Nine army jeeps, all equipped with machine guns, and an armoured tank was provided to escort them to the city airport. Not even the most hardened follower of SSC Napoli would have attempted to take on such a force. Bruised but elated, the pride of Lancashire finally bade a bloody arrivederci to Naples. On returning to Burnley, the headlines in the local paper summed up their fiery encounter with the Neapolitans.

'See Naples and die'!

Three years later they were at it again. This time it was against poor unsuspecting Swindon Town in the inaugural Anglo-Italian Cup final held in the San Paolo. On Thursday 28th May 1970, 55,000 watched first in dismay, and then growing anger as the English underdogs ran Napoli ragged, roaring into a three-goal lead. Finally, after seventy-nine minutes it all proved too much to bear as once again the legendary Neapolitan short fuse ignited and riots broke out on the terraces. Fires were started; seats were ripped up and thrown onto the pitch. The Swindon players watched in amazement as a full-scale battle ensued between the war-weary, baton-wielding police and supporters. All a long way from the sleepy picturesque settings of their hometown. As mayhem erupted all around the referee was left with little option but to abandon the game and award the trophy to Swindon. Not surprisingly the presentation took place well out of sight of the rioters who seemed intent on razing the San Paolo to the ground!

That same year controversy erupted once more when with Napoli closing in on their first title, sinister events occurred at the San Siro in Milan that caused cries of corruption in Naples. In Neapolitan footballing folklore it became known as the 'Bag snatch at the San Siro'. An all-or-nothing clash against Inter with the winner likely to clinch the title. With the Southerners leading 1-0 at half-time through their Brazilian talisman Jose Altafini, the game turned on it's head in the second period when the home side were awarded an imaginary penalty that defied belief by referee Sergio Gonnella. Napoli stopper Dino Panzanato was again in the forefront of battle as he was alleged to have fouled Inter great Sandro Mazzola. The resulting spot-kick was slammed home by another Milan legend, centre forward Roberto Boninsegna, to set up a tense finale. Boninsegna had not yet finished with the Neapolitans and in the closing moments he stabbed home a gut-churning winner to break their hearts. Following the final whistle an outraged Panzanato had to be physically restrained by his teammates from attacking Gonnella who was swiftly ushered away out of harm's way. For the Southerners it all stank to high heaven. How do you defeat an enemy that never took to the field and yet still retained the power to influence? Their spirit shattered, SSC Napoli ultimately finished in third place with Inter taking the championship and neighbours' AC grabbing runners-up.

It hardly got any better.
Stricken by mounting debt, Napoli's new President Corrado Ferlaino was forced to cash in on some of his major assets, and to the absolute horror of Naples, a reluctant Ferlaino sold off the family jewels to Juventus. Jose Altafini and Dino Zoff moved North to Turin in a deal that allowed the club to stay afloat. Decades of overspending had finally seen Napoli hoisted by their own petard. It was the eternal struggle. Forever at the races, but never backing the winner. In typical Neapolitan street theatre fashion both Zoff and more significantly Altafini returned to haunt them in an infamous final encore. Basking in the twilight of a glorious career, Jose Altafini enjoyed a sumptuous golden summer at Turin. In the 1972-73 season, it was his 200th league goal in the last match of the campaign that clinched yet another Scudetto for Juve. He also would have one last role to play in the eternally tragic history of SSC Napoli. Cast as chief villain in the despised colours of their most bitter rivals, the Brazilian would deliver the ultimate coup de grace to his one-time love. For time immemorial, until their volcano decided otherwise, Jose Altafini's name would be spat out with venom in Naples. He would become known as 'Core Ngrato' ('The ungrateful heart'). Towards the end of the 1974-75 season, SSC Napoli and Juve were involved in one of the tightest finishes ever to an Italian championship. The title had all but come down to one match played in the Agnelli's personal fiefdom of Turin. The atmosphere inside the Stadio Comunale was electric. In a show of amazing loyalty and sheer defiance the Napoli tifosi had

infiltrated around the ground to vastly outnumber the home supporters. With many thousands of Neapolitans living in Turin and employed by Agnelli's Fiat Company, tickets were easily snapped up. The Comunale was draped blue and white. It appeared as if all of Naples had descended upon Turin to make sure their team did not again fail them. Many years later this scenario would again appear, only with a happy ending. In a rousing encounter the home side drew first blood on nineteen-minutes when winger Franco Causio struck to give Juve a half-time lead. Once more the title looked set for Turin, then, with thirty minutes remaining, SSC Napoli's beloved captain, Antonio Juliano, smashed home an equalizer and bedlam erupted in the Comunale. Juliano had set up a grandstand finale. The championship became a shootout, nothing less, next goal wins! The Neapolitans roared forward as immortality beckoned. With the home team looking spent and Napoli creating chances at will, only the magnificent efforts of goalkeeper Zoff, a one-time Southern idol prevented a massacre. At last the title appeared Naples-bound. As the clock ticked down and Juve were holding on by the skin of their imperial teeth, many in the Stadio Comunale sensed it was not to be Napoli's day. As Neapolitans held their breath and prayed for a goal, fate once more transpired against them. High above San Gennaro looked away, his hands tied, it was happening again as one of their own, Jose Altafini delivered the knockout punch. Altafini latched on to a clearance on the edge of the Napoli goal and without feeling or remorse for his former love smashed home to leave them cursing their old flame. There was no time to come back, the final whistle blew and the sound of collective grieving amid the Napoli tifosi was felt back in Naples. Again, the city wept.

The following season saw little consolation gained even with a comforting, 4-0 thrashing of Hellas Verona to win Lo Coppa Italia for a second time. Overall, it mattered little, for the Southern hordes lay grieving. Jose Altafini had not only broken hearts, he had come indecently close to destroying their spirit. Yet, still they rose once more to keep the faith. Mocked, abused and derided as mere barbarians and a sore on the face of all Italy, the followers of SSC Napoli licked their wounds, dusted themselves down, sang their songs and prepared to fight another day. Great players came and went. One of the best was legendary Dutch master Rudi Krol. He arrived in 1980, and under Krol's leadership, inspired by his immaculate fifty-yard passes sprayed delightfully around the field, Napoli earned a third-place spot. However, even this achievement was dulled by Juventus winning the title in Naples on the penultimate Sunday of the season, when to half of Turin's delight the Neapolitans were forced to play host to the gloating celebrations of the Grand 'Old Lady'. To make matters worse the 1-0 victory came courtesy of an own goal. Many present in the San Paolo that day swore as the ball crossed the line, Vesuvio itself let loose a groan of bitter disappointment. Naples wept, how many tears did a city have to shed? The years rolled on and still the trophy cabinet lay bereft of the title. History decreed that a club with such resources and a fanbase such as SSC Napoli, the third largest city in Italy would one day triumph, but when? Always tomorrow? Love, hate and love again. Amore.

It was four years before Maradona.

CHAPTER FIVE

EL PIBE DE ORO

The Naples night come laced with lurid tales of debauchery and decadence that would have made the Borgias blush. In the Hotel Royal, women flowed freely as the alcohol and the white powder. As one left another came. An entire floor was given over to Diego Maradona and friends and each night it rocked in true orgiastic style. Anything went, staff stayed tight-lipped at what they witnessed for they recognised the faces of some of those who kept Maradona company deep into the witching hour. The word got passed. It was thought best to keep your fucking mouth shut. A hotel once renowned for it's hospitality and clientele was turned overnight into one unholy den of ill repute. So, it was with great delight that the dignified figure of the Royal's Maitre De, Ettore Bosse, received word from Napoli officials that his most famous guest was moving out. The sighs of relief could be heard all across Naples.

The district of Posillipo, perched high on the top of sea-ravaged cliffs, offers it's residents enchanting views of the bay and Mount Vesuvio. It was home to the more affluent members of Neapolitan society, both legal and otherwise. Judges and politicians lived alongside corrupt government officials and drug barons. The smell of freshly-laundered cash lingered amidst the sweet aroma of exotic flower bowls and lemon groves. Sprinklers drenched immaculate green cut lawns, giving fresh life beneath a scorching Southern sun: clean money. The great, good and downright scandalous. Neighbours deemed fit for this dubious king with a crown of thorns. Posillipo would play host for seven years to Maradona and his band of freeloaders as they attempted to drink Naples dry.

At first, he turned up his nose at the luxurious two-floor apartment in Via Scipione Capece, given to him by Napoli that came with a personal downstairs gym and a huge garage for his fleet of cars. Maradona claimed he would only vacate the Royal, if accommodation similar to the mansion he had inherited in Spain became available. In Catalonia, the lurid tales of drink and drug-fuelled orgies that took place there had already catapulted into the realms of Catalan legend. They christened it 'Dodge City'. Maradona's rented residence in the rich neighbourhood of Pedrales. If the Barcelona newspaper gossip columns were to be only half believed it was nothing more than an incestuous pit inhabited by Argentinian demons and whores constantly wasted on drugs and drink! A description wildly colourful and off the mark? To a point, but it was true some of the Maradona clan's antics that allegedly occurred in Pedrales, caused even the most open-minded Catalans to shake their heads in disbelief. Dark whispers, tall tales of prostitutes queuing to enter, copious amounts of wine and white powder flowing freely. Crazed goings on in the giant size swimming pool which had been repainted at Maradona's request with Barca colours. Orgiastic frenzies the likes hardly associated with the sombre and serious residence of Pedrales. Porn movies shown on huge screens. Screeching cars way past midnight blasting out music as they raced. All this and at it's very heart a partying Diego, who desired something of similar size and stature.

When it was explained to him that this was impossible due to the overcrowding in Naples and the sheer lack of space,

he grudgingly moved himself and his clan uptown to Posillipo.
One reason more than any other saw Diego change tact when told.
In 1980, to the abject horror of all Naples, the miracle of San Gennaro failed to transpire. Many feared this an omen for impending disaster. While the rest of Italy laughed and dismissed such nonsense as Neapolitan witchcraft, the ground exploded in nearby Irpinia on the 23rd November. 3,000 people were killed in a fearsome earthquake, 7000 injured and 250,000 people left homeless. It was catastrophic. The area was devastated, billions of Lira and medical aid poured into the South, but the Camorra ripped off most in an array of cunning and malicious schemes. No sooner indeed had the re-housing projects began than the lead engineer in charge was shot for refusing to accept a pay-off. All the while the homeless were left with no option but to pay the Camorra protection money for the ramshackle dwellings they were forced to live in. Naples was also rocked on it's heels as the earth trembled along the coastline. For most Neapolitans these tragic events came as no surprise. Sadly, no one heeded San Gennaro's warning and death and chaos descended upon the region. Four years on and thousands of people in the surrounding areas still lived in tents and makeshift homes, as there was no room in the already over-populated city. It would have harmed Maradona's reputation if his petulance became public knowledge. Aware of how important it was for Diego's image to remain untarnished, Jorge Cyterszpiler argued that it made more sense to go quietly. However, on being informed of what happened in Irpinia, Maradona had already made his mind up. So, the king had a new home: the court jesters turned up the ghetto blaster, the

neighbours pretended not to mind and life for Diego carried on in it's own inimitable way.

All this apart, when the time arose to adorn the light blue of SSC Napoli, Maradona did so in a way that exhilarated and charmed the footballing soul. He became every Neapolitan's brother, every girlfriend's lover. His picture adorned the bedroom wall of every youngster in the city. An infatuation that was healthy for the heart, wonderful for the ego. but ultimately deadly for the soul. For something so intense could eventually end only one way. In tears.

The week following the epic victory against Udinese and courtesy of Maradona, the Neapolitans staged a smash and grab raid in Florence, home of the great South Americans Daniel Passarella of Argentina and the Brazilian Socrates. On an ice rink of a surface at the Stadio Artemio Franchi, with bright specks of snow melting under a winter sun, the 'Viola' of Fiorentina were beaten by a fantastic effort on forty-nine minutes from the Argentinian as he played a clever wall-pass with striker Luigi Caffarelli, before firing his club well clear of the relegation zone. Caffarelli was one of many Napoli players who began to shine in the wake of Maradona's sudden surge into top gear. His clever link-play with the dancing feet of the Argentinian bursting deep from midfield was becoming an integral part of Napoli's play. It proved to be the only goal and the Fiorentina tifosi, the Collettivo Autonomo Viola, seething at losing to the Southerners acted in typical fashion by attempting a full-scale assault against the gloating Neapolitans at full-time. Strangely, both shared some common ground, an unholy, rabid hatred of Juventus, but when at each other's throats across the battlegrounds of Serie A, this mattered little as they sought ways to outwit the Carabinieri and ignite World War Three on the beautiful ancient streets of the Medici's Florence. Unlike the Neapolitans, whose loathing for the 'Old Lady' stretched back decades and came etched with social and political reasons, the Fiorentina following hated Juve for entirely footballing matters. Two years previous all of Florence was convinced that sinister tactics had been employed and someone at Juve's behest had bribed officials to rob them of the championship on the last day of the season. A penalty by the wonderful Irish schemer Liam Brady gifted Juventus the Scudetto after Fiorentina saw a goal controversially ruled out. It was one if allowed that would have handed them the title, but it was not to be and the Florence skyline was lit up crimson red for three nights as riots erupted across the city. At the time such scenarios occurred with disturbing frequency in Italy. A dark hand, meddling and fixing. Many were caught taking poisoned gold, amongst the most famous Paolo Rossi, whose goals led Italy to victory in the 1982 World Cup. History now recalls that during the eighties match fixing was rife in Serie A, and nowhere more than in the South. Everything and anyone could be got at. In time, SSC Napoli would also appear to suffer the same torment as what befell Fiorentina.

In the month of February, the Neapolitans began a steady climb up the table. Respectable draws were earned with league leaders Verona and away to the impressive Sampdoria in Genoa. In both matches Napoli held their own and after extracting revenge against Torino in Naples with goals from Maradona and Caffarelli, European qualification became a distinct possibility. Following an away draw on the lakes of Como, earned with yet another Maradona penalty, the Neapolitans prepared to play host to struggling Lazio. It was in this game that their number ten shown the full extent of what he was truly capable of when the mood arose. An occasion so memorable that those lucky enough to attend would never tire of boring their children with the fantastic tale of when Maradona put the Romans of Lazio to the sword, in the glorious amphitheatre of the San Paolo. No lions or tigers, just Diego.

It had been ten years since the legendary Welsh-born Giorgio Chinaglia led Lazio to their only Scudetto triumph to set half of Rome ablaze. Since winning the championship, this club that once proudly boasted Benito Mussolini amongst it's most fervid supporters had suffered the indignities of match fixing scandals, relegation and years of mediocrity. So, it was no great surprise that again they found themselves involved in a battle royal at the foot of the table to avoid Serie B. It had proved a traumatic campaign for the 'Biancocelesti' ('The whites and skies'). Lazio had begun poorly and slowly as the months passed, collapsed like a pack of cards to turn into a broken rabble. In a desperate gamble to turn the grim tide they hired legendary veteran Argentinian manager Juan Carlos Lorenzo. The controversial sixty-four-year-old Lorenzo was in his third spell as coach of Lazio and a reputation for win at all cost tactics went before him. This man, who would stoop to any level to see his team achieve victory, prepared for one last throw in Serie A. During a career which stretched back four decades and included a period managing his country in the 1966 World Cup finals (Antonio Rattin and all), Lorenzo earned everlasting notoriety when he led Argentinian champions Estudiantes to unprecedented success, culminating in winning the World Cup Championship The chaos, violence and thuggery involved saw Lorenzo's ruthless doctrine castigated and reviled, but in an age where the result was everything, he became a wanted man and Lazio lured him to Rome. There, he earned the eternal gratitude of his tifosi by regularly beating hated cross-city rivals Roma and finally qualifying for Europe. But after a series of embarrassing altercations against English sides Arsenal and Ipswich in the UEFA Cup, where Lorenzo wound his team up to such an extent that they attacked the Arsenal players in a restaurant following a game in Rome, he was reluctantly forced to bid arrivederci to the ancient Capital. Now, sadly for the Lazio cause, Juan Carlos Lorenzo's fire had waned and the man who took his seat on the bench in the San Paolo was a mere shadow of the fanatical character whose teams had once terrorised and conquered the world. The Roman tifosi had prayed that someone with such a vast wealth of experience would help them pull off a miraculous escape. Sadly, Lorenzo was a man handed the keys to a car after it had already crashed. His arrival failed miserably to inspire and by the time Lazio arrived in Naples, plans were already underfoot for his replacement. The relegation trapdoor was looming and a disgraceful surrender at home to Udinese where they were thrashed 4-1 saw the supporters turn savagely. Defeat by the Neapolitans and the ringing of the death knell would be heard loud two hundred miles away in Rome. Rino Marchesi did not relish the idea of twisting the dagger any further into the bleeding, open wounds of his beloved former club. Marchesi had played for five years with Lazio and they still held a special place in his heart. However, the Neapolitans who waited with bated breath for a raging Maradona to send the Romans home weeping did not share such feelings. For them the only decent thing to come out

of Rome was the Autostrada winding it's way back South. Neapolitans had grown weary of self-righteous, crusading politicians crying crocodile tears for their city. Rome represented everything they detested, an arrogant, aloof central government that had washed it's hands of Naples and all her ailments. Overcrowding, a spiraling crime rate and a poverty level unsurpassed anywhere in the Western world. All mattered little,
for Romans eyed the Mezzogiorno with nothing but contempt.
There's an old adage in Naples. 'God helps those who help themselves'.
Where Neapolitans saw themselves as resourceful and relying on their streetwise wits to survive, elsewhere they were seen as lazy, foul, unkempt, lacking in morals and having no respect for authority. Well aware the Camorra held sway and called the shots in the murky waters of Neapolitan politics, Rome's hierarchy were always suspicious and reluctant to sanction financial aid to a city deemed unrulable and so openly abused. The uncollected tax revenue from Naples alone ran into billions. Extortion rackets strangled the life out of any business that dared to chance a dream. A law unto themselves, a culture apart. A place whose heart and soul lay shackled in the cruel and ruthless chains of the underworld. The Mezzogiorno was best left alone to rot.
Such attitudes by outsiders tarring all Neapolitans with the same brush infuriated the vast majority who wished only to earn an honest living. Hammering the living daylights out of Lazio and banging another nail into the relegation coffin would, in a small way, offer sweet revenge. For despite all the grandeur of Rome – the Coliseum, the Vatican, St

Peter's Basilica, the Spanish steps, the Sistine Chapel – Napoli possessed their own wonder in Maradona.
The Biancocelesti entered into the lion's den.
A city expected: they were handed a typically warm Neapolitan greeting with 86,000 tifosi screaming abuse and demanding Roman blood. Vesuvio rumbled in gruesome expectation. The teams broke away for a brief warm-up before battle commenced. Juan Carlos Lorenzo, a man who had seen it all in his many years, feared the worse and crossed himself, praying for the day to go well. No one was listening and Lazio's descent into footballing hell began. In a storming first half Napoli threw everything they had at the besieged Lazio defence. Fernando Orsi in the visitors' goal was peppered with shots as the home side carried the game to them. The noise from the crowd soared high towards the heavens whenever Diego Maradona received possession. He appeared to ignite jet fuel as he tricked and weaved past hapless Lazio defenders. The haunted expression of Lorenzo on the touchline told it's own story as the bewildering Maradona twisted the rearguard of Calisti, Filisetti, Vianello and Padovino first one way then another. The stadium swayed, ebbed and rocked with delight as their favourite son wreaked mayhem. Each foray by Napoli into the Romans' half came tinged with memories past, of slurs and chants suffered, flags that waved *'Cholera'* in their faces after the earthquake of 1980. Well fuck you Rome. Fuck you.
Half-time came and swiftly disappeared with the Neapolitan tifosi dancing throughout, singing the name of their hero. The siege was relentless and finally a breakthrough occurred when a terrible backpass by the centre-half Vianello was read by Maradona, who took the ball in his stride before lashing a vicious strike past Orsi

into the top corner of the net. The white shirts dropped to their knees. A brave stand had been broken, as had their spirit for a fight. With the travelling Lazio supporters fearing the worse it duly happened when an own goal by Filisetti left Orsi helpless to double Napoli's lead. The Rome-born goalkeeper pounded the Neapolitan earth, the game was up. Juan Carlos Lorenzo stood motionless as bedlam erupted around him; his mind was already back home in Argentina. Before he departed Italian shores, a fellow countryman was about to hand him a going away present that he would never forget. On eighty-four minutes, Diego Maradona scored a goal that would live forever in the memories of all present on that long-gone Sunday afternoon. From forty-yards he smashed a dramatic half-volley past a disbelieving Orsi. As the ball screamed into the net delirium broke out on the terraces. Around the stadium people danced uncontrollably in the aisles. The San Paolo was in a state of hysteria as Diego disappeared beneath a heap of bodies smothering him with thanks. Players, club officials, ballboys, even a hysterical Napoli policeman joined in. The goal-fest wasn't over. Maradona had not yet finished with the traumatized Romans. Three minutes from time the hat-trick was completed when he scored again. This time a curling effort direct from a corner that once more Fernando Orsi failed miserably on. The magical little Argentinian had dipped back into his box of tricks to end a depressing and humiliating day for Lazio. 4-0 and so much for a thousand years of history and all the grandeur of Rome?
El Diego had ended his first season on Italian soil with an impressive third place in the goalscoring charts, finishing only behind the great Michel Platini and Allesandro Altobelli with an outstanding tally of fourteen goals. A

reputation that had become tarnished after his brief nightmare sojourn in Barcelona was enhanced. Naples was seen to have got itself a bargain. To the delight of their followers Napoli finished a respectable eighth position and could hold their heads high. Further highlights included another rampaging performance in the San Paolo, this time a revenge mission against Inter Milan, two goals from Daniel Bertoni inspiring them to a sparkling 3-1 victory. Towards the final weeks Juventus went South and were lucky to escape with a draw. Neapolitan honour had been duly served. The last game saw Fiorentina beaten 1-0 in Naples and a wonderful ovation for the team at the full-time whistle. Diego Maradona had dragged SSC Napoli kicking and screaming out of the relegation mire and into mid-table safety. A seed of hope had been planted under heavenly blue Neapolitan skies and was already beginning to flower. For once life under the volcano was good. As for the championship, that darned elusive Scudetto.
Maybe next year?

CHAPTER SIX

IRREVERSIBLE SUNRISE

Under a jet-black Neapolitan sky that glistened with stars and a striking full moon, the port of Naples entered the midnight shift. Lit by torchlight, scurrying figures whose faces lay masked hurried towards the waiting ships. Freight lorries sat empty on the quayside: their owners nervous, fretting, and eager to be loaded and away. As a city slept the Camorra went to work. Contraband smuggled from far and near. From Sicily, their good friends in Palermo, Africa, and the Balkans. Drugs, cigarettes, alcohol. Rolex watches, even human cargo to be used for prostitution and labour was unloaded down plank-ways to be whisked away under the dead of night. Nearby, port officials and night watchmen played cards, their palms already crossed with silver. Armed lookouts along the seafront kept a wary eye for Carabinieri patrols, their Uzi machine pistols hidden from sight. On a dark beautiful canvas lit by moonlight this is business, Camorra style: the midnight shift.

Princes of the Forcella. Don Vittorio Giuliano was the father and founding member of a family dynasty that ruled secretly over the Forcella district of the city for twenty years. His was a clan united by blood that dealt in blood. As a child in post-World War Two Naples rubble, Vittorio had little choice but to mature fast through his tender years in order to survive as a Scugnizzi (street kid). Vittorio would run errands for the neighbourhood Camorristi. He listened enthralled as the old time guappos related crazy tales of legendary characters from the Neapolitan underworld (some fantasy, others frighteningly real), who refused to answer to anyone except God and San Gennaro. Rome least of all. Young Giuliano dreamt that one day men would talk of him in such hushed tones of awe. As a teenager, Vittorio formed his own street gang and quickly got a fine reputation as a good earner. Rich pickings could be found in the city's seaport, a window to the world and here Giuliano excelled. A little planning, greasing of palms and soon he and his gang were making a small fortune from smuggled contraband, mostly cigarettes, robbed from visiting ships. At nineteen, Vittorio Giuliano's luck ran out when after insulting a policeman in public he found himself behind bars. It was hardly a serious offence, but with Giuliano's activities well known it proved a perfect opportunity to get him off the Naples streets. A mistake and one that the Neapolitan authorities would come to regret, for during his time in jail this young hood from the slums of the Forcella saw his ambitions soar. Up to that time Giuliano had only been playing at being a gangster, but once forcibly enrolled into Naples 'University of life' he was given the finest education possible. On release, Vittorio gathered around him trusted young men as he began expanding his business interests to the gambling, prostitution and protection rackets. A move into the murderous, if lucrative heroin and marijuana drugs market handed them the necessary funds to secure their future by paying off those who had vowed to bring them to justice. No one or nothing was allowed to stand in Giuliano's way as he carved up the Forcella to make it his own. Rival gangs in the districts faced the option of coming under the wing of this new kid on the block or being wiped out. Those who chose to fight were shown no mercy as the name Vittorio Giuliano became feared and respected not only in the city, but also across the entire region of Campania. The wise Don Vittorio married the daughter of a local bigshot who bore him many sons. This delighted Giuliano, for in a place like the Forcella, where betrayal and death lurked around every corner, he needed blood clan. In Naples, almost anything could be bought except blind loyalty. Such a rarity came only through family. Luigi, Carmine, Guglielmo and Rafaele would all follow in their father's footsteps. Come the eighties and with Don Vittorio in semi-retirement, his offspring prospered to carry on the family business. Ruling their kingdom with a disturbing concoction of a kind hand and senseless brutality, they resembled a Neapolitan institution and were as close to royalty that Naples could muster.

Sitting next to the city's main railway station, the Forcella was more Third World than European in appearance. It came as an immediate eye opener for quizzical tourists who foolishly contrived to discover for themselves the real Naples. Known locally as the Kasbah, it was firstly established as a main base for the flourishing Neapolitan black market during the Allied wartime occupation. There, anything for the right price could be bought. Never a question asked. An unwritten rule was always that the Giuliano clan received a cut of anything sold. The consequences for those few foolish enough to ignore was severe. An utter contempt for the authorities was such that any attempt made to bring them to heel was met with the deadly hail of Kalashnikov bullets and a barrage of kidnappings, car bombs and pay-offs.
The Forcella was off bounds, for it simply was not worth the price in blood that would be spilled in trying to clean it up. Many Napoli football tifosi supplemented measly

incomes by hiring their services to the Giulianos. These ranged from peddling contraband, drug trafficking, arson, and, when the call came from above, the ultimate act. For those brave enough to take on the Camorra, the threat of assassination became a constant companion. Shopkeeper, businessman, lawyer, politician, it mattered little. A bomb, bullet or knife awaited anyone who dared oppose them. Come the eighties, the Vico Della Pace was the heart of their criminal kingdom. Also known as the 'Casino Forcella'. A Camorra sanctuary and the private residence of Luigi Guiliano, the then head of the family clan. From the outside resembling only a simple Naples' backstreet three-storey residence building, but inside it was nothing short of a palace. No accounting for taste. Three floors of the finest dirty money could buy. Unadulterated, nouveau-rich Neapolitan style. A marble stairway, velvet red carpeted throughout. The finest antique furniture, priceless paintings by the greatest Italian artists, even throw in a couple of grand pianos. No expense spared. What could not be bought was stolen. Once the client had been vetted by heavily armed guards and allowed through the bombproof door, they were greeted by a huge statue of the Madonna. On permanent loan from the Vatican. The first floor's main function was to serve as a gambling paradise for millionaire members. An exclusive clientele list of Naples' finest degenerate gamblers. All took place in a grandiose hall with a huge tromp d'oeil depicting a terrace on the sea, and green gaming tables filled with decks of cards, playing chips and a gold roulette wheel. Only the best for players with money to burn and lose. On the second floor was a billiards hall and an alcove leading to a gold-plated bathroom. This was dominated by a lavishly, monstrous oyster-shape bathtub later to be immortalised in a photograph taken of Diego Maradona with the Guiliano brothers. Next door was three luxurious bedrooms and in one of these sat a false wardrobe that gave access to a trapdoor taking you to the roof if ever in need of a swift getaway. Above, on the top floor was Don Luigi's living quarters. Off limits to all but blood. Below all three levels in the basement was the brothers hang out/headquarters. Here family business was dealt with. This was in all but name a war bunker with enough firepower piled high to kick start a revolution in the South. It was also home to several hidden entrances that led off to secret passages into the city. Here was where the unofficial government of the Forcella ran their criminal fiefdom. Woe betide any whoever dared take liberties. Anyone…

As if cursed, Jorge Cyterszpiler stood once more on the edge of financial ruin. A series of amateurish, commercial enterprises to promote his client's name in Barcelona had seen his reputation as some manipulative whizz-kid in tatters. More importantly Cyterszpiler now realized his job hung by the slenderest of threads. The twenty-six-year-old knew their time in Italy had to prove worthwhile off the pitch. He simply had to turn *Maradona Productions* into a profitable organization and be seen doing so. Make some real cash to keep the boss happy. Diego's blind assumption that money grew on trees meant many a sleepless night tossing and turning for the Argentinian. Whilst Maradona lived it up with his love of Naples nightlife, a twenty-plus entourage, a Ferrari, a Rolls Royce, a Porsche, a luxury yacht, plus an insatiable appetite for women and cocaine, Jorge Cyterszpiler sweated buckets looking for the next paycheck.

Theirs' was a friendship formed when both were teenagers. Where Maradona caused palpitations in grown men's hearts every time he stepped onto a football pitch, Cyterszpiler was a sad figure of fun, an overweight youth, forever miserable and cursed with a straggling limp, a sad legacy of a childhood ravaged by polio. Such misfortunes saw him lapse into a dark period of depression. It was only when a concerned family friend persuaded Jorge to accompany him to a nearby football match that his true vocation in life called. Playing that day was a fourteen-year-old from the back of beyond called Diego Maradona. After finding the courage to introduce himself to the young Diego, an enduring friendship between the two began. The raggedy kid from the dustbowl shacks of Villa Fiorito, and the middle class Jewish boy from one of the leafier suburban areas of uptown Buenos Aires. Many a night Maradona escaped the hardships of Villa Fiorito to stay over at his new-found friend's house. They would talk until the early hours about hopes for the future. An unlikely double act, but close nonetheless and sharing a wish to be the best at what they did. After securing for himself a business degree Jorge Cyterszpiler was asked by Diego Maradona to become his manager in all matters financial. A touched Cyterszpiler said yes whole-heartedly to his amigo and together their journey to the stars began. Maradona trusted his friend implicitly with not just hard-earned dollars, but more importantly the financial security of his family. At first this was deemed by Cyterszpiler as a privilege, but as time went by and Diego started to act like the spoilt kid in the playground, wanting all the best toys, it developed into a heavy burden. He, much as anyone was blinded by Maradona's genius and sadly it blurred him from the harsh realities that the books always had to balance. Fortunately, the transfer to Naples, hoped Cyterszpiler, would give him the perfect opportunity to grab hold tight of the reins, have a long think, pay off standing debts and ensure the money started to roll in. This once dumpy kid who everybody laughed at, or worse pitied, was ready to make his own mark in the wonderful, weird world of Maradona. Jorge coveted dollar bills like Diego loved a ball. He was determined to impress by showing true business acumen and wring every last Lira out of Neapolitan pockets. Flood Naples high streets with Diego Maradona products, sit back and watch the money come rolling in. Unfortunately, much to the Argentinian's distress, somebody had already beat him to it.

Carmine Giuliano was thirty-two-years-old and a Camorra Prince of the City, when Diego Maradona streaked like a bolt of lightning into his midst. His nickname 'Il Lione' (The Lion), was well deserved. Although Giuliano appeared just like any other young Neapolitan male with his wavy black hair and demonstrative swagger, the eyes gave light to his true character. Dangerous, all seeing, mysterious and downright frightening. The signing of the legendary Maradona was viewed as an ideal opportunity for rich picking by the Camorra. As Diegomania erupted across Naples, 'Il Lione' marshalled together his huge army of hustlers. With Neapolitans keen to be parted from their cash for anything with the player's name emblazoned upon it, the gangs cleaned up. For as blessed Diego Maradona was with his talents, so, the Camorra were equally gifted in what they did. Keen also to lure Maradona into their inner circle, the brother's Giuliano devised a plan. It was one deemed simple but effective. They would laud him with kind words, reverence and a respect reserved only for a king. It was time to throw a party. Show the new boy who really ruled Naples.

At seeing Neapolitan vendors and peddlers on every street corner selling all types of unlicensed Maradona-themed goods, Jorge Cyterszpiler became driven to despair. An indignant Cyterszpiler fumed and rather foolishly began making public noises threatening to sue whoever was behind this unofficial merchandising campaign. Naples had become awash with Diego-related hats, cups, scarves, flags, T-shirts, posters and bed sheets. At the city's heart in the Bassi. Naples' most poverty-stricken slum area, entire families worked day and night in airless tiny one-room flats to cope with the mass demand. No one complained for business had never been better. There was food on the table, Napoli were winning and nothing else mattered. There appeared only one individual in the entire city unhappy with proceedings. However, Cyterszpiler's hard stance softened quite dramatically when representatives of the Camorra paid him a visit to 'recommend' that it would be in his best interest to stop making threats, for such arrogance from an outsider would not be tolerated. It was politely explained to the perspiring Jorge Cyterszpiler that 'The poor people of Naples should be allowed to make a living.' Frightened for his life, Cyterszpiler swiftly changed tact. He was smart enough to realize that although the message was delivered in a calm and friendly manner, the next time would not be so amicable. In this place like no other, business was conducted in a manner that could not be taught in any school or university. For twenty-six was no age to meet your maker and he hardly relished the idea of being throttled with his body hurled over the side of a fishing boat into the bay of Naples, as food for the fishes. Jorge Cyterszpiler had been handed an unforgettable lesson in the ways of his adopted city.

Though hurting badly, it was one to take on board and simply move on.

Theirs' was an invitation dreaded but never declined. A fleeting view through a half-opened door at a world and it's people, for whom normal rules of society did not apply. In the early weeks of January 1986, on a bitter, cold January morning, two young emissaries from the clan Giuliano went to Napoli's training complex in Soccavo on the city's edge. Known with typically, ironic Neapolitan humour as the 'Paradise Centre' it was hardly worthy of a side with ambitions to win Serie A. Quite simply it was a dump. Run down to the point of antiquated, the centre was a constant source of bitterness amongst the players. As ever at Soccavo, security was tight as hundreds of Neapolitan tifosi milled around, desperate to catch a glimpse of their hero. The Camorra messengers appeared like any other of the supporters gathered at the main gates. But these two were different, for after a whispered conversation with a huddle of burly Napoli security guards, they were ushered through to be granted an audience with the normally untouchable Diego Maradona. The Argentinian was approached with great courtesy and informed they were there on behalf of Carmine Giuliano to invite him to a party being held in nearby Nola. The message to Diego Maradona conveyed in the hushed tones of a servant speaking to his king. It was explained that his presence would be deeply appreciated by Don Carmine and the brothers who wished to extend the hand of friendship. How could he possibly refuse? Though aware of their notorious reputation and how they earned a living, Maradona felt no qualms in gratefully accepting, for he and the brothers had met briefly many times on his countless sojourns in Naples' fleshpots and drinking holes. The opportunity to attend was viewed by the player as an ideal chance to mix with those who were just like him. Men whom had dragged themselves kicking and screaming from a lifetime of poverty to earn money, power and, ultimately, respect. Whom had refused point blank to accept the hand fate dealt them. To rage against God's will. That the Giulianos chose to live their life outside establishment rules saw Maradona's admiration for them increase no end. The brothers had come from nothing to Princes' of the City. The Forcella belonged to them, no argument. A kingdom within. A childhood spent in the shattered wastelands of Villa Fiorito, where only a heaven-sent gift for football helped Diego Maradona escape, saw him recognize kindred spirits, blood brothers in the Giulianos. He would later say of those early years in Argentina, 'If you had money for food you ate, and if you didn't, you didn't.' Unknown to most and shrouded in the swirling fog of Naples politics, Camorra money was hugely instrumental in bringing Maradona from Barcelona. Only those skilled in the ways of Neapolitan intrigue knew the truth. For the substantial investment the gangs expected much in return, not least the opportunity to be seen in his company and to bask in Maradona's illustrious shadow. To impress women and dazzle friends. Like a dangling puppet on a string, he would be made to dance for their amusement.

Nola: 1985. The gleaming array of Jaguars, Porsches and Ferraris littering the parking area of the palatial villa chosen to host that sumptuous occasion hinted heavily at the glittering guest list. Politicians, actors, rock stars, judges, even respected men of the cloth, the church's finest, mixed openly with a fearful cast of characters who served the Giulianos in any number of ways. From the loyal foot-soldiers patrolling the surrounding ground, armed with machine pistols and Alsatian dogs at their heel, to the lawyers who robbed more with one briefcase than mere guappos could ever dream of aspiring to with their guns and knives.

The beautiful people came out to play.

Vintage champagne served in crystal glasses, the finest caviar from the Baltic Sea. Pesce Spada (swordfish), Arogasta (lobster), all freshly caught. Endless lines of cocaine on a silver platter. It was a display of wealth and arrogance that dared the authorities to come and take them on. Lavish, extravagant, shocking, outrageous. Even in this mad, live for today city, nobody ever threw a party like the Giulianos. With regal pomp and gangster's swagger, Diego Maradona made a dramatic entrance. Feeling every eye in the building upon him, the king of Naples breezed through the front door, lapping up the adulation. This was his kind of world: Don Carmine Giuliano stepped forward out of the crowd to welcome his guest of honour into the fold. He kissed Maradona on both cheeks before embracing the smiling Argentinian to great applause. Carmine raised his glass calling for a toast. He ushered a photographer to capture the moment for posterity, wrapping an arm around Maradona as he did so. A flash went off and the cameraman quickly checked the snap was good before disappearing through a waiting exit into the Naples night. They had him.

As the evening wore on the dance floor filled with a dazzling concoction of drug and alcohol-fuelled, Versace-clad revelers dripping in jewellery. Diego Maradona amongst them. Like Scarface in football boots. The

dazzling neon rays illuminated diamond-studded shirts, sparkling gold bracelets and chains of the party goers, as they appeared determined to dance through the night, until the sun rose once more over Vesuvio the next morning. Away from the madding crowds the Giulianos attended to family business. There were those present who came seeking justice. A daughter's dishonour cleansed on the end of a fishhook. The brothers gave equal concern to all matters, either large or small, for they considered themselves the true law in the kingdom of Forcella. Diego Maradona partied long and hard as any. His glass constantly refilled before he ever had the chance to finish it, the white powder forever nearby if the desire arose. There was never a need to seek female companionship, for they sought him in droves. Like a preening alley cat that had the cream, Maradona took his pick. Throughout the night endless photographs were taken of the footballer with the brothers and other dubious family acquaintances. At the time it appeared all harmless fun, high spirits, but when the bad times came and Diego refused to perform, when the puppet strings were tugged, they would return to haunt him. Though early in his time in Naples, what happened that night set in motion momentous events from which, ultimately, there could be no turning back. As morning came and revellers staggered to their cars, home to bed, bright specks of sunlight appeared to cast large shadows over the steep slopes of the volcano. An Irreversible Sunrise had broken for Maradona.
He was well and truly hooked.

CHAPTER SEVEN

CROWN OF THORNS

In times gone by on a path laden knee deep with flowers, the triumphant Roman General took the tumultuous acclaim of thousands who lined the roads of ancient Rome, to honour and welcome him home. Senate law forbade the parade of an army through the city gates, so the General, all-splendid in a uniform of purple toga lined with gold and silver braid and etched with scenes of the victorious battle, entered in a single chariot with just a lone slave known as a lictore for company. The lictore had one purpose only: in order to prevent his master from thinking he was in any way God like, he would whisper constantly into his ear the words, 'Remember thou art only a mortal.' Holding high an ivory scepter that lay sculptured into an eagle's head, the General acknowledged the baying crowds who paid homage to the conquering hero. 'Remember thou art only a mortal,' uttered the lictore time and again. The General looked proudly on, the words hardly registering. 'Remember thou art only a mortal, remember thou art only a mortal, remember, remember...'

When the Pope met Diego. They watered down the Communion wine and warned the Vatican nuns to stay in their rooms. As San Gennaro prayed from a high for his boy not to embarrass him, Diego Maradona set off to Rome to meet the Pope. Maradona had received a Papal invitation for a private audience with his Holiness, Pope John Paul II, who himself was renowned as a goalkeeper of some standing and repute in his younger days in pre-World War Two Poland. Maradona journeyed to the

Eternal city with his family, girlfriend Claudia and agent Jorge Cyterszpiler. All excited at this opportunity to meet face to face with the Holy Father. They arrived at the Vatican to face a blazing charge of cameramen, journalists and photographers who were all eager to capture for posterity the moment the leader of the Southern barbarians entered onto the blessed grounds of St Peter's Square. Naples watched live on television as their favourite son was ushered through the paparazzi hysteria for a private meeting with the man given the arduous task of following in the shoes of the Fisherman. Dressed in a jet-black leather jacket with smart white shirt and black tie, Maradona caused Neapolitan hearts to burst with pride as he ventured beyond the Swiss Guard and into the sacred inner sanctums of the Vatican. Naples regarded him as one of their own. This was equally an honour for them as for him. On meeting his Holiness, Maradona smiled politely, but appeared visibly nervous throughout, his laughing eyes trying desperately to conceal secrets that would have made even the Borgias, those infamous past residents of the Vatican, cross themselves with red-faced embarrassment. Pope John Paul towered above Maradona as they engaged in polite conversation. The Pope's amiable patter, friendly manner and disarming smile took pity on the clearly ill-at-ease footballer who appeared to expect at any time someone to jump from behind a curtain and denounce him as a fraud. Diego's mother watched with pride. Dalma Salvadora Franco Maradona felt her eyes well up with tears. As for his girlfriend, Claudia, she smiled serenely as her boyfriend was lauded with plaudits for a clean-living lifestyle and for being an inspiration to all young men. Diego shook the hand of the Holy Father and accepted a set of blessed Rosary beads as a gift. He himself appeared close to tears. It was all a fine example of how effective the Maradona publicity machine operated and the truth was hidden and tampered with to suit a particular image. The Vatican had been duped, or if they knew the truth showed no intention of revealing it. For it suited them also to have the greatest footballer in the world parading his faith every time he scored a goal by making the sign of the cross and giving thanks to the Lord Almighty for divine assistance. What better publicity could there be?

Another lesser known side of what occurred on that long-gone day in the Vatican is much more Diego-like. In the early spring of 1985, after playing in the San Paolo for Napoli against Sampdoria, the Maradona clan set off Sunday night for the capital. Once in Rome, whilst his family settled down at one of the city's finest hotels, Diego and Jorge hit the clubs! Despite an early appointment the next day with the Pope our Argentinian friends indulged themselves with the best Roman nightlife had to offer. Lavish doses of cocaine, wine and call girls saw them come five in the morning both absolutely wasted. Whilst Jorge realised the time had arrived to try and get just a couple of hours sleep before the grand meeting, Diego decided against it and partied through.

Come the time, it was a bleary eyed-still wired Maradona who travelled alongside an equally tired Cyterszpiler to the Vatican the next morning. They were met in the square by the rest of the family. Diego's mother and father looking at the state of them with a mixture of anger, horror and despair. After being escorted into the Pope's private area by the Swiss Guard, Maradona found waiting for him a long line of bishops. Everybody wanting to meet the legendary Argentinian. After shaking every bishop's hand, finally Diego and Cyterszpiler were escorted into the

Pope's own private residence. There, along with his Holiness's personal assistant they sat and waited for the Pope to appear. By this time Diego was in a bad way. The cocaine comedown making him sweat and paranoid. He was shaking and this was noticed by Cyterszpiler.
'Are you okay Diego?' he asked.
Maradona whispered into Cyterszpiler 's ear. 'I need another line Jorge. Otherwise, I'm not going to be able to get through this.'
Cyterszpiler nods and tugs the arm of the Pope's assistant. 'May I have a quiet word?'
The assistant nods and the two men stand to go talk in a corner.
Cyterszpiler speaks quietly. Almost in a whisper. 'Diego has a problem with his stomach. Do you by any chance have a bathroom nearby?'
Nodding, the assistant points to a door. 'Of course,' he smiles.
'The Pope's private one over there. Please be our guest. Use that.'
Cyterszpiler smiles in thanks. 'Grazie your grace. He is simply nervous.'
Diego swiftly heads over. He shuts the door and pulls out a vial of cocaine, lines it up over the Pope's sink and snorts it. Once done, beaming and full of life again he exit's back. Suddenly, the huge double doors to the residence open and Pope John Paul heads in. Diego stands and goes to greet him. Grinning manically.
'Diego, it is wonderful to meet you' says the Pope. 'And smiling my son.
Always smiling.'…

'Ciao Corrado!' In the summer of 85, with an entire city ready to wage war on his command, Diego Maradona went in search of Napoli's supremo Corrado Ferlaino eager to pick a fight. A successful second half of the season in which he carried SSC Napoli almost single-handedly out of the relegation zone and into mid-table safety meant he felt confident that demands for the forthcoming campaign would be heeded. After all, what was a mere President when compared to a king? Ferlaino was relaxing in his office when suddenly the door swung open and in waltzed Diego Maradona. The dumbstruck President sat open-mouthed as Diego sat himself down, treated himself to one of Ferlaino's Cuban cigars, and greeted him with a cheery 'Ciao Corrado, we have got to talk?' Maradona began by making it clear that unless Ferlaino made a heavy investment in team rebuilding he was off. Diego put the fear of God into his supremo by wickedly suggesting he would seriously consider offers from elsewhere. Milan and Turin, being just two of the places thrown into the one-way conversation that caused the President to shift uneasy in his seat and wonder why the hell he had ever brought the troublesome Argentinian to Naples. A perturbed Ferlaino listened with growing fury as he found himself being lectured on how to get rid of the players whom the fans booed and replace them with better. Totally flabbergasted by Maradona's crazed assertion that it was he and not himself who ruled the roost over the city's football club. His piece said Maradona swaggered off, leaving behind a shaking, ashen-faced Corrado Ferlaino, speechless and seething with rage. Ferlaino watched from his window as Maradona's sleek black Ferrari sped away into the city. Although regarded by his fellow Neapolitans as heaven sent, the President remained convinced this cocky

Argentinian upstart had horns. He was of the old school, that players were seen and never heard. Mere servants of the club, not this fellow. Maradona had rewritten the rule book. President Ferlaino had bought himself a heap load of trouble and there was little he could do about it. Corrado bit his tongue for he knew that given enough rope Maradona would almost inevitably go too far. Only then, when the love affair was over, would revenge be had. As the lynch mob gathered at the gallows and the noose was tightened around the player's neck, maybe the same one that was being prepared for him, then the President would have no qualms about kicking away the chair. Until then he would try and resist the urge of having Maradona thrown into the volcano.

Rino Marchesi was proved correct in assuming his stay in Naples would not be long-term. His contract in the Neapolitan hot seat was not renewed and replacing him was the coach from Como, hard-nosed disciplinarian Ottavio Bianchi. Marchesi joined the long list of coaches who had tried and failed to bring success to the Neapolitan hordes. In came the stern Germanic features of forty-four-year-old Brescia-born Bianchi, who was a former Napoli player. He understood the pressures that went with such a role for his time in Napoli colours coincided with one of the Neapolitans' rare flirtations with success in the 1960's. Bianchi saw then at first hand the expectations and hopes of a city that lived and breathed Calcio. The slightest hint of glory and the people of Naples would be awoken with a passion unlike anywhere else in Italy. How great would it be for him to be the man that stirred the southern giant back to life? Bianchi carried with him from the Northern lakes of Como the well-deserved nickname of the 'Iron

Sergeant'. A deep-thinking man, he had devised a masterplan to win SSC Napoli the Scudetto and earn for himself an everlasting place in the hearts of all Neapolitans. Marchesi's game plan failed because it relied almost completely on the genius of Maradona, but not Bianchi's. He understood substantially more than just the dancing feet of the Argentinian was required if the dream was to be realised. For though no one doubted Maradona's role as the undisputed shining light of Napoli, even the brightest of stars needed a supporting cast of proven quality to perform to their true measure. Four months previously in March, at a secret location in the enemy territory of a plush Milan hotel, Corrado Ferlaino met secretly with Bianchi to secure his services. In a cloak and dagger operation designed to keep the Italian press at arm's length, Ferlaino thrashed out a deal with Ottavio Bianchi to prise him away from his beautiful villa on the banks of Lake Como and plunge him into the mad, crazy hotbed of Naples. Bianchi did not come cheap; amongst his vast wage demands was a guarantee that he be allowed a free hand in the transfer market. Bianchi handed Ferlaino a list of players required for the forthcoming season. The President assured him that he would do all in his power to acquire them, and indeed proved true to his word. Class acts such as the talented sweeper Allessandro Renica from Sampdoria and the explosive centre-forward Bruno Giordano from relegated Lazio were lured to Naples. Most surprisingly, from Serie A champions Hellas Verona, experienced goalkeeper Claudia Garella was persuaded to leave behind the sumptuous surroundings of Verona to play his football in the Southern Peninsula. Renica had impressed the previous seasons in Sampdoria's two clashes with Napoli. As for the exciting Giordano, his was a somewhat tainted background after he found himself caught up in the betting rigging scandals that rocked Italian football in the early eighties. Bruno Giordano was banned for two years with no appeal, whereas others such as Paolo Rossi were shown leniency, thus being allowed to partake in the 1982 World Cup finals, with dramatic consequences. Claudio Garella was needed to replace Napoli's keeper and long-time servant between the posts, Luigi Castellini. Garella had played in all of Verona's matches during the title-winning season and his performances had been instrumental in their success. The rivalry between the two cities was poisonous and Ferlaino's success in tempting the formidable Garella to move South was hailed as a brilliant signing and one in the eye for the hated Veronese. Ottavio Bianchi offered Corrado Ferlaino his hand, promising to see him soon in Naples. Little did Ferlaino realise how much he had gained on that miserable, damp, rainy Milan afternoon in winning the services of the tactically astute Bianchi. For in a short time he would grant every Neapolitan on this planet from Naples to New York to Rio their heart's desire.

There was a rotten stink and something had turned sour in the royal court of King Diego. The laughter had ceased. It had become obvious to all in the player's entourage that his behaviour and general demeanour to those around him was of someone suffering wild delusions of self-grandeur. The boss had turned into a bastard. The public- persona paraded by Maradona of a family-loving, God-fearing individual who lived only to bring joy to the people of Naples was in serious danger of being derailed by the man himself. The arrogant trait acquired by Maradona of referring to himself in the third instance and the petulant manner in which he treated those closest to him infuriated family and friends who tended to suffer the worst of his bad moods. One who felt the wrath of this petulant king with a crown of thorns more than any was his long-time girlfriend Claudia. At first a reluctance to believe the stories and rumours about Diego stemmed from the simple fact that he was the love of her young life, but as she experienced up close Maradona's metamorphism from mere mortal to Neapolitan idol she finally admitted defeat. Exhausted and humiliated by her partner's many indiscretions, Claudia fled Naples and returned home to Argentina nursing a broken heart, their stormy ten-year relationship seemingly at an end. The mist had cleared on the looking glass and what she saw filled her with horror. A man she despised had replaced the boy she once loved. Still not satisfied and appearing hell-bent on ridding himself of all those closest to him, Maradona struck again. For Jorge Cyterszpiler, lady luck would again conspire against him. The 1986 World Cup Finals were to be held in Mexico and the head of *Maradona Productions* had flown to it's capital beginning negotiations with a host of media and advertising companies, busy falling over themselves to sign up the greatest player in the world to promote their various products. All were prepared to pay handsomely to have Maradona's name and face emblazoned upon their screens, logos and on billboards. Cyterszpiler was swamped with agents desperate to gain his client's service. Free from the restraints of Naples and it's all-demanding Godfathers, the Argentinian felt certain his horrific run of bad luck was finally over. Jorge Cyterszpiler was on to a winner. Diego was gold dust, not only on the pitch, but commercially off it, equally so. *Maradona Productions* had hit the jackpot.

Then, came the earthquake. On Thursday 19th September 1985, at a little after 7.15 am, a devastating earthquake hit Mexico City. The loss of life was overwhelming as many thousands perished under the rubble and carnage of fallen buildings. Cyterszpiler was in his hotel when all around fearfully shook. It was like the end of the world. The irony was not lost on him as he thought it typical of his luck spending every waking hour under the murky eye of the brooding hulk of the most menacing volcano on the planet, only to find himself in the midst of a frightening natural disaster the minute he leaves it's shadow. As chaos reigned in the city and rescue squads fought desperately to free those trapped under the huge mass of debris, all communication to Mexico City was down. Finally, after a long delay the phone lines were patched up and Cyterszpiler received a call from Naples that changed his life forever. The words hit him like a bolt of lightning careering wildly into a falling tree. To his infernal horror Maradona had sacked him.

To court Diego's attention, a Chinese whisper propped up with equal measures of half-truths and exaggerations was used to bring down Jorge Cyterszpiler from his esteemed position at Maradona's side. Acting on the back of mischievous, second-hand Neapolitan rumours that came laced with jealousy, he turned on one of his most trusted and oldest friends. Without trial or jury Cyterszpiler was given the axe and cast adrift. The so-called crime, an alleged business transaction in which he was accused of personally profiting from, so ripping off his boss in the process. True or false, it was irrelevant; the verdict upon him had been passed. On returning to Naples, a seething Cyterszpiler immediately sought out Maradona to demand an explanation. In a furious encounter the player refused to listen to his manager's please of innocence. Acting the part of betrayed friend, the King of Naples produced a bravura performance of bitterness, anger and tears that matched anything he ever produced on a football pitch. For in Maradona's eyes Jorge Cyterszpiler had committed the ultimate sin and betrayed his trust. There could be only one punishment, he was out. It was time for new blood. As the thorns in his crown cut the skin what Diego Maradona needed more than anything a calming influence in his life, a steady hand.

Unfortunately, breezing into Naples International Airport with a wink and a smile for the impressed air hostesses was the larger than life thirty-eight-year-old fellow charismatic Argentinian, Guillermo Coppola. Coppola's appetite for making money was matched only by an insatiable lust for cigars, good wine and bad women. In no time he made a huge impression on Maradona, who came to regard him as a world-wise older brother. He was a man of wonderfully dry sardonic humour and endless charm, equally at ease in any company, either kings or peasants. Coppola loved to think that he cut a 'Bella Figura' (Beautiful figure). His appearance was that of a handsome old-time Latino gigolo making his living in the seedy tango dance halls of 1950s Buenos Aires.

An awe-inspiring reputation for making money from dust was first established in Argentina where he negotiated for a host of the country's top players, driving a hard bargain and ultimately always succeeding. Offers of employment poured in not just from the football world, but also from major banking and financial institutions that recognised such precious talents. Despite approaches asking him to name his price, Coppola was not tempted. For his 'work hard, play harder' attitude to life made the offer to go and

manage Maradona in Naples utterly irresistible. It was a God-given opportunity to indulge his favourite pastimes in a place that was heaven on earth for such as he.
Before pleasure came business and Coppola wasted little time ingratiating himself with his new paymaster as he strove to make Maradona further fortunes. The wily Coppola negotiated a lucrative deal with a local television company for the player's own weekly show. More importantly he began to test the water with Napoli for a further extension to Maradona's present contract.
Maradona Productions was shut down and in it's place, rising phoenix-like from the ashes, rose DIARMA with Guillermo Coppola at the helm. Diego Maradona may have solved his money problems, unknowingly, in Coppola, he had bought himself a heap load of trouble. As for a grieving Cyterszpiler, he packed his bags and returned home to Argentina. That he would later be proved innocent of any misdemeanour mattered little. Maradona had already begun to commit the grievous error of bowing to his own image. Unlike the conquering Roman Generals of old, Diego Maradona did not have the luxury of a slave to remind him of his mere mortality. 'You've fucking changed Diego.' Instead, he surrounded himself with freeloaders and sycophants who only ever told him what he, Maradona, wished to hear. The roars of the adoring Napoli tifosi ringing incessantly in his ears: 'Diego, Diego, Diego!' The Argentinian risked losing sight of who he really was, and the memories of childhood poverty back in Villa Fiorito that had once kept him grounded no longer worked. The crown of thorns had already begun to prick deep. Maradona thought he was a God.
'Remember thou art only a mortal.'

CHAPTER EIGHT

A LOATHING SUPREME

Maradona hit it and the San Paolo exploded! At 5.27, on Sunday 3rd November 1985, Diego Maradona finally cast off a twelve-year-old curse over his adopted city of Naples. As the ball crashed into the net the roar from across the terraces told it's own story, for the games between SSC Napoli and Juventus were never just simple football matches, they came laced with bitter memories of battles past and supposed injustices. Struck with vengeance and a devil's swerve, Maradona's shot set Naples alright. La Vecchia Signora were down. For the first time in twelve seasons Juventus faced defeat on Neapolitan soil. There was eighteen minutes left to play. The prayers to San Gennaro began, it was to be a busy day for the patron saint.

On 1st November 1897, all Neapolitans awoke to find their worst nightmare become real. Two students from Massimo D'Azeglio Grammar School for young men in Turin, brothers Eugenio and Enrico Canfari had decided to start a football team. Being grand gentleman, they desired a name worthy of their good selves. They chose Juventus, the Latin word for youthful energy, strength and vigour. From small acorns, so began a hundred years and still counting of 'La Vecchia Signora', the dear and derided 'Old Lady' of Italian football. Six years passed and in 1903, on a business trip to Nottingham, England, a Juve committee member was so taken by the colours of Notts County that he bought up an entire kit of black/white striped shirts and took them home to Turin.

Two years later, wearing their newly-adopted strip the first national title was won. It would be the first of many.

On 24th July 1923, the modern birth of Juventus took place when the phenomenally wealthy Agnelli family took majority control of the club and began what would be an enduring tale of success, controversy and intrigue. With the financial muscle of the family business, Fiat, put to good use, Juve soared in both power and size. They came to be viewed as the team of the establishment, with supporters not just in Turin, but across all Italy. A national institution. Helped by referees, always appearing to get the breaks. Hated, adored with equal measure. Black and white shirted heroes or the devil's spawn. Nowhere were they despised more than Naples. The first clash between the two took place there on 21st November 1926. Juventus won 3-0 and four months later, when the return game was played in Turin, it proved lambs to the slaughter as the home side smashed eight goals past the beleaguered Neapolitans. So, it began. Mischievous rumour-mongers told of the Agnelli clan using the almighty influences in higher circles to court favours for their club. In Naples, this was regarded as fact and in a city that lay forever stricken by poverty and crime, an unhealthy concoction of bitterness and jealousy developed throughout the years towards the affluence of the North, and in particular flourishing Turin. The animosity tended to show itself most vividly whenever the two cities met on a football pitch, and with the Neapolitans' frustration maddened by their team's inability to snatch the championship away from the Northern powers of Turin and also Milan, these games between the haves and have nots, produced bouts of mass violence, a generation before the English believed they had cornered the market in football hooliganism. The supporters of SSC Napoli and Juventus had been at each other's throats for decades.

The 1985-86 season dawned, and in typical fashion Diego Maradona wasted little time falling foul of new coach Ottavio Bianchi. His reputation as a strict disciplinarian who ruled with a rod of iron and not one to suffer fools cut no ice with Maradona who refused to bow to no man. The Argentinian took great delight in telling all at the time, 'You could not beat a smile out of Bianchi with a stick.' The training ground at Soccavo proved a battlefield as Naples' finest took an instant dislike to the new boss and all at the football club watched and waited to see how the man who had acquired the nickname of the 'Iron Sergeant' would deal with this prickly stone in his shoe. From the off Bianchi was determined to make an impression and in an early meeting with the Napoli players he laid down his rules by instigating a fierce fitness regime that bore more resemblance to the Foreign Legion. Bianchi understood his immediate impact had to be substantial and decided from the off to go for broke and tackle his most troubled and prized asset with all guns blazing. Ottavio Bianchi's first clash with Diego Maradona became instantly the stuff of Napoli legend.
A sullen Maradona was pulled aside by his new boss and ordered to partake in a special exercise. It involved him sitting on the floor and having to sweep away with either foot a ball thrown by Bianchi. Maradona was having none of it, he argued it was the opposition's job to try and bring him to earth, no one else's. The Argentinian refused point blank to go along. Ottavio Bianchi warned the player that if he did not do so they would have problems all year. Maradona simply laughed in his face.

'Right, and you will have to go!'
Hardly wishing to commit career suicide, Bianchi shrewdly backed down. After conversing with his President on how to deal with his troublesome star, Bianchi realised that Ferlaino himself was nervous on taking on a player who in Naples yielded an all-ensuing power that extended beyond a mere football pitch. He decided to let the matter ride, for the moment. Though it could have been different for in that same summer Bianchi tried desperately to prise away from Juventus, legendary midfielder Marco Tardelli, and the explosive Polish forward Zbigniew Boniek. If successful he may well have held a good enough hand to triumph in his battle of wills with Maradona, but they simply scoffed at their Southern cousin's motley attempts to buy two of Turin's ageing, but still superbly talented stalwarts. They had shown in the past a willingness to do business with Napoli only when it suited their needs. Tardelli and Boniek would be sold, but not to the Neapolitans. 'La Vecchia Signora' laughed their heads off at the sheer cheek of Naples. Had they forgotten their place in the greater scheme of things? Surely history had taught them they could be seen, maybe heard, but never treated fucking serious.

The utter deep contempt in which the Southern capital was held in Turin could only be measured in the depths of hate that engulfed encounters between the two cities. Juve had won the title an extraordinary sixteen times to Napoli's none. The signing of Maradona disturbed, but hardly caused shockwaves in Turin. For the Juve tifosi remained convinced they still held the ace card in French midfield maestro Michel Platini. The Gallic genius held few equals on the playing fields of Serie A, and a majestic showing in the 1984 European Championship when Platini as Captain led France to victory on home soil made it hard to disagree that he was alongside Diego, the world's best. Except that is in Naples, for they would rather argue the world was flat.

As for Diego Maradona's spat with Ottavio Bianchi, a serious rift was quickly averted. There was enough spitefulness directed towards Napoli's direction from elsewhere, they could ill afford friction within. A show of unity was called for. Both characters knew that if the dream of the Scudetto was ever to be realised, all Neapolitan ships had to sail in the same direction. Finally, a deal was grudgingly struck between the two. Neither would rock the boat. On 8th September 1985, to the delight and relief of all Napoli tifosi the time came once more to get the ball out.

The Neapolitan crusade to capture and bring South that elusive championship resumed and as ever the footballing Gods showed a wicked sense of humour by handing Ottavio Bianchi an opening match against his former club, the team from the Northern Lakes, Como. In a hard-fought contest Napoli sneaked home 2-1. Goals from the new boy, Bruno Giordano and Naples' other Argentinian Daniel Bertoni gave Bianchi's men the points. This kick-started a seven-match unbeaten run that saw the Neapolitans enjoy one of their best ever beginnings to a Serie A campaign. Amongst these was a truly ruthless 5-0 dismantling of reigning champions, the much-despised Hellas Verona at the San Paolo. It was a consummate performance by SSC Napoli and for one player in particular, Diego Maradona, it repaid Verona with interest for the humiliating drubbing suffered in the opening game of the season past. 'Lavatevi' was washed away in a shower of goals. With Maradona hurtling into top gear and a superb showing by the increasingly impressive Giordano up front, Neapolitans watched in awe as the team produced a display of attacking prowess not witnessed in Naples for many a year. Maradona had failed to shine during Napoli's early good run. His troublesome left ankle, a torturous memento of the Argentinian's lamentable time in Barcelona caused him terrible agony. Only the frightful, temporary cure of a dreaded cortisone injection enabled Maradona to play on, although, even then, this only dulled the pain and come the aftermath of the contest, away from the roars and adulation of the terraces, he suffered intolerably.

Then came the cocaine to soothe. Like a fairground carousel run on white powder that once on was now become ever harder to get off.

Hellas Verona had endured a painful beginning to their reign as champions. Osvaldo Bagnoli's much lauded team had failed to recapture the form that saw them sweep aside the old order and capture the title. Also, others had begun to look upon them in a new light and theirs' had become a much sought-after scalp. The Veronese won only two of their first seven games, struggling in ninth position. The momentous events in Naples on 7th October 1985, saw them hit rock bottom as the Neapolitans cut loose in bloodthirsty, rampaging manner. A first-half strike from Bruno Giordano was scant reward for the home team's total dominance. It was only in the second with Diego Maradona wreaking mayhem that the goals began to flow. Playing just behind Giordano and Daniel Bertoni, Maradona proved impossible to handle for the Verona defenders as he came at them from deep. Ottavio Bianchi watched on from the dug-out with his usual hang-dog expression. If he was happy with proceedings Bianchi refused to show it. Three minutes after half-time the superb Salvatore Bagni broke from midfield to add a second and open the floodgates. On the hour Maradona proceeded to bring the house down when from thirty-five yards he crashed home a ferocious half-volley that dipped with great venom into the net. On seeing this the San Paolo became a madhouse! Maradona set off in celebration to be swamped by jubilant team mates. The blood-fest was in full flow. Three became four, then five, as Daniel Bertoni with a double and Eraldo Pecci helped to stain the visitor's yellow shirts with further humiliation and wanting just to get the hell out of Naples. SSC Napoli had been a team on a mission. Revenge had proved a dish served sweet and best, Neapolitan style. This 5-0 massacre of the champions moved Bianchi's men to within four points of leaders Juventus. The race was on. The times they were definitely changing, but not just yet in Turin. For some things it appeared, were carved in stone.

As if fired by jet fuel, Juve had raced out of the traps, threatening to disappear over the horizon with a frightening opening sequence of seven straight wins. Their team was an impressive concoction of the finest that world and Italian football had to offer. Only the best was ever considered good enough by the Agnellis' to represent them, and they came no better than Giovanni Trapattoni. The forty-five-year-old Trapattoni enjoyed a fine playing career as a talented ball playing, left-sided midfielder for AC Milan and Italy.

He was hailed as being the only player capable of man-marking the great Brazilian Pelé by honest means. A famous 3-0 win for the 'Azzurri' against the mighty Brazilians at the San Siro, when he had the dazzling South American under lock and key for the entire ninety minutes, earned Trapattoni huge praise. Both in Italy and Brazil, where his tough, if fair handling of their hero saw him lauded with plaudit's. However, anything achieved on the field would be dwarfed by his future staggering exploit's in management. 'Il Trap' as he became known had been in Turin since 1977, and during that period enjoyed unparalleled success. The Sardinian-born Trapattoni molded his teams with the typical Italian philosophy of Catenaccio defence laced with swift counter-attacking football. In his eight-year reign Juventus had won four national titles, a European Cup Winners' Cup, UEFA Cup, and a runners-up place in the European Cup final. Indeed, the bulk of Italy's 1982 triumphant World Cup-winning side came from Trapattoni's side, with the majority featuring in the 3-1 final victory over West Germany at the Santiago Bernabeu in Madrid. Dino Zoff, Marco Tardelli, Antonio Cabrini, Claudio Gentile, Gaetano Scirea, Paolo Rossi. The names read like a who's who of Italian football. Come 1985, and Juventus remained a formidable force. The veteran goalkeeper legend Zoff had finally lost his battle with Father Time and retired, but the backbone of the team remained in place. In attack they had been reinforced immeasurably by the fantastic pace and skill of Danish winger Michael Laudrup. In midfield, Michel Platini remained to add that beguiling touch, which only those truly blessed possessed. As an artist paints pictures on his canvas board with the swish of a brush, so Platini played his football. With the wily, all-domineering defender Gaetano Scirea sweeping and organising at the rear, Juve appeared unbeatable. In Turin, there was already early talk of going through the entire season unbeaten. They had clearly not counted on Maradona. The 'Old Lady' was due in Naples for a much-anticipated showdown.

Sunday 3rd November 1985. Juventus travelled deep into what they considered bandit country, the Mezzogiorno, to defend a proud twelve-year unbeaten record against a side they refused to even contemplate as serious rivals. To do so would in their eyes hand the Neapolitans undue recognition, for they saw them as nothing more than thieves, scum and vagabonds. Their banners told of *'Mafioso'*, the songs of *'Cholera'* and *'You're the scum of all Italia'*. It was deadly, spiteful, racist and cruel. The brave, foolhardy, and sheer lunatic fringe of the Juve tifosi who risked life and limb to travel South and support their team in Naples did so with an escort that would have done justice to a visiting American President. A Carabinieri helicopter flew above their coaches.

Nothing was ever too much trouble for the Neapolitans in their eagerness to make their enemy from the North feel unwelcome, even to the point of the ballboys, all young apprentices of Napoli, receiving instructions (out of earshot) to make life difficult as possible for the Juventus players. If the home side was winning they were told to take their time returning the ball back onto the pitch. Juventus were not just playing against eleven players for SSC Napoli that day; an entire city was plotting to take the Bianconeri down. Unlike all others who felt a bond with Juve in Naples, Giovanni Trapattoni wished to return to Turin with more than just his neck intact, he desperately desired the points. For twelve seasons they had gone to Naples to leave unbeaten and unbowed, if at times a little battle-scarred. Juve had received a hammer blow to their fierce pride in losing the championship title to Hellas Verona the year before and Trapattoni was determined to win it back and return the Scudetto to it's rightful home in

Turin. A win over the Neapolitans would go a long way in achieving that goal. 'Il Trap' was confident his iron-tight defence would prove unyielding against what many were claiming to be the most lethal attacking force in all of Italy. A victory for Juve would leave Napoli trailing in their wake by eight points. Not to mention the dramatic effect on morale in suffering another defeat against their most hated foe. The week previous the Neapolitans unbeaten record had crashed in Turin against Torino when a wonderfully struck free-kick from Maradona came too late to save them going down 2-1. A second loss against the city's other side would have been calamitous. As kick off grew near a draw was being widely touted inside the San Paolo by those who considered the fact that both sides simply could not afford to lose. A game of cat and mouse was predicted. Could the much-vaunted Juventus rearguard contain the on-fire Maradona? Would Platini produce a piece of magic and steal the points? Was Giordano truly good enough to outwit the canny Scirea? All of Italy waited to watch live on television as the two tribes of Naples and Turin prepared once more to lock horns. A sense of history, raging hatred and a treacherous, rain-lashed surface. Naples on the edge. Throw in Maradona, Platini and you had a cast worth dying for.

It proved a contest worthy of such an occasion. Twelve years of pent-up frustration came pouring out in a first half that saw Napoli launch a blistering all-out assault on the Juve defence. Inspired by thousands of screaming, crazed Neapolitans, Diego Maradona led the charge, but unlike most in this passionate red-hot city this particular 'Old Lady' kept her virtue intact against incessant advances. On a soaked surface covered in pools of water, Maradona was still able to lift his followers to heady heights of dizziness as he electrified the stadium with every touch. Juve held firm. Gaetano Scirea was magnificent as he deployed his defensive forces with all the tactical genius of a five-star General. As the contest entered it's last quarter a draw appeared the likely outcome.

Then, it happened.

The tricky footwork of Daniel Bertoni enabled him to burst into the Juve area, only to be sent crashing to earth. As the crowd howled for a penalty the referee instead awarded an indirect free-kick for obstruction twelve-yards out from goal. The indignation and disgust that poured down from all corners of the stadium eased when Diego Maradona stepped forward to take control. A city held it's breath as midfielder Pecci tapped the ball sideways for Maradona to curl a stunning shot past the keeper Stefano Tacconi into the net. Hit with vengeance and a devil's swerve! From an angle that appeared impossible this adopted Son of Naples, a street-wise rascal had hoodwinked the great and good of Turin. Mayhem reigned in Naples! off soared Maradona to accept the acclaim of his adoring tifosi as the San Paolo bathed in a glorious lather of joy and excitement. No one ever played a crowd like Diego as he appeared close to tears with the emotion of the moment. His was the ultimate performance in time of ecstasy. The moment the ball hit the Juve net was later memorably described by one supporter present that day. 'It was fucking divine! The crowd were on the pitch, the policemen were on the pitch. God, was on the pitch!' Through a cloak of darkness, a small chink of light shone. On the other side lay redemption, the lifting of the twelve years curse. His battle plan in tatters, Trapattoni screamed instructions from the touchline to his players, urging them forward. Now, it was

the Neapolitans' turn to hold what they had. Juventus swept forward in desperation, Michel Platini and Michael Laudrup suddenly coming alive on being released from shackling defensive duties to play their normal game. Many in the stadium could hardly bare to watch as the visitors staged a last gasp fightback to save the day. Tempers inevitably flared and Brio of Juve along with Napoli's Bagni were both dismissed for fighting.
The seconds ticked down and with the crowd whistling and pleading for the referee to end their torment, he finally called time. 'La Vecchia Signora' had been beaten. Carnival time descended upon Naples. The Juve players made a hasty retreat from the celebrations that were erupting in a mad frenzy around them. The dark clouds that enveloped the Gulf of Naples since first light finally cleared, and a dot of blue sky broke through. An eye to the heavens. Even San Gennaro wished to view his city in it's moment of joy. Car horns blazed triumphantly across the bay. The Napoli tifosi took to the roads to show their delight at beating Juventus. Trucks filled with flag-waving supporters set off across the Peninsula to share their triumph with those who could not be present. In Naples, hundreds of Vespers sped along the seafront past the historic ancient fortress of Castel dell'Ovo, roaring out Maradona's name. Down every alleyway and crumbling tenement of the Forcella and Spanish Quarter, Neapolitans indulged in that rare event for their club, a victory celebration over Juventus.
The spell had been broken.
One totally underwhelmed by events unfolding around him was Ottavio Bianchi, who remained as ever stone-faced. Bianchi was shrewd enough to realise the setback which befell Juve on the day, and the jeering of gloating

Neapolitans that accompanied Trapattoni's men as they made an inglorious exit from the San Paolo would ultimately serve only in spurring them on to win back the Serie A title. Naples may well have won a famous battle, but the war was far from over. They would bite back with a vengeance.

As for Diego, he was off into the night. The sultry, arousing air of downtown Naples, where devils and fallen angels offered great temptations, proved irresistible. His every whim, desire and fantasy could be realised. A city sat for eternity on death row, it's fate forever hanging on the moods of a bad-tempered Mount Vesuvio had long since lost any inhibitions. Live for today, as tomorrow is a distant dream. They were dancing in the streets and alleys of the city, for Diego Maradona had lain to rest the curse of Turin. Anything, was now deemed possible. Anything.

CHAPTER NINE

CRISTINA

Amore. In his short time in the bay of Naples Maradona had surged through the willing female population of this city with the same ease that he scythed past the tightest Serie A defence. The crazed notion that he had become romantically attached to a local 20-year-old Neapolitan girl called Cristina Sinagra was genuinely thought absurd to those amongst his entourage who had witnessed at first hand his night-time antics. For ever since his long-time girlfriend Claudia had fled Naples in tears and returned to Argentina, Maradona had not so much played the field as sowed his wild oats with all the gusto of a young stallion on heat: he was simply insatiable! How they flocked. Diego's goal against Juventus had elevated him above seventh heaven. He had turned water to wine. There were those in the city who now thought him a God. Other who saw him off-stage knew better. It was all an illusion. A deception. This was no fucking God who was making their dreams come true on a football pitch. The Boy had horns. Beware of false idols.

A week on and still drunk on euphoria after their historic victory over Juventus, the massed legions of Napoli tifosi descended on Milan for what was yet another do-or-die clash with an age-old adversary, the aristocrats of Internazionale. Inter was a formidable side that bristled with world stars. The wonderful poise and technique of West German centre-forward Karl-Heinz Rummenigge, the fleet-footed 'Azzurri' striker Allesandro Altobelli and sublime Irish midfield maestro Liam Brady were the pick of an attacking crop. La Grande Inter! The followers of the 'Neazzurri' ('blue and black stripes'), held those from Naples in lower regard than the dirt on their designer shoes. The twice-yearly sojourn by the Southerners to Milan was greeted with the same amount of wrath and enthusiasm that would have been shown a plague of rats. The Milanese looked upon Neapolitans as barbarians lacking in true Italian virtue and character. That Naples was closer to the shores of Africa than to their own city handed the Inter tifosi ample ammunition to launch a hail of verbal slings and arrows at the Southern invaders. Their banners aimed low:

'Clean the steps before leaving'.
'Soap and water, wash yourselves'.

The Neapolitans replied in typically whimsical fashion.
'Milan, Turin, is this Italy? It is better being Africans'.

The appearance of the two teams to do battle was barely visible as coloured smoke bombs engulfed the San Siro. A freezing Milan fog that had settled itself on the pitch meant the early stages of the contest could hardly be witnessed by any on the terraces. Nothing much was missed as both began with caution. After a nervy, opening period the stalemate was broken four minutes into the second half when a long, hopeful cross into the Inter penalty area by Bruno Giordano, was met by Diego Maradona, who outfoxed two defenders, chested the ball down and with unerring accuracy slashed a left-foot drive past goalkeeper Walter Zenga into the bottom left-hand corner. Maradona ran with arms outstretched to the thousands of Napoli followers who had prayed during the arduous trip North to witness such a moment. A Neapolitan God in football boots slaying his city's many enemies. Emotions overflowed both on the field and off when a bottle thrown from the terraces laid low Napoli's goalkeeper. As tempers frayed the red mist came down and a horrendous tackle by Milanese defender Mandolini broke the leg of Neapolitan midfielder Ruben Buriani. Such was the severity of the foul Buriani never again played top class football. As the battle raged matters worsened when Giuseppe Bruscolotti and Allesandro Altobelli squared up to each other and came to blows. A besieged referee was left with no option but to send both off. Finally, the sides reverted to playing football and fifteen minutes from time, with Inter fighting desperately for an equaliser to save face, pressure told when the magical left foot of Liam Brady grabbed a point from the penalty spot. The game finished 1-1 honours shared. With each starting the day four points behind Juventus there really was only one winner, for in Turin, Juve had resumed business as normal with a 3-1 victory over Roma. Inter and SSC Napoli had simply cut each other's throats.

The following week at the San Paolo an early wonder strike from Diego Maradona against Udinese looked set to spark a Neapolitan massacre. Pibe De Oro executed a wickedly bending free-kick from the far touchline into the top corner when all others on the pitch expected him to cross it into a crowded penalty box. A repeat showing of the 5-0 Verona performance looked on the cards, but it failed to materialise as a strange malaise settled over the home side. Maradona found himself under siege every time he received the ball as Udinese defenders lined up to kick lumps out of him. The Argentinian was scythed down with relish and a disturbing regularity. It appeared a vendetta as the foul count mounted steadily throughout the first period. With a referee seemingly blind to what was occurring, Napoli's number ten finally cracked and went looking for revenge. Five minutes into the second half Maradona saw red. After being floored one too many times from behind, the Argentinian sprang up from the floor and head butted his worst tormentor, Antonio Crismanini. With Crismanini collapsing theatrically and rolling around on the turf like he had been shot, there was little option for the referee who, after such a blatant show of retaliation by Maradona, was forced to order the leading man off the stage in his own theatre-house. As frustrations mounted in the San Paolo the inevitable duly occurred when Udinese snatched a soft, late equaliser ten minutes from time. The final whistle brought only muted boos; somehow it was all so predictable. Sadly, in Naples nothing is ever as it seems,

In time a disturbing epitaph of this game reared it's ugly head. In the summer of 1986, whilst conducting a drugs investigation, Turin police listened in on a recorded tapped phone call between Napoli's general secretary Iallo Allodi and his counterpart at Udinese, Cordi. What they heard astounded them. The conversations centred around the above match between the two clubs in Naples on Sunday 10th November 1985. They spoke of an agreement to ensure the game finished a draw and that Udinese players would be assigned to wind up Maradona and get him sent off. Allodi was already a notorious figure in Italian football and had earned a dark reputation as the ultimate fixer. His speciality was rumoured to be the gift of a gold watch for any referee willing to do business and allegedly his past paymasters at Inter Milan and Juventus offered whatever necessary to gain an advantage. When all became public, Allodi obviously denied such damning allegations, only to duly resign! His parting line was, 'I have always been a clean man.' The evidence proved overwhelmingly otherwise. A sorry tale.

Seven days later Napoli travelled across the deep boot of the South to the Adriatic coast, where they took on lowly Bari at the San Nicola stadium. Two goals by Bruno Giordano handed the Neapolitans a 2-1 victory helping them forget the unfortunate setback against Udinese. They followed up with a fine 2-0 victory in Naples against AC Milan. Strikes from the lethal Giordano and a second from the wonderfully, combative Salvatore Bagni, proved sufficient to send them back North with tails planted firmly between their legs. The news from the Stadio Comunale that a Michel Platini effort had won the points against Sampdoria to keep Juventus well clear left them feeling deflated. One small step for Naples, two giant steps for Turin. So, it continued until the Christmas break when hostilities ceased momentarily for Yuletide season. Juve were six points ahead of Napoli and Inter. They were chasing the wind. Like one of Agnelli's finest Ferrari sports cars, they stood revved, purring and set to disappear over the horizon.
Again.

The many who basked in Diego Maradona's shadow, feeding off the scraps, enjoying the high life, watched in awe and a little jealously at the footballer's incredible popularity with the young ladies of the South. There were times when his living quarters resembled an Arab sheik's harem as huddles of starry-eyed girls, some lusting; others ambitious would be brought before the king of Naples so he could take his pick. Those not chosen would be led tearfully away. Though such was Diego's rapacious appetite, their time would come again. So, it was with genuine, open-mouthed disbelief that his inner sanctum greeted the sight of Cupid's arrow striking him in the heart. Maradona knew twenty-year old unemployed accountant Cristina Sinagra through his sister Maria, who lived below him in the ground floor flat of his apartment in Posilippo. Maria feared greatly for her kid brother as she watched him go through life as if blindfolded on a high wire, staggering and without a safety net to break his fall. She saw in Cristina someone who just might be capable of bringing him down from the tightrope and away from the madcap circus that surrounded his every move. This softly-spoken girl from the backstreets of Naples would in time earn the approval of the most powerful member of the clan Maradona. His mother. Being accepted by Tota was an accolade reserved for only a chosen few outside the blood family. Almost immediately the two sparked and what began as a purely platonic relationship swiftly developed into something more. Diego fell in love with Cristina because she represented everything opposite to the world he lived in. Innocent, honest and pure. She made him feel safe, cleansed almost, appealing to a side of him that many close feared had gone forever. The happy-go-lucky young kid from the rundown shacks of Villa Fiorito playing football from dawn till dusk. The lad who adored his mother and father. This new life, though filled with earthly goods, was devoid of the one thing money could never buy. Genuine friendship. The Kingdom of Maradona was littered with crooks, con-men and two-bit hustlers who all drank from the well of his talent. Prettier than strikingly beautiful, Cristina's entry into the epic saga of Diego's life was a much-needed breath of fresh air. She was not after him for anything and that to a man who had lived his

young life surrounded by sycophants and hangers-on meant so much. So, the king of Naples retired from public life to spend nights in with his new girl. Theirs' were simple needs, a pizza and a video. Just when all seemed peaceful and the nightclub owners of Naples were enjoying the relative calm, a thunderbolt struck Maradona when Cristina announced she was pregnant.
Suddenly, all was dark, swiftly as love came, so it vanished. Maradona felt betrayed, the stirrings of paranoia again gripped his every thought. The crown of thorns pricked once more and Diego disappeared into the Neapolitan nights. With his strutting Versace-clad posse dressed to kill, acting up like they owned the world, never mind Naples, Maradona cruised the bay looking for action. A disc jockey would announce their entry, 'Benvenuti Diego Maradooona!' The air would electrify, hearts would miss a beat. To the sensual, pounding rhythm of the Salsa drum, every girl in the club would attempt to catch his eye. Maradona would simply smile at a bevy of willing Neapolitan beauties, for that was all it required. His leeching entourage slapped high fives, the boss was back. Cristina Sinagra's desperate pleas to Diego Maradona for him to acknowledge the pregnancy fell on deaf ears. His only response was in telling her to get rid and have an abortion. A beleaguered Cristina found herself being frozen out by people she had once considered family. Personal opinions counted for nothing as the clan closed ranks around their boy. She was forced to leave the Maradona household and return home in floods of tears and shame-faced to her parents. Cristina had every intention of having the baby, for her to consider otherwise was unthinkable. Diego Maradona's abject denial of his responsibilities as a father would return to immeasurably

haunt him as around the city rumours flew of the indiscretion against one of their own. In a place so densely populated, no one was ever out of earshot, out of reach. Behind every wall, in every doorway and half-open window, nothing was missed. What began as the distant echo of a faraway wind grew to resemble a raging hurricane as Naples debated furiously the actions of their king. There was a saying. 'Children are children'. Nothing was more precious to Neapolitans than their young, for the footballer to act in this uncaring manner was seen as an insult to all those who came to regard him as heaven sent, a saviour to lead Naples in it's eternal struggle against the North. The treasure of San Gennaro, a gift from the Gods. It appeared now that was no winged horse soaring over Vesuvio taking Maradona to his Coronation at the church of San Paolo. It was a simple helicopter. He had stepped over a line that Lords, Princes and even Kings had reason to fear crossing. Naples possessed the capacity to spit out heroes with the same ease it embraced them. For the first time doubts were cast about the true character of Diego Maradona. The natives were restless, there was unease beneath the volcano.

The more fanatical of the Napoli tifosi considered such talk as treachery, heresy even. The idle chatter of madmen. In their eyes, Diego could do as he pleased, it was his city and people. To even hint at the suggestion of their king being forced to abdicate from his crown was met with derision. For the young from the districts of the Forcella, Spanish quarter, Fuorigrotta, Sanita and San Giovanni, all breeding grounds of the Napoli hardcore following, Maradona was their life. Ravaging unemployment, drugs and heart bleeding, devastating poverty, the Camorra. A miserable, weekly existence only made palatable by the mouth-watering thought of watching Maradona rip to shreds their Northern tormentors every Sunday afternoon. These were Diego Maradona's foot soldiers, loyalty unquestionable, driven by blinded faith. Dare any who tried to take their king away from them. 'Lo potenza della speranza', ('The power of hope'). This was what Maradona gave to those who struggled to survive in one of the most dangerous cities in the world. Lose that and they had nothing.

As a madman pursues a fleeting butterfly so Ottavio Bianchi's team continued their obsessive, incessant pursuit of leaders Juventus. Naples was allowed to dream when in the opening month of the New Year, Juve managed to scrape together only a measly three points. This brief flicker of hope was extinguished when Napoli themselves hit an iceberg and slipped even further. A run of four games in which only two points were won proved disastrous. An embarrassing 1-0 defeat at home to Pisa, followed by a 2-0 loss in the Olympic Stadium against Roma saw the gap rise to nine points. Their cause was hardly served when Bruno Giordano broke his collarbone in a motor bike accident. Giordano's prowess in front of goal was badly missed as he was sidelined for several weeks. Vital matches that had to be won suddenly began to be drawn. Most importantly, Diego Maradona's increasing jaunts back to Buenos Aires, in preparation for the forthcoming 1986 World Cup Finals in Mexico left him jaded and a shadow of his true self. Napoli's once rapier cutting edge had been blunted. As Maradona's form fell away, so did Neapolitan title hopes. The great honour of being chosen to lead his nation into battle rested heavily on Maradona. It was a responsibility he did not take lightly.

Naples was in his heart but Argentina was blood. The national coach Carlos Bilardo had gone public with what was expected from Maradona. 'My team is Diego Maradona and ten others.' Such talk only increased the intense pressure that was heaped onto his shoulders. Everybody wanted a piece of Maradona. The manner of the humiliating defeat by Brazil four years previous that ended their reign as world champions left an indelible mark on the Argentinian psyche. The Brazilians had indulged themselves with great delight twisting the dagger deep and the sending off of Diego Maradona for a rash over-the-top lunge only added to the pain. The sight of the twenty-one-year-old trooping off, head down in tears proved an abiding memory of a match infamous in Argentinian sporting folklore. It's people ached for a shot at redemption, and no one more than Maradona.

As the challenge from the South faded Juventus pulled smoothly away from the chasing pack. The Bianconeri looked set to triumph once more. With the Scudetto gone, the fight for European qualification began and on 23rd February, SSC Napoli ventured way up North to champions Verona, where in a stirring encounter they fought back from 2-0 down to earn a courageous draw. Maradona appeared inspired. Stung by criticism of recent performances he took on Verona single-handedly. Looking back to his magical best the Argentinian led a rip-roaring second half showing by the Neapolitans.

It was his penalty hit with nonchalant ease that halved the deficit. With time ticking away, Maradona headed in a scrambled equalizer that sent the travelling hordes of Napoli tifosi into frenzy. The Brigate Gialloblu stood in grim silence as they watched the wretched Southerners dance with delight on their terraces. For them it had been a horrendous season and as Maradona ran across and blew kisses to the one end of the Bentegodi stadium bathed blue and white, it finally plunged the depths.

Torino went South and were given short shrift with a 3-1 drubbing for their troubles. Goals from Bagni and Cafferelli helped them on their way as Naples bade farewell with many a two-fingered salute. 'La Granata' left Naples and returned to Turin the colour of their shirts. The much-anticipated grudge, return match with Juventus in Turin finished a 1-1 draw. In a game littered with nerves and petty fouls, Napoli led at half time through an own goal by Juve defender Brio, only for the home side to hit back early in the second with an equaliser from fellow stopper Favero. Trapattoni's team had looked decidedly edgy as the finishing line drew near. Then, on 16th March, as Napoli beat Internazionale at the San Paolo, in a gruelling contest settled only by a single penalty from a newly bearded Maradona, the real story unfolded in Rome, where at the Olympic stadium, Juve were thrashed 3-0 by closest rivals Roma. 'La Vecchia Signora' were rocking. The 'Old Lady' was beginning to show her age. Suddenly, with just five games remaining the difference in points at the top of the table had been reduced to just two. Alas, for third place Napoli, their seven-point's deficit left them needing a miracle of San Gennaro proportions to take the title. The chase for the championship lay between Roma and Turin. Naples, as ever, was again left to lick it's wounds and dream what might have been. This was confirmed a week later when a 2-0 defeat at Udinese mathematically ended their chances. Two finely taken goals by the Italian striker Andrea Carnevale finished off Napoli once and for all. Bianchi watched on, resigned to defeat, but admiring the skills, pace and strength of the young curly haired Udinese centre- forward as he cut a swathe through his defence. As a full house of 40,000 at the Stadio Friuli wallowed in Napoli's misery, Bianchi made a note of the name. Carnevale.

There was something very Neapolitan about it!

In the end Turin got to stage a victory party, but only after Roma had given them the fright of their imperial lives. Juventus would also go on to lift the European cup for the first time, but tragically it would be stained with the blood of Heysel, as supporters of both Liverpool and to a lesser extent Juve, dragged themselves into the gutter in horrific manner. As for Napoli, a place in the UEFA cup was earned in bravura style as their team wound up the season with four straight victories.

The highlight was a much-deserved 2-1 victory against AC Milan in the San Siro with a winning goal scored by Maradona, that bore glorious echoes of events to follow in Mexico. A pass from Giordano was snatched upon by the Argentinian on the edge of the Milan box, and in the midst of half a second, Maradona dummied, sidestepped three defenders, before hitting a thunderous low drive into the net. His work for the season with Naples was done, Argentina and a place in World Cup folklore called.

CHAPTER TEN

MEXICAN DAZE

On landing in Mexico, Diego Maradona found himself pursued relentlessly by the world's media as his every word, move and gesture was analysed and dissected across the globe. It resembled a circus, but with no clowns or jugglers, no knife throwers, no acrobats. Just a stocky-built little footballer with a crowd winning smile and blessed with the ability to make the finest defender appear a drunken fool. To make grown men lose sleep and catch their breath. To the beat of the drum roll and trapped in the flashing, blinding haze of the worldwide spotlight, Maradona prepared to prove himself worthy to stand alongside the legends of the past. Di Stefano, Puskas, Eusebio, Cruyff and Pelé. All great names, illustrious and famed. Given time, Diego would not just join such esteemed ranks, he would leave them in his wake. Naples would prove just a kingdom fortress, there remained a childhood dream to be realised for the kid from Villa Fiorito. Maradona was set to conquer the world.

Matters took on a turn for the manic when word from Naples reached Diego Maradona that a seven-month pregnant Cristina Sinagra, surrounded by lawyers, family and friends, held a press conference to declare the footballer as the father of her child. Hell, hath no fury like a Neapolitan female scorned as Cristina demanded Maradona underwent blood tests to prove once and for all he was responsible. Acting like a cornered alley cat, Diego lashed out and denied all. But the damage was done and unable to believe their good fortune, the Italian press went for the kill. Any opportunity to hammer him was taken with bloodcurdling relish. The headlines screamed out moral outrage. Once more and without really trying too hard Maradona became public enemy number one in his adopted homeland. In a vain attempt to escape the rising football fever that had gripped Mexico City, the Argentinians based themselves on the outskirts of the capital in the seemingly peaceful surrounding of the suburbs. Though such was the charismatic pull of Maradona, they found themselves under daily siege by an army of media and supporters that turned them into virtual prisoners at the training facilities of team Club America. Press conferences resembled wild scenes of bedlam and hysteria as a mad flurry of cameras, microphones and tape recorders were endlessly thrust within inches of the player's face.

They flew like bullets…
'Diego, are you the father?'
'Diego, do you love Cristina?'
'Diego, how is your ankle?'
'Diego, look this way!'
'Diego, Diego, Diego, Diegoooo!'
It was a fucking madhouse.
Grouped with world champions Italy, Bulgaria and South Korea for the opening rounds, Maradona showed explosive form as Argentina began with a 3-1 victory against the Koreans. Though not on the score sheet he was instrumental in all three goals, running amok amongst his terrified opponents. Having no answers, the men from the Orient resorted in attempting to kick lumps out of him, but this was easier said than done as Maradona, dynamic, cunning and firing on all cylinders, sped away from flailing tackles and last gasps lunges. Despite his fine form

the critics were scathing in their comments regarding the alleged average quality of fellow teammates. Maradona reacted furiously in a post-match interview, 'I hope everyone pays us more respect when we get to the final.' Watching on worryingly was Enzo Bearzot. Given half an inch the little maestro would undoubtedly wreak similar havoc against his Italian team if the threat wasn't curtailed. Yet, how do you down a missile that appeared impregnable to all known defences? With Gentile retired, Bearzot had only one player left in the squad blessed with the capability and know-how to stem such danger. He required an edge, someone on the inside. In a tactical switch that sparked shockwaves across all of Italy, Enzo Bearzot announced that the dubious honour of curbing the threat of Diego Maradona had gone to team-mate and close amigo at Napoli, Salvatore Bagni. It was claimed by Northerners that this adopted Southern Terroni would not show the necessary heart and aggression for such a difficult task. The proud blue shirt of the 'Azzurri' demanded nothing less than total loyalty, a willingness to stop Maradona at any costs. In the end the doubters in Milan, Turin and all cities past Rome were proved wrong as Salvatore Bagni went for his Napoli team-mate with unrestrained passion and fire. A fascinating duet between the two ensued with Maradona finding himself hunted and harassed repeatedly throughout the contest. No quarter was given or asked as each gave their all in an enthralling one-to-one encounter. The Argentinian escaped only once from the clutches of his Italian shadow, but it was sufficient for him to grab an equaliser after Inter's, Altobelli, had put the world champions in front from the penalty spot. It was typical Maradona as he hit a sweet left-foot volley low past 'Azzurri' goalkeeper Galli to secure a point. The game ended in a 1-1 draw and the final whistle saw the two players embrace warmly sharing a quiet joke. There was still totally unwarranted criticism in the Italian press that Bagni had gone easy on his friend, but considering Diego finished the match limping and with his shirt in tatters, the evidence proved otherwise. The Neapolitan blood brothers had given all and more for their respective countries. Yet, the facts do remain some Italians would only have been satisfied if Bagni had pulled a gun out and shot him. In Naples there was great satisfaction at the outcome. Honour had been served; their boys had not let them down. The end result also suited both nations as it all but secured qualification for the last sixteen.

Next was a date with age-old foes Uruguay.

The Uruguayans have a word. Garra. Roughly translated it means 'To stand strong, be a man'. In an impressive World Cup history this small nation of three million had repeatedly battled against overwhelming odds to triumph. Twice world champions, Uruguay achieved their greatest ever result in 1950, when true Garra was shown to clinch the trophy in front of 200,000, fanatical Brazilian supporters in the footballing cathedral of the Maracana. The host nation was left grief-stricken as legendary Uruguayan Captain Obdulio Varela led his countrymen to an astonishing 2-1 win over Brazil, a result that left the Brazilians crestfallen and plunged the country into a state of national mourning. A victory over Maradona's Argentina would be exalted equally so. Following an honourable 1-1 draw against West Germany in their opening group game, the Mexican skies collapsed on Uruguay, when they fell victim to an emerging Danish side that thrashed them 6-1. Three goals from Verona hit-man

Preben Elkjaer, and a strike from Juve's devastating forward Michael Laudrup, helped to provoke unmerciful criticism back home for beleaguered coach Omar Borras. As emotions ran high his family were forced into hiding and given twenty-four-hour armed protection by the authorities. Borras was deemed the luckiest man alive when results elsewhere saw only a point required against Scotland in their final game to secure qualifications for the next round. That Uruguay's fate still lay in their own hands after what befell them against a rampaging Denmark, meant they could ill afford to waste such a God-given chance of redemption.

The Uruguayans were about to stretch the mythical Garra to it's limit's.

With a brutality more suited to a brawling street gang they acted like crazed madmen in their desperation to ensure progress. Omar Borras wound up his team to the extent that the South Americans went crazy hacking, mauling, spitting and intimidating in order to grab the needed point. The mood was set after just fifty-five seconds when defender Jose Batista scythed down Scottish midfielder Gordon Strachan from behind to leave him writhing in agony on the turf. Acting with almost indecent haste, the Spanish referee Joel Quiniou flashed a red card from his pocket and sent the startled Batista off the field. This proved only to further incite the Uruguayans and one of the darker chapters in World Cup history gloomily unfolded. In a strip of all white, Uruguay performed more like devils than angels as the squalid showing dragged their country's proud name into the gutter. The Scotland manager Alex Ferguson swore, stomped, raged and ranted on the touchline at the antics of his opponents and the Scots' own inept play and apparent lack of courage to overcome such tactics. Some of the Uruguayan mischief-making defied belief as they hurled water bags at the referee and his officials at half-time on leaving the pitch. Needing to win in order to qualify, an insipid Scotland surrendered meekly to go out with a whimper. Only the manager showed traditional Scottish fire as he tore into Omar Borras on the touchline who was urging his men to waste time. Afterwards, a straight-faced Borras, with a shrug of his shoulders commented, 'I could not see what all the fuss was about?' On hearing this Ferguson gave full vent to his feelings at the post-match press conference when in typical unrestrained manner he declared, 'If Borras sit's there defending his team, he is lying, cheating and uttering a load of rubbish. I can't even wish him luck.' FIFA acted swiftly. Uruguay were fined 25,000 Swiss francs and threatened with expulsion if they dared misbehave again. As for Borras, he was barred from the touchline for one game and banished to the stand for the showdown against Argentina. A sorry and turgid episode. This latter-day battle of the River Plate took place sixty miles, Southwest of the capital, in the picturesque city of Puebla. Set against a wonderful mountain backdrop in a beautiful tree-lined valley gorge, Puebla was referred to by native Mexicans as the 'City of Angels'. In ancient times, the Aztecs thought this land sacred and touched by their many Gods. Here on July 16th 1986, at the Cuauhtemoc stadium a modern-day idol sprinkled his gold dust upon such blessed soil. Argentinian cheers soared towards the heavens as Diego Maradona appeared hell-bent in taking on the Uruguayans single-handed. With the hatchet men from Montevideo out only on bail and every tackle scrutinized, they were forced to clean up their act. A stage was provided for Maradona to exhibit his full repertoire of skills, whilst being free from the worry of being kicked senseless. Playing on the shoulders of Argentina's two attackers, his roommate Pedro Pasculi and the tall, elegant Jorge Valdano, Maradona ignited from deep leaving Uruguayan defenders scattered in his wake. From a high in the Director's Box, Omar Borras screamed instructions through a walkie-talkie to his bench, but it was to no avail as the Argentinian number ten sliced through his team at will, causing panic. It came as little surprise that three minutes before the interval, Argentina took a well-deserved lead when a move started by a Maradona dribble, ended with Pasculi firing home from twelve yards past Uruguayan goalkeeper Alves, to delight their supporters. With Italian referee Luigi Agnolin, keeping a terse eye on every Uruguay challenge, their thirst for battle waned as they appeared only intent in trying to avoid an embarrassing scoreline. This was a scenario that never could last for the weight of history between two such historically bitter adversaries meant that old habits died hard. If not at all. Twenty-five minutes remained when the skies above Puebla suddenly turned a deathly black. Without any due warning, a terrifying electrical storm erupted. As the heaven sobbed, jagged streaks of lightning ripped through the night-time sky, a brief prelude to a roaring thunder that shook the surrounding mountains. It appeared to act as a wake-up call for the Uruguayans, who having played with unnatural calm finally decided they would not go down without a fight and damn the consequences. The gloves came off and battle commenced in all it's fury in the 'City of Angels'.

Grown weary of being made to look ridiculous by the alluring sorcery of the opposing number ten, the Uruguayan defenders resorted to type and went in search of Argentinian blood, one in particularly. On a treacherous swamp of a surface the tackles flew in on Diego Maradona, but with an unerring capacity to conjure Houdini-like escape routes out of seemingly impossible situations, Maradona showed remarkable courage as he refused to curtail his dynamic bursts into enemy territory. The Argentinian Captain was on a mission. The more they kicked, the more determined to ensure that those across the River were taught a lesson they never forget.

Hurtling over legs, skating across a rain splattered, drenched pitch, twisting, exploding past defenders, the ball obeying his every command as it appeared tied by invisible string to his dancing feet. A master class from the greatest player in the world. With the referee blowing to end the game the Uruguayans finally brought Maradona to earth, but quickly he was lifted up by adoring teammates and embraced in a bear hug by coach Carlos Bilardo. In Argentina, they had begun dancing in the streets. The revellers roared out his name, an unofficial National Anthem, 'Maradoooona!' A war cry adopted in Naples but born in Buenos Aires. He was their boy. Uruguay would go home missed by no one; as for the Argentinians, their reward for victory was huge as another monumental encounter lay ahead.

England.

In Naples,
 there exists a little-known card game called Scopa. It is played by men of questionable values who care little how they win. At Scopa's dark heart lay rule number one. 'Always try and glimpse your opponent's hand'. To triumph it is expected to lie and cheat, but always watch your back, cover your hand. Armed with this archetypal

Neapolitan tactic Diego Maradona prepared mentally for the biggest match of his life so far. To beat the English by fair means or other, it mattered little, for the bitter humiliation suffered in the South Atlantic still cut deep in Argentina. Maradona was viewed in his country as the one man capable of restoring national pride by slaying the bullying British bulldog. A Falklands War Part Two scenario was stirred up by rabid tabloid hysteria in both nations as a dangerous patriotic fervour took hold. Maradona was referred to in the Buenos Aires-based newspaper Cronica as, *'Our Exocet'* whilst it's equally classless English equivalent's the Sun proclaimed, *'It's war Senors'*.

The Daily Mirror called to *'Bring on the Argies'*. As kick-off grew close a simmering, powder keg, hostile atmosphere left a bad taste in the mouth as old images of the conflict were dredged up on television and replayed constantly. With neither set of supporters not of the ilk to walk away from confrontation, the Mexican police prepared for the worst. In the pre-match press conferences, the managers' Bobby Robson and Carlos Bilardo spent more time fending off questions that had absolutely nothing to do with football, but each knew deep down what was at stake. Sometimes, football really is more than just a game.

Maradona refused also to be drawn. 'I am here to play football nothing more.'

Look,' he exclaimed wearily to an English journalist from the Times, who questioned him repeatedly on the thorny issue of revenge. 'When we go on the pitch it is the game of football that matters and not who won the war.' Fine words from the Captain as he tried to defuse a potentially explosive situation. Sadly, it was only akin to taking a pin out of a grenade and covering the fuse with your thumb. No matter what was claimed in public, there remained a hidden agenda. Former England manager Ron Greenwood hardly helped the situation when asked his opinion on the best way to stop Maradona? He replied, 'First you pull out a handgun!' The quarter-final would be in the legendary surroundings of the Azteca stadium in Mexico City and huge security measures were taken to ensure a bloodbath did not occur on the terraces. The 'Rule Britannia' hordes of Saint George and the notorious Argentinian hooligans 'Barras Bravas' would have needed little prompting if the opportunity arose to go for each other's throats.

Bobby Robson's battleplan focused almost completely on blotting out the threat of Diego Maradona. Robson knew that any attempt to simply man-mark him was doomed to failure, for such was his explosive form there was not a player on the planet capable of dulling the threat for ninety minutes. Instead, England would attempt to block him out by numbers, crowd him, and cut off his air. Plans were made, tactics discussed and the battle lines were drawn. 'Don't let the little bastard breath,' implored Robson at the final team talk. Little did the English realise the full extent of what they would be up against. For Maradona would surprise them all. He would be employing an entirely different set of rules. Scopa.

High noon. Sunday 22nd June 1986. A staggering crowd of 114,580, gathered at the Azteca to witness this titanic struggle between two nations that judging by the stern looks etched on the player's faces understood fully the magnitude of what was at stake. There were no neutrals. The Mexicans in the stadium threw in their lot alongside the South Americans with a rowdy, rampant enthusiasm as they chanted the name of Argentina's number ten with unbridled passion. Maradona had no borders, it was a worldwide religion. As the teams stood for their respective national anthems, Diego glared down past his compadres and gave the white shirts of England what could best be described as a murderous look of disdain. The intent was clear to all who witnessed the moment. Whether people liked it or not football was war. The kid from Villa Fiorito was up for this match like no other in his career. To thunderous applause they broke for a brief warm up before the match commenced. Both Captains were called to the halfway line by Tunisian referee Ali Ben Nasser for ceremonial duties. Maradona and England's thirty-six-year-old veteran goalkeeper Peter Shilton exchanged the slightest of handshakes which was polite nothing more. Each could have done without a touching of palms. Shilton and Maradona attempted to stare each other down. The Englishman all seriousness, the Argentinian wearing a joker's mask, a worrying half-smile. Like he had already read the script. With the stadium close to emotional meltdown the game began.

'Trompe l'oeil' ('Tricks and deception').

After a turgid opening period with both teams appearing to be overcome by the sheer enormity of the occasion, events exploded wildly into life on fifty-one minutes. A badly misjudged hooked clearance by English midfielder Steve Hodge succeeded only in sending the ball spinning back into his own penalty area. Sensing the danger, Peter Shilton rushed out to clear, only to be challenged by a jumping Maradona, who, with a mischievous flick of the wrist erupted into infamy. Blessed with all the cocky charm of the finest streetwise Neapolitan hustler, Argentina's number ten struck to steal a goal. A sleight of hand invisible to most punched the ball over the head of England's goalkeeper to set ablaze this magnificent footballing arena. Shilton's momentary expression of quizzical disbelief bore comparison with a man who had just seen his wallet snatched. In order to stoop low, the Argentinian had leapt high to infuriate the hated English with an infamous stroke of gamesmanship. A stunned Shilton knew what had happened, he blazed with anger. 'Ref, no please, he used his hand, he used his fucking hand!' Ben Nasser was not for turning, he pointed to the centre-circle. 'The Hand of God'. A likely story, for it was no divine intervention on the football pitch that day, just a twenty-five-year-old footballer called Diego Maradona, sporting a knowing grin after succeeding in getting away with the biggest scam of his young life. In Naples they danced with joy, for it was clear they had taught him well. As Maradona ran off to soak up the adulation of the crowd he glanced nervously over his shoulder at the referee and the melee that ensued. Close friend Jorge Valdano ran over to embrace him and with a finger over his mouth gestured 'Sssshh', as if suggesting. 'Don't push it Diego!'

High in the packed Azteca stands amid delirious Argentinian and Mexican supporters, Maradona spotted his father and gave a clenched fist salute. Further below, knots of England followers, most bare chested or wrapped in union jacks with faces contorted, raged, ranted and swore blindly at him. 'Fuck you Maradona. Fuck you!'

He smiled back. Argentina led. All hell had broken loose in Mexico City.

The referee appeared oblivious to protests as he waved away shell-shocked English players. A furious Shilton had run after him pointing to his hand but Ben Nasser was unmoved. The goal stood. A disgusted Bobby Robson pleaded with officials on the touchline. The England manager knew. He just knew. A footballing crime of the highest order had taken place in the Azteca and the English could do nothing about it. Ali Ben Nasser never again refereed another international football match. Before matters could calm down Diego Maradona struck once more, this time with the greatest goal ever scored in the history of the World Cup.

Racked by a sense of injustice and disbelief, England, still in a state of shock, simply did not see Maradona coming as he received the ball just inside his own half and took off on a mazy, weaving run towards their penalty area. A flurry of white shirts pounced, only to be turned inside out and left trailing in the Argentinian's wake as he hurtled clear over the halfway line and into the history books. Across Argentina, and in the back-alley café bars of Naples, they watched mesmerised. Surely 'El Diego' could not beat them all? Maradona dribbled at high pace past panicking, retreating English defenders and bore down on a waiting Peter Shilton. The crowd in the Azteca rose as one to their feet in mounting excitement. A final desperate challenge by Terry Butcher appeared to have put him off balance, only for Diego to throw Shilton a dummy at the last and switch the ball to his other foot, before finishing coolly with a flashing low shot into the net. The Azteca exploded in disbelief and delight. Argentinian commentator Victor Hugo Morales sobbed with joy as he screamed, "What planet are you from that you can leave so many Englishmen in your wake? Thank you, God! For football! For Maradona! For these tears! For this 2-0!'

The sly and the sordid equally applauded as the beauty and the brilliant by those who revered this stocky little figure with Godlike status. All across his homeland and in Naples were in raptures. In fact, every part of the planet where nobody cared about, a Third World, even Fourth. Maradona's world, his people, they were crying tears of joy. All danced, hugged or simply stood in shook. What the fuck had their boy just done? Their boy. Their Diego! Since that day, thirty-two years ago, there has been a million words and more wrote about this goal and still none can do it justice.

Though stung badly by the bittersweet circumstances of Diego Maradona's first and the sheer bloody genius of his second England found the strength from somewhere to come roaring back. On the brink of elimination and with nothing to lose, Bobby Robson threw caution to the wind. Off came midfielders Peter Reid and Trevor Steven, both victims of Maradona's whirlwind, to be replaced by two young, gifted, if unpredictable wingers, Chris Waddle and John Barnes. In a heart-stopping final half-hour, Barnes in particular almost saved the day as he terrorised the Argentinian rearguard with his electric pace and guile. When in the mood and firing on all cylinders, the enigmatic Jamaican-born forward possessed the talent to take apart the finest defence. Nine minutes remained to play when a typically devastating run and cross from the Watford man was met by Gary Lineker who swooped from close range to smash a header past Argentina's keeper Nino Pumpido. 2-1 and game on. Suddenly, amidst the Union Jack clad mass throngs on the Azteca terraces hope now sprung eternal. The incessant nasal roars of 'God save the Queen' sprung from amongst them. With Argentina clearly rattled, hanging on by the skin of their teeth, Barnes again soared down the left flank and hit an inch-perfect cross for Lineker. As the English centre-forward appeared a certainty to equalise, the defender Jose Luis

Brown somehow got there to prevent a certain goal. It was so close and was to prove England's last chance to save the day.

Finally, the full-time whistle sounded and the Argentinian players went in search of their Captain. After, in the sanctity of the dressing room, Diego Maradona led the celebrations as he wrapped himself in his country's flag and along with team-mates sang a boisterous rendition of the National Anthem. Nobody bothered to mention their Malvinas…

They didn't have to.

Late in the game, England centre-half Terry Butcher had motioned to Maradona if he had punched the ball over Shilton? With a wry smile, the Argentinian Captain simply pointed to his head. Questioned afterwards, Maradona caused outrage amongst the English journalists when he claimed with straight face and all mock innocence it was not he, but indeed 'The Hand of God' who soared high over Peter Shilton to score the first goal. With a wicked glint in his eye, Diego told one reporter, who repeatedly tried to force him to admit the said indiscretion, 'Go and cry in a fucking church amigo.' Seemingly enjoying himself torturing the Gringo newspaper hacks, a teasing Maradona finally admitted with an ironic smile and slight shrug of the shoulders that it was, 'A little bit of the hand of God, a little of the head of Maradona.' How they raged. suddenly, as was his wont, and again without trying too hard he had earned an entire new audience to despise him. Not that Maradona cared, for despite all aired publicly the victory in the Azteca was indeed payback time for what occurred in the South Atlantic. A war without guns and bullets, but a war nonetheless. A semi-final date with unfancied Belgium lay in waiting and after beating England, Argentina feared no one. For destiny, and if you were to believe their Captain, God himself was in their line-up! Against such odds the Belgians did not have a prayer.

So, it proved.
Just three days on from the historic victory over the English, the Argentinians stepped out again into the vast cauldron of the Azteca stadium to take on the blood red shirts of Belgium, the dark horses of the tournament. An impressive run to the latter stages saw the Belgians collect the scalps of highly-fancied Spain and a USSR team that was seen by many as the best in the competition. A mixture of experience in players such as Eric Gerets and Jan Ceulemans, added to a dash of youth in the wonderfully talented Enzo Scifo, meant they could not be taken lightly. Again, the hugely partisan audience of 110,420 that had gathered once more in the Azteca came with the intention of seeing the European side, the bad guys, put to the sword by their hero. Diego Maradona was in the best form of his life, in any era unplayable, unstoppable. Mexico had simply been blessed by being handed the platform to watch a genius at the peak of his powers. Twice now this country had been fortunate to witness greatness in their midst. The glorious summer of 1970, being the other when Pele exploded in wonderfully, evocative yellow drenched technicolour on a world audience. Though they would rage against the light for close to an hour and show huge heart Belgium's fate was never in doubt, for truly great players have a moment in history when it's clearly their time. The 1986 World Cup finals were without question Diego Maradona's. Ever the

showman, Maradona produced a few party tricks in the opening moments to keep his adoring following happy, but mostly the first half was spent probing, plotting and searching for a weakness in the opposition's rearguard. Superbly organised by the wily old coach Guy Thys, the Belgians dug in. Theirs' was a game plan, simple but crude. Hold out until after extra time then try and win the match on penalties. It was akin to throwing a party on a railway line. Against any other it may have worked, but this was Maradona. Sooner or later they were going to get flattened.

On the eve of the semi-final, Belgium goalkeeper Jean-Marie Pfaff claimed they could handle Diego. He might have appeared to have a valid point as the man himself in the opening period seemingly bore the look of a player disinterested. Neapolitan deception. *Trompe l oeil.* Then, as against England, when all seemed peaceful the train appeared at breakneck speed to splatter all on the track as he awoke from apparent slumber to break Belgian hearts. Showtime. It was time to go to work. Just when Belgium had dared to dream, Maradona tore menacingly into their penalty area to clip a gloriously low cross-shot past the fingers of a despairing Jean-Marie Pfaff to ignite scenes of wild celebrations across the Azteca. The unerring technique and precision required to score such a goal took the breath away of all who witnessed this moment of sublime ingenuity. With the battle plan now in tatters and looking bereft of spark and the necessary guile required to claw their way back against such a formidable team as Argentina, Guy Thys' men appeared resigned to the inevitable. It duly occurred twelve minutes later when Maradona finally put them out of their misery with a touch of magic that bore easy comparison with his previous work of art against the English. Picking up the ball midway inside the Belgian half he found himself shadowed by a blazing shower of red shirts. All eyes both on the pitch and off fell upon him. A drop of the shoulders and two, three, four defenders were left for dead. Exploding into top gear Maradona scythed through a heap of bodies and roared onwards into the penalty area. Once more the Azteca rose as one: he was at it again! Still surrounded by a seemingly impenetrable mass of red and forced wide of the goal, Maradona produced from nowhere an astonishing left-foot shot that screamed past a bemused Pfaff into the net before wheeling away in triumph.

A Mexican daze.

Amongst the ecstatic, delirious crowd going mad on witnessing such a moment was England manager Bobby Robson, who although still smarting from Diego's 'bag snatch' against his team, typically stood and applauded Maradona's breathtaking goal. Shortly after the hat-trick was almost completed when he went through again, only this time to fire inches wide of the far post. On surviving this particular Diego close encounter, Jean-Marie Pfaff glared daggers at his tormentor before breaking out in a huge smile. It was no disgrace to be beaten by such as he. Pfaff's pre-match comments had returned to haunt him. The full-time whistle saw Jean-Marie Pfaff go in search of his destroyer only to embrace and wish him all the best for the final. Diego Maradona appeared genuinely touched by Pfaff's sporting gesture and the two men left the pitch arm-in-arm, deep in conversation. A World Cup final awaited Argentina against a team whom loved nothing better than to spoil a party.

CHAPTER ELEVEN

KING OF THE WORLD

Diego Maradona was many things to all. A cheat and chancer, maker of dreams, Devil and a God. With the ball at his feet he possessed the magic to lift entire continents off their seats and gasp in wonder and adoration. There were those who simply loved and admired, others who loathed and raged, screaming venom at the mere mention of the fucking name. Maradona. Whereas believers lit candles and bowed before his image. Opinion varied wildly. How do you measure greatness in a man and a footballer? The 1986 World Cup Finals hardly supplied answers, instead they only added to the myth and mystique. King of the world or streetwise hustler made good? With the greatest prize of all at stake the time came for Diego Maradona to show his true hand. Again.

Argentina's opponents were to be a West German team managed by the legendary Franz Beckenbauer, (Der Kaiser), that had proved to be typically efficient, if hardly spectacular during their crab-like crawl to the final. Some spoke of cannon fodder for Diego Maradona to savage at will. Others were warier, for history dictated that the Germans never laid down for anyone. Far superior teams than Argentina had been put in their place by these resilient, never-say-die characters over many decades of World Cup competition who would fight to the very end. They loved an ambush. Great players such as Puskas and Cruyff had seen their hearts broken at the last. Would the same fate now befall Maradona?

With their football no better than functional the Germans came out of the first round with sufficient points and few new admirers. Behind the scenes chaos reigned. Beckenbauer was left with little option but to send the reserve goalkeeper Uli Stein home after he scathingly referred to him as, 'Humpty Dumpty!' Not content with insulting the coach, Stein had also torn into his teammates previously by claiming, 'They played like a bunch of cucumbers,' in warm-up matches. Matters hardly improved as the tournament began when a German tabloid alleged stories of prostitutes being seen leaving the players' hotel rooms. There was also the problem of a bitter fall-out between two of their most experienced stars, centre-forward Karl-Heinz Rummenigge and goalkeeper Harold Schumacher. Both had newspaper columns back home and could not resist the temptation to let fly in the other's direction whenever the opportunity arose. Embarrassed and outraged by the team's antics Beckenbauer exploded with rage when West Germany failed to live up to expectations in their opening two first-round games. Words such as 'Stupid' and 'Garbage' were used to describe their showings against Uruguay and Scotland. That they managed to qualify out of the group surprised even their manager who was forced into a public apology by the German FA after his uncharacteristic outburst. In his entire illustrious career, Der Kaiser, had never faced such a daunting challenge as in attempting to drag these maddeningly, frustrating Germans to the pinnacle of world football. A side packed full of talent but laced with niggling injuries and personal vendettas that threatened at any time to make them implode. Come the knockout phase, only a last minute free-kick from one of their few impressive players Lothar Matthaus saw off unlucky Morocco. Then, in the quarter-finals, a drab affair against host nation Mexico was settled miserably by a penalty shoot-out, in which the nervous Mexicans in front of their own people totally went to pieces and missed four of five attempts. Thus, sending the nation into mourning and handing the game to the Germans. The semi-final in Guadalajara pitted them against the exuberant, but ageing French Musketeers of Platini, Tigana, Fernandez and Giresse. Billed as a re-match of the classic duel in Seville during the last World Cup, when West Germany came from 3-1 down in extra time to finally as ever win on penalties. This time around it proved much more comfortable for Beckenbauer's dogged team. After a truly exhausting epic contest against Brazil, France were already a spent force and an Andreas Brehme free-kick, allied to a last-minute breakaway from centre-forward Rudi Voller, put paid to the French to secure a fifth World Cup final appearance. It spoke volumes for German mentality that despite nowhere near the class of former sides, sheer guts and determination enabled them to claw a path to within ninety minutes of becoming world champions for a third time.

Preparation to deal with Diego Maradona hinged on paranoia after witnessing his momentous exploits against England and Belgium. For the coach he remained the last major obstacle that stood between him becoming the first ever to win the trophy both as player and manager. 'Maradona is the best player in the World Cup, the best in the world. We will do our best to put him out of the game, but it is almost impossible.' Though respective of all the Argentinian forwards, none put the fear of God into Beckenbauer like Maradona, so much that he sacrificed his best player in attempting to make the game a ten-a-side contest. Der Kaiser placed his trust in the twenty-five-year old Bayern Munich dynamo, Lothar Matthaus. Here was the archetypal German midfielder, fast, strong, shoot with either foot, fine technique, intelligent and well disciplined. Most importantly capable of taking on the malevolent cunning and guile of Maradona. The Bayern man possessed nerves of steel. By attaching himself limpet-like, Matthaus hoped to snub him out like a cigarette butt. It would be a battle royal and to the winner would go the thirteenth World Cup.

Unknown to the outside world, Maradona finished every game in searing agony as his accursed left ankle inflamed wildly during the fury of battle on the pitch. Only the ominous sharp prick of the cortisone needle enabled him to withstand the pain, as knowledgeable defenders knew exactly where to hit. The manager Carlos Bilardo had little sympathy with his Captain, for he graduated from the Argentinian school of thought that winning was all that mattered. During his career as a player with the infamous Estudiantes side of the late Sixties, Bilardo built a reputation as a notorious hard man who took no prisoners, most memorably assaulting Manchester United's Nobby Stiles with an outrageous head butt during the 1968 World Club Championships. Carlos Bilardo was ruthless in his all-consuming desire to attain legendary status as the man who won back the World Cup. To do so it was imperative the Captain was on the field. There was nothing he would not stoop to in order to make this so, for without his coveted number ten the cause was hopeless. Argentina needed Diego Maradona like a flower needed rain. Without him they would wilt and die under the blazing Mexican sun. Maradona's own passion and determination

to play and lead his nation to glory meant he was his own worst enemy, for dark tales surfaced that whatever Diego was given to continue performing might have drastic consequences in later years. In his case the term 'dying to play' could well have been frightfully apt.
In Buenos Aires, thousands of posters on every street corner declared unequivocally, *'MARADONA PRESIDENTE'!* A local priest from Villa Fiorito, Monsignor Jorge Caseretto, claimed he had received a message from God saying that 'The Almighty himself was a Maradona fan and that everything was arranged. They would prevail over the Germans.' As exclusives go it took some beating. In Naples, once the 'Azzurri' had been eliminated, every Neapolitan immediately shifted allegiances towards Argentina and rallied behind their king. On the eve of the final Diego Maradona spoke well in praising Beckenbauer's men. 'They play like a real team, they never give up and it would be ignorant not to have the greatest respect for them.'

So, at the Azteca Stadium on Sunday 29th June 1986, Argentina and West Germany fought out a thrilling climax to what had been a truly absorbing and dramatic Mexican fiesta of football. In the history of the World Cup no player ever dominated an entire tournament like Maradona. His goals and performances had overshadowed all. Only West Germany stood between him and a place amongst the game's immortals. Only the Germans, a familiar tale. Again, drawn to the wonder of Diego Maradona like a dragonfly to a flame, the Mexicans firmly nailed their colours behind fellow Latinos, Argentina. A local banner spoke for the entire nation.
'Maradona, why was you not born in Mexico'.

Huge swathes of blue and white gathered joyfully with their green and red clad hosts to decorate the spectacular wide-open terraces of the glorious Azteca, as both sets of supporters joined forces to roar Maradona's team over the finishing line. With genius there were simply no borders. Neither ocean nor deserts could separate as Maradona united football lovers across the globe. Except maybe Brazil, and, of course England.

With the Argentinians in traditional blue and white and West Germany in change shirts of green, the game began. In a ploy no doubt planned in the dressing room beforehand, Argentina launched a callous pre-emptive strike against Lothar Matthaus in an attempt to break loose the chains on their Captain. The opening moments saw the hunter become the hunted as defender Giusti tracked down the German midfielder to stamp viciously on his ankle. A furious Matthaus was fortunate to escape serious injury and on twenty-three minutes extracted sweet revenge by slicing down Maradona from behind for which he was duly and deservedly booked. From the resulting free-kick played high into the German penalty area, Harold Schumacher could only watch in horror as he failed to punch clear and Argentinian centre-half Jose Luis Brown soared high to thunder his header into the net. 1-0. A stalemate then took hold as a disappointing first half ensued. Argentina was content to just sit back and hit on the break. Their opponents appeared hesitant to open up, dreading that the South Americans would strike out and score again. Maradona worked tirelessly for the cause, his footballing brain forever scheming to entice German attention upon him and release fellow team-mates to do damage.

Finally, as the second period began, Beckenbauer's men realised they were in a World Cup final and started to chase the game. The almost inevitable then duly occurred nine minutes after the interval when a clearance from an Andreas Brehme corner saw the Argentinians fly like the wind on the counter attack. A typically breathtaking twist and turn by Maradona, followed by a clever pass to Hector Enrique had the Germans racing back in panic. Enrique placed an exquisite through-ball that was latched onto by Jorge Valdano who sped clear into the penalty area and with great assurance swept the ball low past the advancing Schumacher to surely clinch the World Cup for Argentina. Valdano disappeared beneath a blue and white mountain of joy as all the players and those on the Argentinian bench raced onto the pitch in celebration. A sense of hysteria took hold. Maradona sank to his knees and raised both hands in prayer. The Germans were on the floor. A grim-faced Franz Beckenbauer bore the look of a man resigned to defeat as he stood arms folded on the touchline, watching the cavorting of the South Americans. Carlos Bilardo gestured wildly at his players to keep their concentration for the game was not yet won. The small scatterings of German support lay silent, steadying themselves for the inevitable. West Germany rallied, Lothar Matthaus was released from marking duties on Maradona with orders to push forward. Fifteen minutes from time the mood changed dramatically in the Azteca, when from a corner Rudi Voller flicked on for Rummenigge who slid in to grab a goal back. Sensing blood, Der Kaiser's men threw everything they had left at a back-pedalling Argentina. As against England, from appearing to be coasting they found themselves fighting for their lives in the closing stages. With Bilardo close to a heart attack on the touchline and their Captain unable to break the siege, it just had to happen. Another German corner and with millions watching around the world in total disbelief Rudi Voller broke Argentinian hearts as he stooped low to head home an equaliser, 2-2! Argentina looked to have blown it.

The old adage of never underestimating the Germans had again proved true. Extra-time loomed. As a child Diego Maradona had once proclaimed that his greatest wish was 'To play in the World Cup and be a champion for my team.' That dream in no short time had been reduced to tatters as West Germany launched their barnstorming comeback. As Argentina stood on the brink of disaster this irascible, magical, little street urchin, who plied his trade in Naples, but whose heart lay ensconced in Buenos Aires, produced one last stroke of wizardry to save the day. Six minutes remained when Maradona in centre-midfield delivered a parting gift to Mexico 86. In the blink of an eye and surrounded by green shirts, he played the most outrageous volleyed pass to send twenty-two-year-old Nantes midfielder Jose Burruchaga racing through to fire unbelievably past a despairing Harold Schumacher. 3-2! The Germans fell to their knees, this time there was no way back. One punch too many: cruel as it was beautiful. The thirteenth World Cup final ended and Carlos Bilardo was a man possessed as he sprinted onto the field to embrace his Captain. Every photographer and camera focused on one man, Diego Maradona. He and his team were champions of the World.

On receiving the trophy, a beaming Maradona was hoisted shoulder-high by his adoring countrymen and carried around the stadium. A nation's honour had been satisfied, now all that remained was the keeping of a promise made

to a city and it's people that had adopted him as one of their own. Diego Maradona had shown that he possessed the power to make dreams come true. The time had come to end Neapolitan misery and finally win that elusive Scudetto.
There was unfinished business in Naples.

Post note. The Golden Ball
It came as no surprise to anyone that the award for the tournament's best player, the golden ball, went to Diego Maradona. The Argentinian World Cup winning Captain cut a proud figure on it being awarded to him. This trophy meant an awful lot to Diego and to keep it safe the golden ball, along with a host of other precious, valuable possessions was placed into a Rome high security bank vault that was said to be impregnable. In 1989, three years later, on a dark Roman evening, a gang of masked figures blew a hole in the side of the bank large enough to drive a bus through and in they swarmed to empty it. The thieves got $1.48 million of Maradona`s possessions alone, including the golden ball All Italy was aghast, but none more than Diego Maradona, for amongst the items stolen was also twenty ridiculously expensive watches. In order to try and retrieve his property a seething Maradona visited one of his new-found amigos. An extremely powerful and high-ranking member of the Camorra, Don Salvatore Lo Russo, head of the notorious and much feared Miano clan in the North of the city. The two had become close and Lo Russo was trusted enough by the player to ask for on a couple of occasions if he could supply him with cocaine for personal use? Something which Don Salvatore was always only happy to help with. To this man Maradona asked if anything could be done and the Neapolitan

Godfather assured his Argentinian friend that he would make all enquiries. For 'El Diego' was one of their own. It would be an honour to help retrieve what was rightly his. Don Salvatore did indeed do as promised and discovered in no time that 'Maradona's 'lost property' did in fact reside in Naples and was in the hands of the Picuozzi clan of the Spanish Quarter. 150,000,000 Lira was sent to them for their safe return. Word was sent back to Don Salvatore from the Picuozzi that they were prepared to do business over the watches, but regarding the golden ball, impossible, for it had already been melted down into golden bars. In the end the watches were returned with the money as a gesture of goodwill. The Picuozzi did not want a war. On being informed of the bad news by Don Salvatore, Maradona was wise enough to know how things worked and not to kick up a fuss. For this was Naples, even kings had to behave.

CHAPTER TWELVE

CAPTAIN

Giuseppe Bruscolotti was a man born with the blue blood of Naples flowing through his veins. Signed from neighbouring Sorrento back in 1972, Bruscolotti had shared the pain of the tifosi time and again as Napoli fell at the last hurdle. He had played in the infamous 'Core Ngrato' match when former hero Jose Altafini broke Neapolitan hearts. Nobody ever gave or suffered more than he for the cause. That fateful day when Bruscolotti was made Captain saw the tough, fierce-tackling defender shed tears, such was his passion for the club. So, it was with heavy heart and grand sense of duty that this Napoli legend Giuseppe Bruscolotti passed on his mantle of leader to Diego Maradona in exchange for the promise of the Scudetto. Maradona embraced Bruscolotti and with the handing over of a baton, dipped in the hopes and broken dreams of past generations, the Argentinian took the precious armband vowing not to let Naples and this proud warrior down. He would prove true to his word.

Over the ages, Neapolitan folk ballads have echoed across oceans and continents. Known as the *Canzoni*, these haunting melodies tugged at the heartstrings as they told tales of love lost and found, of a yearning for the old country. Made famous by the legendary Italian Tenor, Neapolitan-born Enrico Caruso, classics such as *'Funiculi-Funicula'*, *'Return to Sorrento'* and the incomparable *'O Sole Mio'* helped romanticise Naples as a city like no other. Perhaps though the greatest *Canzoni* of them all was

performed at the San Paolo footballing cathedral by a massed chorus of thousands back in the mid-Eighties.
'Oh Mama, Mama, Mama, oh Mama, Mama, do you know why my heart beats so fast? Because I have seen Maradona, I have seen Maradona, and Mama, Mama, Mama, I'm in love!'
A perfectionist like the genius Caruso may have baulked at the lyrics, but as a native of Naples he could never have argued with the passion in which they were sung, for something remarkable was stirring under the volcano. With Diego Maradona at the peak of his powers, a rare and fearful sense of optimism had taken a grip. The Napoli tifosi knew well it was now or never for the Scudetto. Reinforcements in attack had been provided in the fast and lethal forward Andrea Carnevale, who so impressed as the two sides met late in the previous season when he scored twice in a 2-0 win for Udinese. Recruits were also sought to add fire and guile in midfield. From Avellino, came the tenacious Fernando De Napoli, whilst in a shrewd show of business acumen, Ottavio Bianchi secured from Triestina in Serie B, the ball-playing skills of Francesco Romano. With these two alongside Salvatore Bagni to help fire the bullets, Napoli now possessed a team to rival any in Serie A. All that remained for coach Ottavio Bianchi and the Napoli faithful was to get their Captain back in one piece, firing on all cylinders. Special prayers were offered to San Gennaro to keep a wary eye on Diego Maradona. Save him from temptation, bad luck, dangerous women but mostly from himself. In Naples, huge pride was taken from his incredulous performances though worries about Maradona's state of mind now he had reached the ultimate pinnacle. Ability was never in question, it was whether Diego possessed the necessary strength of character to

carry on producing miracles in the colours of SSC Napoli? After the history-making adventures in Mexico, Maradona returned to Argentina for a holiday before travelling onto Naples. Little did he know what awaited him on home soil for after landing at Buenos Aires, Maradona was greeted in truly hysterical manner as the entire city turned out to welcome home the conquering hero. A triumphant motor cavalcade paraded Argentina's favourite son through the streets with thousands lining the pavements waving flags, chanting the name of their beloved Captain. He was taken to the Presidential Palace at Casa Rosada, where on a balcony with Argentinian President Raul Alfonsin, in a showering blur of a sky thick with blue and white confetti, a delighted Diego Maradona proudly showed off the World Cup trophy to his blood people. The kid from the back alleys of Villa Fiorito had come a long way.

Once more in the arms of the man she loved was Claudia Villafane. A reconciliation had occurred and much to Claudia's joy, Diego Maradona was back in her life with a promise to behave and settle down. That Cristina Sinagra was due at any time to give birth to his baby was not lost on Claudia, who appeared to waste little time in getting pregnant. However, domestic bliss for Diego was not yet on his agenda as the partying in the wake of Argentina's momentous victory continued at full hilt. Finally, taking a much-needed sabbatical, Maradona retired to his parent's house where in a rare moment of tranquility, two young local boys with a ball found the courage to chance their arm and knock on the door to ask if he would join them for a kick about? Unable to resist, Maradona led them into his mother's garden where he spent an hour enjoying making their dreams come true playing with them. The lads stood mesmerised as Diego all but made the ball stand up and beg. A wonderful tale they could relate to their grandchildren. And they theirs'.

On Sunday 14th September 1986, the Neapolitans trecked North and re-started their Serie A campaign against newly-promoted Brescia. It took their Captain just forty-one minutes of the opening 1986-87 season to confirm that SSC Napoli's all-obsessive, burning desire to win the championship was close to being realised. With his back to goal, Diego Maradona took a prodded pass from Salvatore Bagni exquisitely on his chest and tore with malicious intent towards the penalty area. In almost nonchalant manner, he slipped past two defenders before taking aim and slamming a terrific drive past the keeper. The Brescia players stood transfixed; whatever had swarmed amongst them was surely not human? Those who had dared to doubt hung their heads in shame. Diego had returned in the mood. He soared towards his adoring followers punching the air, thanking the Almighty. Pure theatre. A seething Northern crowd sat outraged but secretly admiring this barbarian king from the South. The final whistle brought great scenes of rejoicing amongst the Neapolitans whom had infiltrated all around the ground. The long journey home to Naples was bathed in the magical memory of Diego Maradona's winner. The omens were good; it promised to be in the words of another famous singer of Southern Italian extraction. Francis Alberto Sinatra, *A Very Good Year.*

On the eve of Napoli's opening home fixture against Udinese, Diego Maradona received word that although expected still shocked him to the core. Cristina Sinagra had given birth to a bouncing baby boy and just to ensure there was no misunderstanding, she went live on National television to announce, 'I will name him after his father. Diego Armando.' To call the child this in Naples was akin to naming him Jesus Christ. Cristina appointed one of Naples' most respected lawyers Enrico Trucillo, to go after Maradona. This he did with a vengeance for even before the cord had been cut on the child, Trucillo issued a paternity suit against the alleged father. Enrico Trucillo had forged an entire career as a protector and fierce advocate of the underdog's cause. He was also said to possess an enormous ego. The opportunity of bringing Diego Maradona to heel was one Trucillo would relish. When challenged, Maradona was again adamant the baby was not his. With the media circus giving the story colossal coverage on television, radio and newspapers, there was nowhere to hide. His apartment in Posilippo became a prison as the lens of the paparazzi descended en masse to the player's door. Up trees, on roofs, above in helicopters, the cameras clicked and flashed, his every move watched. Across all Italy this sensational storyline of a King denying his own blood caused huge controversy. It was a scenario greeted with delight by those who loved nothing more than sticking the knife into Diego Maradona. The next day he played one of his worst matches to date for the Neapolitans as Udinese held them to a 1-1 draw in Naples. A thunderous twenty-five-yard strike by Fernando Di Napoli proved the only highlight of an insipid performance by the home side. From the beginning, on appearing from the tunnel Maradona looked reluctant to even set foot on the pitch. His mind elsewhere, the normally incisive passing lacked it's normal penetration and accuracy. Also missing was the terrifying, electric spurts forward. There was simply no spark. He appeared lost, afraid of his own shadow. Suddenly, in front of a capacity crowd at the San Paolo, Diego Maradona looked to have been swallowed up by the life he had created, the pressure and expectations were strangling him. The Napoli tifosi watched horrified as he struggled to find form. They roared his name, sang the songs, but all to no avail. Maradona knew he had been given a son, but with Claudia expecting also, his thoughts were in turmoil. The King's lot was not a happy one. The one escape from the madness was out on the football field where Diego's only worry was opposing defenders wishing to kick him senseless. This was a minor irritancy in comparison to what he was forced to endure off pitch. After the match a depressed looking Maradona was smuggled out of a side door by his entourage who hustled him through the media wolves that stood ready to devour. There was no getaway though for as he sped off into downtown Naples with Claudia alongside in a jet-black Ferrari, the jackals followed. Maradona might lose them for a while, but in the end his scent proved overwhelming. They would always find him.

To add insult to injury, further heartache followed in the manner of an ignominious exit from the UEFA cup in Southern France, at the hands of unfancied Toulouse. A lone goal from new boy Carnevale was cancelled out by the French on home ground when a similar score-line led to a penalty shootout after extra-time. Ironically, it was two of Naples most favourite sons that failed to convert the spot-kicks as Napoli went down 4-3. First Bagni, then Maradona, to the utter bewilderment of team-mates and more so himself, hit his spot-kick against the post. The sad sight of their Captain in floods of tears and inconsolable meant no tifosi could possibly point a finger of blame upon him. Indeed, his popularity increased to even higher levels of adulation. Whatever cynicism had been cited regarding Maradona's complete devotion to Naples disappeared. He was truly one of their own, a treasure of San Gennaro. For an interview to the RAI Italian television station in the immediate, miserable aftermath of defeat, a visibly emotional Diego Maradona thanked the Napoli fans for their unyielding support. This was not Maradona simply playing to the gantry; he desperately wanted to repay their loyalty. There had been a banner amongst the Neapolitans reading: 'Diego, you are one of us'. It reminded the player of the blood oath he had sworn to the young tifosi whose lives he had so indelibly touched in many ways. It was a debt Maradona intended to honour and in a short time he would have them dancing like dervishes in the backstreets of Naples.

Stung by the embarrassing loss at the hands of Toulouse, Napoli's title charge took on an almost frenzied quality. Diego Maradona was back and ablaze. The reborn enthusiasm evident in every exaggerated gesture and mannerism. Soaked in Neapolitan passion, he cast his diminutive, but captivating presence over Serie A. They embarked on an unbeaten eight-match run that included four goals for Maradona. Two were vital winners at Sampdoria and Roma. A penalty finished with ridiculous, cocky ease secured a hard fought 2-1 victory at the Luigi Ferraris stadium in Genoa. The abiding memory of the game was an instance on the touchline, a rain-drenched swamp of a surface Diego Maradona teased, mocked and beat every Sampdoria player who had the temerity to try and take the ball off him.
In Roma's Olimpico Stadium, Maradona's classic piece of control and astute finishing a minute after half time from a

scything through pass by Bruno Giordano earned them the points. Before the game began the Argentinian performed a remarkable display of ball juggling in the centre-circle that caused gasps from the terraces. It proved a bitterly fought contest played out against a spectacular, dramatic backdrop of Roma red/yellow and Naples blue. As ever, when in Rome, the Neapolitans had to earn the right for every tackle, pass and goal scored. This result shot Napoli to the top of Serie A, but unfortunately the joy was tarnished by having to share their lofty position with an unwelcome old foe. A reluctant Juventus shifted their imperious backsides to allow the great unwashed room upon the pedestal. A showdown waited in a city and stadium that was nothing short of hell on earth for all Neapolitans. On Sunday 9th November 1986, all roads led to Turin.

Juventus were under new management. Giovanni Trapattoni's dramatic decision to divorce the 'Old Lady' and move to Inter Milan opened the door for former Napoli coach Rino Marchesi. The affable Marchesi had glimpsed both sides of the coin. He understood the history, emotions and sheer hatred that existed in confrontations between these two giants of the Italian league. The black/white stripes of the mighty Northern Industrial heartland of Turin versus the sky blue of the downtrodden, irascible, troublesome, but always proud Southern capital of Naples. In an unprecedented show of mass support, the Napoli hordes converged on the Stadio Comunale. With the vast number of Neapolitans employed in the city working for Agnelli's Fiat, ferocious backing was always guaranteed. The epic events of 9th November, would echo through eternity as the Southerners descended like an invading army onto their most hated foes. The gigantic housing estate of the Mirafiori, built in close duration to the grey, foreboding car plants housed the tens of thousands who plied their trade for the Agnelli family. It bore the look of a little Naples, as those who lived there chose to show the true colours and follow the heart as the dream of Scudetto began to grow ever increasingly real. The scheming Agnellis' original ploy for their workers to spend all week toiling for a motley sum of Lira, only to then hand back the cash to support the family's hobby horse Juventus, thus self-servicing the monster, fell short when it came to the exiled Southern Brethren. For though far from under the shadow of great Grandfather Vesuvio, the passion never left. The Agnellis' might have owned the bodies, but for those who kept the faith, they were damned if he would ever wrestle away their souls. What price a mere paycheck in comparison to watching Diego Maradona? The opportunity had arisen to not just glimpse a shooting star but to ride aboard till it's journey's end. There was something in the air.

Well before first light the blue-clad tifosi of the Bulldogs, Fedayn, Blue Tigers and the massed ranks of the CUCB were en route to Turin. Fifteen thousand made their wary way North by car, coach and train to swell the numbers of their Neapolitan brothers already ensconced behind enemy lines. It was an outrageous twenty-nine years previous, on 24th November 1957, that SSC Napoli last won in the league on Juventus territory. Many of those from the South who went to witness with their own eyes Diego Maradona end this witchcraft over their team would not even have been born on that long-gone day. The time had come to lift the curse.

With three-quarters of the Stadio Comunale bathed in the blue-white of Naples, the away side attacked from the kick off. Ably supported by his trusty, swashbuckling Lieutenants, Giordano, Carnevale and Bagni, Maradona led the charge. Roared on by their astonishing following, the first half belonged almost exclusively to Napoli as they dominated possession. Juventus were forced to retreat and defend, yet for the away side, it still remained worryingly scoreless. Five minutes after the interval normal service between these two embittered adversaries appeared to be resumed when keeper Claudio Garella could only push away Juve defender Antonio Cabrini's shot, and from six yards the deadly left foot of Michael Laudrup followed up to lash the ball into the net. It was a goal totally against the run of play and a savage kick in the teeth for the visitors. A sickening sense of reality washed over the Neapolitans. They had dared to dream. An inherited, fatalistic outlook on life that sprouted from waking up each day in the menacing shade of Vesuvio meant they half expected disaster to strike. Not so much paranoid, but more resigned to inevitable failure. Little could anyone have known what was set to unfold, for stirred by an overwhelming sense of indignation inflicted upon them, not just that day but in years gone by, Ottavio Bianchi's men set about Juventus with unreserved venom. Though no way to treat a lady, 'La Vecchia Signora' found herself trampled on as a Maradona inspired Napoli to take more than just her honour. The Neapolitans attacked, driven, sick of failure, determined to rid themselves of this ancient thorn in their sides. Since James Poths and Emilio Anatra took up the mantle many decades ago, SSC Napoli had witnessed some wonderful players, but none held more passion and desire for the cause as those whom finally put paid to the curse of the dreaded Juve on that sweet November afternoon. On seventy-two minutes Bruno Giordano let fly a crashing twenty-five-yard drive that was tipped magnificently over the bar by goalkeeper Steffano Tacconi. As the clock ticked down the incessant pressure told at last, when Tacconi, after making an array of breathtaking saves to keep the Neapolitans out was finally beaten. A richly deserved equaliser arrived from a Francesco Romano corner, as the unlikely figure of centre-half Morenio Ferrario stabbed home a shot from eight-yards. Greeted with more relief than joy by the Napoli faithful, they would at least take pride in a point. A minute later from a Maradona corner, Allesandro Renica flicked on for Bruno Giordano to smash a thunderous, arching volley at the far post past Tacconi, and into the realms of Southern legend. Bedlam erupted in the Comunale! A deep-throated roar tinged with Neapolitan dialect rose like a crescendo across the terraces. The great and good of Turin shifted uneasily in their plush seats. This was so much more than just a simple game of football. Lose this match and the genie could well be out of the lamp and free. A shift of power tilting towards a city like Naples was unthinkable for the Northern aristocrats. But it was happening! The blue shirts continued to storm forward. With sheer trickery and pace Diego Maradona ripped past Juve players causing havoc. They wanted more: to win was not sufficient, the weight of history between these two teams demanded a true cleansing of the pain. It came on ninety minutes when the galloping left full-back Giuseppe Volpecina charged upfield to smash the ball low past a forlorn Tacconi to ignite incredible scenes of rejoicing amongst the Napoli supporters. It was a momentous victory. But for the heroics of Steffano Tacconi, Juve's

humiliation could well have been on a scale unthinkable, for the final scoreline of 3-1 saw them escape lightly. Not that it mattered to those whom ventured to Turin fearing the worse, for in this most unlikely inhospitable and hostile of venues, Neapolitans found paradise. Many stood with tears streaming down their faces, unable to take in the enormity of the victory, one that would live forever in the history of SSC Napoli, and perhaps more importantly, in the hearts of their devoted tifosi who were fortunate enough to witness it live. In the eyes of their beloved city they were all heroes for a day. The Stadio Comunale was theirs' alone as the Juventus fans slid away red-faced. They had no desire to witness the gloating and jubilation of the arch-enemy taking place in their midst. An enduring memory of the game was the sight of a track-suited Juve ball boy leaping with delight every time a Napoli goal hit the back of the net, celebrating for all his worth. Lest to say he was later found to be of Neapolitan origin and was not on duty for the next home match in Turin! In a typically sporting gesture a gallant Michel Platini made a point of shaking Maradona's hand before trooping dismally off the pitch. In spite of the gut-churning hatred between their respected cities both men shared a healthy friendship and respect. Platini was struggling with long-term injuries and this proved to be the final season for one of the greatest footballers ever to grace the world scene. He would be missed, but not in Naples. A changing wind had blown up from the South.
'Il crollo dell'impero bianconero'. ('The falling of the black and white empire).

The following day saw the hugely influential Corriere dello Sport newspaper jubilantly declare: *'Il Napoli in trionfo!' ('Naples triumphant')!*
The equally prestigious Gazetta dello Sport hummed a similar tune: *'Maradona canta Volare!' ('Maradona sings Volare')!*
Another, Guerin Sportivo handed Maradona an unheard ten out of ten marks for his masterful performance.
This was still a championship fight in it's infancy. Napoli were only two points clear of the chasing pack and half a world away from the finishing line. History had taught Neapolitans many things, but none more than that the championship could never be considered won until the final whistle of the season had sounded, your enemy runs out of options and the power to corrupt no longer matters. Yet, there was real fear in the North that Napoli would take the title. In Turin and Milan, they had already begun to steady themselves for what was slowly becoming the inevitable. For so long Naples had been like a tempestuous, unruly younger brother who though truly talented, was never going to possess the necessary drive and ambition to make anything of his life. But as Diego Maradona continued to conjure up miracles on a weekly basis, the question had to be asked. With Juventus struggling and the Milanese unable to mount a serious challenge, just who was going to stop them?
After a welcomed two-week grace for international fixtures, battle recommenced in Serie A, on 23rd November, when lowly Empoli travelled to Naples fearing a beating, and ultimately receiving one. Waiting for them was a Napoli side fired up to ensure they consolidated their position as league leaders. On a horrendously soaked, rain-lashed Sunday afternoon, with dark clouds hovering

gloomily over the bay, the visitors walked into the eye of a Neapolitan storm. Not deterred by the miserable conditions, 85,000 gathered at the San Paolo in typically warlike mood. The anthems of the various clans soared high into the sullen skies, electrifying the arena. Rockets whistled precariously in all directions, blue flares engulfed the terraces. Flags adorned with images and tributes to Maradona lay spread in huge numbers across the stadium. Others spat out insults to their dear friends from the North. One such banner claiming,

'Odiamo Tutti' ('We hate everyone').

This was no idle boast. That all outside their city walls despised them mattered nothing to the hard-line tifosi who revelled in the notoriety.

In what had become an important pre-match ritual Diego Maradona embraced the club physio Salvatore Carmando and kissed his head. The two were close and for Carmando it is a friendship he remembers fondly. 'It all started before one game when we just embraced. Diego kissed me on the head and said 'Thank God,' and from that moment he never stopped doing it. I never had or wanted anything in the form of money, ours was a relationship based on pure friendship. From the first moment he saw me working Diego fell in love with my hands. He was enchanted by how I treated his muscles with my family production ointment handed down to me by my father. With him I also went to the 1986 World Cup as a personal masseur. He, sometimes there 'lent' me to players like Valdano and Ruggeri, I loved him like a brother. I still do.'

Maradona joined Andrea Carnevale in the centre-circle to begin the contest. What followed was nothing short of a mismatch as the white shirts of Empoli were ripped to pieces by a Napoli team playing like champions-elect. The early stages saw Maradona create a clear chance for Carnevale with a beautiful flick on, only for him to fluff the opportunity when it appeared easier to score. Shortly after Salvatore Bagni swept a ferocious drive against the bar as the pressure mounted. Endless corners hit by Maradona on the left and the impressive Francesco Romano from the right caused mayhem in the Empoli penalty area with their pinpoint accuracy. Then, the most remarkable miss from Andrea Carnevale, who only six yards out with an open net to aim at somehow contrived to shoot wide. Yet to score in the league for Napoli, Carnevale hung his head in despair. Finally, on twenty-six minute the Captain took matters into his own hands and calmed the nerves. A free-kick from the edge of the box by Diego Maradona was curled deliciously out of the goalkeeper Julio Drago's reach and into the top left-hand corner to ignite the San Paolo. The defender Allesandro Renica picked the ball out of the goal and smashed it high into the Naples sky in delight. Drago never had a chance. Suddenly, it was vintage Napoli: another free-kick, this time thirty-five-yards-out. Maradona fooled all in the arena as instead of letting fly, he passed short to Renica who flashed in a left foot shot that Drago tipped spectacularly around the post. Still, they came: a majestic volley from Romano foiled only by an equally remarkable stop from the under-siege Julio Drago. Fiesta football! With the Neapolitans in full cry another goal had to come and on the stroke of half-time Andrea Carnevale opened his account when he ran clear to fire the ball past the beleaguered Empoli keeper. It became a question of how many as the second period went much the same as the first. A third came on sixty-eight minutes when Maradona and Bruno Giordano combined beautifully for Carnevale to grab another with a far post header. Minutes later a wonderful pass from the inventive Romano was finished with a touch of class by Bagni, who drilled a terrific left shot past a totally fed-up Drago. Four goals to the good, and all that remained before the final curtain closed at the San Paolo on an exhilarating showing, was for Diego Maradona to perform a last encore. Firstly, an astonishing back flick that bewildered two Empoli players, for he produced it in mid-air! Then, came the main event. Maradona dribbled past one white shirted defender, and as another rushed in to challenge, he dragged the ball clear, controlled with his instep before spinning a remarkable pirouette and speeding away downfield. The church of Maradona rose as one to salute yet another moment of wizardry. These were heady days in Naples. The Napoli tifosi prayed that a happy ending awaited, for far too many tears had been shed over the decades. There was only so many times that a city and it's people could be made to suffer. Surely, if there was a God, he would prove merciful and end Neapolitan torment. Another year in Purgatory or the Promised Land? Naples pondered it's fate over the coming months, for if there were a cause likely to unite the warring clans of the mighty North it would be one that meant denying them the honour of a first Scudetto. Neapolitans feared an unholy alliance with regional feuds temporarily forgotten as Milan, Turin, Florence, Verona and others plotted to bring down SSC Napoli. The mere suggestion of Diego Maradona and his ragged band of Southern Terroni, bandit's and thieves all, disappearing with the title into the badlands of the Mezzogiorno was causing shudders in the Northern corridors of power. Had the genie already slipped through their fingers?

On Sunday 4th January 1987, hostilities resumed after the shutdown for the Christmas holidays, and even before the decorations had come down in Naples their lead had vanished. The league leaders restarted their campaign in 'La citta dei fior', ('The city of flowers'). There was no more beautiful city in all of Italy then Florence. Here, amidst the splendour of this medieval, architectural masterpiece of spellbinding cathedrals and priceless art galleries, Napoli's title dreams were given a vicious jolt of reality with a 3-1 thrashing by Fiorentina. A capacity crowd at the Stadio Artemio Franchi exploded in joy as their beloved 'Viola' hit the Neapolitans with a lightning two-goal blast in the opening half hour that left them on the floor. Strikes from former Napoli player, Argentinian centre-forward Ramon Diaz and Florence legend, Giancarlo Antognoni, hero of the Fiorentine terraces, left Ottavio Bianchi's men looking shell-shocked. The elegant midfield maestro Antognoni had controlled midfield and carved the traumatic visitors apart with an exquisite display. His adoring followers sang in tribute, *'Voi vincente lo Scudetto, ma noi abbiamo Antognoni!'* *('You may win the title, but we have Antognoni').*

A fuming Bianchi ripped into the team during the interval for their lack-lustre showing, demanding more from the below-par players. Five minutes into the second period his harsh words reaped dividends when a revitalised Diego Maradona swooped to end a fine sweeping move with a clever finish at the near post. Eclipsed in the first half by the sublime Antognoni, Maradona suddenly began to play as only he seemed capable. But despite the re-emergence of their Captain, it was the home side that looked more likely to score again. All hopes of gaining a point disappeared in the dying moments when with Napoli throwing everybody forward, including the goalkeeper, Fiorentina's Paolo Monelli broke and hit a superb drive from his own half over the head of Claudio Garella to deservedly seal the win. An embarrassed Garella stood red-faced as the ball flew into his net. The fervid celebrations of the Florence tifosi behind the goal in the Curva Fiesole verged wildly towards euphoria as they erupted into a passionate rendition of their club anthem, *'A Lei Fiorentina.'* The despondent Neapolitans with flags at half-mast filed out of the stadium. Maybe this team was just like the rest over the years that had kissed the badge, but come the moment of truth failed to deliver? Elsewhere, Juventus and a rejuvenated Inter Milan under Trapattoni won to close the two-point gap. The dramatic scenes of their supporters rejoicing on hearing news of Napoli's defeat in the Artemio Franchi, matched easily the ecstatic 'Viola' following whom danced in delight long after the final whistle had blown. It was a Northern thing: Game on. So, began from that moment a race to the finishing line. Along the way Napoli would be pushed, elbowed and knocked from their stride, but could they remain standing? For their many enemies were after them with a vengeance. In a post-match press conference Ottavio Bianchi issued a war cry by claiming that his players possessed the necessary 'Courage and heart' to bounce back from this defeat. Seven days later Napoli responded to their manager's comments in the best possible fashion as they hammered relegation haunted Ascoli 3-0 in the San Paolo. After intense pressure the goals finally came in the second half with twenty-three-year-old local boy Ciro Muro breaking the deadlock on the hour. Fellow midfielders Romano and a late strike from Salvatore Bagni once more put Napoli two points clear as Inter crashed at Verona. So much for Northern brotherhood, as sometimes the urge to bash your neighbour proved just that little bit too tempting. How the Neapolitans laughed as maybe, just maybe Diego Maradona's promise to Giuseppe Bruscolotti to deliver the Scudetto was set to be realised. Then, a history littered with heartache and disasters meant nothing could ever be taken for granted. They had blown it before and few would have been surprised if it happened again.

CHAPTER THIRTEEN

TOUCHING HEAVEN

Still they feared to dream. In Naples, many of the elder and most hard-bitten supporters of SSC Napoli refused to even contemplate the idea of the team winning the championship. Their lives had been full of endless torment, the scars of disappointment and betrayal suffered over torturous seasons past. An epic saga of heartache and tears, that, if ever put to music would have graced the most tragic of Italian operas. A living nightmare, but one they were now so agonisingly close to being awoken from. Touching Heaven? Neapolitans could only pray. Night would soon turn to day in Naples in a most extraordinary way.

When Maradona drank the grass. Spring had come and as March showed it's sunny face, Sampdoria travelled South to Naples eager to throw a rusty spanner in Neapolitan title hopes. A full house in a hostile San Paolo raged with passion and furore. Some indulged themselves by burning an Inter Milan flag for the benefit of television cameras. However, they were shocked into silence on thirty minutes when the visitors, through their whiplash forward Lorenzo, had the temerity to take the lead. Lorenzo smashed home past Napoli keeper Claudio Garella from eight yards. Moments later he should have scored again, only to blaze wide when faced with just Garella to beat. The home side appeared fraught with nerves, never had the stakes been higher. The game restarted and immediately Diego Maradona in typically mesmerising fashion received possession, a jink, a turn, a look up, pass, then in the blink of an eye he was gone. The fanatical tifosi of Napoli watched his every move. Their eyes forever upon him. He was their world, every waking hour, Maradona, their food and drink, lust for life. Nothing else mattered. Diego Maradona once claimed that with the ball at his feet he had the power to dim the sun. Few in Naples at the time who watched him ply his remarkable talents would have disagreed. Six minutes later, the long legs of Napoli's adventurous full-back Giuseppe Volpecina tore menacingly down the left touchline. Glancing up Volpecina clipped a fine cross into the Sampdoria penalty area that screamed out for a blue shirt to attack it. As the San Paolo held it's breath, Maradona broke like lightning from his marker and hurtled himself low to the ground to thunder a wonderfully-placed driven header past keeper Pellegrini into the net. How the Argentinian ever reached the ball with it being so close to the turf, never mind score, was itself miraculous. Maradona had once more cast a spell to bewitch his followers and make them dance like madmen on the grand old steeped tiers of this footballing cathedral. Where their boy was concerned Neapolitans had grown accustomed to Maradona's sublime genius and wizardly illuminating every other Sunday afternoon at the San Paolo; maybe even a little blasé. But on the 1st March 1987, it became apparent that strange powers were at work. A goal to be forever cherished and immortalised in Neapolitan folklore as the time *Maradona drank the grass!* In this captivating city of extremes that gave birth to the legendary child puppet Pulcinella, later to become famous as a lovelorn accomplice of the femme fatale Judy, Diego Maradona had again proved there was never a show without Punch! A 1-1 draw was earned and the

Neapolitans remained four points clear of the chasing Northern wolves.

Next stop, yet another perilous trek up-country, this time to the region of Lombardia and the city of Bergamo to take on relegation-threatened Atalanta. The tifosi of Atalanta viewed the Neapolitans with the same sneering contempt as the followers of Milan, Turin and Verona. Sat in indignant isolation on the far Northern Italian border, the people of Bergamo had little time for it's own pompous near-neighbours, but even less for the Southern rabble that trampled across the length of Italy plundering highway supermarkets and arriving on their precious streets not scared to pick a fight. And how they would always get one! The black and blue brigade of the Atalanta hardcore forever willing to show the Neapolitans some true Northern hospitality. At the Stadio Atleti Azzurri d'Italia, in front of a packed house of 27,000, set against a dramatic, if disturbing background of wailing police sirens, baton charges, choking tear gas and violent scenes of all-out tribal warfare erupting on the terraces, Bruno Giordano kept his nerve to hand SSC Napoli a priceless 1-0 win. A mesmeric dribble by Maradona left three Atalanta players for dead before he crossed for Giordano to crash the ball high into the net at the near post. The thousands whom had endured the treacherous journey to roar their teams on were doubly ecstatic when news filtered through that sworn enemy Juventus had been held to a shock draw at home to Ascoli and Inter had been thrashed
3-1 in Genoa against Sampdoria. Though hardly out of sight, they were well clear as the win in Bergamo stretched Napoli's lead to five points. The chasing pack gnashed their teeth, spitting blood. The Southerners stood on the verge of a monumental achievement, for barring a collapse

of biblical proportions, the Scudetto was going South. Though not yet won, the title was for the first time ever harder to lose. Then again, no one in Naples required a history lesson.

With each week as the title became more of a reality Neapolitans from across the globe were drawn back to their blood country. For the game against Inter Milan at the San Siro a huge Napoli banner bearing the words: *'Forza Napoli New York'* flew high and proud. In a ferocious encounter against the wily Giovanni Trapattoni's Inter, the game ended in despair for Napoli five minutes from time when Milanese defender Giuseppe Bergomi smashed home from five-yards out to hand the 'Nerazzurri' a crucial 1-0 win. Terrible marking in the visitors' defence was punished in the cruellest manner possible. In a fascinating battle of wits between the managers, the Neapolitans looked to have saved a point with the last kick of the game when Diego Maradona's flick-on found Bruno Giordano, only to see his header magnificently tipped over the bar at close range by Inter keeper Ferri. The final whistle blew. Amidst rabid abuse and blinding smoke bombs, the Southerners lead was reduced back to three points. Suddenly, with eight games remaining, and Juventus along with the rapidly-emerging Roma winning to pile intense pressure on Maradona and his team, all was still to play for. Before the gates of Heaven were entered an unholy trilogy of matches against three of their most despised rivals awaited the Neapolitans, Juventus, Hellas Verona and AC Milan. There lay their fate. First up was a date with an 'Old Lady' in Naples. It had been a dismal first season for Juve coach Rino Marchesi. The former Napoli man was hardly helped by the unusually insipid form of his flamboyant midfield maestro Michel Platini, who had struggled throughout the campaign. The thirty-two-year-old Platini still possessed all his characteristic flair, but physically he was on the wane. A succession of bad injuries had gradually taken their toll. For five seasons the Frenchman graced the footballing arena of Serie A with breathtaking artistry in the black and white, winning a treasure chest of medals and trophies. Two Scudettos, a European Cup, the Cup Winners' Cup, Supercup, the Intercontinental Cup and the Coppa Italia. A remarkable record. A unique treble haul of European Footballer of the Year awards and also three-times top scorer in the Italian league meant Michel Platini would be forever remembered in Turin as a true legend. Sadly, for Juve, as the showdown in Naples dawned, the swashbuckling Platini's fire was in it's dying embers. Only a flicker of the spark remained. The heart and mind were willing but the body said no. The owner of Juventus and self-styled king of Turin, Gianni Agnelli once claimed of Platini with whom he became close friends.

'We bought him for the price of a bread loaf but Michel was like caviar.' The tifosi of 'La Vecchia Signora' prayed that their beloved number ten had enough left for a final swansong in Naples. Juve's reign as champions hung by the slenderest of threads. For them to relinquish the crown in of all places, Naples, was considered to be an aberration. Unthinkable. A humiliation to compare with the ragged, bloodthirsty peasants of the French Revolution staging public executions of the aristocracy. The Neapolitans sharpened their guillotine, they had waited a long time for such a mouth-watering scenario. A win for Napoli would enhance their dreams of glory and finish off the challenge of a team who had tortured them since the dawn of time.

As if lit by a rush of electrical current, a rain-lashed San Paolo hissed, fizzed and crackled with nervous anticipation, it's wide-open terraces awash with blue and white as smoke bombs the colour of Naples erupted like thunder, engulfing both ends of the stadium. Then, from the bowels of the arena the sides appeared to do battle in Serie A's match of the season. As the teams warmed up the ever-likeable Marchesi, in a long trench coat, chatted amicably to the Neapolitan ground staff who appeared genuinely happy to meet up again and shake the hand of their former manager. In comparison, a grim-faced Ottavio Bianchi, in a grey bubble jacket and normal hound-dog expression, took to his seat on the home bench. Bianchi's stern features were etched in concentration for the task ahead. For him, smiling was a rarity that only showed itself when he grimaced. Rino Marchesi had chosen to man-mark Diego Maradona with the experienced, tough defender Luciano Favero. The twenty-nine-year-old Favero carried on his broad shoulders the hopes of the majority outside Naples' walls in his task to tame the Argentinian. Immediately, Napoli went on the attack with local boy Luigi Cafferelli, roaring down the right wing and raiding full-back Volpecina, rampaging on the left. Juve were forced back in the early stages as the Neapolitans swarmed all over them with swift, incisive attacking play. Whenever they attempted to keep possession a cacophony of wolf whistles and a hail of boos swept down from the terraces. To the delight of the home crowd Michel Platini's attempts to break the siege failed when two of his normally accurate long passes went astray. It would be a long and weary day for the Frenchman. On fourteen minutes Juventus defender Manfredonia hacked down Napoli's bustling centre-forward Bruno Giordano, thirty-yards from goal and found himself fiercely lectured by team-mate Caricola for giving away a free-kick in such a dangerous position. For this was Diego Maradona territory. Taking up his predictable place, Maradona fooled all and tapped the ball sideways for sweeper Allessandro Renica to fire a shot, skidding low under a woefully, blundering Steffano Tacconi that sneaked like a thief in the night over the line. On a rain-sodden surface the keeper's mistake was perhaps understandable, if not appreciated by his seething Juve team-mates who lambasted him. It was an error unacceptable in games of this magnitude with so much at stake. As the huge San Paolo electric scoreboard flashed up 'goal, goal, goal, goal, goal', a red-faced Tacconi hung his head in shame, praying for the ground to open and swallow him up. Naples was unforgiving on being handed the opportunity to taunt their fiercest tormentors, for it happened so rarely. The game belonged to Napoli as Bagni, De Napoli and Romano in midfield outclassed their Turin counterparts. Allied to a scheming Maradona who probed in typically menacing fashion on the edge of danger. Threatening a killer pass or a scything one-two. Forever a second away from causing a riot, lurking ominously, patiently stalking his prey. Every time a Juve move broke down the Neapolitans sped away on fearful counter-attacks. The blue of Napoli sprang forward and the striped shirts of Juve trailed in their wake like chasing rabbits! On the touchline Rino Marchesi's pre-match, happy-go-lucky demeanour was replaced by that of a man watching his house burn down. The nightmare continued as a ridiculously sloppy back pass from an out-of-sorts Platini, was latched onto by Giordano, whose rasping drive was turned away for a corner by Tacconi. Michel Platini tried desperately to make amends for his own below-par showing when he skipped past three tackles but could only watch in despair as his shot flew hopelessly high over Claudio Garella's goal. An animated Marchesi screamed instructions to his inspirational Captain Gaetano Scirea as Juventus earned a much-needed respite with a corner kick. From this Aldo Serena missed by a whisker from eight-yards out as he turned and lashed a shot inches wide of Garella's goal. Given the chance they were still dangerous. As the half-time whistle dawned Platini produced a sprinkling of magic to make space and deliver a wonderful cross into the Neapolitan area for Serena. With time to spare the much-lauded Turin marksman woefully mis-kicked and was forced to watch in abject horror as the ball bobbled horribly away from him to be cleared by a Napoli defender's relieved boot. Showing full vent to his troubled state of mind, Michel Platini launched a tirade of abuse at his young colleague who looked on non-plussed. The San Paolo was no stage for a Juventus legend such as he to show his frustration as the laughter and mirth that greeted the Frenchman's tirade confirmed.

The second period began with the slavishly incessant Neapolitan war cry of 'Diego, Diego' resonating in passionate tones over the vast open terraces and beyond. Maradona, as ever responded immediately to this call to arms by slashing through a bevy of Juve shirts to lay off a pass for Francesco Romano to let fly a vicious twenty-yard strike, saved spectacularly by Tacconi. The keeper leapt somewhat dramatically through mid-air to grasp the shot to his midriff as if to show the mocking Naples crowd what he was truly capable of. Sadly, for him they already had his measure and simply responded to such histrionics with ironic cheers and sarcastic applause. Steffano Tacconi's card was already marked. With the normally ice-cool

Marchesi caught up in the frenetic atmosphere of the occasion and reduced to a fraught figure frantically shouting orders from the dug-out, Juventus showed only remnants of their true class. But they were not champions for nothing and Platini strode elegantly forward to lash a fine long-range effort tipped inches wide of the post by Garella. To howls of derision around the ground the 'Old Lady' regained albeit, for a short time, her normally regal composure. The seventeen-year-old Juve prodigy, Sergio Buso, produced a wonderful drag-back on the edge of the Napoli penalty area to create space and play in an advancing Michel Platini on the right wing. Platini's inch-perfect cross towards the near post was met superbly by the glancing head of Serena who stooped to head past Claudio Garella with true flourish.

1-1. Aldo Serena soared jubilantly over the advertising boards, only to find himself surrounded by hordes of angry Neapolitan officials, photographers and policemen appearing less than pleased with his antics on Naples' soil. Behind that same goal in the Curva South, many of Napoli's hardcore tifosi, the South Boys, stood ready to greet the Juve player into their midst with a frightful relish. Realising immediately, he had overstayed his welcome, Serena wisely skipped back onto the pitch to continue celebrations with delighted team-mates, who shrewdly had not followed him beyond the relative safety of the white line. The South Boys shrugged their shoulders. Another time and a close shave for Aldo Serena. Just when all in the San Paolo expected Juventus to take control of the match, it was Napoli who shrugged off their disappointment to lift themselves and pin back the visitors with a barrage of frenzied assaults. Ottavio Bianchi had acted fast in bringing on Andrea Carnevale to link with

Giordano and Maradona. The coach's intent was clear, to attack and seize back the initiative. Sensing panic amongst the ranks, Scirea raged at his fellow defenders, imploring them not to lose concentration as the home blue shirts swarmed, darted and dashed with increasing menace. As the pressure mounted, it was inevitably Diego Maradona who engineered a route through. His beautifully clipped cross was flicked on by the powerful Giordano to the far post, where substitute Carnevale pounced to scramble the ball back across goal for Francesco Romano to smash home.

Naples went mad!

Bianchi again moved fast as he made another tactical switch. Off came Giordano to a rapturous reception from the Napoli faithful, and to tumultuous acclaim around the stadium Napoli stalwart Giuseppe Bruscolotti came off the bench to enter the fray and add fire and fury to the Napoli backline. The mean-faced Bruscolotti sprinted towards his position, an ominous proposition for any Juve attacker faced with the gruesome task of beating him. The remainder of the game was played out in a fervid atmosphere of desperation as SSC Napoli fought tenaciously to protect their slender lead. The tension dipped and rose alarmingly as Juve roused themselves for a last-ditch attempt to save their season. Neapolitan hearts were placed firmly in mouths when a reckless Renica foolishly gave away a free-kick on the edge of his own area that allowed Michel Platini the opportunity to save face for Juventus. An unholy silence gripped the San Paolo as Platini lashed in a shot that rebounded off the Napoli wall, only to deflect back and awarding him a second chance. This time the Frenchman let fly a fierce low drive that flew inches wide of the post. Naples took a huge gasp of air, a collective sigh of relief. So often in the past this man had broken their hearts. Secretly, they admired Platini; Neapolitans knew their football, but that wasn't to say they did not hate him with a vengeance also. In the closing moments a poignant, maybe even tragic incident in the centre-circle occurred that confirmed Michel Platini's star had finally fallen from the skies. Receiving possession, Platini found himself literally mugged by a blaze of blue shirts that left him slumped unceremoniously on his backside as they sped away with the ball. The Frenchman remained on the turf with head between his knees. Surely at that instance, this once great footballer decided the time had come to say au revoir, leave them wanting more: the roar of the crowds, bathed in magical memories and adulation. A legend of 'La Vecchia Signora'. To vacate the arena, kicking and screaming, dragged off, embarrassed, red-faced, was unacceptable. Platini did exit stage right at the end of that season in the same manner he played his football, with typical class and poise. Yet, all mattered little on that long-gone day in Naples. For to all present it had become blatantly obvious Michel Platini was yesterday's news.

Off soared Napoli on a lightning counter-attack, with the lung bursting Giuseppe Volpecina careering away down the wing in full, spectacular, looping stride. Juventus defenders were left chasing in his wake as the exciting Volpecina looked up and hit a magnificent ball for Diego Maradona to launch himself through the air with a diving header at the far post, only to be foiled by a remarkable reflex save by Tacconi at the last. A breathtaking slice of football by all! The dying seconds of the game saw Juve camped inside the Napoli half, but it was not to be their day. A sea of exploding blue and white at the final whistle swept over the San Paolo. News elsewhere that championship rivals Inter Milan had been held to a draw by Torino and Roma losing at Udinese, meant the lead was stretched to five points with just six games remaining. The hero of the hour, Francesco Romano, found himself mobbed at the end by his fellow players and a colourful array of Neapolitan characters that found their way onto the pitch to join in the revelry. Napoli President Corrado Ferlaino had watched the game unfold from the touchline, he himself near to nervous exhaustion as the Scudetto grew so close it could almost be smelt. The whiff of success drifted through the Naples air. The President stood on the verge of immortality as the man who stood at the helm when Napoli conquered all. His ego was such that he could simply not let such an opportunity pass. As the cameras rolled and photographers clicked away, President Ferlaino lapped up the limelight. After the legendary 3-1 win in Turin a historic double was achieved over the 'Old Lady' that itself demanded celebrations of previously unheard-of magnitude. Uncharacteristically, the city failed to soar into carnival mood, for there remained a haunting reluctance to indulge whole-heartedly when the nightmare scenario of everything being lost at the last still existed. Of the games left to play for SSC Napoli an arduous journey North to Verona taking on the despised Hellas stood out by far as the most difficult, yet, with their team in such fine form the Napoli tifosi felt convinced of returning home with a decent result to all but clinch the Scudetto.

But disaster once more was set to befall them.

To the disgust of their manager and supporters SSC Napoli went meekly like lambs to the slaughter at Verona. A shambolic first half performance littered with slack passing and frightful defensive errors were seized upon and punished lethally by a rampant home team that scored three times without reply. In a hair-raising atmosphere of unrelenting hatred and vitriol at the Stadio Bentegodi, Osvaldo Bagnoli's Veronese ripped through the nervy Neapolitans with bloodcurdling relish. Ottavio Bianchi watched on horrified as his side, to the sheer delight of a yellow and blue-drenched Bentegodi arena found themselves put to the sword like Christians of old in the Coliseum. Could it have been that fate had decided they were born to suffer?

A murderous rout ensued. Amidst countless close shaves and near misses in the Napoli area, a bullet header from Verona midfielder Pacione, allied to a wicked deflection off Allesandro Renica for a second goal, stunned the Neapolitans. A penalty converted in clinical manner past Garella five minutes from half-time by Verona legend Preben Elkjaer put the game well beyond the away side. A second period was made worse by news of Inter going in front at Avellino through Allesandro Altobelli to hand them a 1-0 win and cut the Southerners lead back again. A bad day had by all of Neapolitan persuasion. The Veronese hardcore of the Brigate Gialloblu taunted their rivals with a song hated by the Southerners.

'Senta che puzza, scappano anchi I cani. Sono arrivati I Napoletani'. ('Get that smell, even the dogs are running. The Neapolitans are coming').

Hitting back in archetypal fashion the travelling Napoli ultras unfurled a banner to warm Naples' hearts and to enrage their hosts:

('Veroneses, Guinea pigs from laboratory')!

So, as their team laid down and died on the pitch, Neapolitan honour was seen to be served as all-out war ensued off it, on the terraces and outside the stadium.

Following the match horrific scenes of violence erupted on the streets of Verona with thirty-eight of Napoli persuasion arrested. Luckily, as the fighting raged no one was killed, but it was not for the want of trying on both sides. Two cities, two tribes and two worlds apart.

As the season drew towards it's dramatic finale the humiliation endured in Verona caused many Napoli tifosi to question the team's mental toughness in being able to hold their nerve. Even Diego Maradona was not immune from the finger pointing and criticism as feeling ran high in Naples following the unacceptable surrender against the Veronese. Doubts were raised regarding where Maradona's priorities lay as he flitted constantly between Naples and Buenos Aires to be at the side of his heavily pregnant girlfriend. The Argentinian refused point blank all orders to remain in Italy and on the 11th April 1987, Diego Maradona and Claudia Villafane were blessed with a baby daughter whom they named Dalma. Whilst Maradona was in Argentina, intoxicated with the joy of playing happy families, back on his adopted soil, Neapolitans fretted about their King's state of mind. Looming large was one of the most important matches in Napoli's history against AC Milan at the San Paolo. It was a game they had to win, anything other than two points could well have proved disastrous with Trapattoni's Inter smelling Neapolitan fear and moving in for the kill. Never had they been so near, yet frustratingly so far away. The city of Naples needed Diego Maradona like never before.

Coming into land at Naples International Airport, the luxurious private jet carrying Maradona and his entourage back to Southern Italy from Argentina veered low over Mount Vesuvio, and all aboard gazed down into the

hypnotic, mysterious, foreboding crater of the volcano's dark heart. The legendary poet Goethe once wrote of Vesuvio,
'A peak of hell rising out of paradise'. A terrifying black abyss that one day, nobody yet knows when, would erupt and destroy all who lived their lives in it's deadly shadow. Maradona was not in the best of moods. Well aware of the mudslinging hurled towards him, viewing such talk as a slap in the face and a blatant lack of respect after all he had given for the Neapolitan cause. In an interview for a British television company working on a documentary of Napoli's title challenge, his tormentors kopped for both barrels. Stung and hurt, Maradona opened his heart.
'Naples is a beautiful city but it has lots of negative aspects too. I don't like Neapolitans worshipping me more than they would their own mother or God. I honestly don't understand that attitude. I also think they are wrong in claiming Naples is the most beautiful city in the world. I just disagree. Naples could be far more pleasant if it's inhabitants were more disciplined but, Neapolitans will be Neapolitans. Maradona has not travelled fourteen thousand miles to come and correct their faults. I simply have to accept this way of life. It is not up to me to say anything; okay, every Sunday I do my bit to make them as happy as possible, but, that is all.'

The sacred church of San Paolo was agitated as a strange sense of foreboding gripped it's packed nerve-wrecked congregation. A full house of tortured souls feared the worse. Déjà vu, they had been there before. So many times in the past SSC Napoli had been dealt a decent hand only for them to play the wrong card and lose all. The tifosi prayed, pleading with their Holy Saint for it not to happen again. Come the Sunday morning of the game and churches across the city heaved with Neapolitans desperate to gain an edge. Naples eternal twelfth man. San Gennaro was forced to work overtime as the fantasy of the Scudetto loomed ever closer. The sides led by their two great Captains Diego Maradona and the regal figure of Milanese sweeper Franco Baresi entered the arena. Amidst scenes of bedlam Maradona cut a fraught sight, full of nervous energy as he limbered up with a rapid succession of feverish quick sprints. Surrounded as ever by hustling crowds of snapping cameramen and photographers, he bore the look of a man with a point to prove, his face etched in total concentration for the job ahead. On forty-three minutes, Diego once more had the Neapolitans claiming they were not worthy and falling in worship at his feet. Napoli were already one up with a goal scored by the head of Andrea Carnevale, when their Captain produced yet another beguiling moment of genius. Showing wonderful skill and technique Maradona swept past Baresi and his defenders before exquisitely rounding Galli in the Milan goal to fire into the net. Crowds who had gathered to watch on television in the alleyways, houses, bars and cafes across the bay erupted as he raced towards his adoring subjects in the stadium to receive their acclaim. Speaking later after the game, one Neapolitan trying desperately to sum up the magnitude of Maradona's to Naples claimed, 'We should have known better. You cannot criticize Maradona for in doing so you criticize God. And you cannot criticize God because he is above all else.'

Napoli's Giordano should have wrapped the points up when his header from close range flashed against the bar. Then, what had appeared a comfortable victory suddenly turned into total panic when with eleven minutes remaining, Milan's centre-forward Pietro Virdis beat Garella from a wide angle to silence the San Paolo rigid. As the scoreboard flashed up news of Inter going in front at home to Fiorentina, the atmosphere on the terraces became increasingly tense. If the 'Rossoneri' managed an equaliser in Naples and Trapattoni's men managed to win, then SSC Napoli's lead would have been cut to a single point and just three games left to play. With nothing to lose AC Milan threw caution to the wind and swept forward in droves. The home crowd whistled and sweated buckets of fear as they struggled under the Milanese onslaught. With many hardly able to watch happenings on the pitch, there was a mass explosion of relief as the final whistle blew. A situation had now arisen that meant in just a week's time Napoli would be crowned champions if they won at Como and results elsewhere went their way.

In Naples, the red, green and white of the Scudetto badge was being etched onto thousands of decorative souvenirs ready for this moment of ultimate triumph. Neapolitan confidence was at an all-time high that the title was finally coming South and the biggest celebrations in their city's history was imminent.

Surely, they couldn't lose it now?

Close to ten thousand Napoli tifosi descended like a plague of blue locust upon the idyllic mountainous surroundings of the Northern lakes. From first light the massed ragged hordes reached the beautifully picturesque Como. Many took the opportunity to rest on the tree-lined banks of the lakes and catch up on some much-needed sleep after an exhausting twelve-hour journey from Naples. The tranquility and clean air of Como was a stark contrast for

lads used to the noise and humdrum of their own city. Appalling poverty, the backstreet stench of rotting garbage, choking pollution from exhausts of the never-ending traffic jams. The seemingly never-ending lines of cars, buses and coaches entering Como from the South, laden deep with singing, unwanted Terroni, began to cause concern to the local authorities, whom suddenly realised this was no ordinary travelling entourage of football fans. It was an invasion: Naples North! Extra Carabinieri special units were drafted in from surrounding areas to ensure the visitors were kept in hand. Polizia helicopters buzzed constantly above the town, watching for the slightest hint of unrest. An almighty Southern army from the badlands of the Mezzogiorno on the march and in every Northerner's face. Armed to the teeth with weapons of faith, hope and Diego Maradona, the Neapolitans came, saw and conquered, the songs anthemic, memorable and tragic. Many tifosi in quiet moments found time to call on their patron for divine inspiration. As kick-off drew agonisingly near, sirens wailed and tensions reached fever pitch an ancient silent prayer was whispered:
'San Gennaro aiutaci tu!' ('San Gennaro please help us')!
This was a club like no other. Touching heaven.

Molte Grazie Carnevale! On the lakeside, in the small but electrifying surroundings of the Stadio Guiseppe Sinigaglia, SSC Napoli fought out a priceless 1-1 draw to ensure only a point was now required to win the championship on home ground in seven days' time. It had been a gruelling afternoon for the away team when after a determined, but nervy showing they found themselves a goal down on the hour and facing disaster. Inspired by a fired-up Maradona, Napoli drew a veil over the disgrace of

Verona to lash back. The Argentinian had foraged throughout, kicked and slashed at senseless, but never yielding. From the occupied terraces of the Sinigaglia the tifosi laid true their feelings as 'Diego, Diego, Diego' thundered out over the stadium and across the vast Lake Como. Only fourteen minutes remained to play when history was made and Andrea Carnevale controlled the ball on his thigh six yards out to lash the ball into the net and send the sweating, praying but forever vocal Southern legions delirious. In that instant the dream became real and all of Italy prepared for the inevitable. The home fans watched on incredulous at the antics and mad hysteria breaking out amongst the followers from Naples. Outside the ground thousands of Napoli tifosi without tickets and denied access exploded in joy. Even President Ferlaino received a kiss off an ecstatic Neapolitan as celebrations raged. It was surely understandable, for never had a goal by SSC Napoli been greeted in such fashion as that of Andrea Carnevale's.

Heaven on Earth loomed large, so why not go mad?

Even the eternally dismal features of Ottavio Bianchi, who it was said never even smiled on his own wedding photographs, leapt high in delight at seeing the ball hit the net. Come the final whistle, Bianchi punched the air, for he knew! Nobody would beat them in Naples, not now. Back in their home city mayhem reigned. With no television coverage of the game crowds stood together huddled round rigged-up radios on every street corner, listening with eyes shut, imagining the action, praying and fingers crossed. Elsewhere, to make the day beyond reproach, Inter were humiliated 1-0 at relegation-battling Ascoli to all but end their title challenge. In a blinding thick mist of flares igniting high above the Como skyline, Diego Maradona,

Captain of Napoli led his team-mates over to thank their supporters for what had been a remarkable turnout. Maradona appeared overwhelmed by the emotion of the occasion, his eyes welling with tears. The quest for the Scudetto was almost at an end, Maradona was set to lead the Neapolitans into the Promised Land.
Everything would be decided in Naples.

CHAPTER FOURTEEN

BELLA GIORNATA (BEAUTIFUL DAY)

Sunday 10th May 1987. Morning. Never had a night passed so agonisingly slow for Neapolitans. Finally, as a blazing sun rose on the far horizon, illuminating fishing boats lost only seconds before on a black sea, the most beautiful day dawned in Naples unlike any in the history of this most put-upon, vilified, but always charismatic city. In churches and cathedrals, services began early with priests rushing through sermons, knowing well the hearts and minds of normally subservient congregations lay for once elsewhere. Outside the sacred walls the noise and furore of Napoli tifosi bellowed loud, forcing devoted men of the cloth into trying to shout out the word of God over Naples' own Earth-bound saviour, Maradona! It was no contest. Hiding their precious blue Napoli shirts beneath angelic white flowing gowns, pensive altar boys glanced nervously at watches as the mass rumbled eternally on. Spluttered coughs from a clearly agitated audience, shuffling uneasily with prayer books, made it apparent that the urge to pray was overtaken by the overwhelming desire to indulge in more earthly pleasures. Sometimes, even the Almighty had to be put in his place. SSC Napoli were calling, it was time to head for the San Paolo.

For once the harvest had responded well and not reaped a bitter crop. There would be music, dancing, song and wine as every Neapolitan was handed the undeniable right to go crazy for a day. That they did so with such gusto and energy surprised few as the city geared up to party like it was the end of the world. Bakers put up stalls under lemon groves to shelter from the sun. They gave away spaghetti allo Scudetto! White and green pasta with red sauce. The back streets of Naples were awash with expectation, her ancient monuments, statues, crumbling tenements and churches festooned with swaggering displays of Napoli colours draped proudly. Naples' narrow, poverty-stricken sun-less alleys splashed with joyful masses of light blue bunting and flags as the city prepared to self-explode. Every building anointed, nothing was missed, for this was going to be a carnival the likes of Naples had never before experienced. Sixty-one torturous years of being pilloried, laughed at, cheated, abused and mocked. Revenge would be sweet on those who had indulged so wholeheartedly in Napoli's misery. Naples braced itself. Riotous scenes of unheralded revelry set to descend upon a people whose spontaneity, passion and happy-go-lucky approach to life had helped them survive the despairing hardships of their every waking hour. The time had come to unlock the chains and go mad!

Of the chasing pack only Inter Milan were left to offer a challenge, though even they clung by the slenderest of threads. Inter trailed by three points with only two games remaining. It would have taken a catastrophe of biblical proportions for the Neapolitans to be dragged back into sight. A single point was all Napoli required against Fiorentina to take the title. No one in the city dared doubt that the most momentous time in their history was just a few hours away. To even hint all would not be well was viewed as treacherous talk by locals who refused to consider such a dreadful, dark scenario. Napoli's trials and tribulations, her despair, joy and aspirations, touched with heartfelt emotions every house, doorway, window and laundry-strewn balcony of the city. The Neapolitans' all-enduring, romantic attachment with their football club had finally reached it's rainbow's end. A love affair unconsummated, until now. Unbeaten all season at the San Paolo there appeared little reason to worry, but woe betide Ottavio Bianchi's team if by some devilish turn of fate, they threw all away at the last. The world would not be a big enough place to hide.

Well before midday, the Spaccanapoli fell into a wildly, delightful, chaotic melee. For once the traffic jams that plagued the city failed to irk as a deafening crescendo of blazing car horns drifted high over the bay, echoing far across the Peninsula. The Centro Storico (Old town) the cradle of the city, Naples' ancient heart, from the Forcella to the seaport flooded with tifosi pouring onto the streets. Traffic policemen, La vigile, on horseback with the black uniforms, red braid and dashing white bands across their chests, smiled at the euphoria erupting around them, laughing as fellow Neapolitans wrapped Napoli scarves around the necks of their horses. They even joined in the songs and chants by blowing on whistles adding enthusiastically, if rather tunelessly to the endless choruses. An unofficial truce was declared as the Polizia joined forces with the many sicari (cutthroats), spacciatore (drug dealers), and scippiatori, (motorcycle menaces), well as the countless thousands of honest decent Neapolitans, in the shared hope that their football team prevailed. For one day only, they would be as one.

The Neapolitans' inherited fascination with fireworks and love of unnerving loud explosions would soon become apparent as they prepared to light up the Naples skyline with all manner of apocalyptic concoctions. Some legal, most not and more suited to a battlefield than for celebratory purposes. Many cast serious misgivings on the city surviving in one piece as the nightmarish, fearsome array of garish, looking rockets were revealed. The more worried inhabitants crossed themselves as they prayed for protection from what was set to rain down upon them. Armageddon may have loomed but no one really cared. There was even an idea by some enthusiastic, most possibly crazed Neapolitans to fire rockets down into Mount Vesuvio when the festival was in full swing. Luckily, at the last moment sense prevailed, and it was decided not to provoke the raging fires that burned eternally in the mouth of the volcano. It would have been the ultimate irony and so typical of Neapolitan ill fortune, to be wiped out in a firestorm of death and destruction in their finest hour by Vesuvio blowing it's top.

Across the city every wall lay plastered with pictures and tributes to those responsible for bringing joy to Naples, their names lovingly scrawled in letters ten feet tall. Garella, Bruscolotti, Ferrara, Bagni, Ferrario, Renica, Carnevale, Di Napoli, Romano, Volpecina, Caffarelli and the allenatore Bianchi. Though all were admired and loved, none came even close to matching the adoration showered on the Captain, Diego Maradona. For this had become his city and people. Maradona's features were smeared on every house and shop window. Life-size mosaics of him decorated major vantage points around Naples, none more eye-catching than that which covered the main entrance of Stazione Circumvesuviana, a railway station linking the capital with the devastated, if captivating ruins of Pompeii and Herculaneum. Here Maradona shone in all his pomp, a glorious technicolour effort that showed him arched over the ball, about to wreak havoc against his opponents. The more fanatical of Neapolitan tifosi carved small, beautifully formed chapels out of stonewalls to worship their idol. Because of his exploits on the football field, Diego Maradona had in many Neapolitan's eyes become even more important than the city's patron San Gennaro and the Virgin Mary. A mantle he was hardly worthy of, but though never a saint, Diego Maradona had proved a saviour for a people who invested their dreams in him. None more than he had brought about this day of wonder.

Between the palm trees of the Piazzale Tecchio they came in their hordes towards the San Paolo. To illustrate the all-consuming desire to be seen as a separate state, if not country, from the despised, faraway despot regimes of Turin, Milan and all points Northern, the Neapolitans adopted the flags and traditional dress code of the American Confederacy dating back to the Civil War between North and South. A mighty Southern army of Johnny Rebs dancing like madmen in the Naples sun, forever the underdog, 'Solo contro tutti' ('Alone against everyone'), but at last jubilant after handling the enemy one almighty knockout blow. Payback time on those whom had given them hell since the dawn of time. Four hours before kick-off the ground was already packed. The official capacity of 86,000 was boosted by streetwise Neapolitans whose furbo (cunning) saw them entering by all manner of untoward means. They came in disguised as policemen, mascots, first aiders, even priests and nuns. Never had the home of SSC Napoli been graced by so many members of the Holy Faith. For whom on this day when the Almighty had never been needed more would refuse entry to a servant of God?

To have a ticket for the San Paolo was regarded in Naples as a day pass to heaven, a heart soaring glimpse into paradise. That the grim foreboding peaks of Mount Vesuvio had vanished in the misty aftermath of erupting fireworks was seen as a good omen by superstitious Neapolitans who feared greatly their volcano's evil eye. They chanted the monster's pet name of *La Buonanima, (the Good Soul),* in an unveiled attempt to appease Vesuvio's good nature. But still it maintained an aura of impending doom the menacing glare. *Il Grande Cono. (The Great Cone).*

For Gennaro Montuori, the acknowledged leader of Napoli's most well-known Ultras, the CUCB, this was a day he had waited a lifetime for. On the eve of the showdown against Fiorentina, Montuori spoke of his hopes for all to go well both on and off the pitch. 'For ten years I have been leader of the Ultras. I have always been against violence and disorder in the stadia. It is too absurd. The stadium is a theatre where you experiment in folklore. This is a stage for true supporters, for friendship. And above all to express your love of the game. We must not let football waste away. Why turn a party into a tragedy? This is an appeal we ourselves make to the rest of the Napoli fans. When we win tomorrow and claim the title the San Paolo must explode, but with joy!'

Bloodied, battered and scarred from countless confrontations with their Northern foes, the foot soldiers of the CUCB intended to stamp their own indelible mark on the day's events. For many weeks Gennaro Montuori's boys had secretly planned a spectacular display of devotion to SSC Napoli and their birthplace. They had with great care designed a banner of previously unseen size and stature bearing the green, white and red of the Scudetto. Montuori was determined his Ultras would command centre stage at the San Paolo by unfurling a masterpiece which would be talked about and envied by rivals for years to come. In the eyes of Gennaro Montuori, on this Bella Giornata for Naples, no one deserved some long overdue recognition more than his lads from Commando Ultra B.

The plane carrying the Fiorentina team landed at Naples International Airport to be greeted with the same warmth a backstreet Neapolitan butcher shows the neck of a lamb as he slits it's throat. Theirs' was a mission to bring an entire city to it's knees and keep the championship alive for at least another week until the final game of the season. The opportunity to complete a historic double over the champions-elect after thrashing Napoli on home ground was a mouth-watering prospect for the visitors. As Naples and it's inhabitants drowned in a raging sea of overwhelming euphoria, the 'Viola' prepared to pull the plug and leave the Neapolitans looking foolish. The immeasurable weight of a bitter rivalry down the years meant the men from Florence would never lie down in the San Paolo. Naples would not be given the title on a silver platter, the war may have been won, but there remained one last battle still to be fought. In the Fiorentina team was a handsomely, gifted, precocious twenty-year-old called Roberto Baggio. This scraggly young kid who arrived in Florence from lowly Vicenze, looking in need of a good meal would in a little time set Italian football ablaze with his erring sleight of foot, wonderful vision and a devastating ability from set pieces to either blast or bend the ball into the net. He enchanted the 'Viola' tifosi who immediately took him to their hearts. A true *fantasista*. Few doubted that Baggio possessed the natural ability to one day walk with footballers of Maradona's ilk. Comparisons with Naples finest proved inevitable. He also wore a number ten shirt, the most coveted in Italian football, and both were kings of their domain. If the Argentinian was the Southern star, then Roberto Baggio was undoubtedly the brightest of Northern Lights. Sporting a stylish ponytail and a flamboyant image, both on the pitch and off, the nickname of 'Il Divino Codino', ('The Divine Ponytail'), proved remarkably apt for this outrageously talented footballer. Baggio was all set to embark on an illustrious career that would hold more than it's fair share of triumph and despair.

With red lights blaring and sirens wailing, a Polizia motorcycle cavalcade escorted the Fiorentina coach, bumping and bullying through the hellish turmoil of Neapolitan traffic to the San Paolo. Alongside them, Napoli tifosi rode with a suicidal bravura on motorbikes, gesturing the two-fingered salute before roaring off, chased by enraged Carabinieri. Nothing could ever compare to the utter confusion and chaos of Naples' roads. In certain parts of the city there even existed traffic lights with the colour orange. They held no purpose except that Neapolitans felt it helped to brighten the place up! Equally, pedestrian crossings were regarded with contempt by locals, who tended to use them only to scare the living daylights out of tourists! Old men would plant their chairs on the pavements and play cards while eagerly anticipating scenes of carnage and mayhem. It was felt the best way to cross a road in Naples simply step out into the traffic and stare the driver down, daring them to hit you! Sometimes it worked, sometimes?

As kick-off grew closer, Napoli security staff turned rough in their desperate attempts to clear the pitch. Matters were hardly helped when a parachutist adorning the Napoli emblem on his chute dropped from the sky into the centre-circle to rapturous applause. This was the signal for the CUCB to unravel their tour de force. Soon to enter the Guinness Book of Records, this badge of Scudetto against a striking blue azzurra background cut a magnificent spectacle. Appreciative gasps from across the stadium rang out as it's sheer scope became apparent. Entire segments of the heaving terraces disappeared beneath it. In salute fellow Neapolitans unleashed yet another devastating salvo of rockets upon the unsuspecting heavens. The stadium shuddered, many glanced worryingly skywards, convinced they were about to be blown off the face of the Earth. Gennaro Montuori watched from the running track encircling the pitch with tears streaming down his face. For these were his boys. It was from here that Montuori rallied the troops by loudspeaker, leading the chants, songs and organising the legendary choreography of which the Napoli tifosi were famed for, their banners expressing with typical eloquence, biting satire and ironic humour the feelings of all Neapolitans on that day of days.

'Napoli, the Immensity of the Heavens is not enough to express our love for you'.

'The Blues, you're Beethoven's Tenth'.

'Maradona illuminates like the sun our once sad Sundays'.

'After God, Diego and Napoli, long live the South'.

'Children of the sun snatch the championship from the children of the cold'.

'Naples has three beautiful things. The Bay, Vesuvio and Maradona'.

'In the sky of Naples there any many stars, but Maradona's shines the brightest'.

'May 87, A New Empire is Born'.

Finally, the gloriously short and sweet: *'Excuse the delay'.*

To a tumultuous reception worthy of their divine San Gennaro, Diego Maradona led his team into the Naples sunlight. A city wept tears of joy. Maradona ducked, weaved and sprinted between the congested hordes of photographers that pursued him, their cameras flashing only inches away from his face. The Argentinian caught sight of Napoli's physio Salvatore Carmando and in what had become a legendary, albeit, theatrical, pre-match ritual rushed to embrace him. Despite being surrounded by a brawling circus of excitable Neapolitans, all exaggerated mannerisms, flailing bodies and utter confusion, the highly superstitious Maradona made sure he and Carmando shared their quiet moment before battle commenced. Salvatore Carmando was in tears. Being Neapolitan meant the overwhelming emotions of the day took their toll upon him. He, more than any knew the suffering Maradona endured with cortisone injections that had increasingly threatened to curtail his career. As the needle pierced the skin, causing the entire body to writhe in agony, Maradona simply gritted his teeth and took the pain. Carmando

witnessed the affection in which team-mates held Diego Maradona. Away from the prying lens of the paparazzi, he was capable of remarkable, spontaneous acts of generosity and great kindness. How he risked injury on the many dustbowl surface/football pitches across Naples playing in charity matches, much to the chagrin of his club. The hospital visits to sick children weighed down with gifts. Their faces lighting up on seeing Maradona in the flesh. Him paying for an operation on a young girl whose face was horribly disfigured, insisting it not be made public. These were not the actions of a man with horns. Then, there was the tail to the head, the flipside of the coin, an enigma. Those outside Naples who tended to regard him as nothing more than a creature from the gutter were always guaranteed ample ammunition to fire the bullets. Maradona moved as if nothing ever stood in his way. An inherent hatred of all things authoritarian saw him spark and rage against any who blocked his path. Whether it be a referee, politician, policeman or President, Diego Maradona treated all with equal contempt. He would do whatever he wanted, whenever he pleased, the outrageously decadent lifestyle away from football with nightly excesses of cocaine, whoring and drink, hardly the preparation required for a top sportsman. But who was he hurting more than himself? The road to self-destruction lay in the mind of the beholder. Salvatore Carmando always felt he had no right to judge. Diego Maradona had more than any earned the right to follow his own path. That he still held the power to enrapture on a football pitch amazed nobody more than Carmando. It was a sad miracle.
A miracle nonetheless.

'Perhaps, now they will love me?' The President of SSC Napoli Corrado Ferlaino bathed in the fawning adulation of his fellow Neapolitan as they queued to pay homage. There was little chance of a car bomb running his evening on this May Day. Only three years previous Ferlaino had been the most vilified man in the entire city. Now, they stood in line to kiss his hand. From sinner to saint, the man who brought Maradona to Naples, who oversaw the Scudetto finally heading South. Those same faces that once wished him dead now declared undying love. For eighteen torturous years the embittered President endured savage abuse from Napoli tifosi who viewed his handling of their club with suspicion. Many were convinced Ferlaino was bleeding Napoli's finances dry to pay for his ailing construction businesses. They knew well of his rumoured connections with the Camorra, but in a city where football and more importantly SSC Napoli mattered so much, this was not sufficient to save him from the wrath of the mob. Corrado Ferlaino had to deliver; to be forever on the brink of extinction and continually having to sell their best players in spite of being amongst the best-supported clubs in Italy was not good enough. Timely remainders were delivered forthwith to Ferlaino in the manner of a succession of car bombs and explosive devices detonating outside the San Paolo. Then, like magic came Maradona! So, as the President blew kisses to his adoring followers on that unforgettable, fine Neapolitan afternoon in May, all was forgotten, if not altogether forgiven. A story set to have a fairytale ending.
This was Naples on the early afternoon of Sunday 10th May 1987.

The Match. The rollercoaster that was SSC Napoli moved rolled slowly upwards before freefalling and dropping gloriously into the biggest party ever in Southern Italy. As Neapolitan mass hysteria threatened to soar out of control in a tidal wave of fluttering flags, ear-piercing whistles and banging drums sweeping over the San Paolo, the game began. A first half hour littered with petty fouls and slack passing was illuminated only by a flashing Diego Maradona free-kick that flew inches wide of the Fiorentina goal. As was expected the 'Viola' sat back and dug in, seemingly content with just the occasional foray into Neapolitan territory. As the roar from the delirious terraces continued unabated, almost demanding a breakthrough, it inevitably occurred. Dropping deep to the centre-circle, Maradona eyed Andrea Carnevale with a wonderful through-ball that sliced apart the Florentine rearguard. As all Naples roared him on Carnevale raced into the penalty box and clipped a fine shot past the grasping hands of goalkeeper Landucci to set the stadium ablaze. If there had been doubts, they vanished forever in the fateful moment that net bulged. As ever, Neapolitan celebrations swelled to hugely exotic proportions. Carnevale sprinted across the running track with arms outstretched to share his joy with the delirious blue tifosi, whilst Maradona fell dramatically to his knees, thanking God, kissing the turf. Tears were plenty: Gennaro Montuori sobbed uncontrollably on the sidelines, a lifetime devotion to his team finally reaping rich dividends after so much misery and despair. Behind him the Napoli ultras danced away the heartache and humiliation of yesteryear. Determined to provide a fitting spectacle for such a grand occasion, Napoli blazed forward in search of more goals. The nerves disappeared, in it's place came swagger and pomp, championship football!

News reaching Naples by radio of Inter going a goal down at lowly Atalanta only further increased the euphoric mood sweeping across the stadium. Chants of 'Atalanta, Atalanta' bellowed loud. It was left to the pony-tailed hero of Florence to bring them down to Earth with a bang, when on thirty-nine minutes, Roberto Baggio curled a delicious twenty-five-yard free-kick past the Napoli goalkeeper Claudio Garella.

Suddenly, it had become interesting again. Garella raged at his defensive wall that appeared to dissolve in the face of Baggio's shot. As the half-time whistle sounded, the restless murmurings of the assembled hordes hinted as to the uncertainty of their fate. A disturbing quiet fell upon the San Paolo and though the flags still waved, it was with a slightly more sense of apprehension. 1-1, it was enough, just.

The re-emergence of the two teams for the second period sparked the crowd back to life, but there remained an uncertainty that wasn't present earlier in the day. Cheers came laced with the nagging doubt Neapolitans had tried so hard to block from their thoughts that all would still go awry. Naples' obsession with fatalism once more came to the fore. With nothing to lose Fiorentina opened up to cause consternation on the terraces. The Napoli tifosi watched with hearts in mouths as their team was forced to retreat. 'Fuck the Viola.' It was akin to a drunkard turning up at a christening and drowning the baby. Roberto Baggio was magnificent, all silky skills, probing, looking for the killer pass. Baggio appeared to be enjoying himself tormenting the home defence, the raging torrents of abuse hurled upon him from all corners of the stadium seemingly inspiring to tease them a little more.

The clock ticked down,
slowly seconds turned achingly into minutes, hails of derision from the Neapolitans each time a 'Viola' player touched the ball and made with deadly intent for their half. The last fifteen minutes dawned and the sixty-one-year wait was agonisingly close to being over. By now most in the San Paolo could barely watch matters on the pitch. The dying moments of the contest saw Napoli playing keep-ball in an effort to wind down time.
With 86,000 souls begging the referee to end their misery and the noise level rising to unheard of proportions, at 17.47, the arbitro, Pairetto duly obliged. For a fleeting second older tifosi found themselves thinking back to seasons past, when all was black and Naples' dreams of glory were ridiculed. The insults that had screamed out:
'Lavense'.
'Wash the steps before leaving'.
'Vesuvio wash them with fire'.
'Mafiosi'.
'Barefoot Children'.
None no longer mattered or hurt as the final whistle blew and through the golden gates of heaven Neapolitans poured. May 1987, the other Italy has been defeated, a new empire is born. How sweet a moment for a people and a city that had wished for nothing more. Held forever in contempt, scorned and laughed at, Naples now possessed the biggest putdown line possible.
'Champions!'
Whilst the game was being played a deathly hush had descended all across the bay. The one sound still resonating was of the distant, differing moods of the San Paolo crowd as they suffered ninety minutes of dramatically changing emotions. Nerves, fraught voices

hoarse, pleading for it just to be over. Elsewhere, no one was to be seen and down on the Via Partenope, the seafront, arriving quizzical tourists at the port armed with cameras around their necks, were left wondering just where all the locals had gone? Normal life it appeared had come to an instant grinding halt. Eerie, a thundering silence. All to be heard was the swish of the sea and a far-off rumble sounding like voices in collective prayer. Tranquility in a place that wouldn't know or care for the meaning of the word. The noisiest most crowded, chaotic city in Europe lay dormant and deserted. Neapolitans were around, if not at the stadium, then in bars, café's or at home crowded around televisions and just waiting to erupt. Then, on the shrieking pierce of a whistle it happened, beginning with a single roar of joy, immediately to be joined by a choir of millions racing outdoors cheering, singing, crying, falling to their knees in prayer! Previously, desolate streets only moments before now alive and teeming in unfolding scenes of blue tinted euphoria! Cars, trucks, buildings and terraces swiftly became draped in Napoli colours as exultant Neapolitans embarked on the party of all parties.

Back at the San Paolo, in a blinding, swirling mist of smoke bombs, igniting red flares and earth, shattering firecrackers, the fanatical hordes of blue tifosi also commenced their long-overdue victory festivities. For the first time ever the pride of Naples, SSC Napoli had earned the right to wear upon their shirt the esteemed badge of the Scudetto. The best of the best, the championship insignia of all Italy. On the pitch a beaming Diego Maradona gestured to his adoring subjects with a raised two-fisted salute, before vanishing beneath a mad flurry of backslapping ecstatic well-wishers. First amongst them was Maradona's younger brother Hugo, who had rushed to embrace his older sibling, almost choking him in an all-clasping bear hug. It was a truly emotional moment for the man who though adopted and adored by Naples, always remained in his heart a *Porteno* (native of Buenos Aires). As much that Argentina's victory in the 1986 World Cup was viewed in Naples, a triumph for Neapolitans also. So, the poor people of Villa Fiorito back in Buenos Aires, equally celebrated SSC Napoli's achievements, for Diego Maradona was one of their own, whom they were happy to share with the Neapolitans.

'I consider myself a son of Naples,' said Diego into a pile of microphones shoved into his face. Glancing up, he caught sight of team-mate Giuseppe Bruscolotti making his way towards him through the adoring crowds. If the Argentinian was the talisman in the title finally coming to Naples, then Bruscolotti was undoubtedly the rock on which such foundations were built. A living legend in these parts long before Diego Maradona ever touched ground at the San Paolo, Bruscolotti had led from the front throughout the lean years, a pillar of strength for Neapolitans who despaired as their football club were repeatedly outgunned by Juventus and the Milan clubs. The veteran defender bore the scars of past battles fighting Naples cause, both physically and mentally. His haggard, war-weary features visible for all to see, but the sickness in his heart at seeing his beloved Napoli humiliated by their many enemies not so, except to those closest to him. The courageous decisions to hand Maradona the Captain's armband in exchange for his promise to bring the Scudetto South had come to fruition. As the two came together to share a warm embrace the most hardened Neapolitans wept like babies. The heart-rending sight of this ferocious old warrior shedding tears of joy whilst clinging tightly to Maradona meant all the pain and frustration suffered over the decades was a price worth paying to witness such a moment. The young king had delivered on his word to the old master. With Diego Maradona proudly at their helm, Napoli began a luxuriously swamping lap of honour around the San Paolo, but as hundreds joined in alongside them it resembled more a joyful stampede. A Neapolitan cavalry charge, tinged with blue and heavy doses of delirium. Supporters, photographers and reporters jostled amongst themselves in an attempt to get close to their idols. Maradona picked up a Napoli scarf from the running track and waved it above his head in the direction of the crowd, soaking up the adulation. A banner exclaimed: *'You are as one, San Gennaromaradona'*. The entire Maradona clan were present to witness their boy's moment of triumph. His mother watched on embarrassed as tifosi bowed before her, falling to their knees, thanking Tota for giving birth to the great 'Curly one.' With tears in her eyes and smiling also she implored them to stand back up. No doubt Tota was the proudest lady in the stadium.

On reaching the relative sanctuary of the dressing room, the Captain led all the team in a rousing rendition of the 'Oh, Mama, Mama' tribute song. The Argentinian changed the verses dedicated to himself to ensure each player was serenaded individually by the others. Maradona grabbed a microphone off a television crew and began a series of comic interviews with all of his teammates. But when it came to Giuseppe Bruscolotti, he showed only glowing respect for 'El Pepe', acclaiming him the true Captain of Napoli. Amidst such wonderful scenes of camaraderie and friendship the men who brought about the greatest day in the history of SSC Napoli danced, sang and laughed. All except one. Despite the grateful handshakes, bear hugs and celebratory kisses planted upon him, the coach Ottavio Bianchi refused to partake, keeping a distance, alone in a crowd. In this, his moment of absolute triumph, he remained stone-faced, only ever hinting at a smile. But the dour features of Bianchi misled many for inside burned a footballing heart that lived for SSC Napoli and the city she represented. Deep down none enjoyed winning the Scudetto more than he. Already, his mind was racing ahead to the following season. Bianchi knew well the Northern aristocracy would come after them with an almighty vengeance. They would not take kindly to being humbled at the hands of Naples. It was a humiliation beyond words and that could never be allowed to happen again. But Ottavio Bianchi already had a plan in mind to counteract the mighty forces being lined up against the Neapolitans. Instead of waiting for the inevitable, all-out assault, SSC Napoli would attack from the off! Why wait for the enemy when you can hit them hard, early and blow them away? Magica.

Such was the noise and furore created in the San Paolo on that fateful day, Mount Vesuvio could well have blown it's mighty top and no one would have noticed or even cared. A poet once wrote of the Bay of Naples, *'I want to bring you to a place where the winter is sweet and the summer is fresh. Where the sea lightly touches the land with lazy waves.'* This evoked vivid image of tranquility, serenity and calm. Not on this day when the title finally came South. For though Naples could never claim to be the sanest of cities, in the early evening of 10/5/87, she truly fell into a state of madness. Nowhere was this more so than the backstreet labyrinths of the Forcella, as open trucks and cars inched bumper to bumper in slow, triumphant procession through the winding, narrow streets of the city's ancient, beating heart. Around them flitting and buzzing like fireflies, hundreds of Vespers sped manically, their drivers hooting and hollering in celebration of this, the greatest day. All the pent-up frustrations of living under the thumb of their alleged betters in the North poured out and the Forcella went wild. Many present swore a witch's spell was cast over it's inhabitants, such was the crazed glint in their eyes. Courtesy of the Giuliano clan, the best wine and food was made freely available in abundance as the self-styled 'Protectors of the poor' moved heaven and earth to be seen in a good light on this most special of occasions. It was after all their boy who more than any brought the Scudetto South, and besides, they could easily afford it. Unsuspecting nearby town and villages across the Gulf of Naples found themselves under siege as joyful convoys of Napoli followers swept through their streets in a victory procession. San Francesco, Vico Equense and nearby Sorrento were all treated to a characteristic show of Neapolitan high spirit's. Famed for their beautiful sunsets, lemon groves and rose gardens, the highbrow residents of Sorrento watched in utter disdain the antics of the city dwellers as ramshackle trucks crammed tight with cheering tifosi roared through Piazza Tasso, their historic town centre. They were to be pitied, like the lunatics of an asylum allowed out for the day. Laughed at, derided and, ultimately told to just go away. Back to their garbage-strewn alleyways in the Forcella. Out of sight and mind. Let them have their moment in the sun, for tomorrow normality would once more rear itself and again

Neapolitans would be left with nothing but aching heads and empty lives. But they would have something far more important, the memories of a day set to go down in Naples' history as amongst it's most glorious ever. A song echoed for hours, and later days, weeks and years throughout the city. An ageless *Canzone* called *O Surdato 'Nnammurato, (The Soldier's Song)*, that somehow captured such a special time for all concerned, *'E mme diciste sin a sera e maggio'* (*'And she said yes to me on a May evening'*). This more than any was the soundtrack of Bella Giornata, and even today is regarded as the defining song of those heady times.
'You were my first love, oh first you'll be for me.
Oh, sweet life of mine.'

Napoli's historic triumph appeared to stretch far, wide and even beyond this mortal coil. On a cemetery wall tifosi daubed the words:
'E che ve site perz?' (*'What did you miss'*)?
The next morning, written in chilling reply:
'E chi ve l'ha ditt?' (*'How do you know we missed it'*)?
Dogs bedecked in blue Maradona wigs barked manically at the bedlam around them. Baying donkeys roamed free around the city with the names of Naples most hated enemies placed on placards around their necks. One story claimed that a hundred donkeys had been shipped in from Sardinia for the party. Napoli's unofficial club emblem, the sad-eyed, downtrodden, but always loveable 'O Ciuccio', being used to poke fun against all who had mocked. As the evening drew in and night fell like a cloak of darkness over the Bay of Naples, hundreds of Neapolitans gathered on the seafront to participate in what at first appeared a mass funeral service. To signify the end

of Northern dominance a temporary chapel had been erected housing wooden coffins bearing the names of SSC Napoli's sworn enemies. Turin, Verona and Milan foremost amongst those. After a short charade of mock grieving, huge cheers erupted from the shoreline as the despised Turin mob, Veronese and Milanese were dragged into the ocean before being set alight by flaming, handheld torches and cast off into the darkness. As the coffins burned, drifting out on the high tide, the sky above blazed in a tumultuous kaleidoscope of vivid colour. For the Neapolitans had let fly everything at their disposal that went bang! Bengal Bombs, Roman Candles and the wonderfully named, potentially devastating Maradona Ball were amongst those honoured with a San Gennaro blessing, then launched towards the Southern stars. It began with a culpo scuro (detonation in the dark) and ended with all hell breaking loose! An almighty ensemble of firepower illuminating the heavens, exploding in a glorious cascade above the Tyrrhenian Sea. Blazing red rings of fire glowed, sizzled, and then faded, falling away. Fireworks that crashed, fizzed, sparked and thundered before detonating into a thousand pieces, leaving spilt in their wake glistening trails of lingering sulphur lining the black sky. Below Neapolitans roared in delight at their handy work, drunk, in body and spirit, totally oblivious to the dangers posed to themselves.

'What the hell! To Vesuvio, sooner or later he'll get us all!'

As once forecast, night had turned to day in Naples. Fire engines raced through the streets, dousing rubbish piles before roaring off at breakneck speed to the next emergency. Never had they experienced such a night as their fellow Neapolitans appeared insistent on burning the city to the ground. Those who witnessed this remarkable show of near-suicidal, amateur pyrotechnics from a safe distance on nearby Ischia and the Isle of Capri shook their heads in disbelief and no less wonder at the mad antics of their lunatic neighbours from across the water. Typically, Naples appeared on the verge of being the first city in history to self-inflict total destruction on itself from the air! But on Ischia and Capri they at least looked on the bright side, for them life might prove just a little more tranquil. Where was Diego Maradona? Away from the madding crowds that chanted his name incessantly amidst the hysterical atmosphere of downtown Naples, it was widely rumoured he spent the late night amongst friends at a party hosted in his honour by the Giuliano clan in the discreet surroundings of the village of Nola, on the city outskirts. So, as not to alert paparazzi or unwanted government attention, the venue was kept secret until the last moment. The guests arrived in sleek, black, stretch limousines, surrounded by mean-faced bodyguards and most prized, beautiful, mistresses clinging to their arms. It was said to have been a lavish affair, even by Camorra standards. Against a backdrop of Maradona's finest goals for Napoli being replayed endlessly on large video screens, the finest women, wine and white powder money could buy was on offer to those lucky enough to be present by special invitation. All took advantage of the Giuliano's generosity, none it was said more than Diego Maradona who partied equally hard as the most drunken, delighted Neapolitan, enjoying the forbidden fruits of his hard-earned labour. Many of the gangs had gambled heavily on the back of Maradona's leading Napoli to success, earning themselves huge fortunes. Neapolitans had always tended to bet with their hearts and not their heads when it came to their football team.

Strange those whose daily existence centred on murder and extortion should act like fawning tifosi when in the presence of their idol. Tipping their glasses in salute, hanging on to his every word. For this man not only earned them fortunes, the genius of Maradona had made their dreams come true.

Alas, morning reluctantly broke and Naples grabbed some much-needed rest before throwing itself back once more into fiesta mood. As a new day dawned only the most fanatical tifosi remained partying. Bleary eyed, but steadfastly refusing to let go of the moment, grasping in their hand like a gust of wind, only to watch sadly as it slipped free. Blown away on the ocean breeze. The last of the rockets were fired almost half-heartedly, lacking the thunderous impact of the previous night's extravaganza. A lone thud, spat and spluttered over the bay, whilst sporadic crackles of fireworks echoed rather wearily in the distance. The city that never slept fell for once into serene slumber. Where the dark blue ocean melted into the sky, a red sun lazily rose, and Neapolitans bade a fond farewell to what had truly been *Bella Giornata*. A most beautiful day. They would truly never see it's like again.

CHAPTER FIFTEEN

MAGICA

It was no illusion. There was a blue moon over Naples. Diego Maradona had led Napoli to a peak so high, there remained only one way left to go. The Holy Grail to claim the Scudetto was achieved, but there were those who desperately wanted it back, at any price. Huge face had been lost in the North. Suddenly, a new enemy emerged, stronger and deadlier than any that had gone before. The Neapolitans had to be brought down. Plans were underway to make this so. A man for whom money was no concern busied himself in bringing together a majestic array of the world's best players in Milan. It would be a team like no other, rivalling any of the past great sides. For make no mistake, the exalted red and black of the 'Rossoneri' were coming.

Totonero: (Football pools). It was an open secret in Naples that the formidable Giuliano family ran a clandestine betting syndicate from their territory in the Forcella. Though well aware of it's existence, the authorities never moved to shut it down. Any attempt to do so may well have ended in a bloodbath, such was the Giuliano's hold over their fortress kingdom. Neapolitans poured millions of Lira into the Camorra coffers on a weekly basis. It's advantages for punters included tax-free payouts and the opportunities to play on credit. This alternate back-alley *Totonero* received special attention from none other than the notorious 'Il Lione' Carmine Giuliano. Unlike the vast majority of gangsters who loathed the spotlight, Carmine loved the public adulation of those in the Forcella who regarded him with respect, as a man of honour. One who held the power to give life and take with equal ease. For respect read fear. He also loved to flaunt his close friendship with Diego Maradona. Countless photographs exist of him arm-in-arm alongside the Argentinian at various clubs and parties. Everybody knew that Carmine and Diego were like brothers. He was admired, adored but always feared. The one letter difference between scared and sacred was never more so than in the case of Carmine Giuliano, for when his temper was roused Carmine would fly into a murderous rage, the equal of any Camorristi this city had seen. Ferocious on matters of family business, he ran the gambling rackets with an iron fist. Only those with a death wish dared to tangle or attempt to cross him.

Terno Secco (Hitting the jackpot). It was every Neapolitans' dream to crack thirteen results in the Italian football pools and earn for themselves a fortune. It came as little surprise in a highly supposititious city like Naples, where people carried with them blessed amulets to ward off evil spirits, that there were those convinced *Totonero* numbers came in dreams, placed there by deceased relatives. It was all just a question of translation. For example, if Diego Maradona appeared, he obviously represented number ten. It was said that with the aid of an ancient, medieval practice of numerology called Cabala, believers could try for themselves to pick their own numbers, but to do so was beset with unearthly difficulties. For it was claimed that prickly, troubled souls in the afterlife, who sought only to prevent and spoil would simply play games with any ungainly, amateurish efforts to make sense of dreams. To counteract such an unreasonable, unholy foe, Neapolitans were forced to enlist the help of a spiritualist guide known as a Santoni, (an interpreter of dreams). These self-proclaimed psychics claimed to possess special powers allowing them to snuff out those who led the living astray. Once paid they consulted their required bible, the Smorfia, a mythical book of dreams, that was claimed only Santoni could properly translate. Sadly, in desperate attempts to escape from a poverty-stricken existence, Neapolitans handed over to these spurious characters their cash. Supernatural powers or total fakes? It mattered little, for to outwit mischievous spirit's in the next world was one thing, to second-guess the Camorra was something else. No Cabala, Santoni or even Nostradamus himself could have predicted what was set to occur in Naples.

For Neapolitans, Silvio Berlusconi was nothing less than Nero reborn, a despised modern day Roman Emperor. Born 29th September 1936, to middle class parents in Milan, a bank clerk and housewife, his early days gave rise to unique money-making qualities. As a child young Silvio put on puppet shows, charging entrance fees to fellow students at primary school. To pay for his law degree at Milan University, Berlusconi sang as a crooner of ballads on ocean liners, worked as a stand-up comic and even sold vacuum cleaners. Once enrolled at University, he ghost-wrote essays for those willing to pay a hefty sum for his literary skills. Forever scheming and looking forward, a young Berlusconi, wise beyond his tender years, always made a point of mixing in the right circles. Amongst those he made it his business to befriend was future Italian Prime Minister Bettino Craxi, later to be Godfather to his daughter and a loyal ally over the years in dire times of need. In the 1960s, Berlusconi took out huge loans guaranteed by favourable politicians (old school friends), to create a firm of contractors that went on to build Milano 2. A giant suburban area near Italy's second largest city consisting of ten thousand luxury homes, all supplied with cable television. Two similar suburbs followed as this brave venture proved a huge success. Berlusconi's business empire Fininvest went from strength to strength. As the insatiable desire for money and power grew over the years he went for broke by splashing outright to buy three of the country's main television stations. Such was Berlusconi's bold and brash manner of doing business, the aptly-titled nickname of 'Il Cavaliere' (The Cavalier), was bestowed upon him. He also bought up major food chains, newspaper and publishing markets. Building tycoon, media mogul, there appeared no end to Silvio Berlusconi's ambitions. He was a phenomenon. Italy had never seen a man of this ilk before. His was the Midas touch. A new word came into the Italian language, Berlusconism. People lived in houses built by Berlusconi, watched television controlled by Berlusconi and even shopped at supermarkets owned by Berlusconi. Worried by so much power in one man's hands, the Italian Parliament issued a court order to try and prevent a total monopoly. But Berlusconi's old school tie relationships again came to the rescue when the by-then Prime Minister Bettino Craxi overruled the judges. Silvio Berlusconi, who once had to sing for his breakfast and tell jokes for his supper, had all of Italy dancing to his tune. He was a king without a crown. As ever with Italian high-powered business dealings, dark tales of Masonic corruption and underworld connections were never far away. Berlusconi was no exception. His was a hand in so many pies that almost inevitably the word Mafiosi would come to be whispered. In time these rumours would return to haunt him. Years later he was investigated for alleged involvement in the car bombing of an anti-Mafia judge. But in the mid-Eighties none dared to air such damning allegations.

In March 1986, Silvio Berlusconi made his long-expected move into Calcio, by becoming President of his boyhood team AC Milan. With the debt-crippled 'Rossoneri' verging on the brink of bankruptcy, the cunning Berlusconi bided his time to arrive in their darkest house, riding a tide of Milanese public euphoria. He vowed to make them the number one club not just in Italy, but the world. Always with an eye for the adventurous, Berlusconi astonished all by hiring little known coach Arrigo Sacchi from Serie B club Parma to take the reins.

Born the modest son of a Parma shoe cobbler and only a footballer of modest talent, Sacchi had caught the President's eye the previous season when his team, playing football well beyond their lowly position, sensationally knocked AC Milan out of the Coppa Italia. The stubborn, abrasive but extremely astute Sacchi was entrusted with making real Silvio Berlusconi's vision of a dream team. With a little prompting from above he acted instantly in the transfer market by bringing from Holland two of the world's greatest emerging talents. Firstly, for a world record fee the towering, mercurial skills and speed of the dreadlocked midfield maestro Ruud Gullit. Then, shortly after for the bargain price of £1.5 million, the imperial, imposing figure of Marco Van Basten arrived from Ajax, a prodigy of the great Johann Cruyff and a striker unmatched in the modern game. The best of his generation. Tall, powerful, lightning fast, sublime technique and blessed with a wondrous gift to score goals from any angle. In this audacious double swoop, Sacchi, whether through luck or genius had initiated a significant shift of power back towards the North. For he had bought gold. President Berlusconi also ordered work to begin on an ultra-modern training complex to be called Milanello. Here, no expense was spared to provide his players with the most sophisticated medical and conditional facilities money could buy. The Milan supreme had only one instruction for his coach, to take the Scudetto back from the Southern peasants and return to it's rightful home in the San Siro. Only then would Berlusconi feel he had his crown.

In the deep South, events in Milan hardly raised an eyebrow. The sun-drenched summer of 1987, was a glorious time in Naples as Neapolitans basked in their newly-crowned mantle of champions. But there was one who refused to rest on his laurels. Ottavio Bianchi showed clear intent of how his team intended to play by buying from Brazilian champions Sao Paolo one of the most feared strikers in South American football. Antonio De Oliviera Careca. Bianchi's battle plan was already set in stone.
The Neapolitans would defend their title by taking the war to their enemies. It would be a three-pronged all-out attack christened MAGICA by the Napoli tifosi. MA for Maradona, GI for Giordiano, CA for Careca. The twenty-seven-year-old Brazilian international bonded instantly with Maradona off pitch and along with the exciting, bustling Giordano, this electrifying threesome would wreak havoc amongst Serie A defences. With the blue tifosi now convinced more than ever that Diego Maradona walked on water, his star in it's highest ascendancy, the Argentinian's street-wise guru, Guillermo Coppola attempted to strike while the iron was hot to squeeze Napoli for every Lira in their bank account. Coppola

reacted fast to try and secure for Diego a further five-year extension to his present contract worth a staggering $23 million. Strong rumours of Silvio Berlusconi planning to steal Diego Maradona away to Milan swept through Naples like the proverbial plague. It caused unease. It made people sick. Quickly, they gathered momentum, there were rumblings in the city and the locals were worried. Just what the hell was going on? When negotiations began with Coppola, a man he despised, a determined President Ferlaino was desperate despite the odds against him to drive a hard bargain. The Argentinians' demands were truly outrageous and quite simply impossible. A stalemate swiftly occurred, Naples held it's breath. No Neapolitan really believed Maradona would ever in a thousand years leave and break their hearts into a thousand pieces by betraying them.

None, and yet.

In great secrecy after much heart-searching Maradona agreed to a rendezvous with Silvio Berlusconi. He always spoke well of Berlusconi calling him a 'Gentleman and a winner.' Yet, despite behind so impressed by the Milan supremo, Maradona felt a move was simply impossible. It was akin to trying putting out a flaming Vesuvio with a fire extinguisher, then, jumping in. The Argentinian understood. 'In my heart of hearts, I knew I couldn't play for any team in Italy that wasn't Napoli,' he would later say. Only then to add dryly, 'Because the fans would kill both me and whoever bought me!'

He said as much to Berlusconi. 'If it comes off we'll both have to leave Italy. You're going to lose business because the Neapolitans are going to bust your balls every day, and I'm not going to be able to live.' Each agreed it simply was not possible, however, such interest was gold dust for

Coppola and with a nod and a wink from Berlusconi, he made his move. Napoli were staying in Milan preparing for a game. A Mercedes was photographed taking Coppola to a mansion owned by Berlusconi for a meeting. The word was leaked of Coppola being told by Milan that they wanted Maradona when his contract expired, at any cost. Without even asking about his current salary, they had offered to double it. A friendly journalist wrote this and upon reading it Corrado Ferlaino began sweating profusely. That same day of publication, the President accepted all the outrageous conditions demanded and more. Once agreed, a beaming Coppola turned up at Maradona's house with a black Ferrari F40-apparently the only one in the world at the time as a gift for the player! Not that Maradona needed more money for Coppola's management had totally transformed his fortunes. He had his own TV programme on RAI that paid $250,000 per month. A $5m sponsorship deal with Hitochi, a Japanese clothing line. Other endorsed products included school stationary for children, confectionery, and a strange kind of cold coffee drink! He even shot a television advert for Japanese Asahi beer on the stepped edge of Mount Vesuvio! Executives knew the value of his fame. Maradona's name sold. On occasions, he would ask for and mostly get rare car models. One time, Diego requested a Mercedes that was unavailable on the Italian market. Sometime later, Coppola called him from outside the apartment in Posillipo and told Diego to look out on his balcony. There stood the car! Maradona went down, exchanged hugs, got the keys, jumped inside and marvelled at it like a little kid on Christmas morning. There was also a Naples Mercedes dealer who gave him a brand-new sports car every six month. Not forgetting a

Neapolitan master cobbler who vowed to give the captain two pairs of handmade shoes every month so long as he stayed. Not off the shelf for the king of Naples, but luxury footwear that would cost normal customers a small fortune. Only the best for Diego.

Life was good!

Though unsure of whether Napoli could even afford it, Corrado Ferlaino knew the alternative of refusing and allowing the player to move North was akin to signing his own death warrant. The President had finally resigned himself to the fact that it was not he who ran the football club, but Maradona and his Argentinian sidekick, playboy manager. Weary of fighting a losing battle and being everybody's fall guy, Ferlaino had reluctantly agreed to Coppola's outrageous demands. When the club announced news of Diego's decision to extend his contract, wild celebrations once more erupted in the city neighbourhoods. Could life have possibly got any sweeter for the Neapolitans?

The flamboyant Coppola poured himself a huge drink on the veranda of his favourite haunt, the Hotel Paradiso on Naples waterfront, and sat back to work out his cut of the deal. What was it to him where the tall tales of Berlusconi's interest in Maradona originated? Chinese whispers they claimed? Diego would never dare even dream of Milan. The truth as ever, different. Finally, on 11th December 1987, Diego Maradona signed a six-year-contract worth $16 million. Coppola's cut was substantial. He declared that 'Maradona's children would eat caviar for the rest of their lives.' Money from sand.

On Sunday 13th September 1987, SSC Napoli, with the badge of the Scudetto proudly ensconced upon their shirts, went North to the foot of the Apennine Mountains to begin defending the Serie A title. Newly-promoted Cesna bore the nickname of 'Home of the Popes' due to the remarkable coincidence of three Holy Fathers hailing from the town. Even such a divine background failed to help their cause when in a hard-fought contest Napoli scraped home 1-0 with a goal from the redoubtable warrior Salvatore Bagni. Seven days on the champions took the field in Naples receiving a reception worthy of their illustrious achievements. Onto the sacred turf of the San Paolo strode the footballing kings of all Italy to face Ascoli, yet another team fresh up from Serie B. The visitors included in their line-up a young man who in name and appearance was rather familiar to the gathered 86,000 crowd. Hugo Maradona. Stories persisted that it was Maradona Senior who put up the money to help cash-strapped Ascoli purchase his younger sibling from Argentinos Junior. It was an emotional occasion for the Maradona clan and all were present in the stands to cheer both on. Diego had spent the week building up Hugo's confidence by claiming he possessed the potential to be as good if not better than him. Sadly, it was just a case of brotherly love. Hugo Maradona was attempting the impossible in trying to do justice his ridiculously demanding surname.

The Captain of SSC Napoli had only one, maybe two challengers to the title of the greatest ever. Comparisons, if only even jovial between the brothers were beyond cruel. For if Diego was cut from diamonds then Hugo as a footballer was moulded from clay. Ascoli's Argentinian number ten appeared miserably out of his depth in the cut-throat, if technically brilliant chessboard arena of Serie A. Indeed, handing him that particular shirt only served to

highlight Hugo's limitations when compared to the opposing number. With a small stocky frame and black curly hair Hugo was similar to Diego in looks only. That blood is thicker than water was truly evident in Diego's overwhelming support for his brother, but in footballing terms they evolved from different planets. Napoli won 2-1 with the two brother's paths hardly crossing. Indeed, the closest they came was at the final whistle to embrace and swap shirts. Hugo's time with Ascoli would be short and after making only thirteen appearances that one season impressing no one, he disappeared into the sunset. Later, to resurface in Spain for a brief period with Rayo Valladolid before finally finding his true level in Japan, where the surname alone guaranteed Hugo a decent payday.
But there was only one Maradona.

Great excitement in Naples occurred when the draw for the European Cup was made, for it handed Napoli a glittering start against the legendary Spanish champions Real Madrid. The Neapolitans' first venture into this prestigious competition saw them play the opening leg away in the majestic surroundings of the Estadio Santiago Bernabeu. None more than Diego Maradona relished the opportunity to put one over Real, for during his brief ill-fated foray at Madrid's fiercest rivals, Barcelona, the Catalans had indoctrinated him into the evils of *'Los Madrilenos,'* the white-shirted demons. To them Real Madrid were devils on earth. The European Cup campaign began in surreal surroundings at the Bernabeu when due to crowd disturbance the previous season, Real were forced to play behind closed doors in front of empty, echoing grandstands. In a vain attempt at gaining the merest of home advantage, the Spanish champions placed hundreds of scarves and banners over the terraces. It became known in Madrid folklore as *'El partido del silencio'* ('the match of silence').

Sadly, for Napoli it was they minus new boy Careca who struggled in such a dreadful atmosphere, sliding to a dismal 2-0 defeat. After the game Maradona was furiously upbeat. He declared to hordes of the waiting world's press that, 'Napoli would triumph on home soil even if Puskas and Di Stefano in their pomp were still playing!'

Two weeks later an estimated 100,000 blood-crazed Neapolitans gate-crashed the San Paolo, in a concerted attempt to ensure their side received sufficient support to drag back the two-goal deficit suffered in Madrid. Every single vantage point was taken. Never in Napoli's turbulent and at times violent history had anything even come close to resembling the inferno that blazed under the volcano on that special night the great Real Madrid came to Naples. When selecting his team Ottavio Bianchi threw caution to the wind by throwing in a host of forward players. Bianchi hoped the rabid atmosphere stoked up on the terraces would unnerve the visitors, leaving them open to his brave, if dangerous, do-or-die strategy. As the tifosi roared for Spanish heads on poles, Diego Maradona led the charge. From the first whistle they threw themselves upon the Real defence. Neapolitan dreams of European glory flickered briefly when on nine minutes new signing, defender Giovanni Francini from Torino set the stadium alight when he marauded forward to grab a vital early breakthrough. The stage appeared set for a grand Neapolitan comeback of epic proportions, only to be cruelly snuffed out by the lethal, Madrid centre forward Emilio Butragueno, 'El Buitre' ('the vulture'), who swooped to kill the tie dead a minute before half-time.

Though hardly the outrageously gifted team of old, the Spanish champions had enough in their locker to hold off frantic Napoli efforts in the second period to get back in the game. It finished 1-1. At the final whistle home players walked sullenly off, heads down, whilst the *Madrilenos* celebrated their battling backs-to-the-wall performance. Maradona had been well held and Napoli were out.

The tifosi went home deflated, for so many years they had waited to see their team in this tournament, taking on Europe's elite, only to see them crash and burn before ever taking off.

President Ferlaino watched on in cold fury from the stands. The result was a disaster for the club, not only in football terms, but financially also. A fortune was earned in gate receipts for the visit of Real. Though after all had received their cut, little remained in the pot. SSC Napoli was like a cow to be milked for all it's worth, then discarded when sucked dry. Players, agents and the ever-present invisible black hand of the Camorra hung like a noose over the San Paolo. Even at such a young stage of the season it became apparent that a second Scudetto was required just to make the books balance. With Diego Maradona and the title on board Napoli was an oil tanker that, although leaking, was sufficiently patched up not to sink. But what if the title was lost and the Argentinian abandoned ship? All bets were then off. There were no lifeboats, just prayers. Many, many of them. Ferlaino was a worried man.

The stinging, bitter taste of defeat at the hands of Real Madrid was swiftly cast aside as SSC Napoli roared back and exploded into a sensational rich vein of league form. Top spot was quickly claimed with their opening five Serie A games all won. It was breathtaking, swaggering football, highlighted by a ruthless 6-0 demolition in Naples of poor unsuspecting Pescara. Only 2-0 at the break, the away side suffered humiliation in the second half. A full house paid homage to the blessed Neapolitan holy trio of Maradona, Giordano and Careca, who opened his account as Napoli went goal crazy.

The week following at the Stadio Olimpico in Rome, AS Roma ended Napoli's run holding them to a draw. On the ancient, historic banks of the Tiber, yet another goal from impressive new full-back Francini earned the champions a share of the spoils. Come the final whistle and the Roma tifosi celebrated the 1-1 result like they had won the game, giving rise to just how much SSC Napoli was now respected. Brushing off their close shave in the capital the Neapolitans remained unbeaten till Christmas, opening up a four-point gap at the top. Juventus were also beaten in Naples with a last-minute penalty from Diego Maradona. A draw looked on the cards after veteran defender Antonio Cabrini smashed home an equaliser to level a Fernando De Napoli strike in the first half. But as the crowd hushed in nervous expectation, Maradona with unnerving ease scored to send the San Paolo delirious. For the third game running 'La Vecchia Signora' were beaten. Words could never describe the feeling of sheer elation and satisfaction that swept through the city as the black and white stripes were sent packing with tails between their precious legs. It was a great time to be alive in the place they claimed you had to see before you died. Lesser teams than the loathed 'Bianconeri' were not just turned over, they were hammered out of sight, collapsing under the sheer ferocity of the champions' firepower. The despised Hellas Verona suffered a 4-1 mauling under the volcano with Maradona, Bagni and two from Giordano all on target as the Napoli forwards tortured the Veronese defence.

The goals flew. A magician's potion brewed in Naples, it's mystical ingredients brought from afar but soaked in Neapolitan passion. Bianchi's inspired signing of Antonio Careca, who could not stop scoring had proved a masterstroke. It was Salsa football. Especially at the San Paolo, where Careca found himself swiftly granted hero status and serenaded with his own tribute song:

'Come on Careca, Careca, Careca. Throw the bomb, throw the bomb'.

This was not an honour given lightly. If Maradona was undisputed king of Naples, then Antonio Careca was it's Prince charming. The beating drums of Napoli tifosi set the tempo and rhythm for Magica to come alive! The craft and lightning pace of 'La Bomba' was a perfect foil for the genius of Maradona. His unerring eye to deliver a killer pass whilst in full flight was heaven sent for the fleet-footed Brazilian. With Bruno Giordano all strength, poise and presence, Naples was in dreamland. The much-vaunted challenge from Silvio Berlusconi's bankrolled AC Milan had so far failed to materialise as they were left trailing in the wake of SSC Napoli's blistering start. The two would go head to head in the first week following the Christmas shutdown. All roads led to the San Siro as Italy waited with bated breath this clash of giants. The Milanese desperately needed to win, it had become imperative the champions were dragged back in sight. Any other result and such was Napoli's form, it was odds-on a consecutive Scudetto would be heading to Naples. The sheer quality of their football meant only those with an inbred hatred of Neapolitans or a simple-minded fool would have bet against them retaining their title.

But already it was whispered the decision had been taken that this would not be allowed to happen. That those ruling from the shadows who with one hand gave and the other took were ready to break the hearts of their own. In Naples, the power of the Camorra meant everything and anyone could be bought. Politicians, policemen, judges, priests and footballers. All came with a price. Affairs of the heart mattered little, it was just business. Deep in the Forcella stood a masterpiece of early sixteenth-century architecture, the classic domed church of Santa Caterina. On her blessed walls a picture of Napoli's championship-winning team lay pasted. In normal circumstances the much-feared wrath of the local priest meant this would never have been tolerated, but such was the love and esteem in which these men were held the poster was left to hang. Scrawled across it was the word *Sacro*, meaning sacred. For the unsuspecting city of Naples, the irony of this would in a short time become almost too painful to bear.

CHAPTER SIXTEEN

FATTACCIO
(FOUL DEED)

Amidst the flowers and beauty of Naples beat a rancid heart. Carmine Giuliano was concerned for the Camorra was not in the business of losing money. Plans were made. 'Il Lione' knew he would have to act fast and with great discretion offer the legendary hand of Giuliano persuasion. 'Be my friend, for you do not want me as a fucking enemy.' When the time came nothing was more certain that everything would be ready. To their eternal shame it was alleged the traitor's sold their souls in Vesuvio's shade. The four whose names were whispered, vehemently denied betrayal, presumably to avoid being lynched. It was a fattacio beyond contempt. The heavenly blue skies had turned a ghastly black over the bay. Sadly, it appeared that even those who gave redemption were ultimately not beyond temptation. For in Naples even the angels had dirt under their wings.

On Sunday 3rd January 1988, a new empire came of age in the North. 80,000 Milanese tifosi, awash in red and black bayed with unrestrained joy as a Ruud Gullit, inspired AC Milan wiped the floor with Serie A champions SSC Napoli. In a consummate performance, the guile and craft of the tall, slender, explosive Gullit destroyed the Neapolitans, taking Milan to a momentous 4-1 triumph. In doing so he totally overshadowed Naples' own lauded world superstar Diego Maradona in a much-hyped personal duel between the two. The twenty-six-year-old charismatic Dutchman's laidback approach to life off the pitch was in stark contrast to his attitude once he crossed that white line. With more tricks up his sleeve than a bar-room card shark, the deceptively casual Gullit handed the Southerners a heady dose of their own medicine.

Yet it had all started so well for the champions as they began the game full of confidence, passing the ball around with supreme ease. On eleven minutes their reward came when Francesco Romano fed his captain, and an exquisite Maradona chipped pass left even the accomplished Baresi flat-footed, as Antonio Careca raced clear to chest down and volley with marvellous aplomb past Milan's goalkeeper Giovanni Galli. With arms outstretched Napoli's number seven ran to salute the thousands of travelling Neapolitans going mad behind the goal. Instead of going for that killer second, Napoli uncharacteristically sat back, playing right into Milan's hands. What followed was an unmitigated disaster for Ottavio Bianchi's team and a historic victory for Arrigo Sacchi's mean, moody and ultimately magnificent Rossoneri. The San Siro rocked on it's grand heels as the home side awoke with a frightful vengeance. Ruud Gullit's magical twist and turn enabled him to cross for Milan forward Pietro Virdis, only for him to slash the ball horribly over from just six yards. The tide of battle swiftly swept back in Milan's favour. Sacchi's innovative, high intensity, attacking British style, performed with huge finesse and technique, saw his players incessantly pressing the opponents across the field. Napoli buckled as red and black shirts came at them from all angles. Evani, Donadoni, Ancelotti, aided by attacking full-backs Tassotti and Maldini, rampaged forward, pinning the Southerners back in their own penalty area. With the Rossoneri libero Franco Baresi marshalling operations in front of a well-drilled back four, Arrigo

Sacchi's team passed immaculately, cutting their opponents to shreds. Whenever Napoli had the ball, Milan fought furiously to win back possession. On nineteen minutes attacking defender Mauro Tassotti played in Gullit, whose precise pass back into the box found the all-action midfielder Angelo Colombo to smash home low from eight-yards out past a despairing Claudio Garella. The long blond locks of Colombo disappeared beneath a pile of Milan shirts. It was hard running football played at great pace, but with poise and wonderful finesse. On the touchline Arrigo Sacchi in a long black trench coat danced a jig of joy. Still Milan raged: Evani's header was saved spectacularly by Garella as the onslaught continued unabated. Again, the thick mustachioed Virdis faltered as he shot haplessly over with an open net at his mercy. But such was the overwhelming superiority of the home team another goal had to come and it was Pietro Virdis who at last found his shooting boots. The Milan number eight's weaving run through the Napoli defence finished with him blasting past the keeper to ignite the stadium once more. The bald-headed Sacchi could not restrain himself and ran onto the pitch punching the air. The Neapolitans were being run ragged. On thirty-two minutes a breathtaking move involving six Milan players that swept the entire length of the pitch ended with Gullit's flying header crashing against Claudio Garella's post and rebounding to safety. Harassed, bothered and ultimately overrun the champions staggered like a punch-drunk fighter to the half-time break.
It would prove just a brief respite.
The second half saw no letup in the action as the Rossoneri tortured their opponents, hitting passes long and short with equally devastating accuracy. At the fore was the mercurial

Dutchman Ruud Gullit, leading the Neapolitans a merry dance, tearing constantly down the right-wing wreaking havoc. One incident saw three Napoli players left in a blue, bedraggled heap as Gullit cast his own particular Dutch black magic over the champions. Diego Maradona was not so much upstaged as blown off stage. Indeed, the Argentinian was even forced on the defensive, hoofing clear from his own penalty area as the pressure remained unyielding. Fifteen minutes from time a scything through-ball from the dynamic midfielder Ancelotti put Gullit clear and he rounded Garella with ease, before placing the ball into an empty net. 3-1 and game over. With the Neapolitans having given up the ghost and simply praying for full-time, Roberto Donadoni compounded their misery by beating Claudio Garella with alarming ease from fully twenty-five yards. A terrible bobble deceived Garella who watched in horror as the ball sneaked horribly over the line. Finally, the famed Italian referee Luigi Agnolin took pity on the Southerners and called time on Napoli's agony. The San Siro rose to salute their glorious heroes. Knowing there could be no argument with the result, Diego Maradona and his team left the field with heads bowed. For on that memorable Milan afternoon, there was only one number ten that mattered, and he wore red and black. High above in the Presidential box, Silvio Berlusconi, dressed divinely by Italy's finest tailors took the acclaim of an adoring crowd. Wearing a suit, the price of a Third World country's national debt, Berlusconi, with beaming smile etched on permanent suntanned features, believed he cut a Bella Figura. This was a man who felt nothing of landing his personal helicopter on the training pitch at Milanello in the midst of a training session. How Berlusconi loved the open-mouthed expressions of the players as he made his typically grand entrance. For one whose giant ego was matched equally by a bank balance, this mattered. Resembling in his exalted mannerisms a Roman Emperor of old, acknowledging saluting gladiators, before deciding the fate of their felled opponents. Berlusconi bathed delightfully in fawning adulation. The dramatic gesture of thumbs down, no mercy to his team, as they twisted the sword deep into Napoli was greeted emphatically by the fanatical Milan hardcore support of the Fossa dei leoni. To them their President was God on Earth, returning to purge Italy of this plague that had swept up from the South. For Neapolitans, he was a despot and big trouble. It was all a timely, if unwanted reminder for Napoli that in January the championship was there to be lost and not won.

Embarrassed by their feeble surrender at the hands of a revitalised AC Milan, Ottavio Bianchi's men returned home shamefaced to Naples. Then, seven days later and in typical fashion, with their pride badly stung by the Milan debacle, Napoli thrashed the living daylights out of an unsuspecting Fiorentina in the San Paolo, who must have wondered what they had done to deserve such a mauling. Eager to rid minds of the previous week's humiliation, the Neapolitans put four past the 'Viola' without reply. A typically, swerving Maradona free-kick that flew like a rocket into the top corner, two from Giordano and Antonio Careca, helped ease the pain. After being drowned out in Milan, the Samba drum once more found it's beat. Elsewhere, at the Stadio Comunale, AC Milan ended a fourteen-year losing streak in Turin against Juventus winning 1-0, courtesy of Ruud Gullit. Christened 'Il Tulipo Nero' (The Black Tulip), by his adoring fans, Gullit was magnificent. The larger than life Dutchman had already in his short time in Italy earned cult status amongst the red and black tifosi. Indeed, the confident Gullit showed he possessed more than one string to his bow by performing live with his reggae band, Revelation, to a 3,000 crowd at an open-air concert in Milan. Though it was on the football pitch where Gullit's true talents shone, as he looked every inch a worthy contender for Diego Maradona's world crown. Born to Surinam and Dutch parents in Amsterdam, this was a player unique on the world scene, not only in looks with his extravagant Afro dreadlocks, but, more importantly footballing talent. Two-footed, deadly from free-kicks, forever on the move, arriving unseen in the box causing mayhem. Despite playing centre midfield for Holland, Sacchi preferred playing him wide right, with the electrifying pace of the Sardinian Virdis on the left and Van Basten through the middle. Like so many of the great Dutch players, Gullit possessed a high measure of versatility that saw him capable of performing anywhere to equally devastating effect. Whilst 'Il Tulipo' appeared worth every single Lira of the record fee paid to PSV Eindhoven securing his services, Marco van Basten found himself on the sidelines for long periods of his first season in Milan colours. A troublesome and ultimately crippling ankle injury saw Van Basten reduced to performing just a cameo role in the 'Rossoneri's' title charge, though ultimately it was one that proved spectacular. For when the return match in Naples came around van Basten would all but decide the destination of the Scudetto. In the distance, kicking up dust, the thundering hoofs of AC Milan pounded in close pursuit of the champions. Every time the Neapolitans looked over their shoulder Milan were forever in sight and earshot. Like a dog with a bone Arrigo Sacchi's never-say die team refused to let go. Yet another epic confrontation between North and South sprang from it's roots into full bloom. Insults hurled back and forth from both cities. The Milanese mocked the lowlife Terroni of Naples that they had neither the heart nor strength to retain their one lucky, measly Scudetto. Soon, they would be back in the gutter to be squashed like bugs under the well-polished heel of Milan's boot. The Napoli tifosi retaliated with unreserved venom by claiming the 'Rossoneri' were nothing more than a Berlusconi plaything to be discarded when he got bored. A prostitute, all grateful and indulging to her filthy, rich pimp of a sugar daddy. It became clear to all that AC Milan had leapfrogged Juventus to become public enemy number one in Naples, a mantle regarded by many in the North as a backhanded compliment. 'La Vecchia Signora' were old news. New banners were prepared, songs penned. Each week saw hearts soar and hopes dashed. No love lost, no quarter given or asked by either side and game on.

A ruthless 5-0 massacre of Como at the San Siro with Gullit scoring twice looked to have cut Napoli's lead back even further, only for Diego Maradona to grab a last-gasp goal in Genoa against Sampdoria. With time almost up on a swamp of a pitch at the Luigi Ferraris' stadium, Maradona latched onto a sloppy defensive clearance, dug the ball out of the mud and crashed home from the edge of the box to steal the points for Napoli. Off he slid, diving headfirst in delight with his compadres on a rain-drenched surface, arms raised in triumph. The Neapolitans left it late, but once again when all looked lost Maradona had saved the day. So, it continued with Milan continuing to stalk Napoli's every move. Almost inevitably nerves took hold and points were dropped. But whenever the champions faltered, AC also tripped up. On 6th March, Napoli went down 2-1 at home to Roma. Two goals adrift with just ten minutes left, Careca pulled one back and all hell broke loose in the visitors' penalty area. The dying seconds saw the Roma players almost on their knees as they came under intense pressure, only to be saved by the referee's full-time whistle. As the home tifosi stood forlorn, news reached them of Milan only drawing 0-0 with Verona. The almost beautiful irony of this was not lost on the Neapolitans who laughed their heads off at this unexpected helping hand from the despised Veronese. Such was the wealth of firepower employed by the champions, almost inevitably they pulled away from the 'Rossoneri', and by mid-April they had a healthy four points lead. A 1-0 win earned at the San Paolo against Inter with a stupendous Diego Maradona free kick was deemed exceptional by even his standards. Such was the ridiculously pin-point accuracy of Maradona, Inter's 'Azzurri' goalkeeper Walter Zenga simply shrugged his shoulders as if to suggest, 'How do you expect me to stop that?' Maradona's flashy Samba dance routine with Antonio Careca at the corner flag celebrated a now five-point advantage over Milan. The championship once more looked safe. Appearing hopelessly outgunned, the hopes of Arrigo Sacchi's men was left in the hands of others.

On 17th April 1988, SSC Napoli travelled to Turin to deal with an old thorn that forever pained them. It would prove a defining weekend in the battle for the Scudetto, for no other team in Italy would relish more the opportunity to knock Napoli off their pedestal. 'La Vecchia Signora', the deposed grand 'Old Lady' of Serie A stood ready to wreak revenge. By their own exceptionally high standards Juve's season had been spectacularly mediocre. Lying haplessly adrift in seventh place, Rino Marchesi's team was in a state of readjustment following the retirement of the exalted Platini. Unfortunately, there was no such phrase as 'transitional period' in the Juventus dictionary and the same sense of unease that dogged Marchesi's last year in Naples had returned to haunt him. The Neapolitan hordes descended on Turin in typically vast numbers, but alas for them the sweet memory of the previous season's fixture was not to be repeated as Juve upset the odds to beat Napoli 3-1 and blow the title race wide open. At the same time AC Milan overcame Roma 2-0 to go just two points behind the champions, with a game against Napoli still to come. Leading 1-0 at the break, a fired-up Juventus playing easily their best football of the season tore into Ottavio Bianchi's side, which to their supporter's horror appeared to lack proper heart for a fight. Defeat against their Turin foes could be tolerated, but to lie down before them? Napoli appeared to have blown a gasket, Magica's spell was broken. On sixty-seven minutes to rub further salt into their seeping wounds, the heavily derided Ian Rush earned himself some much-needed breathing space with the Juve Ultras when he pounced to double their lead. The Neapolitan tifosi hardly knew whether to laugh or cry on seeing Rush of all people score against them. He, the object of their jokes and scorn had lashed back to leave them choking on their venom. This had proved a bad day in the North. As sweet their last visit to Turin was, so this time round it had fallen sour. A penalty driven home by Juventus midfielder Di Agostini was the final nail in their coffin. A late effort finished with fine aplomb by Antonio Careca merely papered over an insipid, scandalous surrender by the Southerners. Something was wrong. The

thousands of miserable, downbeat Neapolitans who stood crestfallen on the terraces of the Stadio Comunale smelt a rat. None felt more betrayed than Ottavio Bianchi.
The allenatore's bewildered, shocked expression at the full-time whistle gave rise to the notion that the battle for the Scudetto could be already over. For Bianchi, the shocking realisation that certain players wearing Napoli colours had thrown in the towel left him sick to the stomach. To lose by bad play was galling enough, but to sell your soul and betray a city and it's people who had nothing else was a crime beyond words. Bianchi could only pray his suspicions were unfounded.

Before the Rossoneri trod a fateful path to Naples for their title decider against Napoli, both sides had potential banana skins to overcome. Milan faced city rivals Internazionale at the San Siro, whilst the champions endured yet another perilous journey up-country to take on Hellas Verona. Neapolitans joked that William Shakespeare must have been in ironic mood when he penned his legendary description of Verona as the 'City of lovers'. Outnumbered in a strange land inhabited by even stranger people, many times they were left battered, bloodstained by murderous hordes of the Brigate Gialloblu, and the outrageously biased local Polizia who viewed Southerners with sneering disdain. But the visitors could hardly complain for when the Northerners went South, the abuse was returned with interest. They found to their bloody cost that Naples was not all romantic splendour, singing mandolins and haunting *Canzone*. Choking chaos, stifling heat and the heavy smell of volcanic sulphur forever lingering. Paradise with an edge.

This was the true home of SSC Napoli. Take liberties and their fucking title if you dare. On the pitch a win for Napoli and defeat for Milan would all but seal the Scudetto, however, it was not to be. For as Maradona's brilliant first half strike from the edge of the box guaranteed his team a hard-earned point in Verona, Sacchi's men triumphed gloriously over Inter with goals from Gullit and Virdis. The point's difference was down to one, as the title suddenly became theirs' to touch.
All eyes fell upon the San Paolo.
Three games remained for each side but there was only one that mattered. Both cities braced themselves for one almighty clash. A loss for either in Naples would surely end their challenge. Diego Maradona called on his team and supporters for one last great effort. Neapolitans prayed that the days of Northern bullies coming to their city laying down the law, all pomp and arrogant swagger were over. Ottavio Bianchi experienced a horrific time in the week leading up to the Milan showdown. A fraught state of mind meant everywhere he looked conspiracies loomed. A chasm of mistrust, bordering on hatred had grown wide between the coach and many of his senior players. Surprisingly, one spared his criticism was Diego Maradona. Though neither would ever claim to be remotely close in any way, Bianchi had no reason to doubt Maradona's sheer will to win, for there had been too many times he had single-handedly saved Napoli with a piece of individual brilliance when it would have been so easy for him not to do so. Although the Argentinians off-pitch antics repeatedly reduced his coach to despair, even to the point where he had considered selling him, despite the consequences, there was no doubt whatsoever in Bianchi's mind of his Captain being on the take. Diego Maradona

may have taken many things in his time, drink and drugs, but money to throw matches? Ottavio Bianchi thought not. Of the others? He could not be so certain.

There were reasons that Bianchi did not sleep well at night, for amongst his line-up there were some whose pasts were tarnished by allegations they would rather forget. Though living legends of the Scudetto win and beloved folk heroes of the tifosi, could these leopards have ever truly changed their spots? Bianchi's mind remained racked with doubts. Was the gallant performance at Verona in a most intimidating atmosphere a positive sign that his team's heart for battle had returned? Or simply part of a cruel charade to allow the leading characters in this dreadful masquerade to deliver the final coup de grace in the San Paolo? Something terrible was going on. Strange events were occurring off the pitch involving the Napoli players. Many were sent threats to themselves and their families. 'Do as you're fucking told or else.' Maradona's Porsche was smashed up, Salvatore Bagni was beaten badly and had his car stolen. Eventually, all the squad were given offers they could hardly refuse. Including letters that dead relatives' bodies would be dug up from their cemeteries and stolen. On Naples' sacred turf upon which their dream was consecrated, this disturbing tale would unfold for the entire world to witness. For if the dark rumours that emanated from the Southern capital had any true substance then Arrigo Sacchi was leading the 'Rossoneri' into a supposed bear pit,
with the game already won.

Like all his Milan brethren, Silvio Berlusconi did not trust Neapolitans. With this in mind a paranoid Berlusconi decided on extraordinary measures of security, for if any

city in the world could concoct a devious plot to blight his team's preparation it was Naples. This unholy place where the Devil needed a bodyguard, where snake charmers and voodoo witches earned a good living sat on blankets outside fancy boutiques and antique bookshops. Where double-dealing, intrigue and corruption were part of everyday life. The President was convinced an attempt would be made to bring them down. In order to avert such a scenario, he hired two planes for the journey to Naples, one for the team and the other carrying food, drink and medicine supplies. For the danger that the Neapolitans would poison his superstars by sprinkling something extremely nasty on their food or spiking their water was deemed a real danger by the Milan President. To such an extent he brought along his own personal chef and private legion of bodyguards to supervise all meals served, with no local hotel staff allowed anywhere near. Purposely waiting until the last possible minute, AC Milan went South only on the eve of the game. On landing at Naples International Airport, the two planes were immediately surrounded by an armed ring of Polizia. Amidst ridiculously over-the-top security measures for a visiting football team, the bemused players were ushered swiftly across the deserted runway and onto a waiting bus. Then, with a formidable escort in place, including a Carabinieri helicopter buzzing their every move, they sped off with dramatic red sirens wailing on a planned pre-arranged route meant to avoid the Neapolitan lynch-mobs supposedly lying in ambush across the bay.
Through veiled curtains Ruud Gullit and co dared to sneak a look and gaze in utter bewilderment at an entire city draped in Napoli colours. Every roof, balcony and doorway covered blue. It appeared beyond fanaticism. An

old Lady looking to cross the road happened to catch Gullit's eye as the coach became stuck at traffic lights. Her wickedly insulting gesture to the Dutchman, delivered with heartfelt meaning left all who witnessed it rather shocked, such was the look of hatred ensconced in her cragged features.

As the coach made it's wary way on the seafront, Via Partone, past the dock, it was if everyone had just up and gone! The harbour's giant lifting cranes left abandoned, precious cargo lying stacked high on pallets, untouched. Hulking freight ships stood silent, their goods unloaded. Unknown to the visitors prying eyes reported their every move to a huge welcoming reception of Napoli tifosi waiting to greet them outside their temporary residence of the inaptly named Hotel Jolly! Men, women, children, all armed to the teeth with rocks and rotten fruit readied their aim. On the final lap of the journey the Milanese felt the full warmth of Naples' greeting, for as they entered the city centre the bombardment began! What appeared like the entire population had turned out to welcome these Northerners who dared to take their Scudetto away. Security barriers manned by lines of Polizia, erected to keep out the baying crowds came under fire. All hell let loose as from nowhere thousands pounced, hurling stones, broken bottles, coins, spitting, screaming abuse. Sheltered by a ring of steel the beleaguered Milan players ran for their lives through this gauntlet of hate into the relative safety of the hotel foyer. There, they watched the scenes outside of Neapolitans serenading them with their legendary collection of derisory chants, insulting songs and vitriolic insults. Parentage was questioned. Fathers and mothers either bastards or whores. In a concerted attempt to ensure none of the Milan squad slept that night, the

locals set up camp outside the hotel and began indulging in a raging sea of noise. The despised Silvio Berlusconi already owned their shops, television stations and newspapers. His triumphal talk of a new dawn scared and irritated them beyond words. History had always shown Neapolitans eager to embrace new conquerors, if only to bathe in the misery of the former. But times had changed, they were now kings of their own castle, and Berlusconi with his *Milanisti* puppets would not be allowed to break Naples' hearts. Fanatical Neapolitans beat drums, crashed bin lids and set off firecrackers, indeed anything that banged was put to use. With typical foresight Berlusconi had already made plans to counteract by renting the entire 25th floor of the towering Jolly. There the jeering and cat-calls could still be heard but at least they were out of firing range as catapults and all manner of improvised homemade siege weapons fell short, crashing to earth.
As evening drew in and the Naples black sky became drenched with stars, the frenzied enthusiasm of the Napoli tifosi refused to be curtailed by minor irritants such as tiredness or fatigue. Theirs' was a holy mission, undertaken by the fanatically loyal foot-soldiers of Maradona, blessed by San Gennaro. Thou shalt not fucking sleep. It was almost as if the Neapolitans feared their team was not capable of beating AC Milan, unless they themselves gave all till morning came. But they had sadly misjudged the fierce resilience of Arrigo Sacchi's men. No amount of wailing, hollering, cursing or hooting car horns would rattle the ice cool Baresi and the chilled-out Gullit. For if any team in the world possessed the character to overcome such an overwhelming atmosphere of rancid hostility, it was the 'Rossoneri'. They would give their reply in the San Paolo.

Finally, a reluctant dawn broke and Naples woke with nervous trepidation. Churches as ever rapidly filled, though this time around congregations felt no fervid obligation to rush off to the football stadium. Suddenly, it had become more important to pray. The unspoken rumours drifting like a rotten smell throughout the city appeared to have left it's indelible mark. Nobody wanted or even dared to believe, but such was the doom-laden nature of Neapolitans they feared the worse. So, the most infamous game in the history of SSC Napoli would unfold. Laced with heady doses of drama, passion, tears and despair. The ultimate deception. After over-estimating Napoli's odds at 5/1, the Giulianos would have lost billions in revenue if they retained the crown, such was the vast amount of cash bet by loyal Neapolitans on their heroes. The Camorra operated along the lines that the meek and mild may go on to be saints in the afterlife, but in this world, they were quite simply fools and there to be exploited. It would prove the ultimate betrayal. The assassins were at the gate. The endgame loomed and Ottavio Bianchi could do nothing about it.

For sadly in Naples even angels had dirt under their wings.

CHAPTER SEVENTEEN

ENDGAME

All dreams end. On Sunday 1st May 1988, amidst haunting flares and a crying sea of tears, Naples died a thousand deaths. AC Milan went South to conquer in exhilarating style. Though sick at heart in losing, 86,000 Neapolitans rose as one to acclaim Milan as worthy winners. This in itself was an achievement beyond words for many reporters and journalists present that day in the San Paolo stadium. Such a spontaneous act of sportsmanship by a normally rabid, fanatical support was unprecedented. But if the truth were known it was the lesser of two evils to be seen as magnanimous in defeat. For the alternative in having to acknowledge being undone by the treacherous acts of their own was simply too horrible to comprehend. The Napoli hordes watched in dismay. Just who were these pitiful, fucking strangers adorning the colours of their beloved club? The endgame loomed, Armageddon was at hand.

The cobbler's son had an ace up the sleeve to surprise all. Unknown to any except those in his inner sanctum, Marco van Basten stood on the verge of a sensational comeback from long-term ankle injury. After a lengthy consultation with Milan's medical team. Arrigo Sacchi felt it a worthwhile gamble risking having the brilliant Dutch centre-forward on the bench in the San Paolo. Who better than Van Basten to call on if the need arose for a goal? With the Neapolitans threatening to self-implode through suspicion and unrest, the 'Rossoneri' intended to clinch an eleventh Scudetto badge by winning in Naples, leaving the champions spent. The Milan party had remained wholly unaffected by the hatred and animosity shown towards them by their inhospitable Southern hosts. Several of their players even had the temerity to wave at their baiters as they once more came under fire, making the short but perilous journey from the Hotel Jolly to the San Paolo. The relaxed demeanour of Ruud Gullit spoke volumes, not just for himself, but all his team-mates. There was a wry smile on the face of Gullit as he watched incredulously through his window at Napoli tifosi on scooters racing at death-defying speed alongside them, faces etched in blood boiling fury, spitting venom at these detested Northerners. From the sideways, balconies and open windows the coach was battered ignominiously with rotten fruit. On arrival at the stadium a Neapolitan lynch mob intent on doing them serious harm fought with their own baton-wielding Polizia in near-suicidal attempts to reach the Milan team. Feelings were running out of control under the volcano. Finally, the tifosi, their faces hidden by blue scarves, retreated, they could do no more. The sword of battle was passed on to those trusted in carrying the fight onto the pitch.

Diego Maradona led the defence of their most coveted crown. Little did Maradona realise the overwhelming odds stacked against him. He would find himself hopelessly outgunned. No matter how much courage and determination were shown, some games were not meant to be won. As the late afternoon sun cast towering shadows over the wide-open terraces of the San Paolo, a surreal atmosphere fell upon the stadium. An entire city braced itself for either triumph or despair. Neapolitans had already been blessed with one fairytale ending. Few doubted whether another *Bella Giornata* would be allowed to occur, no matter how many times or hard they prayed.

Maybe God was listening, but sadly it wasn't the Almighty on that Mayday in Naples calling the tune. The strings were tugged and the puppets danced.

Napoli began looking fraught, full or nerves and scared of their own shadows. Such obvious unease spread quickly onto the terraces and in the early stages it was Milan who impressed as they sought to dominate possession, frustrating both the home team and supporters. Against an ear-piercing, deafening soundtrack of boos and whistles, Arrigo Sacchi's superbly-drilled outfit passed the ball in supreme manner. The much-vaunted Magica trio of Maradona, Giordano and Careca found itself isolated and cut off as their midfield concerned themselves more in resisting the 'Rossoneri' onslaught. It was clear that Napoli, who only one year previously had swept all before them in swashbuckling fashion were up against a side that in both style and players were just a little too good. Whilst the champions gave the ball away carelessly, the movement pace and technique of Milan caused gasps of astonishment around the stadium. The Naples clans howled in displeasure, they feared the worse. Maradona tried in vain to kick-start his team by dropping deep but found himself swamped by the seemingly rocket-fuelled midfield of AC Milan who fell upon him like a pack of wolves. Sacchi's men sparked and fizzed, before finally exploding on thirty-six minutes when striker Pietro Virdis pounced on a deflected free-kick to fire a vicious drive past a flailing Claudio Garella, high into the Napoli net from close range. A delightful Virdis wheeled away in triumph, though immensely careful to stay on the pitch and avoid the Neapolitan photographers and officials who stood encamped, grim faced and in murderous mood behind the goal. An exuberant Arrigo Sacchi raced

characteristically onto the field and embraced Virdis. The 'Rossoneri' had cut deep, Naples was bleeding.
On the stroke of half-time Maradona broke free from his Milanese shackles, beat one man, then two, only to be brought crashing to earth by Paolo Maldini, on the edge of Milan's penalty area. The San Paolo soared into life on seeing it's favourite son at last show a flash of his true self. His perfectly flighted free-kick left Milan goalkeeper Giovanni Galli looking leaden-footed as the ball soared gloriously into the top left-hand corner. It was a goal hardly deserved for the Neapolitans who had been outplayed until then. As celebrations raged inside the stadium, a visibly distressed Galli fell to his knees and lent forlornly against the post. His team had gone to Naples and played the champions off the park on their own turf. As the Argentinian danced an exuberant Samba with Brazilian team-mate Careca at the corner flag in front of an ecstatic crowd, Galli watched on in dismay. His shocked features bore the expression of a man wondering just how Maradona had contrived to bend the ball over the Milan defensive wall and into the net when all angles appeared to have been covered? Composers compose memorable symphonies, painters paint masterpieces, authors write magnificent epics and Diego played his football. Pure unadulterated genius. It was a goal that typified Maradona's time in Naples.1-1. The thin dividing line between joy and despair was never more evident as suddenly the San Paolo became convinced Maradona's wonder strike would spur their team on to greater effort. But come the second period Milan again carried on carving up the Neapolitans at will. None more than Ruud Gullit, whose trickery and speed down the right wing made life hell for the Napoli defenders, and especially the left full-

back Giovanni Francini who was exposed constantly and with great ease by the tantalising skills of the flying Dutchman. He appeared unstoppable.

Finally, fed up of being made to look foolish, Francini hacked his haunting tormentor down and was booked by the referee. Taking full advantage, the wily Gullit taunted his opponent, goading him into another reckless challenge that would see him dismissed. As the Naples' crowd screamed vitriol in his direction, Gullit simply laughed in Francini's face, baiting him into retaliating. On sixty-eight minutes Ruud Gullit cast a spell once more on a despairing Francini, twisting him one way, then another, before firing in a cross that was finished expertly by the head of Pietro Virdis. Claudio Garella was left helpless as scandalous marking in the Napoli defence left Virdis with acres of space to pick his spot and grab a second goal. That, Garella stood with hands outstretched in disbelief at the apparent half-hearted efforts of his defenders to stop the Milan forward, fooled few in the San Paolo. Such theatrical gestures and mannerisms were viewed daily on every street corner in the city by conmen and hustlers plying their trades.

Napoli stormed back and Bruno Giordano crossed for Maradona to stab a low shot whilst off balance straight at Galli. Immediately, the Milan keeper threw the ball out to Paolo Maldini, who quickly fed Ruud Gullit to begin yet another lightning counter-attack for this breathtaking team. Throughout the afternoon Milan's number ten had caused palpitations amongst the home crowd every time he received possession. There was still more to come.

Fourteen minutes remained in Naples when the striding, elegant figure of Gullit, with his Rastafarian dreadlocks flowing, raced with deadly intent over the halfway line bearing down on the retreating Napoli defence. Across the emotionally-charged, tortured, massed terraces, Neapolitans squirmed and sweated as their defenders shuffled backwards, looking petrified, caught in the eye of this Milanese onslaught. Gullit soared with outrageous case into the penalty box before crossing perfectly for the Milan substitute Marco van Basten, standing totally unmarked eight yards from goal. His precise side-foot effort beat Garella to make it 3-1. Sacchi's gamble had paid off. Van Basten had been on the pitch for only a few minutes but had returned to make his mark in inimitable style.

A deafening silence gripped the San Paolo. The time and space which the Dutchman was given caused great alarm amongst the blue tifosi. Amidst haunting flares and a sea of tears, the city of Naples died a thousand deaths. Rumours like fresh air were free to spread. But how was it possible for a team that had so spectacularly won the Italian championship only a season previous, to fall so low? Two minutes later Antonio Careca pounced from close range to cut the deficit. Suddenly, the gloom that had settled over the stadium melted away to be replaced by new found hope. Both managers looked close to a breakdown as they raged on the touchline barking out orders. Whilst Bianchi threw his arms manically upwards, urging his team to attack, attack, attack. Sacchi, with eyes almost popping out of his head, cut a near-hysterical figure as he ranted, raved, implored and pleaded with his players not to concede an equaliser. He need not have worried, for with his Captain Franco Baresi in typically commanding form at the back, Milan were ferocious, yet calm in defence. Napoli swept forward in a last-gasp attempt to save face. The dying seconds saw a corner earned and a final chance to score. Marco van Basten received an ear bashing of monumental proportion from his coach for staying on the halfway line in expectation of a breakout, instead of running back to defend. It was not to be. Neapolitan prayers to their patron San Gennaro for divine intervention fell on deaf ears. The referee Carlo Longhi blew for full-time and Milan led Serie A by a point with just two games left to play. Diego Maradona finished the contest lying slumped on the floor, his efforts in vain. As for Ottavio Bianchi, the ninety minutes left him in despair. His team had performed as if drunk on fatigue. Heavy legged, listless and disinterested. A white flag had been raised over the San Paolo.

A city held it's head in shame.

As beaten Napoli players slid sullenly away, embarrassed with heads sunk, the visitors, to their utter disbelief, were handed a wonderful standing ovation. From a ripple to a tidal wave of applause grew. Milan gathered in the centre-circle to acknowledge this remarkable, spontaneous display of sportsmanship from a crowd that would have gladly torn them limb from limb before the game began. For the 'Rossoneri' had been magnificent. Not for Sacchi's team, the defensively minded, drab and dreary Northern tactic of Catenaccio in order to steal a result on Neapolitan soil. AC Milan had come South and exploded in all hell and fury, playing in a composed and thrilling style. With their bravura showing in the San Paolo, Milan achieved something no other side had ever managed to attain. Respect.

It was like seven days on Death Row for the Neapolitans before the title was finally dragged from their grasp. In faraway Florence, against a fired-up Fiorentina side enjoying their moment in the limelight, and the eyes of all

Italy upon them, the dream died. In all reality the thousands of loyal blue tifosi who ventured North to witness Napoli's last stand travelled more in blind faith than actual belief. Deep down they knew it was a hopeless task. Before the game President Ferlaino reportedly paid Napoli's dressing room a visit in order to wish them luck, only to leave hastily after experiencing an atmosphere that he referred to rather disturbingly as 'An unutterable thing.' What Ferlaino actually witnessed has never truly come to light, but it was clear by that time Ottavio Bianchi had lost his players, Bianchi's anger at what occurred over the final months of the season had left him close to breaking point and he was not the type to let matters lie. Amidst fire and fury, a gloating 'Viola' administered with unreserved joy the last rites to SSC Napoli. For Neapolitans it came as little surprise that the man who delivered the final nail into their coffin was a former Napoli player. It was all part of the theatre. Argentinian centre forward Ramon Diaz scored twice in a 3-2 win and broke the heart of his old club. With ghostly echoes of Jose Altafini, 'Core Ngrato', many years before, Diaz finished off the Southerners to leave their supporters broken-hearted and the Artemio Franchi stadium bathed in euphoria. As news of Napoli's defeat reached Milan, 80,000 Milanese in the San Siro erupted. The 'Rossoneri's' 0-0 draw with Juventus meant the title would return North. A triumph wholly deserved. The old order had once more been established, the way of things. But at what price this was achieved will probably always remain shrouded in controversy.

The fallout from this devastating loss fell like acid rain in Naples. Strange tales abounded in the backstreets of the city that the Camorra had bribed a number of players to lose the Milan match and make a huge killing on their illegal *Totonero*. Others claimed that Silvio Berlusconi with the establishment backing and his countless millions, had simply bought the Scudetto off Napoli. All was hearsay, heresy even, but in the immediate aftermath of such a shocking defeat many Neapolitans, still bitter at their loss, believed anything they were told. Wild, weird and wounding, the accusations flew like spears. Only Maradona and Careca appeared to emerge from the debacle with reputations intact. On the rest the jury was out. Both had been undermined by a spurious lack of fight amongst others in blue shirts that simply proved too heavy a burden for even a genius of Maradona's ilk to carry. To make matters worse a civil war broke out inside the club. Fed up with Ottavio Bianchi's authoritarian attitude and well aware of the feelings towards them in the city at that time, an attempt was made to shift the blame of losing the Scudetto onto the head of their coach. Bianchi had finally exploded in all his pent-up fury at those he was convinced betrayed him, For the accused it was the final straw and a number of Napoli players approached Corrado Ferlaino to inform him they were prepared to go on strike if their coach was not dismissed. They had all signed a letter to such effect demanding action be taken. In Naples, such a dramatic event could not stay secret for long and very quickly it became common knowledge. An entire city held it's breath and pondered the inexorable question. The eyes of the tifosi fell on one man. Just where did Diego Maradona's loyalties lie? Although not one of the alleged original perpetrators, it was no surprise that the Argentinian sided with his team-mates by letting it be known to the Napoli hierarchy that he supported their actions. That one of Maradona's closest friends, Salvatore Bagni, was foremost amongst the protestors who wanted

rid of Bianchi, and the small matter that the Captain's own relationship with the coach was at best intolerable, meant there would be a few tears shed by him if he was sacked. An indignant Ferlaino blew a gasket at the sheer arrogance of those he considered still mere employees. As for Diego Maradona, he was told to behave and
to 'Keep your mouth shut' by his President. Napoli's star player was reminded of the recently signed lucrative contract and who paid his wages. Such talk was like a red rag to a raging bull for Diego, as he then in archetypal manner launched a blistering attack on his Neapolitan paymasters by declaring publicly that the President would have to choose between 'Maradona and Bianchi.' A line in the sand was dug. This Southern empire that only a short time before had appeared impregnable now lay in flames. By their own hand the fires had been lit.
Naples was burning.
Diego Maradona's rabid hatred of authority in any manner or form surfaced with a vengeance and he went to war. In a fit of self-righteousness pithy, Maradona flew home to Buenos Aires vowing never to return until Ottavio Bianchi was removed. The Napoli supremo's situation was desperate. Never in all his years at the club's helm had he faced such turmoil. In backing Bianchi, Ferlaino risked far more than just his job. The President's neck was also now very much on the line again. He had experienced before just what the hardcore Napoli support were capable of if pushed. Luckily, for him, the stories at the time which swept Naples regarding a supposed *Fattacio* occurring against AC Milan that was neither his nor more importantly their idol Maradona's doing saw the pressure ease. Others were deemed far worthier of the tifosi's wrath. For in the Forcella and beyond the secret was

already out. Somebody, somewhere had talked and whether it was out of disgust or simple, Neapolitan mischief-making, it had the desired effect for all hell let loose across the Bay. The names of those said to have brought shame to the South were spat out in the city as gossip turned ever increasingly to believable fact. The four accused were goalkeeper Claudio Garella, defender Moreno Ferrario, midfielder Salvatore Bagni and centre-forward Bruno Giordano. In Naples, sunshine or night's shadow they could not hide. All kept an uneasy silence, but privately contact was made with tifosi organisations such as the CUCB to plead their innocence.

Of the four, only Moreno Ferrario's career appeared clear of any misdemeanours. Of the other three? Rumours that Claudio Garella threw matches playing for Lazio were long known, if never proved. Even a twice-former Napoli coach Luis Vinicio, who managed Garella in the late Seventies when both were employed in Rome, spoke out regarding past alleged wrongdoings of the keeper. Salvatore Bagni found himself involved in a mysterious incident during his time at Inter Milan. Five years previous whilst playing away at Genoa, Bagni set up a last-minute winner for Milan striker Graziano Bini in a 3-2 victory. However, instead of being applauded by the rest of their colleagues, both were snubbed and later in the dressing room attacked by team-mates furious with them for ruining an alleged fix. A Milan newspaper got wind of the story and published it, thus prompting the Italian Football Association to order an investigation. However, Inter were found not guilty on the grounds of 'Insufficient evidence'. As for Bruno Giordano, he was caught hands down in the infamous *Totonero* match-fixing scandal of 1980. Italians still to this day shake their heads at the sheer scale of the conspiracy. Giordano was one of thirty-three Serie A footballers who became involved with a corrupt Rome betting syndicate that after being double-crossed by certain players reneging on their side of the deal, took revenge by blowing the lid on the entire sting. On Sunday 23rd March 1980, in stadiums nationwide, the whistle was blown on the largest match-fixing scam the country had ever witnessed. All Italy watched horrified on live television as police officers walked onto football pitches to execute arrests. As the darkest chapter in Italian football history unfolded and sentences were passed, Bruno Giordano was shown little leniency in being handed a two-year ban. Armed with such proof of what these individuals were capable of, was it so surprising that all who loved SSC Napoli doubted their honesty when donning the blue shirt? Many Neapolitans found themselves gripped with feelings of betrayal and paranoia. Everything they had was gone. Then, there was *'Il Lione'*, for with Neapolitans betting billions of Liras on their side retaining the title, a Milan triumph left Camorra families such as the Giulianos' sitting on a mountain of cash once they failed. Maybe, here is where the answer lay? A line from Mario Puzo's epic novel The Godfather claimed, 'Behind every great fortune lay a crime.' It would have been against the very nature of these men to let such a once in a lifetime business proposition pass them by. It was obvious to all that the Camorra possessed the power to bring SSC Napoli to heel. All it required was the will to do so. Yet, despite all the talk, rumours and gossip, there remained no definite proof. Typical Naples.

A promise from the President that he would not be fired saw Ottavio Bianchi feel confident enough to go on the offensive and sack in merciless fashion those whom had called for his head. It also helped when the San Paolo crowd sang Bianchi's name in the penultimate last game of the season. Naples knew who was to blame and it was not him. The coach lived up to his ruthless reputation by ripping apart the title winning team, riddling the club of those he felt guilty of betrayal and of others deemed simply surplus to requirement. But what would they do with Diego Maradona? Bianchi knew only too well that to even hint at selling Napoli's golden boy was quite literally a suicidal ploy. Personal grudges faded into comparison, for in plotting the removal of Maradona, Ferlaino and Bianchi would be attempting to depose a king, who despite many human failings, retained fierce backing amongst his subjects. Maradona held the power in his dancing feet to bring this football club to it's knees. There had to be another way? Corrado Ferlaino roared out in defiance. He gave interviews to all who would listen that he was prepared to hold Maradona to his contract, thus denying him the chance to play elsewhere.

From Argentina, counter-threats hurled back across the ocean. It was all a game, bluff and bluster. Who would break first? Both sides made noises about never backing down, but behind the scenes great efforts were under way to end the stalemate and ensure all emerged from this mess with pride intact. There was also a much darker scenario. Maradona had received death threats from Naples relating to not just him, but his two young daughters. It was only when he received word from the Guillianos' who gave their personal guarantee that no harm would come to Maradona or his children if he was to return that a decision was made. For despite what was aired for public consumption Diego Maradona had no wish just yet to abdicate. As for President Ferlaino, and Bianchi, they knew well that when fully fit and firing on all cylinders, Maradona remained undoubtedly the finest player in the world. It would have been the act of a madman to sell him. As Maradona sat sulking in Argentina, a strife-torn Naples remained unsure of whether their king would ever again see the sun rise over Mount Vesuvio. For the Scudetto, despite it's fleeting beauty, was just a mere dream, one from which all Neapolitans would eventually awake. Maradona was life itself, the air they breathed. Prayers were said for him to see sense but most were resigned to the notion that he had gone forever. They would be wrong for not even on native soil had Maradona experienced the adoration bestowed upon him by his adopted people. For Diego, their love was a craving he simply could not live without. The money was also a consideration as Guillermo Coppola convinced his client that the Italians were good yet for a few dollars more. DIARMA Productions spent like every day was the last. The old adage that the best things in life were free proved untrue in Maradona and Coppola's case as their insatiable, lustful appetite for fast cars, cocaine and beautiful women saw fortunes easily made and lost. Why ruin a good thing? So, a deal was struck. A charade and a simple marriage of convenience. A press conference was called in Naples. Television news crews, photographers and journalists rushed to Napoli's training ground. Word as ever spread swiftly over the bay and hundreds of tifosi descended on Soccavo, laying siege to the complex. In an unreserved showing of loyalty to their king they sang his name loud and proud. As Ferlaino stood ready to address the audience, a familiar chant reached his ears. The Napoli anthem of 'Diego' resonated loudly through the walls. It was, if needed, a final reminder to their President to do the right thing. Or else? As photographers snapped and cameras rolled, a smiling though distinctly nervous President Corrado Ferlaino paused for great dramatic effect before declaring in grandiose fashion. 'People of Naples, Diego Maradona is coming home.'

A last, sad epitaph of this depressing, Neapolitan tragic farce was the sudden, unexpected departure that summer of Napoli stalwart and club legend Giuseppe Bruscolotti. Only twelve months previously in the joyous aftermath of the Scudetto triumph, 'El Pepe' was proclaimed by Diego Maradona as, 'The true Captain of SSC Napoli.' His decision to call time on a fifteen-year career at the San Paolo caused many to shake their heads. Especially, as he was not included in the Bianchi purge. It was claimed by those closest to him that Bruscolotti left a broken man after learning the extent of the treachery within. Whilst adorning the blue shirt, nobody ever fought harder for the Neapolitan cause on the pitch than he, sometimes with a ferociousness verging on fanatical. But when your enemies lurk in dark shadows, undermining a lifetime's work. When they stand beside you in the same colours, only to possess the sole intent of betrayal. Then, it became a battle that even a warrior such as Bruscolotti could never win. The infamous events of Sunday 1st May, caused him a terrible sadness, one to this day he refuses to discuss, preferring instead to keep his own counsel on what he saw and heard. In saying nothing Bruscolotti says everything. Neapolitans did not deserve what befell them on that fateful day. That same summer the miracle of San Gennaro failed to transpire.
Few in Naples were surprised.

Post Script. In 1994, the British newspaper, The Independent discovered fresh new evidence regarding allegations of match fixing relating to the above infamous match between SSC Napoli and AC Milan. It alleged that several Napoli players were on the payroll of the Camorra and in 1988, may have deliberately lost the Italian league championship to help out underground bookmakers in exchange for cocaine and wild parties with call girls. A round of arrests inspired by information supplied by gangsters who agreed to co-operate with the police, suggested corruption at the club went deeper than previously suspected. In Naples, prosecutors summoned virtually all the squad for questioning, along with players' wives and, according to Italian press reports, extracted several confessions. These ranged from local small time Camorra hoods suspected of peddling cocaine and as many as a dozen team members. They also issued a warrant for the arrest of Guillermo Coppola, Maradona's former personal manager who at the time was on the run from police in his native Argentina. Coppola had been recently spotted by a television crew in the Uruguayan resort of Punta del Este, where he had taken refuge following accusations that he ordered the murder of a prominent Buenos Aires night-club owner and suspected drugs trafficker. Back in the 1980s, the prosecutors alleged, Coppola played a role in distributing drugs to the players at Naples. The case against Napoli had been pieced together from hundreds of interviews with petty gangsters, call girls and past and present club officials. There had also been tales of orgies on yachts, wild nights at a discotheque in the hills above Naples and sumptuous dinners with high-ranking members of the Camorra, Judicial sources also questioned the then President Corrado Ferlaino and club manager Ottavio Bianchi. Despite overwhelming evidence, it all just faded away and nothing was ever totally proven. Hardly surprising when considered what was at stake and for who. Today, the accusations remain unproven but only to those who don't want to believe it. On Sunday 1st May 1988, Neapolitans really did die a thousand deaths and a certain few broke their city's heart. Welcome to Naples.

CHAPTER EIGHTEEN

STATE OF GRACE

SSC Napoli 8 Pescara 2. It appeared the demise of Maradona and his Southern hordes had been greatly exaggerated. On Sunday 23rd October 1988, regenerated by an exhilarating lifesaving transfusion of fresh blood, Ottavio Bianchi's revamped Napoli slaughtered a hapless Pescara, who experienced for the second year running a humiliating defeat in Naples. One of the most sensational score lines in Serie A history sent shockwaves through Italian football. Amongst the goal-glut were old heroes joined by the new. Maradona, Carnevale, Careca and Alemao. Many outsiders regarded the tragic loss of the Scudetto to the Milanese as the final nail hammered into the coffin of Napoli's brief illuminating reign as champions. But there was to be many a twist and turn of fortune, both ill and good before they as ever cut their own throats. The epic saga of Diego Maradona's time in Naples was set to hail in even more heady doses of triumph and despair. Yet, during the Neapolitan summer of 1988, few would ever have bet on him being around so long. For the best of times had suddenly become the worst.

It was a sullen, unshaven Diego Maradona who returned from self-inflicted exile in Buenos Aires to Naples. Despite the peace talks all was still not well. There remained unknown to outsiders, rivers of bad blood between himself and the club hierarchy. The Argentinian had always been bigger than SSC Napoli, the problems now stemmed that he acted like it. The prickly small acorns that had niggled him since arriving from Barcelona suddenly became jagged spears. His accommodation in Posilippo, despite being amongst the finest in this city, was now deemed by a foul mood Diego Maradona. 'A fucking cage without bars.' Every time he set foot upon his balcony, tifosi below would scream his name. There was nowhere to hide, privacy was impossible. The adoration suddenly threatened to strangle Maradona. The Naples nights still echoed with the joyful sounds of partying, samba music and laughter. Cocaine and wine flowed freely as ever, but it had become more a necessity to relieve the pain and anger rather than enjoyment. The magic had vanished and he could no longer stay faithful. Amidst great secrecy a fed-up Maradona instructed his manager Coppola to find him another club. Also, the brutal manner in which Ottavio Bianchi dismembered the title-winning side irked Diego. It very swiftly became clear that he had no intention of making up with Bianchi. The animosity between the two proved overwhelming and the utter contempt they now held each other in meant that no matter what deal Coppola and Ferlaino tried to conceive, it became blatantly obvious they could never again work together. A compromise was suggested in which the player would be allowed to train alone, away from the hawk eyes and barking voice of the 'Iron Sergeant'. Hardly a perfect scenario, but one deemed preferable for Neapolitans to Maradona plying his trade elsewhere. Say Milan, or God forbid Turin? The Napoli coach consented only through gritted teeth to such an absurd arrangement. Only in Naples could this madcap charade have been concocted. But when it came to Diego Maradona, normal rules did simply not apply. That he appeared hell-bent on doing all in his considerable power to undermine Bianchi, only fuelled what was an already intolerable situation. For even a hardnosed veteran like he was not immune from the extreme pressure managing a club like Napoli brought. There were those who due to his historic triumph in bringing them a long-awaited Scudetto, still remained wholly loyal to Maradona with a blind faith tottering on fanaticism. The 'Enemies of Maradona' were their enemies. If needed many of these young tifosi would have gladly sided against God or the Devil himself. Bianchi knew he was on borrowed time. Only the momentous achievement in realising every Neapolitans' fantasy had prevented the axe from falling. To take on a king, two weapons are needed in your armoury; the love of the people and a preferable alternative. Ottavio Bianchi had neither and had resigned himself to the only possible outcome. The sack. But Corrado Ferlaino had no intentions of firing Bianchi. After all the riches brought to the table by his beleaguered coach, he believed it a matter of honour to stand by him. The President sought a meeting with Diego Maradona to end this nonsense and ensure peace broke out in Naples. In this city anything untoward that affected his football club never stayed secret long and Ferlaino had quickly become aware of the Argentinian's expressed desire to go elsewhere.

He proposed a deal to suit all.

Call a truce with Ottavio Bianchi, play one more year then and only would he be released from his contract. There would be nothing in writing, a simple promise, a handshake. 'A Neapolitan State of Grace' shall we say. The understanding was clear. Maradona would be free to leave. He reluctantly agreed. It was to prove an olive branch that pricked when you least expected. As the Argentinian in time would discover to his cost.

Diego Maradona's body was if not broken then waning. He had suffered far too many painkilling injections, so many more than were good for him. His battered ankles and leg muscles had become almost permanently inflamed. Before matches he could hardly walk, only to be helped, albeit temporarily, by a club surgeon's jab that allowed him to play. Once a year in an attempt to lift the searing pain, Maradona put himself under the surgeon's knife to have bits of unwanted, leftover cortisone quite literally scraped off his joints with a scalpel. This was the unseen world, the true reality. Away from the adoring crowds, the player both in body and mind was close to collapse. But such was Maradona's ultimate box office appeal, the pressure was on the coaching and medical staff to ensure their Captain took to the field ever week. For how do you replace genius? To take Diego Maradona out of the Napoli line-up was akin to removing a bullet from a gun. That every Sunday in Serie A, he was ruthlessly hacked down, mauled, punched and spat at by opposing defenders under instructions to stop him playing at all cost, meant little to those at his football club who cared only about money, and nothing about the Argentinian's health. He was a commodity, nothing more, to be milked until there was nothing left. God help Maradona if he dared complain. Or even worse, leave before they had bled him dry.
With the President's word that his position was secure, and the bribed, rogue genius of Diego Maradona available for selection, Ottavio Bianchi began the task of rebuilding a team good enough to win back the title. Despite all, Bianchi's enduring love affair with Naples and her football team still thrived with a passion rivalling any young tifosi from the Forcella, Sanita or Spanish Quarter. Though not a

native, the blue blood of this fair city ran fierce through his veins. The coach understood those chosen to wear the Napoli shirt had to possess special qualities. Neapolitans demanded an air of *fantasista* about their footballers. To satisfy this fanatical support Bianchi proved once more a shrewd operator in the transfer market by bringing in players of real flair and imagination to replace those sold during his summer bloodletting. Foremost amongst them was Brazilian international playmaker Rogerio Ricardo de Brito, otherwise known as Alemao. Bought specifically from Athletico Madrid to supply ammunition for fellow countryman Antonio Careca and Diego Maradona, the twenty-seven-year-old Alemao quickly felt at home in the San Paolo. Wonderful dribbling skills and an eye for the killer pass saw this tall, languid midfielder, who played with just the right touch of arrogance and with socks rolled permanently around his ankles, tailor-made to make a huge impression in Naples.

To replace his discarded number one, Claudia Garella, Bianchi turned once more to Verona, signing the experienced goalkeeper Giuliano Giuliani. Also, in a double swoop on Turin, the Torino winger Massimo Crippa and highly rated full-back Giancarlo Corradini were snapped up. From Ascoli came another dogged defender, Antonio Carannante. Finally, the coach wrapped up his spending of President Ferlaino's money by buying Sampdoria's strong-running midfielder Luca Fusi. A new Napoli was born.

Ottavio Bianchi readied himself for yet another helter-skelter ride aboard this out of control Neapolitan rollercoaster. As ever there would be no seatbelt or parachute. Instead, he would ride in the lap of the Gods. San Gennaro willing, Bianchi could only pray he be allowed the chance to reclaim the Scudetto, before freefalling and going the way of so many before him. The early signs were hardly promising for after an opening last gasp win over Atalanta in Naples, the Neapolitans suffered a humiliating 1-0 loss at unfancied Lecce. Then, just when the critics looked set to unsheathe their slings and arrows upon Bianchi's head, a Maradona-inspired Napoli exploded in truly spectacular manner. On 23rd October, all came together when little Pescara went to Naples with some trepidation after being thrashed 6-0 the season before. Never ones to go along with the general consensus that lightning never struck the same place twice, Neapolitans proved otherwise and dished up yet another merciless drubbing for the unfortunate visitors. This time by 8-2! A stunned San Paolo watched in disbelief as Maradona led the line in glorious style with a bewitching, understated, but sensational performance nonetheless. It was a rampant orgy of rip-roaring attacking football. Two goals each for the Captain, Careca, Carnevale and new boy Alemao sliced apart a Pescara team, whose faces with the tally steadily mounting turned equally red as their shirts. The highlight of a 4-0 lead at half-time was a typically wicked, swerving thirty-yard free-kick from Maradona that flew like a rocket into the top right-hand corner to set the stadium ablaze. Further mayhem followed, but again it was Maradona who stole the show when from fully forty yards he cut inside from the touchline, feinted to pass, only then, with the outside of his left foot, clip an outrageous shot that missed only be a whisker. It was a magnificent effort to prove he remained the finest exponent of his trade on the planet. Blessed spontaneity: a bewildering sleight of footwork, miraculous in the making and exemplifying the magic that set apart those touched by angels. The stadium stood as one to applaud.

Neapolitans had grown increasingly weary of the constant bickering between Guillermo Coppola and Corrado Ferlaino as the battle to own Maradona's soul raged. They had no interest in two such mere mortals. Who bothered listening to the carpings of a contemptible Salieri whilst Mozart plied his own heavenly gift? For the countless thousands of Napoli tifosi who basked gloriously in his diminutive shadow, only one thing truly mattered. Maradona was back doing what he did best, making their dreams come true. Despite alleged rumoured longings for pastures new, in the back alleys of Naples, the popularity of Maradona showed little sign of waning, as he remained to Neapolitans a living God.

Three weeks later SSC Napoli topped even their cruel, massacre of Pescara with a ridiculously swashbuckling 5-3 defeat of eternal enemy Juventus in Turin. A home side under new coach, former Napoli and Juve great Dino Zoff, found themselves blitzed in an opening period that saw the Southerners roar deservedly into a 3-0 lead. Two from a rapacious Careca and a third from a rejuvenated back-in-favour Andrea Carnevale (after the selling of Bruno Giordano), saw the massed blue hordes ecstatic. As always in Turin, between these two bitter adversaries, Southern banners and flags lay drenched en masse over the Stadio Comunale terraces. Three minutes into the second half the home side pulled a goal back for what appeared merely scant consolation from midfielder Roberto Galia. Then, shortly after, Juve's sublime Russian international Zavarov shot home past Napoli goalkeeper Giuliani to make it 3-2 and game on. Turin was alight! Sadly, for the 'Old Lady' the fire was swiftly extinguished when Antonio Careca struck once more to complete a memorable hat-trick. Thirteen minutes from the end, Juventus rallied one last time through wide man Luis Di Agostini, only for Napoli defender Allesandro Renica to wrap the points up with a late penalty. 5-3, and yet another superb showing by Ottavio Bianchi's restructured team.

Just when Neapolitans thought life could not get any sweeter, champions AC Milan re-entered their sights. On Sunday 27th November 1988, Arrigo Sacchi's 'Rossoneri' returned to the San Paolo. For the blue tifosi, red and black shirts back in their midst conjured up disturbing reminders of the last time they crossed swords under Southern skies. The controversial events which devastated SSC Napoli on that soiled May Sunday afternoon, still caused sleepless nights in Naples. Many were confused as to what actually took place. Others refused simply to believe for nothing had ever been proven. All was rumour and second-hand gossip. However, Neapolitan belief that the bigger the conspiracy, the easier it was to hide meant serious misgivings remained that something truly rotten had occurred. Deep down they knew. They just knew...
The San Paolo held it's breath as these two great rivals prepared once more to do battle. From the kick-off, both sides appeared pensive, reluctant to open up, preferring instead to rely and wait for their opportunity. For forty minutes it was typical Italian cat and mouse. Then, a lofted pass was hoisted over an unsuspecting Milan rearguard that to their infernal horror was latched onto by an unmarked Diego Maradona. Out came Giovanni Galli to confront the Argentinian, only for Napoli's number ten to leap high and head the ball over the stranded keeper into an open goal from twenty-yards out. The San Paolo

erupted as Maradona raced across the running track to celebrate his fifth strike of the season with the tifosi hordes. Neapolitans rose to salute him. With the referee Luigi Agnolin ready to blow for half-time, a long goal-kick from Giuliani was misjudged for once by the normally impeccable libero Franco Baresi, and Antonio Careca sprinted through to shoot past a despairing Galli, sending the stadium once more into raptures. Shortly after the second half began two became three, when with Milan pressing forward, the home side broke. Sprinting clear into the Rossoneri penalty area, Andrea Carnevale's low shot was half-saved, only for the rebound to fall at the feet of the raiding Napoli full-back Giovanni Francini, who from close range gleefully side footed the ball into the net. A crazed melee ensued behind the goal. Naples had waited long for this moment of redemption, a cleansing of the soul. The Milanese appeared close to collapse: Careca let fly a thunderbolt from thirty-five yards that the overworked Galli somehow managed to tip miraculously over the bar. The visitors were being run ragged. Arrigo Sacchi showed clear his frustration on the bench, angrily waving away a television crew filming his animated features, politely informing them in no uncertain manner to clear off.

Repeatedly, Napoli launched swift, incisive counter-attacks that many times threatened to increase their lead. The San Paolo throbbed with furore and excitement. As he led yet another breakout from a Milan corner, the time came for Diego Maradona to add his own brand of magic to this Naples carnival. Surrounded by red and black shirts, Maradona bewitched them all with an outrageous back-flick to teammate Allessandro Renica that left Baresi, Maldini, Costacurta and Tassotti wondering where the ball had gone? Though Pietro Virdis converted a late penalty to grab his customary goal against Napoli, it was just a consolation for Milan, and twelve minutes from time the unstoppable Careca set the seal on a memorable day for the Neapolitans when he pounced to make it 4-1.

Any other season in Serie A, the Southerners would have been clear favourites to win back their title, but not that year for Milan's other great empire had awoken from it's slumber. The famed blue and black stripes of Internazionale. 'La Grande Inter.' Fuelled by the thunderous, Teutonic heartbeat of twenty-seven-year-old Lothar Matthaus, Inter had begun the campaign in explosive style. Matthaus was lured that same summer along with another established German international, defender Andres Brehme from Bayern Munich. The highly-regarded Inter coach Giovanni Trapattoni had built a powerful team brimming with technical expertise, creativity and experience. Up front 'Azzurri' forward Aldo Serena and the much-travelled Argentinian hitman Ramon Diaz proved a lethal combination. A water-tight rearguard, marshalled superbly by goalkeeper Walter Zenga and defensive stalwart Guiseppe Bergomi, allied with the fire power and lung bursting Lothar Matthaus in midfield, meant they were an awesome proposition for any team in Serie A. As the months rolled on Trapattoni's relentless, all-conquering Inter remained unbeaten, crushing opponents both at the San Siro and beyond in ruthless manner. In order to just hang on to their coat tails, Ottavio Bianchi's side found themselves in the almost impossible situation of having to win every week. Inevitably, the Southerners faltered and when they did Inter slipped that little further out of reach. Though Napoli clung on, desperate to claw them back, their dreams of glory instead turned abroad, to foreign fields and the UEFA Cup. Come New Year, the Neapolitans had advanced to the quarter final stage of that competition to draw, of all teams, Juventus. The sighs of disappointment could be heard loud in both cities. Neither wanted the ignominy of being knocked out by the other, for bragging stakes were just too high. On Wednesday 1st March 1988, the first leg took place in Turin, with Juve gaining a 2-0 advantage to take South. Napoli tifosi were despondent, for their team had not performed in the Stadio Comunale. Two weeks later Naples welcomed 'La Vecchia Signora' with a hospitality befitting the generations of hatred that had existed between them for generations. Juve coach Dino Zoff, who many years before left the Southern capital to take Turin gold, knew his team faced a difficult task, despite the two-goal lead. So, it proved as the Neapolitans ripped into them from the first whistle. An early penalty from Diego Maradona and a second strike from Andrea Carnevale before half-time levelled the tie on aggregate. Only the great pride of the visitors who refused to bow down in the face of this Southern onslaught upon their heads saw them survive till extra-time. Just as a penalty shoot-out loomed large, on 119 minutes a Maradona corner was met by Allessandro Renica who smashed a bullet header past Stefano Tacconi. A nerve shattered San Paolo erupted in sheer unadulterated joy! As the Juventus players lay distraught on the turf, all of Naples wallowed in their despair. A loathing supreme. At the full-time whistle Renica was lifted shoulder-high by his ecstatic team-mates and chaired around the running track to take the acclaim of a delirious crowd. A decent night in the South.

Revenge for Dino Zoff's side came sweet and swift just a fortnight later when they returned to the San Paolo to inflict a devastating 4-2 defeat on the Neapolitans and all but end their Scudetto challenge. On that same Sunday, Inter Milan thrashed Como 4-0 in the San Siro to go six points clear of Napoli. Ottavio Bianchi gave up all hope of catching Inter and turned his concentration fully on the UEFA Cup. For SSC Napoli, a home semi-final against crack West German side Bayern Munich lay in wait. Four days on from the savaging at home by Juventus, Diego Maradona led his team out to face the Bavarians in front of 79,950 screaming blue tifosi in Naples. In an all-red kit, Bayern proved typically tough and resilient German opponents. It was Teutonic efficiency against Neapolitan flair. Played in driving rain, Bayern Munich were in control for the vast majority of the first half, looking by far the better team. A snap shot by Bayern forward Olaf Thon almost handed them the lead, only to be saved superbly by Giuliani. Cruel then, they dropped their guard for a split second and paid the ultimate price. Five minutes before the interval a deft touch from an unusually subdued Maradona let in Andrea Carnevale, who fired home from twelve yards. Bayern continued to impress in the second period as they forced the Neapolitans back with some neat, inventive football. Again, the Germans enjoyed plenty of possession, only for Napoli to strike on the break. From one such move the home side should have doubled their lead when Diego Maradona fed Antonio Careca wide on the left, and his precise pass was met by Carnevale's diving header that thumped ferociously against the post. With all Naples still bemoaning their ill-fortune, Maradona popped up once more to hit a dipping cross into the Bayern penalty area for

Carnevale, whose glancing flick this time soared gloriously into the net. Game over.

Two weeks later, armed with their 2-0 advantage, Bianchi's men travelled to Germany as huge favourites to get through. In the daunting atmosphere of Munich's Olympiastadion, with a passionate Bavarian 65,000 crowd behind them, a fiercely committed Bayern gave all to try and pull back the deficit. Though nowhere near the calibre of past great Munich teams that possessed such world superstars as Beckenbauer, Muller and Rummenigge, the modern class of 89 remained a potent threat on home territory. Sadly, for them, Napoli were just that little better. With Maradona pulling the strings and the lethal Brazilian, Careca, in the form of his life, scoring two goals, the Neapolitans fought out a thrilling 2-2 draw that eased them into the UEFA Cup final.

There they would face yet another German team, VFB Stuttgart. Never had the Neapolitans won anything of note in European competition, For Diego Maradona, winning this tournament presented the perfect opportunity for him to leave Naples, hopefully with the cheers of Napoli tifosi ringing in his ears, wishing him well. Maradona's mind was made up. Make no mistake, win or lose against Stuttgart, he was going. President Corrado Ferlaino's promise that he be allowed to leave meant contact with top French side Olympique Marseilles had taken place. All had gone well, the abdication appeared imminent. Guillermo Coppola had met secretly with Marseilles' controversial chairman Bernard Tapie, who promised to double whatever the player was earning and more. It was the deal of this or any other lifetime.

For nigh on five years Diego Maradona had been centre-stage as the leading actor in a dramatic Neapolitan opera, played out every Sunday in football theatres across Italy. Loved and despised in equal measures, booed, hissed, cheered and adored, villain, demon, hero and saviour. It had all got out of hand. The time had finally come when Maradona just wanted to be human again. He wanted out. Once Upon A Time in Naples. The fairytale was close to being over.

Wednesday 3rd May 1988: UEFA Cup Final. First Leg. Diego Maradona's supposed Neapolitan swansong began in the worst possible manner when after just seventeen minutes in Naples, the Germans took a shock lead through their exciting, long-haired young forward, Maurizio Gaudino. His twenty-five-yard free-kick, hit low, was horribly fumbled by Napoli keeper Giuliani, who watched in abject horror as the ball fell from his grasp and rolled agonisingly over the line. The deafening barrage of noise that had roared like thunder from the 81,000 tifosi on the San Paolo terraces from the first whistle fell silent. As the white shirts of Stuttgart celebrated, Giuliani sat hunched with head in hands. After dominating the early stages with Antonio Careca missing two glorious opportunities, Napoli appeared stung by Gaudino's unexpected, if fortunate, strike. VFB's coach, former Dutch international Arie Haan gesticulated madly on the touchline as he screamed instructions to his team, imploring them to concentrate. Be prepared. For Haan was sufficiently astute to realise that the Neapolitans were about to hit them with everything they had. Inevitably, a siege ensued with a scheming Maradona working overtime, searching for that elusive equaliser. Chances were made only to be woefully wasted. Foremost amongst the guilty was Careca, who appeared for once to have put his boots on the wrong feet.

The second half saw no respite and with the screw turned ever tighter, they finally got a break. On sixty-eight minutes, a scramble in the Stuttgart area ended when a volleyed shot on goal by Diego Maradona was deemed blocked by a German hand and Greek referee Germanakos awarded a penalty. The cheers from San Paolo that swept over the bay were of more relief than joy. Maradona appeared the calmest man in Naples as he stepped forward to beat Stuttgart's keeper Eike Immel with delightful ease and level the tie. Napoli's Captain grabbed the ball out of the net and raced back to the halfway line before replacing it on the centre-spot to re-start the game.

Now they went for the kill.

The visitors' goal led a charmed existence as the ball bounced, whizzed and flew all over, except where Napoli forwards desired it. Close shaves, bad luck and catastrophic finishing, all conspired to drive the Naples clans mad with frustration. German fortune appeared to be holding; then, three minutes from time it finally ran out. Again, it was the wizardry of Maradona saving the day as he dribbled past desperately, lunging, Stuttgart defenders, before crossing from the by-line for Antonio Careca to slot home from eight yards and win the game. It had been close.

Just when all appeared calm and serene in Naples' waters, Diego Maradona surfaced in inimitable style to rock the boat and once more cause an eruption worthy of their volcano. Four days on from the UEFA first leg, Napoli travelled to Bologna minus their esteemed number ten, who claimed to be suffering chronic back pain. Bianchi fumed; genuine or not, he had finally grown exhausted of the Argentinian's every whim and need being pandered to.

Yet, his team-mates and fans still adored him? Could Neapolitans not see, like he, that the myth of Maradona was just that, pure illusion? If this man was truly a King why did he not act like one? Ottavio Bianchi's men lay six points adrift of the all-conquering Inter Milan. With Inter away at Juventus, and the Neapolitans still to play at the San Siro, it became essential they won at Bologna. Without Maradona it was not to be and a disappointing 1-1 score-line proved insufficient as the 'Nerazzurri' also claimed a vital point in Turin. The title was now definitely gone. Bianchi was appalled at Maradona's non-appearance, but by this time had adopted the attitude, 'If he plays he plays.' He knew only too well that Maradona was a law unto himself and interested just in staying fit for the second leg in Germany. The *'Iron Sergeant'* also was set to call time on his historic stay in Naples. Like Maradona, Bianchi hoped Stuttgart would provide him with a fitting farewell. That he never shouted from the rooftops about his passion for the Neapolitan cause did not mean the fire burned any less within.

The rich, dulcet tones of Rai's acclaimed, legendary, television football commentator Bruno Pizzul, welcomed Neapolitans and all of Italy to Germany and the Neckerstadion. By plane, car and train, the tifosi had travelled in their many thousands over the Alps, through Switzerland to follow their team. Across Stuttgart's impressive stadium, huge smatterings of blue lay drenched on the terraces. Even the home dugout was covered in a Napoli flag, put there by mischievous Neapolitans who were enjoying teasing the annoyed Germans from their seats behind. Looking pumped-up and ready for battle, both sides appeared from the tunnel. Many of the Napoli players gazed around in total astonishment at the enormity of support for them around the stadium. The banners were everywhere. *'Blue Tigers', 'CUCB', 'Napoli Platoon', 'Ultra Napoli', 'Sorrento Napoli'* and *'South Boys'* amongst many more.

The fit again Diego Maradona even swapped high fives with tifosi, who using typical Neapolitan ingenuity had managed to infiltrate down onto the running track, posing as cameramen and photographers. Before kick-off, Maradona sought out Napoli's physio, Salvatore Carmando, to plant the ritual kiss on his forehead. It was the manner in which the Argentinian looked worryingly around before he finally glimpsed Carmando that showed just how important this little superstition had become. Not just to both men, but the entire team. Boosted immeasurably by the return from injury of their twenty-three-year-old rising superstar Jurgen Klinsmann, the home side began brightly, brimming with confidence and attacking from the off. With the dashing blond-haired, golden boy of German football adding much needed pace, skill and strength to Stuttgart's forward line, the Napoli defence came under tremendous pressure in the opening stages. The lightning Klinsmann showed a devastating turn of pace down the left flank, only to be sent crashing to earth by full back Giovanni Francini, who appeared in no mood to be chasing shadows. The fight for midfield superiority proved no place for the faint hearted, as tackles and challenges flew high and dangerous. Stuttgart's tall, gangling, Yugoslav defender Srecko Katanec gave the impression of having eaten raw red meat before kick-off as he attempted to start fights with all and any in a blue shirt. On the touchline, home coach Arie Haan raged whenever a decision went against his team. He claimed the

Neapolitans were overly-theatrical in falling to the floor at every opportunity. Each time Diego Maradona received the ball, Haan's face turned a worrying purple, barking out instructions for the Argentinian maestro to be closed down. That Maradona was picked out for special treatment by the Germans surprised nobody, for they feared him greatly knowing that given the slightest inch, he could destroy them.

The Neapolitans were quick to fight fire with fire and retribution was swift when required. On nineteen minutes Maradona was scythed down brutally in the centre-circle by the fired up Katanec, only for the referee to wave play on when Alemao came away with possession. The Brazilian broke forward to play a one-two with his countryman Careca, before racing into the penalty box and stabbing the ball past keeper Immel into the net. With arms outstretched Alemao sped across the running track to salute the fanatical hordes of San Gennaro. The sheer extent of Napoli's support suddenly became apparent as half the Neckerstadion erupted in a wild sea of blue/white flags. Only one man of Neapolitan persuasion appeared unmoved by it all. Ottavio Bianchi sat motionless as around him bedlam raged in the Napoli dugout.

With the overall score now 3-1, the Germans threw caution to the wind and in typical fashion came roaring back. From a corner, Klinsmann levelled with a brave header through a mass of bodies to make it 1-1. On scoring he turned to the crowd, imploring them to make more noise and out-sing their Neapolitan visitors, who momentarily had fallen silent. For what remained of the opening period it was Stuttgart who had the edge, as Jurgen Klinsmann and Maurizio Gaudino left the Napoli defence repeatedly stretched with their fearsome pace and intelligent link play.

So, it was a relief that with only moments left on the clock before the break, the Neapolitans broke out to earn some respite with a corner up the other end. Maradona's initial effort was easily cleared, only to bounce high and rebound towards him. This time the Argentinian headed back into the six-yard box where waiting to pounce was the unlikely figure of defender Ciro Ferrara. Arriving unmarked, the Neapolitan lashed home with great delight a right foot volley past Eike Immel that flashed into the net. Born and raised in Naples, it was a moment that meant everything to Ciro Ferrara. As a teenager, he proudly captained Napoli's youth team to a national championship. The man who presented him that trophy was none other than Diego Maradona. Now, he had given him yet another precious memory to treasure, one never to forget. The look on Ferrara's face as he ran back to retake up his defensive position was one of total incredulity. Back in Naples the wine tasted increasingly sweet, and many a glass was raised to 'Our Ciro!'

The second half began with the Germans still pressing relentlessly forward, but Napoli were holding, and on sixty minutes, the UEFA Cup was finally won. A long clearance was flicked on by Antonio Careca to Diego Maradona, who, after bewitching two Stuttgart defenders, played a beautifully measured pass back to the Brazilian who raced to support him. Sprinting at great pace Careca took the ball in his stride before finishing immaculately with a masterful shot into Immel's bottom left-hand corner. Raiuno's commentator, the wonderful Bruno Pizzul, roared in delight. 'Gol Di Napoli! Grandissimo!'

With half an hour left to play, jubilant tifosi began their victory celebrations around the stadium. Smoke bombs engulfed the terraces. Rockets shrieked high into the

Stuttgart heavens, lighting up the skies. Amidst amazing scenes of Neapolitan revelry, the home side refused point blank to believe all was lost and continued to attack. The forlorn features of coach Arie Haan spoke volumes. Looking resigned to the inevitable, Haan had retreated to the dugout, his earlier fire as he blazed on the touchline apparently snuffed out. A slight glimmer of hope appeared for the Germans when Gaudino's twenty-five-yard shot brushed off Fernando Di Napoli to beat Giuliani, making it 3-2, though still 5-3 on aggregate. Scant consolation. As the dying moments ebbed away, large swathes of German police mounted a human shield around the stadium's running track to prevent any excitable tifosi reaching the pitch. For a Neapolitan fervour/madness had taken hold in the Neckerstadion. A minute into injury-time a horrendous back pass by Di Napoli was intercepted and headed powerfully past a helpless Giuliani by Schaler, making it 3-3. Insignificant, but soothing to German egos nonetheless.

Finally, ending Stuttgart's misery, Spanish referee Armenio called time and a carnival began in Southern Germany. Miracles were common in Naples, but Ottavio Bianchi breaking into a half smile at the full-time whistle was deemed by many of Neapolitan persuasion, reason itself to party. However, the coach quickly resorted to type when he disappeared down the tunnel, leaving his players to bask in the glory. On the pitch Diego Maradona found himself alone, cut off by an incessant barrage of microphones and cameras thrust within inches of his face. Pushed, shoved and manhandled, it became a dangerous farce as he struggled to retain his footing amidst such relentless attention. It was only the intervention of Napoli goalkeeper Giuliano Giuliani, grabbing Maradona away from the paparazzi circus, that allowed him to rejoin adoring team-mates. Immediately, the Captain was lifted high, for they like all Napoli tifosi worshipped the air he breathed and the ground Maradona walked on. Still, the Stuttgart flags waved defiantly to the very end and many of the locals stayed behind long after the final whistle to salute their brave side. A host of white shirts, Klinsmann and Gaudino foremost amongst them remained slumped on the turf, devastated in defeat. Showing great sportsmanship, home supporters applauded the all-singing/dancing Neapolitans clans rejoicing in their midst. Hardly familiar to being shown such respect, the tifosi responded in equally good fashion, a novelty indeed for the visitors. At 22.07, set against a deathly black sky, the giant electronic scoreboard in the Neckerstadion flashed up a huge neon-blue Napoli badge and to the victors went the spoils.

The time came for the trophy to be handed over. Fighting through a frenzied mass of hollering reporters, cameramen and photographers, all desperate for a sound bite, Diego Maradona finally made his way to the presentation table. Wearing a beaming, wide grin, he suddenly found himself confronted by Corrado Ferlaino, who stepped forward from the crowds to whisper into the player's ear, 'We are going to see the contract out, aren't we Diego?'

For just a mere second the Argentinian appeared shocked by what he had heard but recovered instantly. With a wry smile on his face the President moved back into the shadows, leaving the way clear for his Captain to be handed the trophy. In the blinding glare of a thousand flashlights, Maradona raised the UEFA Cup high. A city and it's people unashamedly wept tears of joy. As for their King? The realisation that Ferlaino had double-crossed him hit home like a bullet crashing into his chest. So much for the promise of just one more season. A State of Grace? He vowed to make his President pay for such treachery. Fuming at this betrayal, Maradona plotted revenge. But even though considering himself wise to the ways of his adopted city, little could he have known the terrifying powers set to be unleashed upon his head. For in Naples, even kings did as ordered. No exceptions. Their strings were tugged and they would dance to whatever tune was required. Maradona's misguided/dangerous sense of self-delusion meant he walked unsuspectingly into a viper's nest. To beat the world with a ball at your feet was one thing. Taking on the Neapolitans in their own backyard, armed with nothing but wounded pride was akin to an act of madness. For it was no longer just a game. No rules, no referees and no mercy.

Ultimately, no contest.

CHAPTER NINETEEN

ENCORE

Naples awaited with trepidation the coming storm. The abdication of their king appeared imminent, for Diego Maradona's crown of thorns had pricked so deep the wounds were now visible for all to see. As he sought solace far across the ocean on another continent, it became clear there was to be no happy ending. Just maybe, God willing, before the tragic drop into the abyss they would be allowed a final great triumph. Prayers were said for the salvation of Maradona's footballing soul to help cast away the demons and bring the Scudetto home. Together, one last time with him back to lead them, Neapolitans prepared to rage against the light. Encore.

With the sole aim to engineer a one-way ticket out of Naples and into the welcoming embrace of Marseille chairman Bernard Tapie's, idyllic, Southern, French paradise, Diego Maradona stumbled unknowingly into a Neapolitan minefield. In the closing weeks of the season he withdrew without warning from a game at Ascoli, claiming to be suffering from a stomach upset. Cynics however believed it was all a charade, with Maradona's non-appearance a less than subtle show of support for Ascoli and former Napoli folk hero Bruno Giordano. Following the infamous events of 1st May 1988, and the controversial defeat by AC Milan at the San Paolo, Giordano was tossed like garbage into the dustbin by Ottavio Bianchi's ruthless purge of alleged offenders.

The Rome-born player's past crimes saw him cast amongst the chief villains of this particular, sordid Neapolitan drama. Stones were hurled in Giordano's direction with no real shred of evidence, hard or otherwise. His tainted history meant mud stuck. Blinded by a deep sense of injustice, Diego Maradona's refusal to play against an old friend surprised none who knew something of his true character, for he showed towards those he considered compadres a remarkable loyalty. That Bruno Giordano scored in a 2-0 win to play an integral role in beating the Southerners helped only to fuel a powder keg situation. Rumours were already rife that Diego Maradona wanted out of Naples. A deep sadness, coloured by a sense of betrayal saw for the first-time doubts emerge in the Forcella, and beyond by those whom had loved Maradona unconditionally. An incessant desire and passion for their football club meant the tifosi had been taken for fools before. Maybe even 'El Diego' was just cleverer in hiding his true face? Standing by a former-team-mate was to be admired, betraying your adopted people with a self-centred arrogance was not. Diego Maradona's rabid desire to be rid of Neapolitan shackles could no longer be hidden, and a week later it became clear for everyone to see when all hell broke loose in Naples.

After just twenty minutes of a home match versus Pisa, and to the rising fury of a 70,000 crowd, the Argentinian signalled to the Napoli bench demanding to be substituted. Limping theatrically, Maradona's exaggerated gestures pointed to a supposed leg strain. As he made his way off the field, apparently in severe pain, the San Paolo made it's true feelings known. This incident proved the final straw for a fraught tifosi, who vented their frustration at his girlfriend Claudia and business manager Guillermo

Coppola, both watching on stone-faced in the Presidential Box. As plastic bottles and coins were hurled in their direction, Maradona stared daggers from the touchline. His own ears rang with the deafening crescendo of boos and catcalls raining down upon him. 'The fans who boo me are pure cretins,' he claimed post-match. Memories of the Scudetto and the recent triumph in Stuttgart were swiftly forgotten. It is said that the greatest of love affairs end only through death or betrayal. This was to be no exception. Hails of displeasure poured out from all corners of this crumbling pit of a concrete bowl, though still a consecrated ground for Neapolitans. The legendary terraces of the Curva Sud that hosted the blue/white hordes of the CUCB howled in derision as SSC Napoli, without their inspirational Captain slumped miserably to a 0-0 draw against the already relegated Pisa. Reeling from this monstrous display of public humiliation, an indignant Diego Maradona, blazing with anger, lashed out at the detractors. Furious at the manner in which Napoli tifosi had turned violently on his girlfriend and manager, he launched an almighty tirade against his tormentors. 'They insult my family honour and can go to hell. I am ready and prepared to leave Naples right here and now.' Diego Maradona had begun setting about burning all his bridges. He continued to wage war against all. Maradona's television programme, broadcast live every Thursday evening on local station Channel 21, was used solely as a platform for the player to fire broadsides at Corrado Ferlaino and other foes, mainly journalists who had the temerity to question his actions. A show that was once a simple half-hour love-fest between Maradona and Napoli tifosi became nothing more than a weekly tirade of vitriol and venom. Such increasingly manic behaviour and a refusal to accept the merest criticism hinted heavily of someone out of control.

So, when Maradona flew home to Buenos Aires for the summer threatening never to return, few in Naples were hardly surprised as they had heard it all before. The difference now that feelings toward him had split so profoundly there were many Neapolitans couldn't care less. A newspaper poll in the Forcella, undertaken by Il Mattino, showed that strength of feeling towards the Argentinian was fifty/fifty. Whilst there were those who swore a blood vendetta against Maradona, others claimed they were willing to travel to Argentina and beg their hero to return. In order to try and defuse the situation, safe back on home soil and wholly unaware of just how volatile emotions in Naples had become regarding Diego Maradona's absence, a statement issued on the player's behalf proved a disastrous piece of public relations. That he complained about the treatment meted out to Claudia and Coppola in the match against Pisa was sufficient enough to alienate him further, but what Maradona went on to further claim shocked even the most hardened of tifosi.

'I will not report back to training for Napoli because I am convinced there is a plot against me, my wife, daughters, brothers and parents which places us in real danger. As a man and father, I bear the responsibility of defending the greatest treasure I possess. My family.'

He went on to rage about 'Threatening phone calls' and the mysterious vandalising of a Mercedes car. Most seriously, a break-in at his sister's apartment in which nothing was stolen, but certain objects were simply tampered with. Furniture was re-arranged. At this last allegation Neapolitans gasped, for it was well known in

Naples that the Camorra favoured such action as a warning to those said to have displeased them, a last chance before it got bloody. Without actually saying the player was seen to be accusing the mobsters of intimidation in their efforts to stop him going to Marseille. It was unheard of and simply not done. The Napoli police were fully aware of Maradona's close relationship with the Giuliano's but showed little interest in such allegations. For them the player was reaping what he sowed. Without a shred of proof, they claimed it would be a waste of time investigating. Play with fire and you risked getting burnt by the flames. Dropping hints like grenades that the Naples underworld had threatened his family made many think Maradona bore some kind of death wish as that could be the only possible, logical explanation for such madness. Neapolitans shook their heads. Five years under the volcano and still he did not understand the way of things? It was a most obvious slap in the face for the Giuliano clan, and the dark Princes of Forcella could ill afford to let such a blatant show of disrespect go unpunished. There would be an answer but it was not be with a bomb, knife or gun. The Giulianos, if challenged, could unleash a small army of foot soldiers numbering 500 from their territory by simply snapping their fingers. A more ruthless band of cutthroats it would have been difficult to find. Loyal to the point of fanatical, all orders were carried out with religious zeal. This was the frightening power of Maradona's true paymasters. Luckily, for the Argentinian, it would instead be a subtler strategy used to teach him a lesson in manners. For Maradona, an Irreversible Sunrise was set to break and all but destroy him. Less than a week after the catastrophically-worded statement was released to the world's press, a photograph accompanied with a large piece appeared on the front cover of Il Mattino by columnist Giuseppe Calise. It showed Diego Maradona alongside two of the Giulianos brothers-toasting champagne with a huge grin ensconced upon his face. Taken years before at a party laid on in the player's honour, it was one of countless snapped on many family occasions when he was present. Maradona appeared totally relaxed in the photo enjoying the legendary hospitality of the Camorra and all that entailed with the notorious brothers Carmine and Rafaele stood each side of him. It was blatantly obvious to all who understood how the Naples underworld operated that the picture was only printed with the consent of the gangsters. Il Mattino may well have had access to such material for years but would never have been able to publish for fear of dreadful retribution by the Camorra. They had let it be known in typically conspiratorial manner that Maradona was a friend. A word that in Naples carried sinister undertones. This opening, enduring glimpse of the Argentinian at play with his mad, bad, Neapolitan amigos was carefully calculated to cause most damage to the player's reputation. The caption alongside read as follows. *'It is absurd to think that anyone would want to challenge the Camorra by threatening it's idol.'* The meaning was clear, Diego was one of them. It was crazy to suggest they would hurt him, and he they. With one slight nudge tremendous pressure was placed on Maradona, for it had become clear that a drip-drip policy was about to be put into use by the Giulianos in order to make him see sense and return to Naples. There would be if required infinitely much worse to follow. As all eyes and ears turned towards Argentina the silence was deafening, for Maradona had disappeared off the map.

To escape the rising furore his actions had provoked Diego fled Buenos Aires in secret with his father and travelled 400 miles by car up the Rio Parano to Diego Senior's birthplace. The little fishing village of Esquina. There, he was guaranteed anonymity and time to think. Away from the prying lens of the paparazzi both men spent hours relaxing on the river banks reminiscing about his childhood days, when life was so much simpler. It was left to Guillermo Coppola to stave off the arrows hurtling over the ocean towards them. Realising just how bad the situation had become and how that infernal statement had blown up in their face, he contacted Napoli's President Ferlaino and expressed a wish for peace talks. For once, Corrado Ferlaino rejoiced at holding the upper hand over this cocky Argentinian who had caused him so much heartache. Wallowing in Coppola's discomfort, the President enjoyed making him sweat, before agreeing to a meeting. He ordered to Buenos Aires one of his most trusted aids, Luciano Moggi. A man in his middle forties, with lizard features and skilled in the art of Neapolitan street politics, he was more than a match for the slick, cunning, if for once, clearly on the back foot, Guillermo Coppola.

The formidable Moggi flew immediately to Argentina where he wasted little time seeking out Coppola. He informed him in no uncertain terms that Napoli still held Maradona's signature and were not prepared to waive it for any amount of money. Not standing on ceremony, Moggi also let it be known that on returning to Naples, the player would have to train, travel and rest with his team-mates. No more special privileges such as arriving at away games by private plane, which had so infuriated club officials in

the past. As Coppola tried in vain to make a point and fight his corner, Moggi's revelation that Napoli intended to begin proceedings on a civil lawsuit against Diego Maradona for breach of contract if he did not tow the line in the future completely floored Coppola, for the Neapolitans were assuming there was to be one? Was it simply arrogance by the Neapolitan or were there other forces at work in the shadows pulling his strings? Hardly took a genius to work it out. A rare day indeed when Guillermo Coppola was stuck for words, but the time Luciano Moggi went to Buenos Aires, it duly occurred. He detected in his voice and mannerisms an utter confidence that could only stem from the fact Moggi was speaking not just on President Ferlaino's behalf, but for others of more dubious distinction. Three things had suddenly become crystal clear.
1: Napoli's tough stance could only have been taken with the backing of the Camorra.
2: Financially, they were shot without Neapolitan dollars.
3: Whether he liked it or not, Diego Maradona was Naples-bound. They were going back.
It was with little enthusiasm that Coppola journeyed to Esquina to inform his young master of their predicament. As expected, Maradona exploded with rage on being told. It appeared he was forever destined to be a prisoner of a city that with equal measures shackled him in chains of love and hate. After much soul-searching, tears, tantrums and threats of retirement, he accepted the wise counselling of his father and reluctantly gave up. This was the only man alive capable of making Diego Maradona see sense. A striking resemblance to his boy in looks, if not temperament was uncanny. Diego Senior's reasoning was that his son desperately needed to play football, for it was

the water that gave him life. The Neapolitans had made it clear they would rather see Maradona rot in the wilderness than released him from a five-year contract. It might as well have been written in blood, such was Napoli's determination to win out. Also, there was his problem in fighting off the pounds. Since his early teenage years Diego had been pumped full of cortisone, steroids, painkillers and all manner of injections to ensure he kept playing. These possessed crippling long-term side effects and as time rolled on they were seriously taking a toll. None more than a worrying capacity to pile on weight, for without a strict training regime, his physical condition tended to see him blow up alarmingly. Diego's life was at this time hardly that of a world class athlete. An unhealthy tendency to gorge wildly on junk food, whilst embarking on alcoholic marathons, interrupted only by cocaine binges had unsurprisingly caused a dramatic effect in his appearance. To cover up he grew a beard to hide the double chin and took to wearing baggy clothes in an effort to disguise the huge excess fat gained around the midriff. When pictures of him looking dreadfully out of shape appeared on Italian television, Neapolitans looked on in disbelief. Despite great disillusionment with their Captain, Naples heaved a heavy sigh. They looked close in their king's eyes and saw nothing. The spark had gone out. This wasn't right. Just who was the impostor on their screens? Finally, his father's selling point to Diego Junior was the fact that a World Cup loomed large on the horizon and had to be defended in of all places, Italy. That his country so wholly depended on him was all the immensely patriotic Maradona needed to hear. Playing in hostile cities such as Milan, Turin and God forbid, maybe even Naples, in Argentina's colours was an opportunity worth eating a little humble pie for. However, Diego would make the Neapolitans wait a little more before finally heading back.

Playing his foolish games, he had yet to arrive from Argentina when the Napoli team returned for pre-season training in August, where a new face was there to greet them. As expected Ottavio Bianchi vacated his post to take a well-earned sabbatical, safe in the knowledge he would be forever immortalised as the man who led them to their first ever Scudetto. Admired and respected, sadly never truly loved by Napoli tifosi who struggled in warming to Bianchi's dour persona. History would prove a more astute judge of Ottavio Bianchi's achievements. In time Neapolitans would come to regret treating their greatest ever coach with such little love. To replace him, Corrado Ferlaino swooped for Albertino Bigon. The forty-two-year-old Bigon had enjoyed a wonderful playing career at AC Milan where he made his name as an attacking midfielder of some style and repute. Once retired, he took up coaching with equal panache and won promotion with little-fancied Cesena into the top flight, keeping them there against all odds for two seasons. In the cut-throat world of Italian football, he learned good and fast, so much that the Neapolitans took note and came calling. It was an opportunity the ambitious Bigon could not refuse. With his dashing good looks, confident manner and a remarkable resemblance to a youthful Charlton Heston, Albertino Bigon cut an impressive figure when introduced at one of Napoli's legendary press conferences/riots. The expert handling of the baying press pack as he fended off questions regarding a certain Argentinian in a calm, polite but always articulate fashion was a performance that delighted his President, for it confirmed to Corrado

Ferlaino he had chosen well. SSC Napoli was in safe hands with this man. The new coach was wise enough to realise that despite their present spat, Diego Maradona remained a saint on Earth to the majority of Neapolitans, a Prodigal Son who would be instantly forgiven if he showed the slightest hint of remorse or more importantly, a return to form on the pitch. It would have been foolish to rule out reconciliation, but Bigon was also a realist. Maradona's debauched lifestyle and unfortunate habits meant that he was close to becoming a spent force, verging on meltdown. Already, the physical aspects of his game that at one time made him unplayable had gone. The quick brain and breathtaking skills remained, but the body had become an unwilling vehicle to carry out the required tasks. A great player was still there, but now the effort needed would have to be tenfold anything he had ever produced before. With good grace, Albertino Bigon left the door open for him to return. Whether Maradona could be bothered to walk through it was doubtful.

On September 1st 1989, Diego Maradona and his eternal entourage of loved ones and bloodsucking leeches had boarded a plane to carry them back to Naples, when the player once more blew a fuse on learning that Guillermo Coppola was refused permission to sit with him in first class due to lack of space. Taking this as a personal insult, he stormed back off. This happened time and again as the player, with his pride pricked, seemed hell-bent on making the Neapolitans and all around him sweat by acting like a petulant child. Another incident, he did a little dance on boarding for the world media, only to instantly walk off again as the games continued. Over thirty provisional bookings were made, only then to be cancelled as

Maradona refused at the last to travel. Finally, on the 6th September, amidst a mass human barrage of paparazzi, he took flight back to Italy. Diego Maradona's ill perceived notion that he would be welcomed back onto Neapolitan soil with open arms was horribly misjudged. Determined to show all he had won the battle of wills with his least favourite, surly Argentinian, President Ferlaino organised a press conference at the Soccavo training centre in which only an invited audience of journalists sympathetic to himself were present. It was in all but name a victory parade. 'Maradona is the greatest player in the world,' he exclaimed loudly. 'But precisely because of this he has greater duties than others. A fine of $85,000 has been imposed and now he must get in shape and stop skipping training. No more.' This was later reduced to $24,000. The scathing, public criticism by the Napoli supremo left all Naples waiting for Diego's reply. Maradona's ego was such, it was felt impossible for him not to lash back. Instead, in typically mischievous fashion he issued a statement that from now on a $10,000 fee would be charged for all interviews, cash to be paid up front. Beaten but unbowed, they had still to truly break him. Such arrogance helped only to infuriate the press who prepared to wreak revenge and with the Camorra clans withdrawing their protective shield, Maradona was stalked day and night, his every move snapped by a prying lens and blazed across the front pages.

Based on the Napoli Police recording of the interview:
71 shots: Shortly after returning from Argentina, on 28th September 1989, Diego Maradona, accompanied by his Neapolitan lawyer Vincenzo Siniscalchi, entered the old courts of Castel Capuano. The Naples hall of Justice.

Maradona had been summoned by the famed public prosecutor Federico Cafiero de Raho, who was swift to inform the footballer that he was neither under investigation, nor accused of anything. It was simply for a chat to clear up a few misunderstandings regarding him. These stemmed from just a few days previous when 71 photographs in all of the Napoli Captain had been found in a draw during a raid on the Guiliano family home at Vico Delle Pace. They appeared to show him as their guest on many occasions. The shots were contained in a report by the head of criminalpol Campania, Matteo Cinque. A law enforcement legend in this part of the world. De Raho explained to Maradona that Cinque was concerned that he found it strange to find the presence of Maradona with the brothers. Especially regarding how they made their money. That it was known to all including he surely that the Giuliano's ran the *Totonero,* and someone like Diego in his position could be easily prejudiced regarding recent events in Naples with SSC Napoli. It was dangerous for himself to be seen fraternising with them. Even though Maradona had done nothing wrong, guilt by association in this city with so many still hurting from the Milan debacle could destroy his reputation. De Raha passed the shots over and Diego flicked through them saying nothing. Wary, where was this going? What else did they have, his eyes shooting across nervously to meet Sinciscalchi. Was this all just to shake him up?

On the field Maradona was scared of nothing or no one. His courage equally admirable as the skills on the ball, but this? All after what had just occurred, could it be yet another warning? Facing de Raho, he appeared a scared and uncertain young man and the prosecutor was well aware of this.

'Senor Maradona, in a statement recently you announced about wanting to remain in Argentina, because you were scared of Camorristi threats What kind of intimidations?' Diego knows he has to be careful how answering. 'Judge, that statement I released was because the press said incredible things about my failure to return which just wasn't true. I wanted to say something else. Not to the Camorra, but the fans. I wanted to emphasize my fear for the safety of my family and appeal to Naples society to take appropriate measures to protect them.'

De Raho doesn't seem impressed and the Argentinian starts to worry. More questions are forthcoming and Maradona clearly uneasy decides enough and stands to leave. As he heads off Siniscalchi grabs his arm. 'Diego, you have nothing to hide. Please, sit back down. Let the man ask his questions then we can go home.' Maradona does so and a smiling de Raho continues. Still Diego does not convince and is accused of contradicting himself.

'The delay in returning to Naples?' He repeats, now losing patience. 'The Camorra had nothing to do with it.'

'Tell me about the photos?' pushes de Raho

Maradona again looks across to his trusted lawyer who nods back to him.

'Yes, I know Carmine. I vaguely remember meeting him that first day. It was after training and my friend Gennaro Montuori, our head of the Curva B took me to a fan club in the Forcella. There, I stopped to talk to some of them and was invited to dinner by a guy.'

De Raho shows him a photo of a man in a red jumper smiling alongside Diego.

That's him,' replies Maradona. 'Carmine.'

'Was this at Vico Pace?' asks de Raho, who hands over to Diego the infamous shot of him alongside the brothers in the oyster shaped bath.

'Yes,' he replies. 'I was taken there that evening. Carmine introduced me to his brothers. Nice guys.'

'Have you seen Carmine Guiliano recently?'

'Six months ago at the Rosolino restaurant. I was there for a wedding, again invited by Montuori. But I get invited by fans to various occasions all the time because of my fame. They give me prizes, plaques and gifts for going. That night I had no idea who was getting married. Just so happened that Carmine was there also. Naples is a small city for people like me Senor de Raho. Sometimes you can't help bumping into people whether they be angels or devils. I am Maradona, everybody wants to kiss my hand.'

De Raho studies him closely and blood out of a stone comes to mind. He realises there is little point carrying on.

'Thank you for your help today Senor Maradona. We'll be in touch if I need to speak to you again. Good luck for the season. Forza Napoli yes?' De Raho smiles and holds up the photographs.

'We shall keep hold of these for safe keeping.'

The two men stand and shake hands and then a clearly angry, stone-faced Diego leaves with Siniscalchi alongside him.

This fucking city...

Napoli's campaign was underway and an opening 1-0 win away to Ascoli and at home to Udinese saw them top the table. Albertino Bigon had proved a shrewd judge in the transfer market. Lacking the funds previous managers had enjoyed, Bigon showed a good eye for bargains. From Juventus, the experienced midfielder Massimo Mauro and the powerful, robust Lecce defender Marco Baroni arrived to bolster the squad. Whilst both were good solid Serie A professional players and proved fine additions, neither set the Napoli tifosi hearts beating. The turmoil felt over Diego Maradona remained to cast dark shadows over Naples. Hope sprang from a most unlikely source.

Deep in the murky, hidden depths of lowly Serie C, a young man by the name of Gianfranco Zola plied his remarkable trade to small, but still wonderfully receptive audiences. It was almost if his talents were such that those lucky enough to view it every week made a deal not to inform strangers of this genius in their midst. The vast gulf in both talent and finances between the backwaters of the Italian Third Division and the millionaire, world-class footballers of Italy's upper echelon meant Serie A may as well have existed on the moon. This this kid who still played with great passion for his hometown club Torres, in Sardinia, was that rare exception, a precious gem in a sea awash with mediocrity. With club scouts from the mainland rarely visiting the island, the twenty-two-year old Zola's world class potential remained criminally unexploited at the top level. Only through the kind act of a Torres director, Nello Barbanera, who personally contacted Napoli pleading with them to come view their boy, was he given a chance. After listening to Barbanera lauding huge praise on the player, Luciano Moggi travelled to Sardinia to see for himself what all the fuss was about. After witnessing Zola in action Moggi was blown away and wasted little time signing him up. On return Luciano Moggi said to his President, 'I can assure you we have discovered another Maradona.' It was said Ferlaino did not know whether to laugh or cry.

The happy-go-lucky Sardinian's small, stocky build, deft sleight of foot, strength and devastating forward play demanded comparison to a young Diego. Such talk at one time would have been construed in Naples as heresy. Not anymore. He would not remain secret for long. Deputising for Maradona, Zola made his Serie A debut in the San Paolo against Udinese and impressed from the off with a wonderful all-round display, including a wickedly-hit free-kick that smashed into the crossbar. The little man enchanted the Napoli faithful who instantly christened him 'Zoladona'.

Maradona himself took Zola under his wing and it was something he has never forgotten. 'Diego always used to keep the No10 shirt for himself. However, once we played an Italian Cup game in Pisa, and so I went to take the No9 shirt, but Maradona brought the No10 shirt over to me. He told me that he wanted to wear the No9 to pay homage to his friend Careca, saying he wanted to play once with that number, but I later found out that he gave it to me for the experience. I was very flattered. That was a great gesture. It gave me a lot of confidence.' More of this story later.

Diego Maradona had come to understand that only on the pitch could he win back Naples' heart and once more earn the right to walk between Neapolitan raindrops. It was time to get back to what Maradona did best, playing football like no other. His Trojan-like efforts to regain match fitness saw the new allenatore warn to him enormously, so much that with Napoli defending an unbeaten four-match opening sequence and sharing top spot with Juventus, Bigon named the Argentinian as substitute for an upcoming home game against Fiorentina. The coach was prepared to wipe the slate clean and start afresh. Looking like a sea pirate with his dazzling, gold earring, long hair and bushy beard, Maradona strode across the turf to take up a place on the bench. A first faultering step on the road to redemption.

The reaction to him from home tifosi was warm, if not wholly overwhelming. Support rang out from the Naples tribes of Carmando Montuori's CUCB. High in the heavens, the second section of Curva Sud, a huge banner was unravelled over the advertising boards. *'Diego, El Emperadur Del Mundo.'* (*'Diego Emperor of the World'*). Thousands of Maradona's foot-soldiers, drunk on blind faith and cheap Neapolitan wine paid homage. In their eyes he could still do no wrong. There did remain those in the 80,000 crowd still to be convinced of Maradona's loyalty to the cause. For them it would take an act of forgiveness rare in these parts to accept him back into the fold. A rekindling of Naples' most passionate, enduring love affair had been made infinitely more difficult because of hurtful and damning claims by both sides. Accusations that cut deep. Legendary stubborn Neapolitan pride meant something extraordinary was required to help change minds.

In a disastrous first half against Fiorentina, Napoli were given a footballing master class by a young man already being hailed as heir apparent to Maradona's world crown, Florence's own golden boy Roberto Baggio. A two-goal lead was handed the visitors by the opposing number ten, who though viewed by Napoli tifosi as a dandy boy because of his trademark ponytail, secretly held their grudging admiration. A respect tinged with jealousy for Baggio's wondrous sorcery on the ball, this maker of dreams. For they too were once blessed with one of similar ilk who produced Neapolitan miracles.

The man in question was relegated to watching on animated from the sidelines, roaring encouragement to his team-mates, showing a passion sadly bereft in their performance. Roberto Baggio's first goal caused gasps of admiration from all corners of the stadium as he dropped a shoulder, jinxed, dummied and left the entire Napoli defence for dead, before rounding the keeper Guiliani to slot home with ridiculous ease. Across the San Paolo, a smattering of applause was heard as the most hardened of blue tifosi saluted this moment of wizardry. His second produced only cries of derision from the terraces as Baggio's darting run was stopped at the last by the lunging tackle of Ciro Ferrera to concede a penalty. To a crescendo of boos, he got up, dusted himself down, before calmly scoring to hand Fiorentina a 2-0 half-time lead. Baggio had been nothing short of sensational. He had shown all the hype over him being Italy great hope for the forthcoming World Cup Finals on Italian soil held real substance. Roberto Baggio was in the process of single-handedly taking Napoli apart on their own patch. It appeared game over for the Neapolitans, as in Serie A, no team came back from such a deficit. So, went the logic for this was Naples and here when the mood arose anything was possible. As the spot-kick hit the back of Napoli's net a familiar chant began to resonate loud from the terraces. It began as a whisper and swiftly rose to a crescendo, 'DIEGO, DIEGO, DIEGO'. Nothing like a family crisis to focus Naples' hearts and minds, to heal old rifts and let sleeping dogs lie. With nothing to lose, Bigon instructed his exalted Argentinian to warm up in preparation for the second half. Maradona took to the stage determined to prove there was life yet in the old seadog! With the leading man set to once more tread the boards at his hometown theatre, events

were about to be turned on their head. He gestured to all corners of the stadium with clenched fist and was greeted with a deafening response. Maradona retained the power to have Napoli tifosi eating out of his hand. Though forced to adorn the number sixteen shirt instead of his legendary ten, and still showing signs of an obvious weight problem, Diego's sheer presence had an immediate galvanizing effect on the home team. Players like Careca, Alemao, Crippa and Carnevale, whom had struggled miserably in the first half suddenly came to life. He orchestrated the onslaught from deep, probing, hitting passes both long and short. With Napoli attacking incessantly, rewards came swiftly when a dubious penalty for handball was awarded. The San Paolo held it's breath as all eyes turned towards one man. A Hollywood movie script would surely have had the returning hero stepping forward and blasting the ball into the net. The credits roll…Diego Maradona's tale was never meant to be the stuff of fairytales and to the horror of all Naples, Fiorentina keeper Marco Landucci saved his weakly-hit effort easily. Maradona berated himself, cursing and annoyed, but there was scant time for self-pity. A shrug of the shoulders and it was back to work. Still, Napoli came,
roared on by a crowd seemingly possessed. It was on the hour when after unrelenting pressure the Neapolitans finally got a goal back. A Carnevale cross fired in from the left wing was deflected by luckless defender Pioli past a helpless Landucci at his near post to set the stadium ablaze. 2-1 and game on. A burning desire to make amends for his wretched penalty drove Maradona on. There were moments when he appeared back to his devilish best, creating with ridiculous ease countless opportunities for the Napoli forwards. There was no longer an after-thrust,

that frightening acceleration of pace which once enabled him to leave opponents for dead had gone. Instead his unerring ability to spot a killer pass and bewildering footwork proved equally effective in torturing the besieged visitors. Chances were made and missed, all foiled by the courageous Landucci who at times appeared to be playing Napoli on his own. Maradona also went close, letting fly from twenty-five-yards, only to see his low, swerving shot flash past the post. Fifteen minutes remained when a terrible lapse in the tiring Fiorentina defence enabled Antonio Careca to sneak unnoticed behind them, before poking a shot under Landucci's body that rolled agonisingly over the goal line and into the net. As the Neapolitans went wild, even Rai's television cameras showing the match live across Italy visibly shook as the foundations of the stadium rocked. It had been a comeback inspired by Maradona's introduction and the little man was not yet finished with the visitors. With just three minutes left and the 'Viola' hanging on grimly for a point, the Argentinian delivered an inch-perfect cross onto the head of attacking full-back Giancarlo Corradini, whose diving header won the day as it flew like a bullet past the forlorn Marco Landucci.

Naples celebrated a famous comeback. The ecstatic Corradini ran straight into the arms of Maradona to thank him for his magnificent assist. Albertino Bigon watched on with a look of incredulity at those around him celebrating, old and young like madmen!

So, this was Naples? Such passion!

Around the San Paolo, cries of 'Maradoona, Maradoona' rang loud. It was love again, amore! The full-time whistle saw Florence's beloved Prince Regent, Roberto Baggio, share an embrace with Naples' own royalty in the centre-circle. After a superb opening showing, he and his team found themselves overwhelmed by Napoli's blistering second-half display inspired by the returning hero. The young pretender although highly blessed by the footballing Gods was sent packing in typical, uncompromising Neapolitan fashion. Baggio was good, very good, but he was still no Maradona

To no one's real surprise Diego was reunited with his number ten shirt after the game. Together, for a final time, Diego Armando Maradona and Naples would go up against the North. One last great battle remained to be fought.

There would be no rules.

Encore.

CHAPTER TWENTY

NAPLES' LAST STAND

With heart-wrenching resignation, Napoli tifosi understood they were on borrowed time. All roads spiritually and financially for their club pointed tragically to self-made oblivion. With Maradona back in the fold and still the measure of Neapolitan dreams, hopes remained high for one final fling with immortality. Whereas, once their only concern was Vesuvio spilling molten lava upon their heads, a new fear now gripped. For after being blessed with a taste of greatness, a return to being mere also-rans filled them with dread. In order to survive what lay ahead, something was needed to grasp onto, to take into this impending eternity of doom and despair. A glorious reminder of when they were king of kings. As the curtains closed on SSC Napoli's most glorious era, a final battle dawned. Naples' last stand.

It was Carnival time in Naples! Goals from striker Andrea Carnevale, both made by Diego Maradona, gave Napoli an unassailable 2-0 lead against arch rival's AC Milan. Carnevale: a man blessed with the perfect name for such a grand occasion. Caught up in the fiesta-like atmosphere, the electronic scoreboard in the San Paolo flashed up images of smiling faces. With the contest clearly won, 80,000 Neapolitans reacted with delight when their heroes on the pitch indulged in showboating. Cries of 'Ole' rang out from the crowd as the home side mocked their opponents with a spell of keep ball that had Silvio Berlusconi's recently crowned European champions looking decidedly second-rate. Foremost amongst the tormentors was Maradona who had proved to be the difference between two evenly-matched sides.

Only a fortnight on from the miraculous comeback against Fiorentina, Maradona continued to confound his critics. After scoring a vital, late equaliser at Cremonese seven days previous, he was looking fitter by the week and, having got rid of the hideous beard, appeared to have acquired a new lease of life. Only six minutes remained against the 'Rossoneri', when Maradona raced clear of the Milan offside trap to beat keeper Giovanni Galli with a sublime chip of such genius that for a moment the stadium appeared to momentarily hold it's breath asking, 'Did he really just do that?'

When questioned afterwards on how marking Diego Maradona compared with other Serie A superstar forwards, Milan defender Paolo Maldini remarked, 'When you have played against Maradona, all the others do not matter.' On their most hated foes' soil the Milanese were humiliated 3-0. Love, loathe or admire him, there could be no argument. Those Northerners who prayed they had seen the end of this Southern, turbulent priest shook their heads in dismay. For Maradona was back!

Sadly, this second honeymoon period between player and club failed to last. On 1st November 1989, Napoli were due to play a UEFA Cup second round tie against unfancied Swiss side Wittingen at the San Paolo. A first leg 0-0 draw in Zurich ensured the holders were clear favourites to qualify, only for Albertino Bigon's meticulous pre-match preparations to be thrown into chaos an hour before kick-off when Diego Maradona was sensationally declared unfit to play. Bigon knew well the reasons for this, as it was an open secret around the city that he had returned to the ways of old. In the days leading up to the match, Diego had been conspicuous by his absence from the training ground at Soccavo. The Neapolitan grapevine overflowed with dark and crazed rumours, some beyond belief, others, knowing the characters involved quite possible. A joyful reunion had occurred. Maradona's recent spectacular renaissance saw old friends welcome him with open arms back into the fold. He was family again and Naples' forbidden fruits were offered up in abundance. Aware of a city's eye upon him, the allenatore moved fast. Knowing he could not afford to be seen as weak Bigon showed a ruthless streak by suspending Maradona until further notice. For the first time he realised just what previous managers were up against when dealing with the troublesome Argentinian. Of the thorns beneath the surface. With a talent like Gianfranco Zola now available to call on, it was no longer the nightmare of old and a battle this impressive Napoli coach felt he could win. The opening skirmishes against Wittingen proved traumatic at a nervy San Paolo. With the tifosi pining unashamedly for their idol, the Swiss minnows took full advantage leading 1-0 at the interval. Humiliation was ultimately averted in the second half when Bigon's revamped side roared back with goals from new boys Baroni and Massimo Mauro's late penalty saving the day. But it had been close.

As for Maradona?
Blessed with a little time on his hands, he found himself with a most unexpected date at the altar. Just when Neapolitans thought Maradona could never again surprise them, he announced his decision to make an honest woman of long-time suffering girlfriend Claudia Villafane. The sound of female hearts breaking was heard loud across

Naples Bay, none more than Cristina Sinagra, the mother of his son. Never one for half measures and determined to show Argentina's high society that the kid from the backstreet slums was now their equal and more, Maradona instructed Guillermo Coppola no expense was to be spared. It was jokingly claimed that Claudia's spectacular wedding gown alone, laden deep with pearls, gold braid and specially-imported lace from Switzerland, could well have wiped out Argentina's national debt. With money no object, Coppola moved heaven and earth to acquire for the big day nothing less than Buenos Aires Cathedral. 1,200 invitations were sent out for what became the hottest ticket in town. It was a guest list unlike any other, consisting of the great, good, mad, bad and totally notorious. An extraordinary cross-section of characters. From the dirt and dust beginnings of Villa Fiorito, old friends pulled on their Sunday best, unable to believe their compadre had remembered them. Equally, in Naples, tifosi such as CUCB leader Gennaro Montuori were rewarded for their loyalty. A 747-jumbo jet was hired by Maradona to ferry over the 250 Italian entourage that included, amongst others, all his team-mates and various Napoli staff and directors. They, alongside a heady mix of family, close friends, Argentinian television celebrities, pop stars and politicians, filled the pulpits to await the arrival of Diego and Claudia. Camorra chiefs were also present. From every background, far and wide, all came to pay their respect, for this man despite many faults was at heart decent and if a friend was ever in need, Maradona would always be there for them. A rare gift.

Not since Eva Peron's wedding had Argentina witnessed such lavish scenes of pomp and circumstance. On the day, the bridegroom's obvious foul mood was clear to all, his

pre-nuptial nerves never more apparent than when he punched one of the hundreds of paparazzi photographers outside the Cathedral who had dared to block his path. An occupational hazard when dealing with Diego. Both he and the bride appeared anxious throughout the service, their forced smiles a giveaway to an undercurrent of tension. Maradona cut a fraught figure as last-minute doubts looked to have seriously overwhelmed him. But with a preening best man Coppola alongside, a smile lighting up the cathedral. Pretending all was well and one eye on Maradona to prevent him dropping his shoulder, throwing a dummy, and disappearing into the sunset. Diego remained at the altar. The music began and this glittering ceremony unfolded. Not a dry eye remained in the building as the happy couple were officially declared man and wife. Wild applause accompanied the newly-weds back down the aisle as they made for a rented Rolls Royce Phantom 111, said once to be owned by a certain visitor to these parts, Nazi war criminal Joseph Goebbels. The short journey from the Cathedral to the reception saw thousands of cheering Argentinians lining the surrounding streets to wish the Maradonas' well. Escorted by a police motorcycle cavalcade, the Rolls made it's way to a local boxing arena called Luna Park, one of Diego childhood haunts.
There, 1,500 guests prepared to party away the evening in unforgettable fashion. A famed Buenos Aires eighty-piece Tango Orchestra ensured events went along with a real swing. As the music blasted out nothing was denied those present. A hundred solid gold rings lay hidden inside a huge wedding cake for the lucky guests. Masquerading as waiters, an undercover journalist managed to slip past the tight security barriers to make astonishing claims as to what occurred that night away from the public eye. They

told of fully paid-up prostitutes posing as international interpreters, offering their unique services. Along with the finest champagne and cigars, in sugar bowls on every table cocaine was said to have been openly available to those who wished to indulge themselves. Nothing was left to chance in order that the 'chosen' had the time of their lives. Whether true or just blatantly falsified, all added to the legend of Diego Maradona and the world he had come to inherit. Behind all the self-indulgence, decadence and sheer excess lay one man's all-consuming desire to prove he had arrived. The poverty-stricken childhood of Villa Fiorito remained in his heart, but those times had gone forever. The message was sent loud and clear.
'I am Maradona, and I can do what the fuck I like.'

Back in Naples, there was one who had his measure. The courageous decision to drop Maradona for the match against Wittingen showed Albertino Bigon possessed the necessary bravery to take on and even, if the need arose, sell him. With Italia '90 on the near horizon, Diego realised this was not a man to be messed with. Any lengthy spell out on the sidelines could have proved disastrous. As in Mexico, Argentina's World Cup hopes again rested almost entirely on the shoulders of their beloved Captain. It had become essential he played regularly to ensure being in prime condition for the tournament. Even cutting out the dreaded cortisone injections and deciding instead to play through any pain barrier over the coming months. Whilst the many critics felt they had good reason to question his errant lifestyle, Maradona's courage and sheer desire to play football was never doubted. It was beyond reproach. With Napoli's allenatore not one to bear a grudge and impressed with the giant efforts made by a seemingly remorseful Maradona in training, Bigon handed Diego yet another lifeline. Though woe betide if he let him down again, for waiting in the wings was Gianfranco Zola. A most unlikely vulture, but one who though counting himself amongst Diego Maradona's most fervid admirers, stood ready, if needed, to come and replace the most revered of Neapolitan heroes. Typically, Maradona surprised all in his attitude towards the fledgling Zola. Naples watched in amazement as the Argentinian took the young Sardinian under his wing, sheltering him from those who threatened to lead the boy astray. A master and pupil relationship developed, one that quickly blossomed into a close friendship. After every training session at Soccavo, the two remained behind. Watched by admiring crowds of Neapolitan players, journalists and tifosi, they performed acts of sorcery that defied belief. Maradona would stand in the centre-circle, flick the ball up and purposely smash it time and again against the crossbar. Astonishingly, he never missed! Zola followed suit and though succeeding many times, failed to match Maradona's unerring eye. Diego would show off striking the ball twenty yards, only for it to then curl in mid-air and fly back towards him. This he would do repeatedly across the pitch, each time the same outcome. Zola's efforts to match often ended in frustration, only for the master to wrap a consoling arm around his shoulders, whispering advice. On they would go, one striving for perfection, the other already there. With Diego Maradona back in the team, Napoli's attempts to win back the Serie A title intensified. A much-deserved 2-0 victory over Inter Milan in Naples offered growing proof that the Neapolitans meant business. Both goals came in the last fifteen minutes when the champions' fierce resistance finally cracked. Firstly, wonderful skills by Maradona enabled him to find Alemao on the edge of Inter's penalty area. The fleet-footed Brazilian played a sublime through-pass to countryman Antonio Careca, who from twelve-yards turned and smashed a terrific low shot into the net. Spearheaded by new signing Jurgen Klinsmann, the visitors threw caution to the wind, only to be suckered by the ultimate counterpunch. Six minutes remained when Napoli broke out. With the entire stadium on their feet roaring them on, Alemao stayed calm to feed Maradona a wonderfully weighted pass that the Argentinian controlled delightfully, then with ridiculous ease side-footed past goalkeeper Walter Zenga. Game over and as the San Paolo rocked, Albertino Bigon had that special look in his eyes of a man who knew he was onto something good.

In yet another rousing contest at the Stadio Comunale in Turin against Juventus, a draw earned saw them go three points clear at the top. An early strike by winger Massimo Crippa electrified the fifteen thousand blue tifosi present to give Napoli a perfect start. In a storming second half the 'Bianconeri' roared back. Inspired by their clever, tenacious, Sicilian born centre-forward Salvatore Schillachi, (Soon to be immortalised in Italian World Cup folklore), a deserved late equaliser arrived when Juve defender Bonetti came up field to level with a powerful header from a corner. Points shared between fierce, old foes whose bitter feud from generations past only increased in venom as the years went by. It was a blood thing. From father to son; the eternal battle, North versus South. For Neapolitans, rivals came and went over the seasons. Verona were loathed, Milan despised, but there remained only one true enemy. The accursed 'Old Lady' of Turin.

Napoli continued to set a scintillating pace. However, disaster befell them when in just the third round their brief reign as UEFA Cup Holders was brought to a crashing end by German side Werder Bremen. In the first leg, the home side found themselves two down at the San Paolo, but in a gallant second-half fight back, goals from Brazilians Careca and Alemao looked to have saved face, only for the Germans to snatch a last-minute winner. Whereas, the Neapolitans could have claimed to be slightly unlucky on home soil, the return leg in Germany left them shame-faced and reeling. For the striking green/white-striped shirts of Bremen handed out a 5-1 mauling. A full house of 38,000 at the Weserstadion raised the roof as their team ran riot. Total humiliation. It was without doubt the worst thrashing for years and received with rancid indignation in Naples. The overall aggregate score line of 8-3 to Bremen hardly did them justice, such was the manner in which they had outclassed the Neapolitans.

Here Bigon showed his true worth and quickly rallied the troops. SSC Napoli, minus an injured Maradona on the bench, returned to form and thrashed Atalanta 3-1 in the San Paolo. Gianfranco Zola was simply divine, a playing style reminiscent of Maradona in so many ways. Full of bewildering sorcery, teasing, twisting and turning, a swerve of the hips leaving defenders trailing. Then, to cap a perfect day in Naples, scoring a truly memorable goal, letting fly a magnificent twenty-five yard shot that screamed into the net. Maradonesque! He had been taught well. Nine minutes from time Zola departed from the fray to be replaced by the great man himself. As the stadium rose to acclaim their new hero, 'Zoladona,' a smiling Diego Maradona warmly embraced his young friend on the touchline and the two swapped high fives. These were heady days once more in the South.

He just couldn't help himself.

Diego Maradona's God-given talent to arouse controversy whenever he opened his mouth showed itself again in early December. Convinced that the footballing hierarchy had fixed the World Cup draw to ensure Argentina received the toughest group possible, he went public to suggest it was all a pre-arranged farce. An outraged FIFA President Joseph Sepp Blatter lashed back labelling the Argentinian's comments, 'A very grave offence.' He warned that 'Maradona could well be banned from Italia '90 for his actions.' Blatter claimed, 'It is idiocy beyond belief. Either he is stupid or he is plain bad.' Not that Maradona appeared too perturbed. In reply he said, 'I will apologize, but I am not going to recant anything.' Surprisingly he received huge support from inside footballing circles, for it was long rumoured previous competitions had been rigged in similar ways. Those who called for Maradona's head on a plate after his outburst found themselves facing much unexpected criticism as many rushed to the Argentinian's side.

Questions were asked. Hardly used to being put in his place by the petulant ravings of a semi-literate, streetwise urchin from the backside of Buenos Aires, Sepp Blatter plotted revenge. When asked his opinion of the finest players to emerge from Argentina, he retorted spitefully, 'I know of only one great Argentinian footballer, Alfredo di Stefano.' Maradona had made himself an enemy for life in upsetting the cushy world of FIFA's President/dictator. In time he would pay a heavy price. Blatter would have his day.

On the 10th December 1989, Napoli travelled the short distance to fellow Southerners Bari. Determined to put one over their big city neighbours, the home side set about their task with a passion. They defended an early goal from their exciting forward Monelli with a passion verging on fanatical. Leading 1-0 with only nine minutes remaining, a shock appeared on the cards, only for Maradona to mastermind a piece of magic that produced a cross from which Andrea Carnevale saved Neapolitan necks. Suddenly, with the vast support of Napoli's away following evident, scenes of violence erupted across the entire San Nicola terraces. Soon, a full-scale riot exploded. The local Carabinieri displayed little neutrality as they charged the visiting tifosi with batons and shields. After being beaten back, in went the tear gas. Carnage ensued. The final whistle saw Maradona rushing across the pitch pleading for his supporters to be shown a little leniency, but as the fighting raged it became apparent that the lads from Forcella and the Spanish Quarter were holding their own! With closest rivals Inter and AC Milan both drawing, the gap remained three points. As the Christmas break dawned and footballing hostilities ceased for a brief respite Albertino Bigon had rebuilt and instilled such confidence in his side that a second Scudetto in four years was within reach. This was a journey Neapolitans had undertaken many times before and only once had they succeeded. Aware of the pitfalls that lay ahead, no one in Naples was getting too excited.

When battle recommenced late December in Rome, Southern hopes of further glories received a nasty dose of reality. Playing in all white, Napoli went down 3-0 at the Stadio Olimpico against Lazio. Inspired by one of their own, twenty-one-year-old Paolo di Canio, the home side delighted the fanatical Lazio Ultras with an all-out attacking display. Hard to believe that only a year previous he himself stood on the terraces as a member of the feared Irriducibili, on the Curva Nord. Full of devilish skill and pace, di Canio ripped the Neapolitans to shreds every time he received the ball. Indeed, the 'Biancocelesti' were unfortunate not to win by many more, such was their superiority over the visitors. After the match Diego Maradona, with a shrug of his shoulders and a wry smile was painfully honest. 'We deserved nothing, congratulations to Lazio, they were the better team.' One to forget for all Neapolitans. Seven days later Napoli played host to relegation-haunted Ascoli. A demanding San Paolo, still feeling the bitter taste of defeat in their mouths from the Lazio debacle, cried out for a blood fest. It was not forthcoming as Bigon's men struggled woefully against an Ascoli side intent only on defending for a point. Andrea Carnevale suffered the kind of afternoon forwards dread as the ball appeared determined to make him look ridiculous. Napoli's performance was so poor that the crowd vented their frustration onto a distraught Carnevale, who visibly wilted under the hail of abuse. Finally, on sixty-six-minutes, redemption arrived. A Maradona cross found the leaping Carnevale and his towering header broke the deadlock. Once more how they loved Andrea Carnevale!

One week on further humiliation dawned away at lowly Udinese. Already a goal down, an 86th minute thunderbolt from home striker Mattei looked to have won the day for the struggling Northerners, who were managed by former Napoli coach Rino Marchesi. Then, a footballing miracle of San Gennaro proportions occurred. Though far from home, their patron showed that he had not forgotten his troublesome flock, when for some unknown reason the arbitiro Pairetto awarded the visitors a dubious penalty. With time almost up Diego Maradona swiftly rushed to place the ball before reducing the deficit and giving his team a glimmer of hope. Surrounded by six black/white-striped shirts Maradona set off on a last run. Deep into injury-time the Neapolitans were throwing everything they had left at a panicking Udinese rearguard. Salvation arrived as so many times before in the closest thing to San Gennaro available for Neapolitans here on Earth. Somehow, the magical little Argentinian squeezed a pass through to the far post where rampaging full-back Giovanni Francini stabbed home an astonishing equaliser. 2-2! The final whistle saw the Napoli players celebrate like they had already won the Scudetto. A somewhat shell-shocked Albertino Bigon shook hands with his Udinese counterpart. Though deeply entrenched in the relegation struggle, a rueful Marchesi shared a quiet word with the Naples coach. He knew more than most that when it came to his club, it was always best to expect the unexpected! They left the arena deep in conversation, each with vastly different problems, but both forever cursed/blessed with having SSC Napoli in their heart. To their grave, once in never out. The Neapolitans remarkable comeback against Udinese kept the Milan clubs at bay, albeit by a single point. With fifteen games still remaining and the Milanese approaching top form another classic North/South championship race was on.

A narrow 1-0 home win against Bigon's old club Cesena came courtesy of a goal immaculately conceived by Diego Maradona for Massino Crippa, who with great technique smashed a wonderful shot past the Cesena keeper from ten yards. It was the eye-catching, instant lay-off from the

Captain that caused eyebrows to be raised around the San Paolo. A strict fitness regime designed to have Diego in peak condition for the forthcoming World Cup had kicked in and the Neapolitans were reaping the benefit. Physically Maradona appeared almost back to his best.

Next to suffer were a side genuinely detested in Naples for matters hardly relating to football, a club and it's supporters that regarded themselves as infinitely superior to Neapolitans. From the far reaches of Italy's Northern regions, the hated Hellas Verona came South. Bottom of Serie A and looking certainties to go down, fortunes had changed dramatically for the once feared Verona. It appeared unthinkable as they stood on the brink of humiliation that only six years previous the championship badge of Scudetto had flown proudly over the Comunale Bentegodi. Coach Osvaldo Bagnoli remained at the helm, but even this master tactician had been unable to prevent the drop into the abyss. The players Bagnoli now possessed bore no comparison to those who once graced the blue/yellow shirts of Hellas. Sadly, for all Veronese those days had gone as the Napoli tifosi were swift to remind the derisory number of Brigate Giaboblu who had braved the perilous journey, standing huddled together for safety, in one small, heavily protected section of the San Paolo. The CUCB had arranged a very special surprise for those whom once dared torment them with banners such as *'Stench from the South'* and the infamous *'Lavatevi'*.

The appearance of the two teams was the cue for an immense, perfectly choreographed yellow banana to appear like magic upon the terraces. A typical example of Neapolitan, gallows humour, aimed at the large racist elements amongst the Verona following that indulged in monkey chants and waving swastikas every time Napoli played at the Bentegodi. Recently on their terraces the mocking Giaboblu had taken to wearing surgical masks in games against the Southerners. Payback came with Maradona who appeared determined to put on a performance worthy of what had occurred pre-match. Playing with all his old swagger, enjoyment and enthusiasm, the mesmerising Argentinian set about bringing the arrogant Northerners to their knees. Every darting run came laced with torturous menace. Time and again the San Paolo lay enraptured by their king's dagger like thrusts into the heart of Verona's defence. At one stage, such was his burning desire to entertain the Neapolitan masses, Maradona appeared to be laughing whilst running amok amongst the terrified flurry of yellow shirts. He was at his mischievous best. Every so often he waved at the crowd, even picking out a familiar face! It was personal: every trick, flick and deft sleight of pass was used to inflict wanton humiliation on those whom dared once to disrespect. Perhaps, deep down Diego already knew his time with Napoli was drawing near and therefore was hell-bent on giving Verona something to remember him by? A deflection off Hellas midfielder Giancomarro opened the scoring, but the moment all Naples had craved arrived two minutes before half-time. Racing clear of three defenders, Maradona tore into the penalty box before rounding the keeper Peruzzi and making it 2-0. Off he sprinted over the running track to be as one with his adopted people. Delirium gripped the San Paolo terraces. That strange, fervid atmosphere which only this crazed city and it's inhabitants could generate had again taken hold. The second period simply offered further opportunities to tease and torment the bedraggled visitors. The referee's whistle for full time ended the Northerners' plight. Diego

Maradona's honour had been satisfied. Though still to have a vital say in the destination of the Scudetto, it was to be a long time before Hellas Verona recovered from their eventful journey South to Naples.

February began well with further victories away at Fiorentina 1-0, and yet another barnstorming performance from their Captain against Cremonese on home soil. Maradona weaved ghost-like through the red/white-striped defence to score twice and wreak havoc throughout the entire ninety minutes. His finest moment came with a thirty-yard free-kick that he curled with consummate ease past Cremonese keeper Rampulla into the net. Due to renovation work for the World Cup, this game was played out in an eerie, echoing, half-filled San Paolo. Naples had been picked to host a semi-final venue. A tale soon to unfold. As for Napoli, their true test was still to come, for Milan and Inter lay in wait over the coming weeks. With both matches at the San Siro, the Neapolitans faced their most crucial spell of the season.

On Sunday 11th February 1990, they failed miserably against Arrigo Sacchi's European champions, losing 3-0. With AC Milan's superstars threatening a massacre, Napoli survived a first half only with the blessed luck of San Gennaro. The pressure was such that a goal had to come and shortly after half-time, the winger Daniel Massaro struck from close range. A thundering header from Paolo Maldini and a late strike from the glorious Marco van Basten gave the scoreline a more realistic look as the 'Rossoneri' blasted Napoli out of sight. The Neapolitans' lead had vanished and it was Milan who now topped Serie A. The Red Devils had 'O Ciuccio' by the tail. Few thought they would let it go.

A week later, further misery descended on Naples after just four minutes when Roma defender Nela hit an unsuspected rocket of a free-kick leaving Giuliani standing. The San Paolo was silenced, all seemed to be falling apart. Only Maradona looked up for the challenge, single-handedly taking on the Romans. As the jeering and boos rang out from the terraces even he appeared to lose heart. However, a fifteen-minute respite from the pressure at half-time worked wonders for after the interval Napoli came out a team possessed. It was like a light being switched on in the San Paolo as the players whom had earlier performed like strangers, failing to string two passes together suddenly awoke to what was at stake. Alemao came alive: it was the Brazilian's precise pass that put Crippa clean through, only for the lightning winger to be sent crashing in the penalty area. Striding purposely forward Maradona made no mistake with the spot-kick placing his shot into the bottom right-hand corner. After being on cruise control for almost an hour, Roma suddenly found themselves with a real game on their hands. For ten minutes a blue wave surged forward. Then, Carnevale played a superb through ball that sent Antonio Careca roaring unmarked into the box. What followed was one of the finest goals ever seen at the San Paolo. Forced wide onto the goal-line by the keeper's challenge, Careca somehow produced an amazing shot that flew into the net from what appeared an impossible angle. Already ensconced in tifosi hearts, that instance saw 'La Bomba' enter the esteemed realms of Neapolitan legend. With the taste of Roman blood sweet in their nostrils, Napoli turned up the heat. The on-fire Massimo Crippa was again sent sprawling for yet another penalty. This time around Diego Maradona placed the ball in the opposite side of the goal.

Still not satisfied the San Paolo roared out for more. Attempting to appease their rapacious appetite, Maradona flicked the ball up on the edge of the box and let fly with an outrageous overhead bicycle kick that if successful would have surpassed even Careca's earlier monumental effort. Unfortunately for Diego, the Roma keeper Cervone leapt high and produced an outstanding save, tipping the ball over the bar. A sporting Maradona applauded his opponent. 2-2

After the AC Milan debacle, Albertino Bigon's extravagant, if wholly unpredictable side had recovered some pride. How they had needed it for next on the agenda was a return date at the San Siro against Serie A Champions Inter and it was one they were forced to face without Diego Maradona.

To celebrate the 3-1 victory over Roma, a partying Maradona vanished ominously into the Naples night. When time came to return for training at Soccavo he never showed. The rumours began. A frustrated Albertino Bigon held a meeting with his President as to Diego's whereabouts, but even the all-seeing, knowing Corrado Ferlaino was at a loss to explain his absence. Word was finally received by phone that he was at home looking after his sick daughter, but this cut no ice with Bigon, for more reliable sources informed him that Maradona lay wasted in a notorious Forcella brothel. The allenatore's preparation for Napoli's most important match of the season, one that could well decide whether the Scudetto was returning South, had been thrown into chaos due to the selfish behaviour of Maradona.

A man who claimed endlessly Naples was in his heart. Prior to the game, travelling tifosi scaled the gigantic heights of the San Siro to unravel a huge Napoli banner that was visible across the city. Nothing could have inflamed Inter followers more than seeing the Southern colours flying high over their territory and they sought retribution. Unbelievable scenes of mayhem erupted in the stadium as the two tribes masked by scarves across their faces clashed. Chains, bottles, flares and knives flashed and were hurled before the Milan Carabinieri finally calmed the situation. On the pitch SSC Napoli were handed the perfect start when after just seven minutes Antonio Careca dribbled past half the Inter team as he ran from the halfway line before rounding keeper Walter Zenga and scoring. The Brazilian delighted his tifosi as he danced the Samba routine in front of them, whilst at the same time infuriating the baying Milanese. It would be one of the few times they made it out of their half for the remainder of the opening period saw Napoli pinned back by Trapattoni's powerful, hard-running, skilful side. Jurgen Klinsmann was a nightmare for the Neapolitan defenders. With Aldo Serena alongside him, Klinsmann caused the visitors endless problems. Added to the fearful midfield surges of Lothar Matthaus exploding amongst them, Napoli held on for grim life. Klinsmann was unlucky to see a goal disallowed for offside, whilst Matthaus smashed a vicious free-kick against the post. Plenty of luck and courageous defending saw the Neapolitans reach half-time still leading. Shortly after the break their defence were finally breached when Matthaus crossed perfectly for his countryman Klinsmann to power a fine header past the besieged Giuliani. What followed was nothing less than a siege as the champions went for the winner. From a corner Klinsmann again rose high to grab his second and leave the Napoli keeper pounding the turf. With Inter hitting them from all angles the Neapolitans were run ragged and a final goal came when the tormenting Klinsmann once more crashed in a shot that Giuliani failed to hold and forward Allesandro Bianchi swooped to make it 3-1. The day deservedly belonged to 'La Grande Inter'. Come the final whistle blue/black smoke bombs engulfed the San Siro pitch. Elsewhere, the 'Rossoneri' had gone to Rome and thrashed Lazio 4-0 in the Stadio Olimpico with the inestimable poaching talents of van Basten grabbing a brace. Sacchi's men had opened a two-point gap. The loss of their influential Captain had taken it's toll on Napoli and suddenly a certain Argentinian had a lot to answer for.

Diego Maradona surfaced to find himself in hot water with Albertino Bigon, for he had simply pushed him too far. The atmosphere at Soccavo could have been cut with a knife as the two men locked horns. The allenatore refused to consider him for selection, instead he chose Gianfranco Zola for the upcoming home game against Genoa, one Napoli could not afford to lose. Journalists confronted General Manager Luciano Moggi about the stand-off, but Moggi just shrugged his shoulders, claiming in a resigned manner, 'I walk on eggs around here.' As expected the match with Genoa was a taut affair. In a tense, stifling atmosphere at the San Paolo with the tifosi still singing for Maradona, Napoli looked to be heading for a calamitous 1-1 draw, a result probably enough to finish off their challenge. Once more Zola proved his own weight in gold. Keeping cool when all around were looking edgy, he took aim and cracked a last-minute winner to keep the nervy Neapolitans in touch with AC Milan. Gianfranco was already in danger of becoming a legend in these parts. Seven games remained to play. Many in Naples feared they could not take much more. With the stakes so high

Albertino Bigon decided it was in the best interests of all to forgive and he recalled Maradona.

The city of Lecce sit's deep in the boot of Italy, and on 11th March 1990, played host to Napoli. Lecce were fighting for their lives at the opposite end of Serie A and promised their big city rivals a Southern battle royal. They remained true to their words and it was not until the second half that they managed to edge in front through a Carnevale header. The situation improved even further for the visitors when news filtered through from Turin by radio that Juventus were beating Milan. On hearing this the travelling blue army exploded with joy! Once more they dared to dream. Could it really happen again? Reality did not take long to slap Neapolitans in the face. The yellow/red striped shirts of Lecce simply refused to lie down and twenty minutes remained when their flying winger Pasculi levelled. Overcome with relief, the charismatic Lecce manager Carlo Mazzone raced along the touchline dancing a jig of unrestrained delight to celebrate the goal. Mazzone's celebrations took him within range of the Napoli faithful. Luckily their attempts to lynch him failed and the game finished 1-1. Despite the disappointment for Bigon's team of not being able to hold on for a win, Juve's 3-0 shock hammering of the 'Rossoneri' meant the point's deficit was reduced to just one. All considered, a good day for the South. It went on...

A city divided: AC versus Inter. Neither club desired such a potentially high-octane occasion so late in the season, for there could be only one winner. Events in Milan were put to the back of Neapolitan minds as they had enough on their plate away to Sampdoria. Napoli found themselves under pressure from the off by a home team still grasping on tight to an outside chance of the title. Their explosive pairing of Roberto Mancini and Atillio Lombardo wasted little time testing out whether the Southerners were up for a scrap so far away from home. A stirring contest ensued with both sides creating and missing a handful of chances. It wasn't until thirty-seven minutes that a breakthrough occurred when the creative Mancini cut inside the Napoli box and laid the ball off for his team-mate Dossena to smash a flashing drive past Giuliano Giuliani into the top corner. Shortly after the interval it was the eye-catching Careca who let Neapolitans breathe a little easier when he played a stupendous one-two with Carnevale, before finishing with some aplomb to equalise. A draw suited neither side, so there was no let-up as both continued to attack with little thought of defending. It was end-to-end football that left the crowd breathless and the managers speechless! Just when the visitors looked to be getting on top, a Mancini corner found the balding Lombardo's head to beat Giuliani all ends up. 2-1 it ended. By his own exceptional standards Maradona had not played well, and there were even rumblings amongst his most fervid supporters that maybe he was not the force of old. The apprentice had learned fast. If needed, though with heavy heart, Zola was ready to answer the call from Albertino Bigon. The final whistle signalled great celebrations in the Stadio Luigi Ferrari, and not just from the home crowd. For word came from the San Siro that Inter had beaten AC Milan 3-1. Amazingly, with only five games left to play, Milan, Napoli, Inter, Juventus and Sampdoria remained in with a chance of the title. In the most open championship anyone could remember the dream of winning the Scudetto was causing heart attacks across the length and breadth of Italy.

Juve were in town. If ever there was a game tailor-made for Diego Maradona to silence the doubters and put Napoli's challenge back on track, it was 'La Vecchia Signora' in Naples. In the tunnel shortly before kick-off, Maradona walked along the line shaking the hands of all his team-mates. He and they knew it was make or break time. Lose this game and there was no coming back. Opposite, the eleven men in black/white-striped shirts appeared pensive, knowing full well what awaited those who dared to wear the Juventus colours in this the most sacred of Neapolitan shrines. Together, the two sides made the short walk up the stone stairway, each step seeing the noise level reach higher decibels before the sunlight dazzled their eyes and 86,000 blood-curdling voices greeted their entry into the inner sanctum of the San Paolo. Beat us if you dare.
Welcome to Naples!
Diego Maradona began the match looking more like his old self, demanding the ball, explosive, full of guile and zest. It took him just thirteen minutes to set the stadium on fire. A thunderous drive by Andrea Carnevale crashed against the Juve bar, pinged around, before finally falling to Maradona who swivelled and hit a classic shot that Steffano Tacconi never saw as it ripped past him. On the half hour Maradona brought the house down once more with an archetypal swerving twenty-five-yard free-kick that Tacconi could not even dream about preventing. On the terraces and across the city, Neapolitans fell in homage, pleading forgiveness as Diego shoved a million words of criticism back down their throats for daring to suggest his star was on the wane. As the game wore on Napoli toyed with Juventus, content to just keep possession, torment and humiliate. A dangerous tactic and

one that irritated their coach no end as he screamed at them from the touchline to go for a killer third. Bigon had been right to worry, for with a whole half hour still left to play the exhilarating Salvatore Schillachi was hacked down in the penalty box and De Agostini fired home to make it 2-1. Suddenly, those of local persuasion were no longer laughing. Their teams' over-confidence had left them vulnerable in a way unimaginable only a short time before. With spirits raised the 'Bianconeri' began to play in a manner that scared the hell out of the home tifosi. Neapolitan nerves were finally soothed when an in-swinging Maradona corner found Giovanni Francini and the defender in a mad scramble at the far post stabbed the ball over the line. Game won. Come full-time the San Paolo erupted with delight. The dream was still alive.

Tavolino: A Serie A season was never complete without one notorious incident of Neapolitan skullduggery causing national uproar across Italy. On Sunday 9th April 1990, in the far Northern city of Bergamo, to no great surprise it duly occurred. Napoli were involved in a dour struggle against an Atalanta team fighting to save face after a recent humiliating 7-2 thrashing by Inter Milan. Playing in a rare change strip of red shirts, the Southerners came under relentless pressure on and off the pitch as hails of objects from a hostile home crowd rained down upon them. Twelve minutes remained and a game seemingly fated to end scoreless exploded in truly controversial fashion. After going to take a throw-in, Alemao suddenly fell to his knees, claiming to have been hit by something thrown from the terraces. Television replays showed that a coin appeared to have dropped short, but such was his apparent discomfort it was originally thought that another had

struck him off camera. Napoli physio Salvatore Carmando immediately raced to usher the player off pitch, gesturing wildly to the bench for assistance. Carmando was picked up on a nearby microphone imploring Alemao to, 'Stay down, stay down!' In what looked a rather overtly theatrical act to shelter him from further assault, his teammates crowded around pleading with the highly experienced referee, Carlo Longhi for protection. Gianfranco Zola replaced the stricken Brazilian for the final stages, but still Napoli failed to break the stalemate and despite late pressure the game finished 0-0.
Full-time saw tempers overflow in the stands as rival tifosi attempted to settle the day with their own version of extra-time. As the fighting raged only yards away, Diego Maradona embraced fellow countryman, Atalanta winger Claudio Caniggia in the tunnel area and the two swapped shirts. The wailing of sirens mattered little to Maradona and Caniggia, for to them this was merely a petty, insular, Italian squabble. More importantly, to all of Argentinian persuasion, Italia '90 was drawing ever closer and both men would play an integral role in the defence of their coveted World Cup trophy.

A still seemingly 'dazed' Alemao was taken with great haste to a Bergamo hospital where later that night he was visited by club President Corrado Ferlaino. After spending a little time at the player's bedside, Ferlaino emerged to face the waiting press. Wearing his most doom-laden expression, the President, when asked on Alemao's condition, replied in all seriousness, 'He did not recognise me.' Ferlaino went on to demand the same kind of justice be handed out to Atalanta that so often was shown his club over the years in similar circumstances. The President was swift in claiming that he expected nothing less than to be given the points. Three days later the Italian Football Federation shocked all by coming down in Naples favour, awarding them a 2-0 win. They were left with little option when the arbitro, Longhi, submitted his report in favour of Napoli and through grinding teeth and pounding fists the Federation adjusted the Serie A table to place them level alongside AC Milan with only three games remaining. *Tavolino*: a mathematical rescheduling of the result. A paltry hundred Lira coin had blown the championship race wide open. …Happily, Alemao swiftly recovered….

In the elegant surroundings of the city's countless coffee house and bars, Milanese seethed with disdain at these cheating 'Africanos' from the Mezzogiorno. Not only they cast aspersions South, followers of every club North of Rome did likewise. Local rivalries mattered little in such circumstances for everybody hated Napoli. No neutrals. Not surprisingly, 'Rossoneri' supremo Silvio Berlusconi led the moral outrage campaign. Milan even went to the extent of hiring lip readers to prove Carmando had told Alemao to 'Stay down!' Though all to no avail. Typically, Berlusconi made the most of the situation. He was in the early throes of a political career that in time would lead to the Italian Presidency. 'Il Cavaliere' realised nothing pleased the masses more than some good old-fashioned Neapolitan baiting. So, Berlusconi duly obliged, telling of his disgust at what occurred in Bergamo. Condemned by all except those of Napoli persuasion, the newspapers, television and radio stations vented fury upon Southerners' heads. An overreaction bordering on hysterical took hold, every half-baked insult and cliché regarding Neapolitans was dug up and hurled in their direction. Again, those who hailed from beneath Mount Vesuvio had contrived to almost ignite civil war against their fellow countrymen. Not that they were too concerned for when the Scudetto was at stake there could be only one tactic. Whether by Diego's 'Hand of God' or Alemao's dramatic, dying swan routine, to win was all that mattered. Scopa.

Thirteen years later in an astonishing interview given to Il Mattino (Naples' largest-selling local newspaper), Corrado Ferlaino cleansed his soul and confessed it had all been a set-up. In his own words, 'It was Salvatore Carmando who came up with the idea. The player was actually struck by a coin, but we extended the episode to make a little scene. At the beginning Alemao did not understand what we were up to. It was only after Salvatore whispered into his ear that he played along. Later after visiting Ricardo in hospital, the game continued when I informed the press that he did not recognise me! Afterwards when alone I fell about laughing, for Alemao was perfectly well. We fooled them all!'

As the accusations flew there came only typical defiance from Naples. They had longed ceased worrying about the opinions of outsiders. Despite endless attempts over the centuries to grind them into the dirt, fires continued to rage wild in rebellious Southern bellies. Berlusconi and his ilk could simply go and fuck themselves. With a snarling vitriol and utter contempt Neapolitans spat back, refusing to cower under the well-polished heel of Northern Italy's aristocratic boot.

For all except one there were no regrets. Ricardo Alemao's decision to go along with this charade was claimed to have haunted the highly religious Brazilian for years. So much that a later decision to become an Evangelist priest was said partly due to the guilt he still felt regarding his actions. In Naples, it is claimed behind every man of the cloth a dark secret lurks, a past indiscretion. In such circumstances they were treated with great respect, but also secretly with a crude suspicion. How else explain their decision to refrain from humanly desires? Not Alemao, his fall from grace was well known and richly appreciated by Neapolitans. Nobody ever threw stones (or indeed coins) in his direction. Except that is in Milan and Bergamo. As the vast majority of Italians prayed feverishly for SSC Napoli to fall flat on their faces, they returned to action taking on Bari in the San Paolo. Fired by the overwhelming tirade of abuse and criticism in previous days, Albertino Bigon's team proved irresistible and dismissed their sadly outclassed Southern cousins with a merciless display of attacking football. Maradona, Carnevale and Careca excelled as they indulged in shooting practice. A first-half penalty made and converted by Maradona was scant reward for the Neapolitans' scintillating play. Performing to the gantry Napoli showed off to a watching Italy. Second-half goals by their twin striking duo, both taken in breathtaking style made the final score 3-0, laying down the gauntlet to Milan. Far away in the San Siro, a Daniel Massaro header handed the 'Rossoneri' victory against Sampdoria to place them on forty-nine points with just two games remaining.

On Sunday 22nd April 1990, all roads led North for a fateful double-header that would ultimately decide the destiny of the Scudetto. Whilst Albertino Bigon's men were forced to endure a last, perilous journey up-country to Bologna, AC Milan faced a Hellas Verona side fighting for their lives to stave off relegation. The footballing Gods were in mischief-making mood, for a Hellas win in the

Stadio Bentegodi over Milan would almost certainly hand the title to their arch enemy, should they triumph in Bologna. The ultimate irony for the Giaboblu hordes, but one deemed wholly acceptable if it enabled them to survive in Serie A. In times past, Bologna had prided itself on showing wonderful hospitality to all outsiders, except Neapolitans, and after being greeted with the warmth of a freezing snowstorm, Napoli took swift revenge on their unwelcoming host by roaring into a 3-0 lead at the Stadio Renato Dell'ara. Antonio Careca began the rout in the third minute. In one movement the lethal Brazilian chested the ball down before letting fly an unstoppable drive into the top corner from fifteen yards to cause unbridled celebrations amongst the 5,000 travelling Neapolitans. Careca's stupendous effort was met with dismay by the Milan tifosi in Verona listening intently on radio to unfolding events in the Dell'ara. The gloom doubled moments later when Diego Maradona cut in from the left-hand touchline to hit a tremendous shot low past home keeper Cusin from the edge of the penalty area. Maradona was proving back to his devilish best as Napoli continued to sweep forward. On fifteen minutes Carnevale played in swashbuckling defender Francini to finish with sumptuous ease. On enemy territory Neapolitan songs resonated loud as they stood on the brink of a potentially historical victory. With their game already looking over, all thoughts turned to what was unravelling in the Bentegodi.

On the half hour, Naples fervour temporarily dampened when Milan grabbed a lifeline with Marco Simone's deflected free-kick giving them an undeserved lead over a ferociously battling Verona. With both contenders winning and each having their final game at home, a play-off to decide the title suddenly became increasingly likely. It would not be required for in Verona the second period brought a drama and excitement unmatched in Serie A history, as Arrigo Sacchi's much-lauded superstars self-exploded in incredulous style. With, it was later claimed in true Neapolitan conspiratorial fashion, more than a helping hand from a friend in Naples. Immediately after the break Bologna grabbed a goal back to help ease wounded pride after their first half mauling. The Southerners reply was instantaneous. Who else but a ravaging Maradona crashed in a wondrous thirty-yard effort, forcing Cusin into a miraculous save as he leapt high to punch over the bar. As Napoli went all out for a fourth they were boosted immeasurably on sixty-three minutes when news arrived that Hellas defender Sotomayor had smashed in a header to equalise for Verona. Bedlam exploded in the Bentegodi as they wept tears of joy and relief. The Rossoneri swept back and shortly after, Arrigo Sacchi went crazy on the touchline when Marco van Basten was refused what looked a sure-fire penalty by Sicilian born referee Rosario Lo Bello. A name soon to become demonised in Milanese folklore. An outraged Arrigo Sacchi completely lost his cool. He charged onto the pitch to confront Lo Bello, only to be swiftly shown a red card by the official and dismissed from the bench. Off trudged a scowling Sacchi to the safety of the tunnel, where surrounded by armed riot police he continued to watch as outraged Veronese tifosi attempted to reach him with a hail of coins from the surrounding terraces.

With the clock speeding incessantly onwards, Milan tempers frayed and frustrations overflowed. None more than their imperial centre-forward Marco van Basten, who repeatedly found himself hacked and slashed down by defenders, only for the referee to ignore his many pleas for protection. The normally, well-oiled footballing machine that was AC Milan stuttered badly. Disaster loomed. Unless they scored again a win the following week for Napoli against Lazio at the San Paolo would see a second Scudetto in four years head South into the badlands of Mezzogiorno and Naples. As for the Southerners, the old adage of 'The enemy of my enemy is my friend' had never been more apt as Verona gave everything. Even in their wildest dreams no self-respecting Neapolitan could ever have believed such a scenario possible. A thought equally shared by the Veronese. After being felled one too many times Van Basten cracked and got himself booked for simply complaining. Worse followed when fellow Dutchman Frank Rijkaard remonstrated on his behalf, only to receive a ridiculous red for daring to do so. A melee ensured as an irate, dumbfounded Rijkaard refused to leave the field before being allowed a potentially explosive last confrontation with the woeful Lo Bello, who clearly had lost the plot. Or had he? That Lo Bello appeared to be shamelessly enjoying himself hardly helped to calm tempers. His inept display at times bordered on the ridiculous such was the seemingly one-sided bias. It was only the wise actions of Franco Baresi and Ruud Gullit ushering their team-mate out of harm's way that temporarily calmed the situation. Just when it was thought the day could not get any worse for the beleaguered Red Devils, more gut-wrenching news came from Bologna.

Five minutes remained in the Dell'ara when Diego Maradona fed a delicious pass through for a quick thinking Alemao to beat the offside trap. The so-called 'Villain of

Atalanta' surged on, rounded the goalkeeper and made the score 4-1. The Brazilian looked to have fully recovered from recent events as he lapped up the adulation of the vast travelling support. A miracle recovery? San Gennaro moved in mysterious ways. Whilst Neapolitans danced in jubilation, Milan misery increased tenfold in Verona when an infuriated van Basten finally reached the end of his tether. After yet another decision went against him, the forward took off his shirt and threw it at Lo Bello. Cue the exit. With almost indignant haste out came the card to signal expulsion. Off he went, joining a worryingly ashen-faced Arrigo Sacchi and Frank Rijkaard in the tunnel area. Driven to despair by the alleged injustices being meted out to them, 'Rossoneri' fury with the referee was such, many swore he performed as if wearing the Napoli blue under his supposedly neutral black shirt. Something stunk to high heaven that day in Verona and if the Milanese thought rock bottom had been reached with the departure of Marco van Basten they were sadly wrong. For what happened next left them reeling and on their knees. With time slipping away Arrigo Sacchi's nine men continued to press and carry the battle forward. All shape and method had vanished to be replaced by wanton panic. On eighty-eight minutes, the final nail was hammered into their coffin. A lightning break saw the darting little winger Pellegrini chased all the way by a desperately tired and depleted Milan defence. As the Bentegodi held it's collective breath the scraggly, long-haired Pellegrini took aim and executed a wonderful chip over keeper Giovanni Galli into an empty net. Convinced Pellegrini was offside the Milan players once more surrounded the referee, only to be given short shrift. Costacurta refused to be silenced and as went the script found himself flashed a red by Lo Bello. With just

eight men left on the field the 'Rossoneri' finally threw in the towel. Hellas was still alive! Scores across Italy meant a weeks' grace and the opportunity to fight on, but in the end, they would go down much to Naples' delight.
As for Senor Rosario Lo Bello?
 Due to Berlusconi's insistence and his own safety he was never again allowed to referee a game that Milan were involved in. Many years later when the dust had finally settled and tempers relatively calmed, Napoli President Corrado Ferlaino hinted heavily in an interview to Naples' Il Mattino that he was at the time, 'Very close' to Lo Bello. Ferlaino spoke of 'Good relations.' Comments really that hardly needed interpreting.
Game, set and championship point!
Verona and Naples. Two cities, a world apart in so many ways spontaneously combusted. The full-time whistle in Bologna saw chaos on the pitch as the Neapolitans waited with bated breath confirmation of Milan's fate. Then, it came and the sudden realisation of a second Scudetto heading to Naples hit home. A familiar song broke out amongst Napoli tifosi that belonged exclusively to their fair city. Sung with huge gusto and a heartfelt passion the words drifted high into miserable, grey, Northern skies;
'Oh, my first love, oh first you'll be for me, Oh sweet life of mine'.
Barring a disaster of catastrophic proportions, the title was returning South. The Napoli players found themselves mobbed by hordes of reporters. Their main target was inevitably Diego Maradona, who faced with a barrage of microphones shoved within inches of his face, spoke only in gushing terms of his team-mates. A great victory had been won in the North and a further point against Lazio on home soil would guarantee festivities fit to signal the end

of the world. Alas, for Neapolitans, such a dreaded scenario was at hand. The good times were drawing to an end, but not before one last hell of a party.

Sunday 29th April 1990. Seven days later the inevitable duly occurred and uproarious scenes of revelry descended upon Naples. The 86,000-fanatical congregational in the San Paolo witnessed a lone header from defender Marco Baroni secure the required win over a lame Lazio side that came, saw and did not dare attempt to conquer. Against a breathtaking sea of blue/white flags SSC Napoli were crowned champions. Speaking in the immediate aftermath of the game an emotional Diego Maradona dedicated the title to his father. 'Dedicato a mio Padre.' Maradona had again proved how dangerous it was to write him off. For him, the sense of vindication was overwhelming. Ten months earlier, he had been branded a mafioso and a drug addict. 'I shut them all up' he said. A journalist asked him whether Napoli would not have suffered less had it not been for all the controversies? 'A mi me piace vincere cosí,' he replied. 'I like to win like this.' As did Naples! In just a short time Diego Maradona would be back playing in the San Paolo, only with Argentina's colours and in typically unforgettable circumstances.

Amidst the rising euphoria, the man that delivered the ultimate prize, Albertino Bigon remained the same composed figure who attended his opening press conference only nine months previous, fending off with effortless ease searching questions about Maradona. Bigon's epic achievement meant he entered with full honours the realms of Napoli folklore. A treasured place in Neapolitan hearts forever assured. The entire city spilled out onto the streets. On every corner vendors sold bottles of sea water labelled 'Berlusconi tears' to joyful revellers who snapped them up as mementoes. Baying mules roamed loose with pictures of Milan's hated President pinned to their asses. A 4-0 win for Sacchi's team over Bari played out in a funeral-like atmosphere at the San Siro meant nothing, for the Donkey's had truly bolted. Across the bay a sense of disbelief took hold.

It had happened again! Against all odds Naples had won the day. Yet, where the first Scudetto was greeted with utter joy and great feeling of relief, this second came etched with an overwhelming sense of desperation. An almost painful longing. As night fell, Southern skies once more filled with all manner of breathtaking rockets and flares. The partying went on long and hard, too hard. Three years previously it was perceived as the start of the fairytale. Somehow, this time around it felt like the end. Naples' last stand.

CHAPTER TWENTY-ONE

REBELLION

Only Diego would have the nerve to attempt such a trick. Never in World Cup history had a similar, torturous choice been forced upon a city. Surely this time Maradona had gone too far? For what right anyone, a king even, to demand a people turn against their own? Neapolitans riled in horror, why them? Had they not suffered enough? A banner on that fateful evening in the San Paolo spoke succinctly of their plight: 'Diego, you are always in our hearts, but Italy is our blood.' Naples was split: at a time when they should have been basking in the joy of a second historic Scudetto, Maradona had once more tipped them over the edge. A nation held it's breath, rebellion was in the air. Surely not even Neapolitans would stoop so low?

Italia '90, produced little in terms of spectacular football but more than redeemed itself with drama and controversy aplenty. The fourteenth World cup opened on Friday 8th June, at Milan's San Siro, now the re-christened, and renovated Giuseppe Meazza Stadium, with one almighty upset. In an astonishing shock that reverberated across the footballing planet, huge underdogs Cameroon beat the champions' Argentina. Bidding to retain their golden trophy won four years previous in Mexico City, the Argentinians walked into an African storm. In a courageous performance wholly appreciated by a fiercely pro-Cameroon, 73,780, majority-Milanese crowd, the minnows outclassed, bullied and ultimately battered the reigning holders into submission. Argentina's one great hope Captain Diego Maradona was anonymous throughout. His every move tracked and ruthlessly dealt with by huge green-shirted defenders, who cared little for the great man's health or reputation. From the kick-off, it became apparent that a pre-tournament injury to his left foot sustained during a warm-up match against Israel, had left Maradona in constant pain. He was also suffering badly from an ingrowing toenail. Desperate measures called. Without their legendary number ten the Argentinians were bereft of both quality and hope. So, once more the Captain relented and underwent the torturous stab of a cortisone needle to ensure he played against the Cameroon. Maradona's frustration began before kick-off when Argentina's national anthem was heckled throughout. Against a background of howling derision, Diego's face was of thunder as he listened to his nation's honour being ridiculed, it's flag mocked. All this whilst Cameroon's was cheered to the rafters and greeted with rapturous applause at it's finale. The recent infamous events in Verona and the controversial loss of the Scudetto remained an open would amongst the Milanese, ensuring a special welcome was reserved for the Southern barbarian king, who had dared to wrestle their title away. Never had this famous old footballing cathedral heard such vitriol directed towards one man, this despised Neapolitan despot. With Pavarotti's *Nessun Dorma* supplying Italia '90 a wonderful soundtrack, all that was required in this grand Italian opera was a larger than life villain. Diego Maradona fitted the bill to perfection.

His appearance meant that an occasion normally noted for bringing nations together for once resembled a hate-fest. Appearing oblivious to the hail of abuse raining down upon him, Maradona showed off before battle commenced. Gently he coaxed the ball with his left foot onto the shoulder, juggled four times, back down to the knee, before finally flicking it off to an admiring team-mate. All with such absolute nonchalance. Sadly, for Maradona and his compadres the day from that moment on took an inexorable turn for the worse. After an opening fifteen minutes in which a nervous Cameroon appeared intimidated by their more illustrious opponents, the fourteenth World Cup exploded into life. Awoken to the surprising notion that Argentina were actually nothing special, the 'Indomitable Lions' came out of their defensive shell and went for them with a ferociousness verging on brutality. None more than the toweringly, fearsome centre-half Benjamin Massing, who introduced himself to Maradona with a horrific stamp on his damaged foot, for which he was rightly booked. Picked on constantly Diego got kicked harder than the ball throughout. His shins, calves and ankles constant targets. Indeed, it happened so repeatedly the fouls appeared more like systematic muggings than challenges. The South Americans themselves were hardly shrinking violets when it came to the game's darker aspects and a niggly, violent contest ensued with no quarter given by either team. Cameroon were swiftly opportunistic up front, brimming with energy and skill in midfield, whilst breathtakingly savage at the rear. As for the champions, they looked dire. Their vastly outnumbered supporters in the stadium refused to be intimidated by what appeared the entire world wishing them ill-fortune. An enthusiastic if out of tune Argentinian band tried with an impressive bravado to pretend all was well, but secretly they must also have feared the worst as their team's showing begged loudly to differ. Diego Maradona was misfiring badly. Each touch greeted by piercing deafening whistle from the Milanese, relieved of possession with a worrying regularity and clearly becoming increasingly infuriated at his own inability to grab hold and make things happen. There remained the odd flicker of wizardry to remind them he was still around, but nothing more. The brain was willing, a much-abused body was not. An exhausting, albeit successful Serie A campaign with Napoli had taken it's toll both physically and mentally on Maradona. There appeared nothing left in the tank. On the touchline, Carlos Bilardo looked close to a heart attack watching his team being overrun by an African team showing little respect for either name or stature.

The half-time whistle offered brief respite from what had been nothing short of a mauling for the world champions. In an attempt to ease the pressure Bilardo introduced lightning-fast Verona winger Claudio Caniggia. The tall, blond, long-haired Caniggia was good friends with Maradona off the pitch. There were many similarities between the two. Each hailed from similar backgrounds, plied their trade in Italy and most disturbingly, shared an unfortunate cocaine habit. Caniggia was only allowed to play in the competition at the last moment after being the subject of a police investigation in Italy involving drug trafficking. Once cleared he joined up with the national team, though great doubts remained over his complete innocence. On the field when focused Caniggia remained a potent weapon in Argentina's less than impressive armoury. With a devastating turn of pace and unerring ability to ride a tackle, allied with great skill and finishing, Claudia Caniggia on his day was a world beater. He also possessed a truly annoying trait of falling over whenever an opponent even dared to glance at him. In the early stages of the second half this quickly irritated the

Cameroon players no end and they made certain that if Caniggia did go to ground it was for a good reason. Diego Maradona's total frustration at being unable to influence events around him started to show itself. Not the type to find fault with fellow team-mates, he instead vented his anger at the highly-respected French referee Michael Vautrot. Pleading with typically Maradonesque dramatical gestures, Diego argued every decision, praying it would help stem the green tide. It was to no avail for the Cameroon with nothing to lose simply overwhelmed them attacking incessantly. Only bad luck and fine goalkeeping by Neri Pumpido kept the holders alive. Thunderous cheers greeted every African foray over the halfway line as the hugely biased Milanese roared them on. Events took an unexpected turn on sixty-two minutes when patience finally snapped with the antics of Claudio Caniggia and justice, Cameroon-style, was meted out. Breaking clear from his own penalty area, Caniggia accelerated away at great pace through a host of green shirts before being stopped ignominiously in full flight by an outrageously high tackle from Kana Biyik. Left with little option the referee flashed a red card and Biyik received a standing ovation from all corners of the stadium as he left the pitch. Rather than being deflated this helped only to spur on Cameroon and astonishingly, five minutes later they took a deserved lead. From a deflected free-kick Omam Biyik (brother of the dismissed Kana), rose to crash a header straight at Pumpido, only for him to watch in horror as the ball slipped out of his grasp and over the goal-line. Huge celebrations followed as the Cameroon players cavorted wildly next to the corner flag, with all manner of crazed high-jinks and death-defying forward rolls. African smiles had lit up the San Siro. The expected onslaught from the world champions failed to transpire and much to the despair of their ashen-faced Russian coach, Valeri Nepomniachi, Cameroon continued to carry the fight to Argentina. Defending stoutly and breaking with great menace, a most unlikely upset appeared on the cards. With Maradona reduced to a mere mortal, the South Americans, try as they might, lacked the necessary firepower to trouble their opponents' goal.

Eight minutes remained to play when Nepomniachi played his ace and brought on the legendary ageless Roger Milla. Officially said to be thirty-eight, many scoffed, putting his true age in the mid-forties. All mattered little for in this short cameo Milla terrified the Argentinian defenders whenever in possession with his alarming mastery of the ball and devastating shooting. As time ran down and utter humiliation loomed, all Milan prepared to bask wonderfully in Argentina's and particularly Maradona's misery.

Then, with only moments remaining Claudio Caniggia awoke from slumber to race with deadly intent into the Cameroon half. With his blond locks flowing, Caniggia cut a dashing sight as he soared onwards, leaving in his wake a trail of despairing green shirts. Suddenly, arriving in mid-air and at high speed came the man-mountain Massinga, who, with what appeared measured foresight and deadly relish seemed intent on slicing the Argentinian in two. As Caniggia rolled around in an apparent death throe on the turf, Massinga did not even wait to discover his fate and began the long walk to the touchline. In a remarkable display of support the entire stadium rose to acclaim the defender, who in turn waved to his new-found Italian friends. 'Forza Cameroon' resonated loudly over the terraces.

Left with nine men, the Africans steadfastly refused to buckle and reward came with the sound of Monsieur Vautrot's whistle. Their Captain apart, the beaten champions made a subdued exit, leaving the stage clear for African jubilation. Diego Maradona sportingly went around shaking the hands of his elated opponents. Later, after being rather predictably chosen to partake in a random drugs test, Maradona attended the post-match press conference. In an attempt to win back some much-needed face and still seething at his maltreatment by the Milanese, the Argentinian was at his mischievous best when he declared to a waiting audience, 'I am proud to have played a part in the people of Milan putting aside their racism for a day to cheer on Cameroon.'

The irony of these well-chosen words was not lost on all present. The fact remained the holders had been defeated and victory in the next match against Russia suddenly became essential. Safe in the knowledge this time around they would be amongst friends, the world champions headed South. With the city still in seventh heaven after clinching a second championship title, it was with great joy they welcomed home their boy. The king had returned and Naples rejoiced. Argentina was in safe hands.

Despite only a half-filled San Paolo, Maradona's name was sung with tremendous gusto by Argentinian and Neapolitan alike. On the pitch the red shirts of Russia began brightly with a touch, technique and swift incisive passing that made their opponents appear leaden-footed. On thirteen minutes drama occurred when Argentinian keeper Pumpido was stretchered off with a broken leg following a collision with his own defender, Olarticoechea. On came substitute Sergio Goycochea whose first action was to palm away a Russian corner. From the resulting kick a fantastic header from Oleg Kuznetsov was stopped on the goal-line by Maradona's hand. At first it appeared to be a shoulder, but television replays showed clearly it was the same right arm that felled the English in Mexico. He had done it again!

All hell let loose as the Russians pleaded with the referee for a penalty, but the Swede Erik Fredriksson, as Ali Ben Nasser four years before, were up against an artist schooled in the dark arts of Scopa. Neapolitan black magic, it was no contest. Stunned by such a blatant act of injustice the Russians became dispirited and their stomach for battle waned. It came as no surprise on the half hour when forward Pedro Troglia headed the Argentinians in front. In a low-key affair with neither side overtly impressive, victory was sealed twelve minutes from time when the man who scored the winning goal in Mexico, Jose Burruchaga, latched onto a sloppy back pass by the unfortunate Kuznetsov to make it 2-0 and game over. In between Argentina had again flattered to deceive. Diego Maradona remained a sad shadow of past glories, though sheer presence alone appeared sufficient to inspire a vital win for his countrymen. Throughout the contest Maradona bickered constantly with the referee, appearing more interested in diving and winning free kicks than actually creating opportunities. Hardly the behaviour of a man named recently by his President Carlos Menem, as Argentina's 'Official Consultant ambassador for sport.' This was not the magician who had cast a spell over all who crossed his path in times gone by. Age, injuries and a destructive, self-indulgent, decadent lifestyle had finally taken a heavy toll. It was desperation, the acts of one who had come to realise he was only human after all.

Argentina's final group match was again in Naples where a 1-1 draw with an impressive Romania eased both nations into the second round. Maradona was insipid once more. If Italia '90 was proving witness to the sad demise of arguably the greatest player of all time, it also hailed the arrival of a new world superstar from Eastern Europe. This man known as the 'Maradona of the Balkans'. The pride of the Carpathian Mountains, Romanian Captain Gheorghe Hagi. Against Argentina, Hagi was magnificent, a wonderfully sublime left-foot ripping apart the South Americans at will. Playing in a manner so reminiscent of Maradona in his pomp, the Romanian was awe-inspiring, totally overshadowing the real thing. After yet another turgid performance by the champions, even the most fanatical Argentinian supporter did not hold out much hope of them retaining the title. Drab, dreary and little more than average with the brightest light hopelessly off form, it was felt only a miracle would see them overcome the next opponent in the second-round knock-out phase in Turin. An old friend whom when the two came together the world stopped to watch and both nations held their breath. Brazil

Though not possessing the heavenly talent of past great sides, the Brazilians remained a potent force and were being hailed as clear favourites along with Italy to win the competition. This city, home to one of Italy's most scared relics, the Turin Shroud, prepared to play host to the greatest grudge match of them all, Argentina v Brazil.
For most it was already a foregone conclusion, a mismatch. Argentina were not given a prayer, but in this place where Christ chose to return, another also was hell-bent on showing his true face. Diego Maradona was determined to prove that he too performed miracles and the

whole world would bear witness to his second coming. On 24th June 1990, at the remarkable, newly-constructed Stadio Delle Alpi, 61,381 gathered to watch the showdown between these South American giants. On a sweltering hot Turin afternoon, vast swatches of yellow/gold shirts and flags stretched out in breathtaking style across this space-age stadium. The Rio Carnival had for a day been transferred to Turin. Support for Brazil on the terraces was overwhelming as watching neutrals fell behind them with the same fervid passion as a street kid from the favelas (slums). Everybody, apart from their small-if fanatical support wanted this irritant, boorish bunch of Argentinians removed from the tournament so that the partying could continue right up until the final. Even their own Football Association feared the worse, for unknown to the players they were already booked on a provisional flight back home the following day. As expected, Maradona's name was greeted with a deafening barrage of whistles when read out over the tannoy. It had become par for the course. The Samba drum beat thundered loud, the beautiful girls danced, the band played. Against this spectacular backdrop of passion, noise and colour Brazil began in whirlwind fashion.

Stung by terrible criticism from their nation's media that they were by far the most defensive side ever to leave Brazilian shores, Sebastian Lazaroni's men appeared on a mission, for in the opening period they blitzed Argentina's goal. With players such as Napoli's Antonio Careca and Ricardo Alemao in full flow, Brazil stormed forward. Neapolitan blood kinship appeared to have evaporated when pre-match Careca labelled Diego Maradona, his supposed good friend, as an 'Argentinian Pygmy'. It was the man nicknamed 'Lo Bomba' by the Naples tifosi who in the first sixty seconds burst through to fire a shot that Sergio Goycochea just managed to block. In what was a typically, tempestuous and fiery encounter between these aged old adversaries, Argentina battled courageously through the first half without conceding. Though heavily outclassed, the holders were not going down without a fight. Last ditch defending laced with a tenaciousness verging on fanaticism saw them survive, though in all but the scoreline it had been a massacre. Brazil had created sufficient opportunities to win a dozen games. Their Captain Dunga came closest when he rattled the woodwork with a powerful header, whilst Alemao saw a fierce shot palmed away by the heroic Goycochea, who at times was all that stood between his nation and total humiliation. As the second half unfolded, further gilt-edged chances were created and missed. Amongst Brazilian supporters a muttering of discomfort for the first time could be heard. When Antonio Careca once more shot against the post and Alemao followed up with a drive that cracked the opposite side, a terrifying sense of foreboding grabbed hold.

Maybe it was not to be Brazil's day?

Throughout the entire game Diego Maradona had been like a ghost at his own funeral, desperate to help ease the torment of his loved ones, but utterly helpless to do so. As the battle raged and yellow shirts pinged the ball to each other, ripping through Argentina with effortless aplomb, he was simply invisible. Even the Brazilian fans had lost the urge to boo, such was Maradona's apparent utter inability to hurt them. Eight minutes remained of this epic contest when Maradona, loved, hated, feared and adored, roared back to life. With both sets of supporters stricken by the unbearable tension prevalent in the stadium, the idea of extra time and even the awful possibility of a penalty shoot-out was deemed preferable to experiencing a goal at the last. Agony or ecstasy, it mattered little, for the shock could well have been fatal. Games between these two were often decided by moments of sheer genius that caused eyes to blink and the heart to soar.

It would happen again.

With his back to goal in the centre-circle, Diego Maradona picked the ball up, turned, and accelerated past his marker. A momentary shudder rocked the Stadio Delle Alpi. Suddenly, Maradona was clear and the yards as did the years fell away. Fear gripped Brazilian souls: their worst nightmare realised. He was back! Yellow shirts chased in desperation, slashing, hacking out of mortal terror, but somehow an unerring ability to ride the most ferocious of challenges enabled him to keep possession. As if carried by angels, Diego Maradona soared past three more defenders before laying off an exquisite pass for the unmarked Claudio Caniggia. With the Brazilians concentrating solely on Maradona, they had forgotten about the winger and with space inside the penalty area to pick a spot, Caniggia flashed a superb drive past Taffarel into the top corner. His Captain alongside him, the goal scorer raced over to the corner flag where he fell flat with arms outstretched before being mobbed by ecstatic, disbelieving team-mates. Maradona punched the air, he bore the look of a man reborn. As for Brazil, both team and followers gave off the impression of being mugged. A last chance appeared in the dying moments to save themselves, but Muller lashed over when it appeared easier to score. The final whistle signalled Argentina's first victory over Brazil in four World Cup meetings. In Buenos Aires the celebrating began as they set about proving that not only Rio could party like it was the end of the world. Against all odds and expectations, the still-champion had stolen it.

The 'Holy Water' scandal. A highly controversial, if colourful footnote to this game was provided by Brazilian defender Branco who claimed to journalists' post-match, that he had been 'drugged' from a water bottle given to him in the first half by the Argentinian bench off their physio Miguel di Lorenzo. The game was played at a boiling temperature of 30 Celsius, and Branco had been charged in the opening period to keep Diego Maradona at bay. During a pause in play, the Brazilian took the drink and soon after began to complain that he felt drowsy. Later Branco was simply unable to keep with Diego as he set off on the sensational run for Claudio Caniggia's winning goal. The journalists gave Branco a sympathetic ear, but even his native hacks felt such accusations were too outlandish. Their boy it appeared was simply emotional and sick at heart with being eliminated by their fiercest rivals

All went quiet, then, two years later, Branco came across Argentinian defender Oscar Ruggeri who had played that day at Rio de Janeiro airport. What he told the Brazilian left him dumbstruck. 'Ah, Claudio, that was a good trick we pulled on you back at Italia '90, wasn't it?' Ruggeri admitted there had indeed been a 'special' bottle, identified by its coloured top in the physio's medical kit on that afternoon in Turin. The story might have ended there were it not for Diego Maradona. In 2004, speaking on the programme Mar de Fondo, on Argentinian television. Diego confirmed Branco's accusations were true. His bench did indeed have a 'special' bottle marked up for the

Brazilians laced with the tranquiller Roipnol, and it was this that was offered to Branco when he shouted across at the Argentinian bench for a drink.

Branco claims the effect of the drink was immediate and lethal. The Brazilian felt dizzy, his legs close to collapse and he almost fainted. At half-time Branco begged to be substituted, but coach Lazaroni pleaded with him to stick with it and he played all of the second half. In a last twist around that time, Argentina coach Carlos Bilardo, gave a strangely guarded answer when asked also about the incident. 'I don't know but that doesn't mean that it didn't happen, I can't say for certain that it didn't happen.' However, shortly after, Bilardo came clean and admitted he and a 'helper' did actually mix a drug known as 'Good night Cinderella' and it was passed on to Branco!'

An astonishing tale.

A quarter-final in Florence against Yugoslavia loomed large, however, many were already doing the maths. If the skilful, but unpredictable Slavs could be overcome, the mother of all semi-finals awaited in Naples. Surely the Gods of football were having a private joke, Italy against Maradona's Argentina in the San Paolo? Neapolitans said their prayers and hoped beyond all hope it would not come to pass, but, somehow, they already knew. Diego Maradona was returning home to break their hearts.

After having disposed of the real thing, Argentina now found themselves against a nation nicknamed the 'Brazilians of Europe'. When such wonderful ball players as Robert Prosinecki and Dejan Savicevic were in the mood, Yugoslavia were a match for any team in the tournament. But the highly-fuelled concoction of Croats, Serbs and Macedonians that made up their team meant they were often more likely to beat themselves, a nationalistic self-destruct button pressed on many occasions and one that returned to haunt them again in Fiorentina's Comunale stadium when it mattered most. For this game Argentina wore their dark blue away shirt, black home shorts and regular white socks. The same combination they used in the previous World Cup in ('The Hand of God') match with England. There was something different about their Captain's kit, for he wore Napoli away socks, which were also white, but made by the manufacturer Ennerre, as opposed to Adidas like the rest. It didn't go unnoticed, especially in Naples. Could they love Maradona anymore? Doubtful. 'El Pibe De Oro' was already thinking ahead. After outplaying Argentina for 120 minutes, this bitterly fought quarter-final went down to penalty kicks. During the contest Diego Maradona had fell back into anonymity, his tour de force against the Brazilians appearing now just a sad drunkard's rendition of classic poetry. Sluggish and frustrated, Maradona looked a busted flush, no more than when he scuffed a spot-kick in the shootout that would have put his nation 3-1 up. Taking advantage, the ice cool Savicevic stepped forward and blasted a shot past Sergio Goycochea, making it 2-2. When Troglio hit a post for Argentina next time around, it really did seem as if they were going home. Dezotti netted for Argentina and to the dismay of neutrals, Goycochea saved once more, this time from Hadzibegic to win the tie. With the luck of the devil Carlos Bilardo's team had made it to the semi-finals. An emotional Bilardo joined his players as they took the salute of their small, but boisterous following. That nobody liked them was wholly irrelevant, for the holders were through and hanging on to their trophy for dear, dear life.

Later that same day in Rome, Italy set up the ultimate showdown at the San Paolo when they beat the Republic of Ireland with a lone Salvatore Schillachi goal. No one slept in the Eternal city that evening as the car horns blazed away in triumph. Few were worried that for the first time Italy were now forced to leave the capital and play away from the electric atmosphere of the Stadio Olimpico, where they had been guaranteed incredible support throughout the competition. None believed that a mischievous, even downright rebellious city as Naples would fail to give vociferous backing to the beloved 'Azzurri'. Neapolitans were after all though it begrudged Northerners to admit it, Italian. Their loyalty to the blood country unquestionable, surely? So, all eyes turned South, for in just four days' time, with the world watching on, Naples would be forced to bare it's soul. The 'Azzurri' were on the march! Under the astute management of an experienced coach, fifty-seven-year-old Azeglio Vicini, they had cast away their defensive shackles of decades past, in favour of a more attacking style. With fifty million Italians constantly giving him advice on who to pick Vicini remained focused on the job in hand to mould together a side capable of withstanding the pressures that competing for a World Cup on home soil brought.

The eve of their opening game against Austria saw one paper carrying the headline, *'Failure will not be tolerated'*. His was an Italian team brimming with skill, power and pace. A magnificent defensive stalwart to organise the rear in AC Milan sweeper Baresi, midfield guile from Giannini, Donadoni and De Napoli, whilst in attack, a marvellous array of strikers from which to choose in Serena, Carnevale, Vialli, Baggio and 'Toto' Schillachi, this son of a Palermo bricklayer whose mad, staring Sicilian eyes were lighting up Italia '90. The coach's one true Achilles heel lay with an absurd reluctance to acknowledge the rare genius of Roberto Baggio, choosing instead to select the more solid, harder working Gianluca Vialli. In a first round match Baggio scored the goal of the tournament when from the halfway line he took on and beat the entire Czechoslovakian defence. Even then Vicini remained far from impressed and insisted that the boy from Florence lacked the required mental toughness to play in every game.

However, just when the Italian press were building up a head of steam in their clamouring for the golden boy Baggio to start against Argentina, up popped Diego Maradona to lob a verbal grenade that not only rocked Italia '90 on it's head but threatened to spark open civil war between North and South.

'The Italians are asking Neapolitans to be Italians for a day, yet for the other 364 days in the year they forget all about Naples. The people do not forget this.'

In an unveiled attempt to propel Napoli tifosi onto Argentina's side, Maradona spoke directly to his people, urging them to cheer for their king. 'What has Italy ever done for you?' he asked. Naples reeled: Maradona had issued a call to arms. Opinion was split, a Pandora's Box had been opened. Bitter feelings that Neapolitans had tried desperately to bury whilst the tournament ran it's course returned to immeasurably haunt them.

Maradona's words never failed to arouse the deepest passions and this blatantly cynical ploy to divide and conquer caused even them to consider whether he had finally gone too far? One Neapolitan man when questioned on local television reacted angrily to the suggestions that he should even consider going against his country. 'Neapolitans are more Italian than Italians,' he argued. 'We are Italians and we support Italy.' Whilst there were many who were genuinely horrified at Maradona's remarks, the more fanatical in the Forcella welcomed their hero's words as yet another opportunity to goad their good friends in the North. What better weapon than worldwide humiliation? Tifosi made ready their *'Forza Argentina'* banners. Pre-match, with emotions spiralling wildly out of control, Argentina's flag was torn to shreds outside their training camp at Trigoria, near Rome. Speaking on Rai television an outraged Maradona pledged to avenge his nation's besmirched honour in the San Paolo by knocking out the Italians. There was something in his eyes that caused Neapolitans to sit up and take notice. They had seen that look before, he was serious.

On that fateful morning of 3rd July, Naples awoke in dreadful anticipation of the coming storm. It's people pondered their heart-rending choice. Italy or Maradona? Throughout the day swarms of Argentinians had begun arriving, their numbers swelling dramatically since the smash-and-grab raid against Brazil. Embraced warmly by the locals, spontaneous parties broke out along the Spaccanapoli. Hopes for an unlikely victory over Italy were high for was this not the City of Miracles? Many took the opportunity to visit churches where they whispered quiet prayers to their kind host's patron. Others partook in a different kind of holy pilgrimage, to Maradona's home in the hills of Posilippo. Though perhaps most poignantly a blue/white scarf of their country was placed with great discretion around a statue of San Gennaro. In this hour of need all straws were to be clutched at. Secretly, in more

quiet moments Argentinian supporters feared wanton humiliation at the hands of an exhilarating 'Azzurri'. Their new found Neapolitan friends were quick to remind them that all was far from lost, for they would be playing under Vesuvio's shadow, and here anything was deemed possible.
Anything.
As kick-off drew near and the San Paolo bathed gloriously in the red/green/white of the Italian tricolour, it appeared Maradona's call for Rebellion had fallen on deaf ears. Naples' plight was reflected in the words of one succinct banner. *'Diego nei cori, Italia nel cuore'. ('Diego in our chants, Italy in our hearts')*. The night was still in it's infancy and as a tremendous roar greeted the teams' entrance, those Napoli tifosi who had broken ranks with the vast majority became clearly visible amongst the South Americans, joining in with their singing. Other Neapolitans decided simply not to cheer for either side. It was a strange atmosphere, restrained even. This was a city at war with itself. As the players' names were read out over the tannoy all the South Americans were roundly booed until it came to their Captain, who received a cheer that echoed far over the stadium and across the city. Maradona raced across to the Curva B and blew kisses to his Napoli tifosi before applauding the rest of the crowd. That they loved him was not in question. He had come from the sky and made their dreams come true, but this was blood. Those who did choose to side with the 'Azzurri' did so in the hope that here on sacred turf, their boy could take care of himself.
The game began as expected with Italy quickly finding their rhythm and pinning Argentina back. Once again Vicini risked the vengeful wrath of his countrymen by

leaving out Roberto Baggio, but as the host nation tormented the holders with their movement and pace in the early stage he appeared hardly missed. In danger of being overrun the champions mercilessly hacked down their opponents. Throughout the tournament they had attempted to make up for their dearth of class at any cost. But this was Italy, it was sheer folly to believe they could ever be bullied or intimidated. As tackles flew the 'Azzurri' replied with a bloodcurdling, bone-shattering interest. On seventeen minutes, Toto Schillachi drew first blood when he pounced upon a Goycochea block from Vialli's shot to lash a ferocious drive into the top corner from eight yards. Off he soared with arms outstretched, eyes bulging from the sockets! No matter what became of him afterwards, Schillachi remains to this day the defining image of Italia '90. A shooting star maybe, but a legend forever.

Diego Maradona fished the ball out of the net and sprinted back to restart the game. He appeared to have found a semblance of his old form, probing and prompting in centre-midfield. But it was still Italy who looked by far the better side, their rapier-like incisive passing cutting a swathe through Argentina's defence. Though enlightened every so often by moments of pure skill, the remainder of the first half was a cruel tense affair, with the French referee Vautrot requiring eyes in the back of his head as flare-ups raged. Much to the disgust of Baresi, Maldini and Bergomi, Claudio Caniggia spent most of his time collapsing like he had been felled by a sniper's rifle. It was a grim and brutal, but still an utterly fascinating encounter between two nations with so much at stake. Finding it hard to resist their natural tendency to defend a lead, Italy came under increasing pressure and just before the break a rejuvenated of sorts Maradona let fly a rocket that was saved spectacularly by keeper Walter Zenga. It must have been the Naples air for Diego had found from somewhere a new lease of life. Half-time passed quickly and Italians everywhere suddenly realised the so-far carnival-like road to the final had turned into a crawl. Even the great Franco Baresi was displaying signs of nerves as his usual immaculate distribution went awry. With an hour gone Argentina had opened up and for the first time in the tournament began to play in a manner befitting their status as world champions. The South Americans attacked incessantly, Carlos Bilardo screamed out instructions from the touchline for his players at every opportunity to 'Find Maradona!' By this time Italy had retreated en masse. Vicini looked close to a coronary as he implored his team to push up the pitch, but a combination of nerves and traditional old habits meant they were unable to break out. As the clock ticked down tension inside the San Paolo became unbearable. Individual errors in the Italian defence saw supporters closing their eyes in horror.

On sixty-seven minutes with a full moon shining bright in the black Neapolitan heavens, their worst fears were realised. Almost inevitably it was Diego Maradona who orchestrated the move as he received possession in midfield and laid a pass out wide to the attacking full-back Jose Olarticoechea. Blessed with a little time the defender's cross found Caniggia, whose glancing header dipped over a badly flailing Zenga to land in an unguarded net. Suddenly, with a ragged Italy looking vulnerable and ripe for the kill all bets were off. Not only Argentinians celebrated in the San Paolo, a minority of Neapolitans also could not resist such temptation. Maradona blew kisses to his adoring followers. From the beginning of the competition he had been jeered, whistled, heckled, his anthem abused. Loathed, hated and detested. 1-1. Welcome to Naples!

With extra-time looming Vicini gambled and threw on his joker in Roberto Baggio. 'Il Divino' found himself an immediate target for defender Ricardo Giusti, who was booked for leaving a stud mark up the back of his leg, an induction course Argentinian-style. The seconds ticked down, Vautrot's whistle was greeted by both sides with relief, a brief respite from the overwhelming tension of battle. All inside the San Paolo took a sharp intake of breath before being plunged again into emotional turmoil. The match resumed with the fresh legs of Baggio tormenting the leg-weary South American rearguard, his silky skills leaving opponents two options. Either look foolish or bring him to ground. Giusti was of such mind, for after being left in an embarrassed heap by Baggio, he extracted revenge by punching the exalted Italian in the face. Vautrot immediately flashed the red card, reducing Argentina to ten men. An incensed Maradona harangued the French official. His hands bound in prayer, the Captain pleaded Giusti's case, but the referee simply waved him away. With the Argentinians defending for their very lives and the Italians almost paralysed by nerves, the game inevitably fell into stalemate. Vautrot's decision to call time on proceedings cut like a knife across Italy, for the horrible charade of penalties would be called upon to decide the winner of this searing drama in the San Paolo. On a sweltering, dripping, hot Naples evening, Franco Baresi, Captain of the 'Rossoneri', loyal stalwart to the 'Azzurri' stepped out of the centre-circle to begin proceedings. Baresi, Baggio and Di Agostini all scored, as did Serrizuela, Burruchaga and Olarticoechea for

Argentina. Then, at 3-3, the night took it's inexorable twist when Milan's Roberto Donadoni made his wary way forward. He walked in the doom-laden manner of a man heading for the gallows. It came as little surprise when Donadoni hit a weak shot straight at Goycochea, the line was broken. The spotlight fell on one man and not for the first time in his remarkable career.

Diego Maradona entered centre-stage.

If he scored the Italians would have to convert the next effort or face the ignobility of being eliminated from their own World Cup, and to make matters worse by a man whom they had treated with total disdain from the opening match of Italia '90. With a ridiculous par-nonchalance that beggared belief, Maradona simply rolled the ball into the bottom left-hand corner, whilst Zenga went in the opposite direction. As Diego wheeled away in triumph, Italy stood on the brink. Only Aldo Serena stood between them and utter desolation. Carrying a nation's hopes, the Inter striker stepped forward and hit a woeful penalty straight at Goycochea. With tears streaming down his face Serena collapsed to the floor. In that moment a dream died. Later, he wept live on television begging forgiveness for the miss.

'I wear the sadness of fifty million people on my back.'

The 'Azzurri' were out. On screens throughout the land Italians watched in horror as Maradona led his team on a celebratory lap of honour around the San Paolo. The king of Naples saluted those whom had joined with his countrymen in support of Argentina, for it was not only Argentinians who laughed, danced and sung under Vesuvio's shadow. There were others also who celebrated with glee the host nation's exit. It did not take long for the recriminations to begin. Maradona's post-match comments hardly helped to calm moods, 'I hate to enjoy the sadness of my friends.'

This sarcasm was not appreciated with emotions running high and that night his house was stoned. An angry Azeglio Vicini slammed the level of support Italy experienced in the San Paolo, claiming it was nowhere near what they had received in Rome. Many Northerners cast treacherous glances towards Naples and accusations of betrayal raged. All were vehemently denied by it's inhabitants, however, the facts do remain the triumphant war cries of 'Argentina' echoing over the bay way past midnight on that fateful evening came tinged with a local dialect. Maradona's cunning plan to exploit Neapolitan resentment had worked to perfection. His words heeded by some, if not all.

On 3rd July 1990, Italians cried themselves to sleep for a rebellion had occurred in the South that broke their hearts.

CHAPTER TWENTY-TWO

SNAKEBITE

In the early spring of March 1991, a lone figure walked warily into the grand marble surroundings of Naples' Palace of Justice, demanding to see the city's chief magistrate. He looked nervous, clutching tight on a cigarette, fully aware of the magnitude his actions were about to cause. The man's name was Piero Pugliese, a shadowy figure from the Neapolitan underworld. Pugliese claimed to possess intimate knowledge of a famous Napoli footballer linking him with drug trafficking and match-fixing. He wished to cut a deal, total immunity from prosecution for past misdemeanours, in return promising the authorities a prize beyond their wildest dreams. Exposing the myth of 'El Pibe De Oro'. To dish the dirt on the soiled private world of Diego Maradona, shaking the ground beneath and crucifying him. Like another once upon a time ago, in this part of the world, there was to be no happy ending.

In 73 BC, a gladiator slave called Spartacus rebelled and he and his companions fought for three years against Roman legions who sought to destroy them. It was called the 'Revolt of the Slaves' and after a heroic struggle they were finally outgunned and defeated by the legions of Crassus and Pompey. Not before terrifying Rome. The revolt began after becoming tired of being abused in the fighting/training arena based at Capua. The modern Santa Maria Vetere, sixteen miles from Naples. After killing their guards, Spartacus and seventy other gladiators took refuge on the slopes of Mount Vesuvio, in ravines where it was easy to fortify. There they clashed many times with the local Roman soldiers whom had been handed the unenviable task of bringing them to heel. The fugitives were originally armed only with nothing but clubs, spears and forks, but when prevailing against the enemy would seize their weapons. The Roman Senate swiftly grew tired of these disturbing reports of mere slaves killing soldiers. Forgetting that these same slaves were trained gladiators, (fighting machines), and those alongside them were now being taught how to kill by the same men. An army of three thousand was despatched led by two Rome Quaestors (Magistrates) Gaius Glaber and Publius Varinius, to end the insurgency. Not knowing they were being watched the Romans arrived under Mount Vesuvio at night and surrounded the rebel camp. It was for them sport, no more for the superiority in numbers was simply overwhelming. They would take to their sleep content. The guard went down and taking advantage Spartacus and his small but deadly gladiator army attacked with violent fury. It was wanton slaughter as the ground turned red with Roman blood. Carnage ensued. It became known as the 'Battle of Vesuvio'. Those soldiers whom fled and survived spoke of the sheer ferociousness of the enemy. It had been a rout. Spartacus was a natural leader and from the slopes of the rumbling volcano, a slave revolt turned into a slave war as the gladiator's number swelled with thousands of new recruits. Across the country they swept, freeing slaves, burning and looting everything in their path. All this mass of humanity wanted was freedom from tyranny and a chance to live free. Finally, knowing they could never allow Spartacus and his once enslaved brethren to escape, the Roman senate issued a decree that their finest Generals and armies be used to quell and end this madness. The proconsul Marcus Licinius Crassus in command of eight legions marched out of Rome under cover of darkness and headed South. The wilderness. This Mezzorgiorno. Spartacus had made secret arrangements with the Cilician pirates to take his army to Thrace. It was to cost them almost the entire vast fortune they had acquired in their forays but deemed worth it. The Cilicians with a fleet would meet them in the deep South and there they would cross the Messina strait and freedom. Sadly, Rome had also cut a deal with the pirates, a better one and the ships never shown. Trapped with his back to the sea, Spartacus declared to his gathered army that the only way to become free was to kill every Roman sent against them. As they turned to faced Crassus' elite legions, little did he know Pompey with another huge army was also lying in wait. It was simply impossible odds. The rebels were finally defeated with losses of sixty thousand men. Women and children were taken prisoner and a further six thousand fighters crucified along the Appian Way between Capua and Rome. Spartacus almost certainly amongst them, for he was never identified by the Romans as his followers refused to give him up. They loved a good crucifixion in the city of the seven hills and come 1990, another was forthcoming.

In Rome, on 8th July 1990, at the Stadio Olimpico, an Argentinian side decimated by injuries and suspensions went into a World Cup Final against Germany fired up with a nationalistic passion verging on psychotic. After the tumultuous events of the San Paolo five days previous, Maradona was despised like never before by Italians and when caught on the stadium screen mouthing 'Sons of bitches' in reaction to the crowd drowning out his nation's anthem in a crescendo of boos, open season was declared on Argentina's Captain. A hailstorm of vitriol rained down that shocked even those who were there to support Franz Beckenbauer's team. What should have been a showcase occasion deteriorated into a horrific, ill-tempered affair with the holders by far the worst offenders. The battle-plan appeared simply to reach penalties by any means. To their credit Argentina had achieved the impossible by making the normally boorish Germans the neutral's favourite. Bilardo's men spent almost the entire contest hacking down any opponent who dared to go within twenty yards of goal. Reduced to ten men on the hour when half-time substitute Monzon slashed down Jurgen Klinsmann, they went even further into their defensive shell. Luck ran out with just six minutes remaining Rudi Voeller looked to be tripped by the trailing defender Sensini in the box and the Mexican official, Edgardo Codesal, deciding to put Italia '90 out of it's misery, awarding a penalty. A highly dubious decision with the theatrical Voeller looking to have dived, but still one much appreciated by a rabid, pro-German crowd. Immediately, the referee found himself surrounded by a Diego Maradona-led mob that seemed intent on a lynching if he did not change his mind. Despite the outrageous bullying tactics of the Argentinians as they bumped and pushed him, Codesal kept his cool. Showing equal nerves of steel, Inter full-back Andreas Brehme stepped up to fire low past Sergio Goycochea and surely win the World Cup for his country. Knowing the cause was hopeless, Argentina became even further enveloped in red mist when Dezotti brought more shame upon his nation by grabbing German defender Jurgen Kohler round the throat as he raced away from him with the ball. Codesal's immediate branding of a red card was a sign that the thuggish South Americans had truly plunged the depths. As the final whistle resonated in the ancient capital, Rome bore witness to a public display of emotional turmoil the likes of which no footballer has ever been subjected to. Maradona sobbed uncontrollably. His face etched in sorrow, all to the sheer joy of the Stadio Olimpico who wallowed wonderfully in such obvious grief. In front of a watching world with all eyes and cameras upon him Maradona broke down, both physically and mentally drained. There was nothing left to give. The pressures of carrying Argentina and Napoli over such a long period finally proved too heavy a burden to carry. The tears fell, but here in this footballing-mad country there could be no sympathy for a man who had single-handedly orchestrated Italy's downfall. Diego Maradona's descent into hell had begun.

The Last Act. There was a great sadness on the San Paolo terraces as they watched this slow and heavily bearded overweight imposter in Napoli's, legendary number ten shirt masquerade as their beloved Maradona. Also, there existed much anger for the cause of his malaise was an open secret amongst the tifosi. Diego Maradona was out of control, he no longer trained, preferring instead to spend nights in Naples' red-Light area, whoring and taking cocaine. His team-mates tried desperately to make him see sense, none more than defender Ciro Ferrara, who would go to Diego's house and try to persuade him to attend training sessions at Soccavo. Ferrara recalls, 'I would explain how much we loved and needed him. He'd react and come with me, work the cocaine out of his system and then we'd go off and have a pizza together. Sometimes, when I think back now I wish I'd done it more often.' Sadly, Ciro Ferrara was fighting a losing battle because unknown to him, cocaine had for the first-time overtaken football in the life of Diego Maradona. Even at his lowest ebb Maradona was capable of producing moments of wizardry. A magnificently executed scissor-kick against Hungarian side Ujpest Dozsa in the European Cup helped the Neapolitans to a 5-0 aggregate win and reminded people of the player he once was. After the game he declared in typical robust manner, 'I would play for Napoli in a wheelchair if needed.'

Whispers across the city were that Maradona's time in Naples was short. Matters were brought to a head before a second-round match against Spartak Moscow when he claimed, to the astonishment of the club's medical team, of being injured and so could not travel with the squad to Russia. After being threatened with a huge fine Maradona relented and made his own way at the last. In the end many Neapolitans wondered why he bothered going, for a clearly sulking Diego appeared totally uninterested in influencing events on the pitch. Bereft of any inspiration and far from home, a stuttering Napoli team were eliminated 5-3 on penalties in the Moscow snow. Going out at such an early stage as against Real Madrid two years previous, left Ferlaino spitting blood. Much needed revenue had again slipped through Napoli's fingers. He, like the most fanatical of tifosi was fast losing patience with the increasingly unpredictable Maradona. It could not go on. For when a magician reaches into his hat and the rabbit's refuse to appear what is there left? A spluttered cough, deafening silence, before a slow embarrassing shuffle off stage. The show was coming to an end.

On 22nd November 1990, SSC Napoli played host to Fiorentina. Even at such an early stage, Albertino Bigon knew victory was essential if his team were to have any chance of retaining the Scudetto. After a superb 5-1 pre-season massacre of great rivals Juventus in the Supercoppa Italia, hopes were high of another successful league campaign. But events off pitch regarding their Captain, had an unsettling effect on the team and one win in the opening seven games left them lying in a miserable tenth position. Also, the coach was growing ever weary of the constant backstabbing, political intrigue and in-fighting that existed in the Napoli corridors of power. To such an extent that he was already contemplating a move elsewhere.

As for Diego Maradona?

A late decision to exclude himself from selection on the day of the 'Viola clash' left Bigon almost speechless with rage. The player and his manager Guillermo Coppola had spent the previous evening snorting coke, drinking and partying the hours away with call-girls in a private residence of the Hotel Paradiso. That the home side won 1-0 with a rare Ciro Ferrara goal was of secondary importance, for it was claimed that same night a meeting took place in which President Corrado Ferlaino finally issued the order to deal with Maradona. The love affair was over. He had outgrown his usefulness and become an embarrassment to the city. Plans were put in place, phone calls made and favours called in. So, it began.

The following day an astonishing article appeared on the front page of the prestigious newspaper Gazzette dello Sport. Generally regarded as pro-Neapolitan, the feature by it's well-respected Napoli correspondent Franco Esposito, made unveiled references to Maradona's worsening cocaine addiction. *'A dark evil taking hold. A mysterious illness affecting the world's greatest player.'* Esposito was a journalist with intimate knowledge of the Naples scene. He would have been well aware of what was occurring, but wise enough to realise some things were best left unwritten. That he produced such a hard-hitting piece slaughtering Maradona meant it was clear the green light had been given by those in power to do so. For whatever reason they wanted it to be published. Normally, on the rare occasions such scathing attacks found their way to print, Napoli officials would shout and scream, threatening lawsuit's and blue murder. This time, nothing, just a deafening silence from the San Paolo. That itself spoke more than a thousand words.

It became clear the veiled cloak of protection that had shielded Diego Maradona from prying eyes since his arrival in Naples had been swept away. Whilst performing miracles on the pitch, Neapolitan tolerance with their king knew no bounds. All they asked of Diego was to win them football matches. But, come the end when human failings were revealed and the magic touch had waned, they simply spat him out with venom. The sheer ferocity of what happened next caused even the city's most hard-bitten to wince.

In what could only have been a concerted campaign, a systematic deluge of lowlife pimps, pushers, prostitutes and addicts appeared to denounce Maradona in newspapers across the land as nothing less than a sexually-depraved, drug-crazed maniac. Lurid tabloid headlines screamed out scandalous stories of cocaine-fuelled orgies in Naples backstreet brothels. Italians shook their heads in disbelief; if only a fraction were true, how did he ever find the time to play football? Each day brought new revelations. Some were simply ludicrous and obviously fake. They came, sold their story and disappeared. Journalists who attempted to follow-up Diego's more 'interesting' encounters found not only were the characters involved hard to track down, most simply did not exist. Reeling badly from this almighty onslaught, Diego Maradona's world was rocked even further when an undercover operation by Napoli Polizia recognised his voice speaking on a wiretap, during a surveillance operation against a Forcella based cocaine and call girl racket. The Argentinian was caught red-handed asking for 'Gear' off a well-known local woman called Carmela Cinguerama, who was said to run for the Camorra a chain of seedy establishments close by the city's main port. Although cleared of any involvement with the original investigation, it was felt enough information was available for the government to launch a separate legal action against the player for alleged possession and possible distribution of narcotics. A public announcement was made of this boosting both egos and personal profiles of those adjudicating. Maradona was a huge, if relatively easy catch in a sea brimming with sharks. Having his head on a pole would prove a coup in the ongoing battle against organised crime.

For Piero Pugliese to arrive unannounced on their doorstep, desperate to cleanse his soul was a joy they could hardly have expected. It was a confession that came drenched in blood. Pugliese owned up to a host of gangland assassinations. He also dropped strong hints to interrogators that he was prepared to spill the beans on those who ruled from the shadows. Suddenly, he was entitled to the highest state protection. With such a tempting statement, Pugliese immediately became 'Pentiti' (Turncoat), an inhabitant of the dangerous world of

'Pentismo' (Repentance). A living death sentence shown to those whose efforts to expunge their sins left them facing the merciless wrath of former masters. Times were desperate and corruption was rife. This was a lawless city. Gangster chiefs were blatantly putting forward their own people as candidates in local elections across Naples and winning. Any honourable politician who dared to mention ballot-rigging was ruthlessly gunned down. It had become a matter of survival between good and evil. As war was declared on the Camorra, Piero Pugliese attempted to escape a messy end by telling all.

Prosecutors listened with a mixture of incredulity and suspicion to his stories. He claimed to have been a valued member of Diego Maradona's inner circle, with much sought after duties, such as being a chauffeur and bodyguard. Life with Diego brought many perks, much preferable to previous employment working part-time as a security guard at the San Paolo, whilst allegedly having to supplement income by moonlighting as a hired gun for the Camorra. Pugliese's story began at Maradona's wedding in Buenos Aires, November 1989, where he was approached by Guillermo Coppola and asked to oversee a package that needed delivering home. Pugliese understood immediately the parcel was drugs and not wanting to risk the wrath of his paymasters agreed to go along. Through the aid of an unsuspecting courier who believed she was only carrying paper documents, the cocaine was successfully ferried to Naples. According to Pugliese, he was rewarded handsomely for his role in the smuggling with 20 million Lira paid out of DIARMA's bank account, for which only Maradona and Coppola had signature rights to sign off. Unbeknown to the Argentinians, their Neapolitan employee, in fear of being used as a scapegoat if all went wrong secretly taped meetings between them. A paranoia that stemmed from the Naples streets where trust came only through those related by blood. When confronted, Guillermo Coppola could not deny the transaction due to taped evidence and his name on the cheque. Cool as ever he claimed, 'The money was simply a loan and for the good of Naples' children.' The cash was to start a football school with a promise to be paid back within the month. Where other people had blood in their veins, Coppola had ice.

Serious cracks in Piero Pugliese's credibility as a witness appeared when he changed his story on how the cocaine was delivered to Naples. An absurd statement that it was brought in by Argentina's squad on their way to play a friendly match against Italy, saw officers begin to think they were being led up a blind path. More raised eyebrows occurred when he cast crazed accusations that Maradona had conspired with the Camorra to ensure the Neapolitans failed to retain the Scudetto in their infamous collapse towards the end of the 1987-88 season. That Diego had ensured thousands of Neapolitans, who bet with their hearts on the *Totonero* to win Serie A, would not collect and his gangster friends clean up. Such comments made no sense for it was outrageous to suggest Diego Maradona had thrown matches. As Napoli fell away during that fateful time, it was obvious to anyone that none fought harder than he. Maybe the blame did lie elsewhere? Doubts were aired as previously written in earlier chapters regarding certain individuals. A mystery still to be resolved. Not Maradona, to even suggest such was perceived as the muttering of lunacy. Experienced members of the elite Nulceo One, Naples' finest crime fighting force smelt a rat. They failed to comprehend just what to make of this particular pentiti. Streetwise Camorra hood who was willing to say or do anything to save his skin, or a Neapolitan Walter Mitty character with a death wish, unbridled imagination and living in a fantasy world? If enough mud is thrown some inevitably sticks and as Maradona's star hurtled forever downwards, the feelings of resentment were such, many had come to believe he was capable of anything. For Guillermo Coppola, the heat from all sides had become even too hot for someone of his normally chilled persona to handle. Beating a hasty retreat, he fled home to Argentina. Once on safe ground he declared the split from Maradona had been 'Purely affable and only temporary.' He simply wished to spend more time with his family in Buenos Aires. A pathetic charade of a public statement read, 'Diego Maradona did not and never has taken drugs.' Looking wonderfully tear-stained and quaking with emotion, but super slick to the end, Guillermo Coppola vacates the story. To say this pantomime was greeted with contempt in the Southern capital was the equivalent of calling Mount Vesuvio a teapot. This was the home of street-theatre. Neapolitans knew a con-man when they saw one. The truth being Coppola had left Diego alone to face the lynch mob whilst he ran to save his own neck. As the raging fires of hell engulfed Maradona's adopted city in all it's fury, he attempted to sought shelter on a football pitch. Once, it had been a sanctuary, away from the pitfalls and stresses that being a living God to so many involved. Not anymore; where once they came to admire, now it was to stare and poke fun. The Maradona who skipped beneath the raindrops with a ball tied to his feet by a mystical piece of string no longer existed. Stolen away, never again to be seen. The pitch was now a cage, the stadium a zoo. That he still continued to be picked by Albertino Bigon was for reasons of both pity and the hope that a momentary spark of the old magic might create an opportunity for his badly misfiring side. Amidst the controversy of a horrific season the Neapolitan's title was long gone. All that remained was for the same fate to befall their Captain.

In the end it all came down to pure mathematics. Knowing they could save two years of astronomical wages and escape the nightmare scenario of having to sell him, President Ferlaino prepared to call time on the once exalted, but now disgraced Argentinian's reign in Naples. Years before when an exuberant Maradona swaggered arrogantly into his office to lay down the law on who should or should not be bought, Ferlaino thought then that given enough rope he would inevitably hang himself. That day had drawn ever closer. To be treated with so little respect irked Ferlaino in a way perhaps only other Neapolitans could understand. Back then they needed him. Despite everything that went on behind the darkened veil, Maradona lit up lives, made dreams come true, settled old scores and gave Naples back it's pride. But there was a curse that lurked constantly, nagging, gradually eating away both at body and soul. It was one opponent, despite all his God-given gifts that Diego could not shake-off. In the end that was why they crucified him. For seven years Napoli's shadow army of fixers went to extraordinary length to ensure Maradona's drug-taking never surfaced at post-match doping tests. His urine was either swapped for a clean sample or in a ploy so typically Neapolitan in it's scheming, the player would use a hidden tube from which he could produce a false specimen. 'Close friends' of Naples working in the Italian Football Association always made certain the number ten shirt never appeared in the chosen list at away grounds.

Despite the fire, fury and controversy surrounding his now every waking moment, team-mates still adored their ailing Captain and for good reason. The maestro treated them all like brothers and Maradona was smitten with his said 'apprentice' Zola, more than any other. He attempted to pass on as much knowledge, particularly his free-kick prowess, as possible before it was too late. Relating back to an earlier story regarding Zola. Towards the end in a league fixture at Pisa in February 1991, Maradona again handed over the number 10 to Zola and he wore nine. After the match which ended 1-1, he explained to journalists, 'I gave Gianfranco my shirt because he's the future of Napoli.' Maradona clearly knew time was almost up.

On Sunday 17th March 1991, Napoli played Bari at the San Paolo. It was one of the rare occasions that Bigon played both Gianfranco Zola and Diego Maradona together. That they won 1-0 with a lone Zola goal was totally irrelevant, for what happened in the immediate aftermath would in no short time cause shockwaves across not just Italy, but the entire world. Moments after the game finished a shattered Maradona was approached by the club's chief medical officer Arcangelo Pepe, who informed him he had been selected for testing. Knowing well the safeguards in place, though surprised at finally being chosen away from home, Diego went happily along with proceedings, never dreaming that he was cutting his own throat in doing so. There are only so many times you can twist a snake's tail before it turns around and bites you.

Seven days later in Genoa, Diego Maradona played his last game for Napoli in a 4-1 drubbing by champions-elect Sampdoria, a sad irony being that it was against these same opponents whom Diego scored his first Serie A goal for the Neapolitans. Now, would be the last, a penalty hit with grim conviction into the bottom left-hand corner. To this day Maradona calls that, 'The saddest goal of my life.' Then, it happened, like a nuclear explosion ripping across the Southern peninsula, news broke that Diego Maradona had failed the drugs test administered the week before. Evidence taken from a Rome laboratory showed traces of cocaine in the player's urine. Sensing blood and seemingly desperate to dance on Maradona's grave, the Italian authorities moved with rapid haste in handing out an immediate suspension. His true enemy had at last surfaced, only then did Maradona come to understand the full extent of the conspiracy waged against him.
Snakebite.
The lightning speed of events and the cold, calculated manner in which they unfolded bore all the traits of a traditional Camorra style sting. Without a blessing from the Giulianos' and other influential families, such an audacious *Coup d'état* would never have been undertaken. That it was allowed to occur meant they too had washed their hands of him. What use a lousy cokehead? Diego Maradona was alone, for the first time Naples must have felt like a foreign city. Friends became strangers overnight. Those who once fell at his feet proclaiming, 'Ti amo piu che I miei figli' ('I love you more than I love my children'), now looked at him with nothing but contempt. Aware that this unseen foe would never stop until he was ran out of town, Maradona decided to grant them their wish. The fairytale was over, it was time to go home.

'Vedi Napoli e scappa' (See Naples and run away).
In the early hours of Sunday 1st April 1991, the distant drone of a small jet engine was heard over the beautifully lit up bay of Naples. On board was a tearful Diego Maradona, his family and a small huddle of lifelong Argentinian companions whom had remained loyal to the end. He came from the heavens in the blazing glare of the Neapolitan sunshine and left like a thief in the night under cover of dark. Against a sleek black sky glistening with stars Maradona made his getaway.

The next day at the San Paolo, a spontaneous gathering took place of the Napoli players and backroom staff. All were upset, none more than Gianfranco Zola who broke down in tears and had to be consoled by Ciro Ferrara. The young Sardinian had lost not just a team-mate, but mentor also. Speaking from the heart Zola claimed that, 'It would be difficult to wear that shirt.' Word spread quickly of the King's abdication. In years to come, when fathers related to son's incredulous tales of Maradona's exploit's during the glory days, how it all came to end would surely haunt them forever. The realisation that they would never again see him in a blue shirt suddenly hit home.
'My God,' exclaimed a grief-stricken tifosi.
'What have we done?'

CHAPTER TWENTY-THREE

EPITAPH

On Monday 2nd August 2004, SSC Napoli were officially declared bankrupt and ceased to exist. It appeared San Gennaro had finally lost patience with his Neapolitan flock. No more deadlines, the club was wound up and the San Paolo gates draped in chains. A door slammed shut on seventy-three years of rich history soaked in passion and unrelenting drama. How could this have been allowed to happen? Only four months previous in Buenos Aires, hundreds staged an all-night candle-lit vigil outside the Suizo medical clinic, faces etched in grief, old ladies, children, men, young and old, hoping for a miracle. A priest arrived to administer the last rites but was ushered away by the crowd. They were not yet ready to give up on their boy. A man received a call on his cellphone and yelled out, 'He is going!' Suddenly, all around people fell to their knees and began to pray for the soul of Diego Armando Maradona. Couldn't live together, lost souls apart.

Just six years after Maradona vanished into the Naples night never to return, Napoli were relegated from Serie A for the first time since 1964. Somehow, it had all felt so predictable as years of wanton abuse, mismanagement and outright corruption left a once proud club in ruins. Still the star players had been bought in a vain attempt to appease their fanatical support, but all failed in comparison, for the small, if monumental shadow of Diego Maradona hung like a colossus over the San Paolo. Those who even dared to dream of following in such footsteps were simply wasting their time. Maradona's dynasty was beyond compare and out of reach to mere mortals. It was like throwing a bucket of water at a lightning bolt. Much as Napoli fell apart on the pitch, behind the scene chaos also reigned as the financial status of the club soared out of control. The fortunes earned from the Maradona era were ripped off mercilessly. The debt was close to being out of control and constantly rising.

SSC Napoli had been nothing more than a money-making machine for Camorra overlords, whom when success dried up, washed their hands of it and looked elsewhere to plunder. The players who brought so much success were sold off. As expected Albertino Bigon did not hang around and the Neapolitans hired a promising young coach from Caligari called Claudio Ranieri. With lawyers demanding wages for their clients/players in the dressing room and bankers threatening to pull the plug at any moment, Ranieri fought a courageous fire-fighting campaign to keep Napoli's head above water. The President, who still possessed in his head wild delusions of grandeur deemed this insufficient for a club of their stature and promptly sacked a stunned Ranieri. Marcello Lippi was lured from Atalanta. Lippi was already viewed in Italy as a master tactician and he led Napoli to a UEFA Cup spot. Suitably impressed, Juventus then pounced to snatch him from Naples' grasp. From that moment it became a matter of time. The path to Purgatory had begun.

During the initial early years following Maradona's departure, Napoli remained on the pitch competitive in Serie A, finishing sixth and seventh in the 1993-94 and 1994-95 seasons respectively. This was largely thanks to a talented crop of players, which had been bolstered by the exciting Uruguayan midfielder Daniel Fonseca and talented youngster's Naples born Fabio Cannavaro and Calabrian midfielder Benito Carbone. Unfortunately, the financial meltdown behind the scenes was boiling over. President Ferlaino's disastrous attempts taking on the North had left the club in dire straits. With the pressure overwhelming from the tifosi he finally, reluctantly stepped down in 1993, after twenty-four years at the helm. Only returning a year later to save Napoli from insolvency. Ferlaino's heart when it came to the football club could never be faulted, just his head for business. To stay afloat a fire sale had to be organised with their best assets sold. The great hope for the future, Gianfranco Zola, who carried the dreams of the next Neapolitan generation was sacrificed and transferred to Parma. Though not wanting to go, Zola was left with little choice when explained to him that if he did not leave Napoli were out of business. Thus, tearfully he packed his bags. Zola's move was one that incensed the already bleeding tifosi who blinded by despair turned once more with a vengeance on their President. Again, a weary, battle-scarred Corrado Ferlaino was forced to check under his car every morning. Though hardly a saint, Ferlaino, like the Captain of the Titanic appeared determined to stay on board as Napoli slipped ever further under the waves. He was afflicted. Blind love makes you do foolish mad things. Amore. Joining Zola, youngster Fabio Cannavaro also left for Parma, whilst another of Napoli's favourite son's Ciro Ferrara followed head coach Lippi to Juventus in 1994. Next to depart off the wage bill was Benito Carbone to Inter a year later. These moves only served to confirm what Napoli tifosi dared not admit. The balance of power had shifted back to the North. It was like the Maradona era had never existed.

Their form in the first half of the 1996-97 season offered a slight reprieve when the newly-appointed, former player Luigi Simoni guided them into second place after fourteen games. However, enthusiasm was soon dampened by a dramatic downturn in form and the departure of Simoni, who was jettisoned after a furious President Ferlaino discovered the coach had a pre-arranged agreement to join Inter at the end of that season. Pride in both his club and City, saw Ferlaino feel betrayed by Simoni, so he duly sacked him. Youth coach Vincenzo Montefusco stepped in as the freefall continued unabated. Napoli won just two of their last sixteen games, finishing four points above the relegation zone. A close call. Neapolitan's fatalistic approach to life and their football team meant few saw hopes of improvement and they were right to do so.
Come the 1997-8 season, it turned critical. Some of the scorelines were beyond embarrassment. A horrific 5-0 reverse at Empoli, 0-4 at home to Parma, 6-2 away to Roma, 5-1 at Bologna and 6-3 by Sampdoria in Genoa. It was wretched. Worse was yet to come. Much to the tifosi's anger and disbelief, Ferlaino once more was forced to shed their finest talents as the debt again threatened to throttle them. Napoli were being strangled to death. Three of the best players were sacrificed. The popular Southern born midfielder Fabio Pecchia went to champions Juventus, the exciting Brazilian winger André Cruz to Milan, and the talented French international Alain Boghossian joined Sampdoria. These now gone, the heart of Napoli's team had been ripped out. To add fuel to an already raging fire, a panicking Ferlaino went through four different coaches and thirty-three players.
It was beyond a joke.

An embarrassing, torrid campaign ended with just two wins and fourteen points. Neapolitans spoke of biased referring decisions, faceless enemies in the North plotting to bring them down, but this was a Napoli team hardly in need of such conspiracy theories for they were quite capable of doing it themselves. The unthinkable had become reality. It was just a question of when and where. Relegation arrived in Parma on 15th April 1998, and total desolation descended on Naples when a 3-1 defeat confirmed their drop into the uninhabitable backwaters of Serie B. After 33 consecutive years in Serie A, and just eight on from their second Scudetto, Napoli were down.

Marooned, a giant blue whale beached alone on a sand teeming with termites slowly being eaten away. Neapolitan sadness was matched only in feeling by the spontaneous outbreaks of partying breaking out in Milan, Turin and Verona. They had longed to witness the back of these Southern Terroni, watch them squirm in their lowest hour. The hatred was such that celebrations erupted in the North, the likes of which had not been seen for years. Arriverderci Napoli! See you in fucking hell! After two years of footballing misery, the Neapolitans under coach Walter Novellino, were promoted back. In May 2000, amidst wonderful scenes of new-found optimism, SSC Napoli returned to Serie A. Horns from ships moored in Naples harbour blared out in triumph. Sadly, it was to be just a fleeting return to the top table as the drama at this most operatic and tragic football clubs carried on all guns blazing.

With little option President Ferlaino was forced to push up on the poisoned throne and a new face now sat alongside him in the boardroom. Cruel, false hopes for the long-suffering Napoli tifosi appeared in the manner of Rome born media magnet/entrepreneur Giorgio Corbelli, whom had purchased a fifty percent stake in the club to become joint power broker with Ferlaino. He promised a return to the great old days, of making impossible dreams come true. Neapolitan weren't impressed, too much had gone on and besides, the only one capable of making Corbelli's words sound even remotely true had long left town years ago. There were no fond farewells, more good riddance and fuck you from both sides. No, when it came to SSC Napoli these day it was simply a shrug of the shoulders and shake of the heads. The tifosi had lived the dream and it appeared for how they had ultimately treated their king, the punishment was to endure a living nightmare with their beloved club.

As if content to let Corbelli take a little heat, Ferlaino deferred to sacking the man who had dragged them clear of the Serie B swamp mire, Novellino. In his place came the much-travelled coach known for attacking football, the Czech Zdeněk Zeman. Money was found for a host of exciting players and recruited for Zeman. Striker Nicola Amoruso, wing-back Marek Jankulovski and the return of past favourite Fabio Pecchia. Told by Corbelli to entertain the Napoli masses, Zeman stuck to his well-known attacking principles even when results were bad. It proved a truly disastrous appointment and short-lived and he was fired only six games into the season. No wins, fourteen goals conceded, including five at the San Paolo against Bologna. Ferlaino allowed himself a little smile as the tifosi turned their attention for a while on a red faced Corbelli. Next time around the Presidents' changed tact and turned to the no-nonsense approach of Emiliano Mondonico, a coach whose tactics contradicted wildly to what Corbelli had promised the Napoli tifosi. 'Another fucking fraud' they murmured about their new joint President. Mondonico was renowned for performing minor miracles elsewhere and had famously led Torino to a UEFA Cup final in 1992. Sadly, for all concerned minor miracles were not enough under the volcano. There had been too much poison poured into the well.

In a desperate last throw of the dice, come January, two attacking Brazilian forwards were brought in on loan. The devastating Edmundo from Santos and the clever striker Amauri of Parma. This swiftly backfired with Edmundo injured on his debut and side-lined long term, leaving Amauri left fighting a lone, losing battle up front. No class, no hope, no redemption. To most Neapolitan's real surprise, Napoli were again relegated on the last day after an extraordinary finale saw six teams separated by just two points. Tragically, after just one season in which old acquaintances were made with at times gruesome consequences, both on and off the pitch, they fell once more. A heinous lack of funds for Ferlaino and Corbelli to pay or even buy players proved too much of a cross to bear.

It had become clear to see now that Napoli were dying.

Diego Maradona's harrowing, turbulent journey through the Nineties was an even more self-destructive path than that taken by the Neapolitans. After testing positive for cocaine in his system, FIFA acted swiftly in handing out a fifteen-month ban from all competitive football. Returning home to Buenos Aires, a depressed Maradona fell back into old habits and on 26th April 1991, only three weeks after fleeing Naples, in an extraordinary incident shown live on Argentinian television, he was dragged away in handcuffs by plain clothes officers from a friend's apartment into a waiting mass of cameras. Police officials said their drug investigation was aimed at two of Diego Maradona's friends, Ricardo Ayala and Jorge Perez. Whilst Ayala's apartment was being watched, Maradona made visits on consecutive days before the arrests. Appearing still in a drug-induced haze and trying desperately to avoid being photographed, he sheltered his eyes from a blinding barrage of paparazzi flashing only inches away. Several bags of cocaine it was claimed was thrown out of the window as officers entered. A blatant set-up with the media circus receiving a tip-off well in advance of the arrest. Somebody, somewhere wanted him grinding into the dust. The appearance in court was again a sensational news story as this fallen star awaited his fate. A lenient judge Amelia Barres De Vidal, ordered Maradona to seek treatment and placed him under medical supervision whilst he quit the drug. For two painstaking years he battled against the addiction and for a time looked to have exorcised his demons to such an extent that when the playing ban expired, a surprising old 'friend' resurfaced asking for help. Unbelievably, SSC Napoli made a last-gasp move to stave off the coming storm by prising him back to Naples.

'Napoli soccer has not forgotten it's great champion,' claimed President Corrado Ferlaino. With a remarkable rehashing of recent history Ferlaino attempted to attain the moral high ground by claiming Diego had to return and complete his contract. In Naples, the President was under immense pressure from his volatile tifosi. He knew more than any of their penchant for unremitting hostility if the cause required. A notorious reputation had reached ferocious new heights as Napoli struggled against their impending doom. The disaster that had befallen them was blamed entirely on the shoulders of their supremo. For Corrado Ferlaino, if it meant going cap in hand to his greatest enemy to avoid the wrath of his blood clan, so be it. The alternative was unspeakable. If Ferlaino thought Diego Maradona had even vague thoughts about returning to a place that nailed him to the cross he was sorely mistaken. Instead, for the second time in his career Maradona was Spain-bound.

Famed for it's splendid orange groves, the beautiful Southern city of Seville became Diego's showpiece home for a short period whilst he portrayed his God-given gift for wreaking mayhem in foreign ports. It was a disastrous time for all concerned. Convinced by Seville coach and former Argentinian guru Carlos Bilardo that it was the right move he crossed the water but simply never settled. Indeed, his time in Seville is remembered more for an infamous incident when Maradona indulged in a spot of team bonding and treated his new compadres to a night of debauchery at a notorious local brothel. Also, well-publicised fisticuffs in a nightclub that ended with a wild west-type free-for-all signalled it was not meant to be. A paltry four goals in twenty-six appearances was a poor return for a $7 million investment. Both sides were glad to be rid.

Returning home, Maradona found himself followed everywhere by eager photographers desperate to capture him up to no good. Buenos Aires became a prison. In order to recharge his batteries, he retreated out of sight to a country home in Moreno where for a while peace broke out in the crazy world of Diego Maradona. Sadly, they soon found him and under severe pressure and feeling the strain, Diego finally snapped. A posse of paparazzi had gathered outside the main gates. After asking them to leave and they steadfastly refusing, all hell broke loose. Their constant shouts of 'Diego, Diego, Diego, Diegooo' driving him to distraction. The main in question decided enough was enough. Taking cover behind a car with an air rifle he began taking pot-shots at the unwanted guests. With an aim unerring, Maradona wreaked mayhem, ensuring the next month of headlines on the front of every Argentinian newspaper. Only intervention by an old ally, President Carlos Menem, and massive public support allowed him to escape jail, paying only a large fine for injuries caused. In reality, they would never have dared putting him behind bars for if you took on 'El Diego' in his own backyard you risked revolution.

On 5th September 1993, Argentina suffered the most humiliating defeat in their history. In a vital World Cup qualifier, a 5-0 thrashing by a brilliant Colombian side at their own Monumental stadium, left the 77,000-fanatical home crowd stunned. The men from the mountains of Bogotá and Medellin administered on their aristocratic neighbours the mother of all beatings and delighted in doing so. It was a result that left them struggling to qualify for the Finals. As Carlos Valderrama and Faustino Asprilla ran riot, a familiar chant resonated across the terraces. The crowd began to call for the return of their hero. 'Maradona, Maradona' thundered loud. It was a desperate plea for help. Only one man could save them from disaster. Forever the patriot, he was unable to ignore such a passionate call to arms. On 17th November 1993, although looking a sad shadow of his former self, Maradona led his nation to an uninspiring 2-1 play-off victory over Australia, clinching a place in USA '94. By that time, he was home playing for provincial club Newells Old Boys. Maradona claimed it was a return to his roots, but a $25,000 sum paid monthly into a bank account by Old Boys President Senor Cattaneo, no doubt proved a powerful sweetener. Again, disturbing whispers emerged regarding Diego's health. In just a few months his weight plummeted, the excess fat disappearing at an alarming rate, the face gaunt. The official word was that Diego had undertaken a strict diet with the result he was now far healthier in both body and spirit. The truth as ever was much darker and that summer in North America, Maradona would be found out in front of the entire world.

In Boston, on 29th June 1994, Diego Maradona's world was rocked like never before when it was confirmed traces of the banned substance ephedrine had shown up in his urine and he was being thrown out of USA '94. Argentina had just beaten Nigeria to secure qualification for the second-round phase of the World Cup. Maradona had played astonishingly well, too well for someone of his ageing thirty-four years. FIFA officials had already chosen him to undergo the post-match drugs testing, a drawing of lots picking out Diego's number ten shirt. Suspicions were aroused after the Argentinian's first game against Greece, when the Captain scored a wonderful goal, a typically sublime one-two before shooting devilishly past a stunned Greek goalkeeper. His celebrations caused raised eyebrows around the world as he raced up to a pitch-side television camera and with eyes bulging roared out a death-defying yell. Some called it sheer relief, a reaction to those who sneered that he, 'Maradona' was all washed-up. A busted flush. Others claimed he appeared possessed with demons in his soul, whilst the vast majority of football supporters simply watched on in amazement, mouthing, 'What the fucking hell is he on?'

Once again in the world of international football Diego Maradona had become a pariah, a disgraced figure. His many enemies given fresh ammunition to fire their bullets. At a press conference to give his side of this sad, sordid tale he lashed out, 'They have cut off my legs.' A thinly veiled attack on FIFA and it's dictatorial style Presidency. Years before in the run up to Italia '90, Maradona had caused Sepp Blatter great embarrassment when he alleged that World Cup draws were pre-arranged. In his mind what happened in the USA was payback time, a theory to this day in Argentina and most of the Third World believe as fact. When news of the ban was announced, tens of thousands took to the streets protesting in far off places such as India's New Delhi. For Diego Maradona was the idol of an underclass scrubbed off a post-modern American-driven world map. A God to those who lived in shanty towns, bare foot, poverty-stricken, who watched his goals on battered television beside open sewers. Victims of changing times where materialism was all that mattered. Their cruise missile against oppressors far too powerful to be hurt by slingshots. From Naples' ancient labyrinth of hidden alleyways to the backstreets of downtown Cairo, these were the people who cried when news broke that Maradona had once again been brought to his knees.

Despite being handed yet another agonising fifteen-month FIFA playing ban, and scribes worldwide penning Maradona-related footballing obituaries, the player himself steadfastly refused to step out of the limelight. The adulation was like a drug that without it he would simply wither and die. To the utter dismay of the Argentinian football hierarchy, Diego decided to try his hand at becoming the greatest manager ever. Fuelled with a

burning desire to succeed, Maradona failed in truly spectacular fashion, first as coach of lowly, struggling first division side Deportivo Mandiyu, then, in charge of Club Racing. Both terms lasted together no longer than six months but proved entertaining mayhem as he collected a bevy of touchline bans and fines for speaking his mind in a manner hardly suitable for a living legend. This was Maradona, no hidden agenda or banal clichés, everything flowed from the heart. A fierce passion for football that at times, more than was healthy threatened to explode. One particular discerning rant about a referee he memorably referred to as a 'Gutless coward with no balls,' was pretty typical of what occurred, as Diego went down all guns blazing. As disasters go it took some beating. Frustrated at every turn by the inability of players to carry out set instructions, due to the fact that many were overawed by his sheer presence, or mostly just not good enough, Maradona simply lost interest and instead vented anger at 'Enemies' in the establishment, who sought by any means to bring him down. Forever plotting, scheming, waiting for an opportunity to twist the knife deep. Finally, realising football management was not for him, he turned to another field where his particular, persuasive talents might be of better use.
Politics!
With him at the helm Maradona dreamt of a worldwide international players' union, one that stretched across oceans, over mountains, for rich and poor. All would have their say, a democratic vote. It would be a mighty stick to fight back against the autocratic heavy-handedness of FIFA. Take the game back from the faceless ones. Those who forced them to perform like slaves in the blazing heat of Mexico 86 at twelve noon, all for the sake of television

companies. The players were the artists who sweated blood and tears, they should set the rules. He sent messages to top footballers across the globe urging them to join him in Paris, where at the elegant surroundings of Hotel Le Meridien, this brave new venture would begin. And come they did; Eric Cantona, Gianluca Vialli, George Weah. Others such as Hristo Stoitchkov and Paul Gascoigne contacted Maradona pledging help. Those who actually showed up offered moral support for the Argentinian's noble, if somewhat spontaneous idea. None more than Manchester United's Cantona, who at the time was serving a nine-month ban for karate-kicking a Crystal Palace supporter, who HAD made the dreadful mistake of insulting the volatile Frenchman's mother. Unfortunately, events did not go as planned. A press conference hoisted jointly by both Maradona and Cantona swiftly became prickly, two egos so large that France itself, never mind the conference suite of the Le Meridien would not have proved large enough. As Cantona spoke in philosophical tones of the grand merits of their scheme, Maradona became bored and asked his new-found compadre if he was going to go on all afternoon? Needless to say, the atmosphere soured, and well before the moon shone over the Seine, Diego was off enjoying all the hospitality Parisian nightlife had to offer. This footballing utopia for brothers from the Soweto townships to Madrid uniting together never again saw the light of day. For the bright lights of Paris were calling Maradona. Nothing came before a party.

Shortly after, yet another ill-fated, but highly emotional comeback occurred. This time with Boca Juniors, the club of Diego Maradona's heart. It proved again calamitous as his ballooning weight saw him reduced to an almost comical figure in the eyes of those whose love was not blind. As a child he wished only to wear the famous blue/yellow shirt of Boca, setting fire to La Bombonera with wonderful goals. He would daydream of receiving the ball, skimming a defender, through the legs of another, before soaring into the penalty area and flashing an unstoppable drive that burst the net. The crowd would rise and chant his name, 'Maradonnna!' This Diego had already experienced, but as his thirty-seventh birthday dawned, he could only once more fantasise about such moments. A horrendous sequence of missed penalties and truly embarrassing performances stretched the patience of even the most passionate fan. When he again failed a post-match dope test with traces of cocaine found, few were surprised. On 24th August 1997, it was officially announced and as ever the usual tired, dreary excuses were dragged up by the player's entourage, who lived off his back, picking up scraps, stealing a living. Those who really cared about him, who remembered with tears in their eyes, the fresh-faced kid from Villa Fiorito casting spells on a football pitch, prayed he finally sorted himself out. Sadly, it was not to be. A leading Argentinian Specialist Doctor, Ricardo Grimson became appalled at his refusal to curb the white powder. In an effort to shock and bring him to his senses Grimson broke the news that 'Maradona could die at any moment if he does not quit.' Sadly, a deluded Diego carried on.

'Gods don't die,' they told him. Just one more hit, then another, then …

Three years later, in January 2000, Diego Maradona felt the first larcenous tap of death upon his ever-widening shoulders. As a result of cocaine binges whilst partying in the Uruguayan holiday resort of Punta Del Este, he suffered what was first feared a fatal heart attack. When the grave news reached Argentina, people sobbed openly, it was feared only hours before they lost their most beloved son. For a short time as doctors fought to revive him, his heart actually stopped for twenty seconds, and legend goes in Naples, at that moment Mount Vesuvio rumbled. Neapolitans were devastated; it appeared their boy was mortal after all. Past grudges were forgotten in an instant, for was he not their treasure of San Gennaro? Remarkably, showing amazing powers of recovery Maradona came back. This was one bright light Diego refused to go towards. Only a week later, he was sat up in bed earning a hundred thousand dollars for giving an interview telling of his close shave with 'The Beard' (Maradona's pet name for God). After just ten days in a Montevideo hospital, Maradona was deemed well enough to be flown home by private jet and continue his recuperation at the Sacred Heart clinic in Buenos Aires. Doctor Carlos Alvarez who oversaw the treatment was alarmed at the extent to which his patient's vital arteries had been damaged by cocaine. 'He has flirted with death,' exclaimed an emotional Alvarez, no doubt a football fan. 'Maradona's heartbeat is down to just 38 per cent. It is akin to pouring a kilo of salt down the throat of a person who has hypertension.' For Diego, this was beyond a sickness, the drugs had become a necessity to breathe. He would go to any lengths to acquire them. Matters came to a head when one night a notorious local dealer dressed as a doctor in a white coat was caught red-handed in his private room. Maradona claimed he was simply a childhood friend who had come to visit, but the truth was clear to all. His personal physician Alfredo Cahe knew they had to get out of Argentina or he would be dead within months. Cahe recommended Canada but an unexpected invitation saw them head towards the Caribbean.

Since the Cuban people's revolution of 1959, President, General and founding father of modern day Cuba, Fidel Castro ruled supreme. Even the United States of America, Castro's sworn enemy, whose mighty fist attempted many times to destroy him, had failed to bring about his downfall. No argument, it was Fidel's island. In the early summer of 1994, a fawning Diego Maradona was first introduced to his life-time idol. Both shared a similar political ideology, and despite being a generation apart, the coming years saw an unlikely but enduring friendship flourish. Any opportunity which arose for Diego to talk up the man he called with great affection, 'Il Commandante' was taken. 'I am proud to be a friend of the greatest man in living history.'

Such generosity of words was never forgotten by a man like Castro and in Maradona's darkest hours, he offered his hand. In a blaze of publicity, the Argentinian arrived in Cuba looking horribly overweight but still striding defiantly through the airport foyer. He showed off a tattoo of Castro's trusted legendary, Lieutenant Ernesto Che Guevara emblazoned upon his arm, himself a porteno. Speaking to waiting reporters Diego praised, 'The Dignity of the revolution.' Then, with tears in his eyes and voice cracking with emotion he opened up. 'Maradona does not want to leave this world. I want to live, watch my kids grow up, I vow to beat this sickness.' Alongside him were parents Dona Dalma, Diego Senior and the ever-faithful, suffering Claudia with both daughters. All were smiling, for it appeared the penny had finally dropped with their

boy. Chances of a happy ending suddenly looked a little rosier.
Welcome to Cuba!

The rehabilitation process began. For a while the wonderfully, tranquil atmosphere of the island appealed to Maradona. Convalescing west of the capital Havana, at a health farm, La Pradera, a specialist medical centre that dealt with those deemed untreatable elsewhere, his condition dramatically improved. Under a strictly controlled diet Diego slimmed down, lost two stone and looked to be winning the battle against cocaine addiction. Bizarrely, he even hinted at playing again for Argentina. 'It is true I wish to represent my country one last time. No matter what mistakes I have made with drugs, I am still Maradona. I am still El Diego.' It couldn't last. The inner demons returned and a late night head-on car collision with a bus outside Havana was heavily rumoured to have been caused by a coked-up Maradona losing control at the wheel. Driving on the wrong side of the road, it was a miracle he wasn't killed. Two strikes down, one left. Though denied vehemently by those around him the path to redemption appeared further away than ever.
Over in Naples, they watched with heavy hearts the tragic demise of their boy. In the Forcella where Maradona was loved like no other, he never really went away, for on every wall his face and name still lay lovingly adorned. Hand painted murals with heartfelt messages placed alongside them, one in particular catching a rare optimistic mood for this troubled, but totally charismatic city's, caustic outlook on life.
'The Sun always rises'.

Neapolitans prayed at night to deliver him from evil and back into their hands, let they be the ones to save his soul. It would be Naples' greatest victory. Whether it was simple yearnings for glories past or a guilty conscience at how he left them, a feeling existed that the time had come for reconciliation. For as Napoli languished in Serie B, close to extinction, littered with players not fit to clean Maradona's boots, everything became clear. Despite all that had occurred, it was without question a love supreme. Amore. Made in heaven, divorced in hell. Loved and hated, but how they missed him so.

Attempts were made to heal old wounds.

On 24th August 2000, amidst great pomp and ceremony, SSC Napoli retired their number ten shirt in honour of Diego Maradona. Also, they presented a request to Naples city council that the San Paolo stadium be renamed after their greatest ever player. The club acted on the back of daily newspaper Napolipiu that ran a huge popular campaign. Under intense pressure local politicians wasted little time passing the motion, before attempting to having it officially recognised by central government. Not all were for it. One local councillor Guilia Parenti broke ranks. 'I am full of admiration for Maradona as a footballer,' Mrs Parenti said. 'But his image is one full of both light and shadow. Also, he is still alive, and since we aren't in Iraq, we don't dedicate public buildings to living people.' Finally, it came down to an ancient seventy-six-year-old by-law dating back to the Mussolini era prohibited any public building being called after a person until they had been dead ten years. The despot 'Il Duce' returning from the grave to haunt them. Desperate to appease an infuriated populace, anxious councillors applied for special dispensation. Sadly, Rome was not in the business of helping out a city that viewed state taxes as simply an irritant to be ignored. To Naples' disdain the bill was eventually allowed, but only on the understanding it came into existence a decade after his departure from this mortal coil. Hardly cause for celebrations in Maradona's city. Also, an old acquaintance of Diego's, a certain lady, Cristina Sinagra, was asked her opinion of what should be done? 'From a sports point of view, I don't think I mind and Diego Jr is very keen. But from a human aspect, we would hope that rather than having a stadium named after him, Maradona might be able to go back to just being the great man that he once was.' Beware the biting satire of a Neapolitan woman scorned.

Later that same year, FIFA awarded both Diego Maradona and Pele a joint award as their best Player of the Millennium. The embarrassing truth for the authorities was that votes cast by the public had Maradona winning hands down and delivering a crushing victory to his Brazilian nemesis. An official FIFA internet poll showed overwhelming support for the Argentinian. This could not be allowed as those in power could never live down such humiliation. So, arrangements were made. A dubious 'Special Committee' of experts ensured Pelé tied in the final count, thus sharing the mantle.

On 11th December 2000, at a glitzy ceremony in Rome, the footballing establishment announced the results and few were surprised at the final outcome. To the bureaucrats' dismay Diego Maradona travelled from Cuba to accept his prize and the speech had them reaching for the tin hats! 'Grazie to the people who have voted for me. Grazie to FIFA who have listened to the opinions of the public for without them we are nothing. I dedicate this prize to the most famous Argentinian of all time, Ernesto Che

Guevara, to the Argentinian people and to my family.' His piece said, Maradona vacated the stage to polite applause from the suits' nothing more.

Across the globe in 'Diego's world' they were dancing in the streets.

Though few would ever have dared to admit at the time, there appeared an almighty rush to honour Diego Maradona's achievements whilst he was still round to appreciate it. An onslaught of plaudit's ensued from people whose lives were irrevocably touched and enriched by his extraordinary exploits on a football pitch. No more than on Saturday 10th November 2001, in Buenos Aires, where 60,000 packed out La Bombonera for the official Maradona tribute match. 'El dia de Diego,' (Diego day). It was a fiesta of an occasion at what Maradona himself always referred to as the 'Temple of football.' A huge flag draped lovingly over the terraces of Boca Juniors' stadium spoke for millions unable to be present. 'Gracias Diego'. The match itself was a mere sideshow to the love fest going on around Maradona, with the present Argentinian national team lining up against a Rest of the World XI. Higuita, Matthaus, Ferrera, Francescoli, Valderrama, Stoitchkov, Suker, Careca and Cantona. All threw away egos for a day to pay respects to the finest footballer of their generation. The star of the show performed one half apiece for both sides, his every touch cheered to the rafters as players from both side fell over themselves in a desperate attempt to let Diego score. Though a wretched weight problem was obvious to all, his redoubtable spirit meant he never gave up. This plodding, hapless figure being waved through by opponents, but still unable to produce the moment all in the Bombonera craved. Then, late on Maradona managed to convert a penalty past Colombian madcap goalkeeper Rene Higuita, whose well-meaning if rather obvious decision to dive the wrong way set the stadium alight. With tears rolling down his cheeks Diego took off an Argentinian top to reveal underneath a Boca shirt. Cue unadulterated scenes of mass hysteria! Everybody cried, even the referee. It was that kind of day. 'El dia de Diego.'

A familiar name appeared once more in the colours of SSC Napoli. In 1993, an Italian magistrate's court ruled beyond any doubt Diego Maradona was the father of his one-time girlfriend, as mentioned earlier, Cristina Sinagra's child. That he turned out to be a talented footballer deemed good enough to be taken on Napoli's books had Neapolitans whispering crazy talk of a messiah, a second coming. The enormous hype placed upon young shoulders was in total contrast to actual playing ability. He was good, but not that good. This was no 'Pibe De Oro' Mark II. Diego Senior refused point blank to admit from afar that this 'stranger' was of Maradona blood. He spat insults at any who dared to suggest otherwise.

'I never ever want to talk to anyone about that kid, ever.' On 20th May 2002, he was left with little option when the seventeen-year-old Diego confronted him on the course during a charity golf tournament in Fiuggi near Rome. Left with nowhere to run Maradona simply stared at this young lad whose features resembled so much his own. Then, whether angry, unimpressed or just simple overwhelmed, he panicked and fled. But the powerful notion of a son, after having been blessed with two daughters, appealed and later that day they did meet up. The two walked alone for an hour before embracing and promising to keep in touch. Whilst an overjoyed Diego Junior returned to

Naples, his Pop left for Buenos Aires and a soon-to-be third run-in with 'The Beard'. Once home he returned to type. Despite God granting him precious time to make peace with his boy, still Maradona appeared to have a death wish. Not content with just flying close to the sun, he flew into it, stoking fires, tempting, teasing the Grim Reaper to make his move. Endless white lines of cocaine tapped out and snorted, slowly destroying him. It couldn't go on, for nobody lived forever. Not even El Diego.

Epitaffio. the story ends. On Sunday 18th April 2004, a shockingly bloated, heavily sweating, forty-three-year-old Diego Maradona joined in the chants of the crowd for his beloved Boca Juniors from a VIP box in the Bombonera. The animated antics and gestures so typical of a man whose ailing heart continued to be worn outside his enormous stomach. So entertaining were Maradona's passionate rants and spontaneous bursting into song that most of the people who sat close by spent more time watching him than the actual match. The mood changed in an instant from joyful excitement to blind panic when Diego suddenly lost balance and fell to his knees. With prying eyes trying desperately to catch sight of their fallen hero, terror gripped those closest to him. Was this the end? As Maradona fought for breath an ambulance was called, and with sirens blazing, he was whisked away, swept at full speed through the hectic Buenos Aires traffic to the Suizo Argentina medical clinic. Amidst scenes of bedlam at the emergency entrance, a seemingly dying Diego Maradona was literally thrown into intensive care as concern heightened about his health. He was admitted with blood pressure, a swollen heart and, most worryingly of all, acute respiratory failure. A condition officially described as 'critical' by a sombre-faced hospital spokesman who also worryingly related, 'A feverish Diego Maradona has been heavily sedated and placed on a ventilator allowing him to breathe.'

As the devastating news swept through the capital, every television, radio and newspaper hurtled headfirst towards Suizo. Hospital security staff jostled with paparazzi, eager to capture the death throes of a king. Inside, doctors fought to stabilise Maradona. The situation appeared grim. His people swore it was not cocaine-related, but such words were meaningless considering what had gone before. Only a ghastly silence came from the clinic, no one was talking. Disturbing rumours he was already dead circulated amongst the mass crowds gathering outside, only to be immediately denied by the authorities. As the evening drew in, the night had never felt so long, dark and cold for Argentina. A nation was in turmoil. In an emotionally tear-stained show of unity hundreds joined hands to form a candle-lit vigil around the building. Together they prayed he would somehow find the strength to triumph once more over adversity and pull through. This was surely though one opponent even Diego's powers could not overcome? The unwanted appearance of a priest to administer the last rites was met with a hail of derision by Maradona's supporters. The man of the cloth was told with all great respect that he was not welcome, for they were not yet ready to give up on their boy.

Monday dawned and as Buenos Aires swung into life, every vehicle of any description that drove past the clinic on Pueyrredon Avenue carried the Argentinian flag and honked it's horn in a 'Good luck' gesture.

One flag read. *'Diego, Argentina needs and adores you. Don't go away'.*

Another was from a people who though far away were there in spirit.

'From Naples with Love'. Never was Scopa needed more. Further bad news emerged from inside when it was announced that Maradona had developed a serious lung infection to hamper even further his chances of recovery. Only family and close friends were allowed in to visit the stricken star. Such was the large numbers congregating around Suizo, police officers were forced to cordon off the entire area. His by then ex-wife Claudia Villafane, their two daughters, mother and father and, surprisingly, former business manager Guillermo Coppola, who had somehow wormed his way back into the clan's affections, were escorted through the wailing hordes who chanted constantly Diego's name. A small chink of light shone mid-morning when personal physician Alfredo Cahe claimed he was responding to treatment, though later that afternoon an official medical update threw cold water on such optimism.

'Maradona remains in a critical condition.'

Again, hopes waned. Finally, after a torturous three-day wait a heart-warming statement was released saying he was off the danger list but still faced a long stay on hospital. If what happened next was a miracle then the Almighty truly worked in mysterious ways, for after just a two-week recuperation, Diego Maradona fought back from the brink to declare himself fit enough to be discharged. It was an extraordinary recovery that left the Suizo medical staff perplexed and also dismayed for they knew there would be no next time. This was the last chance to get clean. When leaving, on asked by a huddle of disbelieving reporters as to his true health, a smiling Diego called out, 'Give me a ball and I'll show you I am well!'

Even after everything that Maradona endured, his laughing eyes still hinted at mischief. Once more he had slipped through the Reaper's desperately grasping fingers. Maybe God just didn't fancy sitting at the right hand of Diego Maradona? Who knows where the road will eventually lead? As Maradona bows out, his fate uncertain, few carry hopes of a rainbow's end. For sometimes it's just not meant to be. Three cheers for the bad guy as chances are we may never see his like again.

As for Napoli?
Neapolitans may well have been forgiven for thinking their patron San Gennaro had turned against them for how they had treated their own on earth messiah. In September 2001, the creaking, crumbling, once consecrated, concrete bowl of the San Paolo had to be shut down because of flooding. Thus, forcing the team to play home matches in minor stadiums across the South. With Maradona no longer real, just a mural painted on a Forcella wall. The San Paolo, a sea of tears and a team tumbling ever further down. In the boardroom, backstabbing, treachery and furore was once again in the air. After a bitter and much prolonged, public legal battle, Giorgio Corbelli and his new partner in arms, Naples born, hotel entrepreneur Salvatore Naldi, manipulated and bought out Corrado Ferlaino's shares in the club to take complete control. This time no way back for Ferlaino. Tired, emotionally drained he stepped away. No fanfare, no songs of praise, no fireworks lighting up the Naples night to say arriverderchi. Just 'Ciao Corrado, shut the fucking door on the way out. 'An emotional Ferlaino would later say, 'I have dedicated thirty-three years of my life to Naples and the memories

are thousands and special. But the memories must be placed: life always begins tomorrow morning.'

This great footballing tragedy continued when Corbelli was sensationally arrested in 2002. He and some associates were charged concerning the sale of 300 fake art paintings sold through his Telemarket TV shopping channel. Just days after on Saturday 16th March, SSC Napoli was put into the hands of administrators. The team coach Gigi De Canio speaking to Gazzetta Dello Sport, appeared almost resigned to the chaos when interviewed. 'Unfortunately, it's our destiny here that something new happens every day and we're experiencing a very unusual season.' A typically Neapolitan understatement. The administrator Gustavo Minervini was placed in charge for a year to establish whether there really was any hope, otherwise bankruptcy loomed. So, Napoli descended into an even further never-ending downwards spiral. Finally, they hit rock bottom. The last President standing, Salvatore Naldi simply could not afford to fund it anymore. On 2nd August 2004, the Civil Tribunal of Naples declared SSC Napoli bankrupt with debts totalling €79 million. The very existence now threatened. It there was going to be another miracle then it had to be now.

As the deposed king Diego simply refused to die, so it was that in true, dramatic Hollywood style, SSC Napoli were saved from extinction at the very last by one of their own. Just when it appeared San Gennaro had grown weary of the troubles and strife of his city's football team, a new saviour stepped forward to save their necks. Billionaire movie mogul, Aurelio De Laurentis, the cash-rich son of legendary film producer Dino, received the eternal gratitude of his blood kin by splashing out €34 million to own Napoli outright. Italian FA rules stipulated that any club in bankruptcy had five days to find a buyer. Also, if support was of sufficient size, they could begin again in Serie C1 (Third division), rather than have to scrape through the minefields of amateur leagues. Most importantly, banks would be forced to cancel any money owed. With massive debts this was a blessing from heaven. Suddenly, doubting Neapolitans realised their sacred San Gennaro had not forsaken them after all. For as Napoli's luck turned, he too appeared back on form! One who could tame lions, cure the dead, produce Maradona and bring about two Scudettos'. What price a few measly bankers? For was this not the City of Miracles? 'San Gennaro aiutaci tu.' Now and again their patron liked to remind his flock he was still around.

Welcome to Naples!

It was clear De Laurentis had done his homework, this was the richest owner since Achille Lauro, and arguably the most astute. Napoli had incredible potential, mouth-watering even. In the age of pay-per-view television and an estimated eight million supporters worldwide, maybe life did exist after Diego? Once more something special was stirring under the volcano. The canny Don Aurelio knew how to play the fiddle of his fellow Neapolitans. 'Naples has always been my heart, and we, my people, have suffered like no other. It is time to put Napoli back on top of the world.'

Music to the ears of a city that had all but given up hope. Players were brought in, seasoned veterans, promising local youngsters, all proud to wear that cherished light-blue shirt. They scraped off the dirt, dusted themselves down and began again! It was a fresh dawn, a clean slate that wiped away past failings. Aurelio De Laurentis christened his team, 'A new Napoli!' An astonishing 55,000 tifosi showed up at the San Paolo to witness their first game in the previously uncharted, murky depths of Serie C1. A banner on the Curva Sud ominously declared. 'Juve, we are coming to get you'.

This was no idle threat and all in Turin knew it. They shook their heads. 'Would these infernal Neapolitans ever go away?' The epic adventures of this glorious if tragic club goes on, but no matter what unfurls in further chapters of their history, the seven years of Diego Maradona will never be surpassed. For once upon a time in Naples, Maradona made dreams come true.

What finer epitaph could there possibly be?

EPILOGUE

CHAPTER TWENTY-FOUR

RETURN OF THE KING

(NAPLES 2005)

At first just a small speck over the Tyrrhenian sea, the plane carrying Diego Maradona back to his adopted city drew ever closer towards Naples shores. Any worries that Maradona may have laboured regarding his welcome were soon to be dispelled on landing, for awaiting his imminent arrival at Naples Airport were thousands of Napoli tifosi crowded inside the terminal building desperate for a first glimpse of their Diego. It had been a tumultuous twenty-one years since Maradona's original introduction by helicopter onto the San Paolo pitch, where mass hysteria had greeted his dramatic arrival. Now, amidst similar scenes of delirium he found himself again mobbed by well-wishers. Despite a flood of security and police surrounding him Diego was swiftly swallowed up in a mad sea of both over-enthusiastic media and Napoli supporters.

Bedlam reigned. Cameras flashed and blinded, a thousand voices screamed at once, people scuffled to grab a picture on their mobiles and reporters thrust microphones within inches of Maradona's face. Everybody wanted a piece of the stocky little figure with the huge wide grin, waving wildly and blowing kisses. As Neapolitans cried tears of joy, passing American backpackers gazed quizzically on at the unfolding madness.

From the airport, accompanied by ex-wife Claudia, Maradona was whisked away with a huge Polizia escort to a supposed secret location, but this being Naples, thousands already stood in wait outside the chosen hotel. Word had spread like wildfire across the bay and as Maradona's entourage grew closer the excitement began to rise. With sirens wailing and horns blasting for the locals to let them through it appeared an entire city had turned out to witness with their own eyes the legend that was Diego Maradona. Once safely inside the hotel Maradona headed straight towards a first-floor window, from where he personally led the adoring crowds in a mass Neapolitan communal sing-along. The classic terrace war songs were dusted down and given full justice by the older tifosi who had prayed for this day to come. Not just for the chance to say thank you to the man who made their dreams come true, but also for the new generation of Napoli support. Their children who had heard the tales and viewed the goals on television but never seen Maradona live. To them he was like a mythical ghost, someone who their parents had simply made up for bed time stories. The framed photograph that adorned the living room wall alongside the blessed painting of San Gennaro. Both treated with equal deference. Now, at last they could allow their sons and daughters to see Maradona in the flesh.
'Oh Mama, Mama, Mama'.
In the hours leading up to the game Maradona spoke in gushing terms of his former team-mate Ciro Ferrara, but also explained there was no chance of him playing in his upcoming testimonial. 'I am not playing because I can't manage it,' stated Maradona.
'I had a try but my knee is out of action and needs operating on. But tonight, I am going to be on the field

with my teammates to be close to Ciro Ferrara. He is leaving football, but he will not leave our hearts because he is a great man.'

A glittering array of stars from past and present was in Naples paying tribute to Ciro. Including amongst them were some of the biggest names ever to wear the shirts of SSC Napoli and Juventus. Antonio Careca, Salvatore Bagni, Gianfranco Zola, Zinidane Zidane, Bruno Giordano, Paolo Di Canio, Fabio Cannavaro, Allesandro Del Piero, Gigi Buffon, Gianluca Vialli and Pavel Nedved. In reality, there was only one man the Neapolitans couldn't wait to see.

It was a most wonderful evening for the return of a king!

On Thursday 9th June 2005, after a fourteen-year absence Diego Armando Maradona stepped once more onto the hallowed turf of the San Paolo stadium and 70,000 Neapolitans erupted in a cacophony of electrifying emotion. Flares exploded, igniting the black sky blood red. Fathers whom once fell in worship at his dancing feet held their sons high to catch a glimpse of the great Maradona. Amidst riotous scenes of acclaim set against a dramatic soundtrack of erupting firecrackers that both deafened and worried, Diego Maradona saluted those whom still adored the ground on which he walked. Watching on and cheering loudly as any of his fellow Neapolitans was Ciro Ferrara. Few would have blamed Ciro if he was annoyed at seeing his testimonial match reduced to a mere supporting role for Maradona's return but the truth lay in his heartfelt words. 'He is my gift to the people of Naples,' exclaimed an exuberant Ferrara. 'A present for the twenty years of my career.'

During the interval, to the San Paolo's wonderful surprise, Maradona took to the pitch and was handed a microphone. With tears in his eyes Diego addressed the crowd. A hush swept over the stadium. 'I want to thank Ciro who gave me the chance to come back to Naples, this city and people who have really missed me. – And I have missed you.' Cue mass emotional meltdown! 'Tonight, you have shown me that you have not forgotten about me, and for this me and my daughters thank you from ours hearts. Forza Napoli!' Everybody cried….

Surrounded by the usual frenetic, human melee Maradona's vain attempts at a lap of honour came to an abrupt halt. Though good natured the battery of photographers, cameramen and over-enthusiastic security men who swamped him appeared to irk the Argentinian. Finally, losing patience he broke free of the mad-cap posse and raced towards the terraces to be as one with the Napoli tifosi. After all the good times and bad, theirs' was a love like his that refused to die. As if to soak up the atmosphere and adulation Maradona stood for a second and closed his eyes. The healing was complete, now he was truly home.

A proud city, so poor, ravaged by poverty and unemployment but whose inhabitants lived every day as their last. Neapolitans never bowed to no one and refused utterly the rules of normal Italian society. For such cannot apply in a place that wakes every day praying their eternally brooding volcano doesn't blow them off the face of the earth.

These were Maradona's people and to this day Naples remains Maradona's city. For a short time, he helped them forget their daily plight and for that they will always be truly grateful. Nobody before or since has come remotely close to entering their hearts like him and will never do so.

Diego Maradona came from the sky promising miracles and kept his word.

CHAPTER TWENTY-FIVE

A LIFE TRULY LIVED

On Wednesday 5th July 2017, exactly thirty-three years since Diego Maradona first arrived in Naples, he returned to the city to be made an honourable citizen. On the day electronic banners were placed at every bus stop of the city to show a greeting that read 'Ben tornado Diego'. ('Welcome back, Diego'). As expected, local media coverage of the event was all consuming. The sports papers produced special editions, whilst the Regional TV station Canale 21, renamed Wednesday, 'Maradona Day'. In 1984, 70, 000, Neapolitans had crammed into the San Paolo for his unveiling to begin an outrageous love affair of momentous highs and savage lows. Happily, years tended to make the bad times fade and people's thoughts in Naples lingered only on the glory days. Diego's legacy for what he achieved back then remains across the city in the manner of many lovingly painted murals and tenderly kept shrines. Bottles of his tears on display in café bars alongside a signed shirt, a playing photo and of course accompanying the all-seeing San Gennaro. Devoted love letters to their king scrawled on endless walls. Back in 1991, he may have been forced to flee by private jet, a hapless Cocaine addled mess and broken physically, but Maradona's soul remained. Tainted maybe, but forever visible on any walk down a Naples back-alley. Look, right or left and you would see him. Staring back in the prime of youth. Smiling, hidden in his laughing eyes the secrets of those long-gone days. If only they knew!...
On the eve of the ceremony, fifty-six-year old Diego Maradona spoke of his feelings at a press conference.

'Tomorrow, I will become a citizen of Naples and I thank the council for doing this, but I have been a citizen ever since the first day I wore the number 10 shirt for Napoli. I thank my team-mates, without whom I wouldn't be here today and we wouldn't have won all that we won. I dedicate this citizenship to my mother, my father and all the Neapolitans. Tomorrow will be an unforgettable day for me. Many generations have passed since my time. Now, the Dads' have to find videos of my goals to play to their sons. Even the youngest kids know me in Naples and that makes me very proud.'

The ceremony took place at the Palazzo San Giacomo, Naples' City Hall and as was only to be expected turned into an emotional affair. Diego appeared genuinely touched. 'I thank the mayor Luigi De Magistris for putting me in the middle of all this, and I want to thank Naples because I travel all over the world and no one ever welcomed me as well as the Neapolitans.' As ever Diego could not help himself when it came to those discerning voices who claimed to give him citizenship was a disgrace upon the city. 'I also say thank you to those who didn't want me to become a Neapolitan citizen, because it proves that we can discuss anything in a democracy.'

The mayor De Magistris also spoke honouring 'El Diego'. 'Diego made the Neapolitan fans dream and then turned the dream into reality, so, he deserves honorary citizenship. You will stay our number 10 forever, you'll officially be a Neapolitan citizen. You, Diego, who are the greatest player of all time.'

Cue the curtain call to begin the rousing tributes to Maradona. Those who were young tifosi in the heady days now middle-aged, but the passion never left as the words to the songs flowed from their mouths. In typically mad, heartfelt manner, Maradona buttoned down his shirt, punched the air and joined in. All quickly escalated when he jumped onto the roof of his SUV sitting partially topless to be swarmed by adoring tifosi. 'Whoever doesn't cheer loud is a Juventus fan,' sang Diego, loud and from the heart. Security guards tried in vain to calm matters pleading with him to get back down on the pavement. Finally, he was away, but the night remained in it's infancy for Naples had not yet finished with their favourite son and latest citizen. Far more festivities remained as 10,000 Neapolitans awaited him in the Piazza del Plebiscito.

It began at 9.45pm, as a succession of local musicians took to the stage and paid homage to the one christened 'El Pibe de Oro'. Yet, the audience, though appreciating their efforts had come to see one man only and were growing restless. Chants of 'Diego, Diego' grew louder and more incessant. One too many singers, the last one found himself roundly, if unfairly booed just because he was through no fault of his own, not Maradona. The atmosphere was becoming rowdy in a way that only Naples could aspire too. Realising this the compere tried to appease the crowd, 'Don't worry, don't worry, Diego is here. You will see him soon.' Up went the cheers, their king was close.
Then,
Shortly, after 10.30pm, he made his entrance. Dressed in a black shirt and black suit, Maradona strode about the stage, waving, blowing kisses and soaking up the applause. His wide grinning face and tear-filled eyes projected onto the big screen behind him. A rendition of 'Oh, mama, mama, mama' broke out. Once upon a time in Naples, the song of

those times on the San Paolo terraces. Diego joined in with wonderful gusto leading the delirious mass chorus. Next over the PA system came Opus' 'Live is Life'. The legendary You-tube video clip of Diego dancing along whilst making the ball sing during a warm up against Stuttgart back in 1989. The lyrics belted out by an adoring audience many not even born when Maradona was lighting up the San Paolo with his God given talents. Tearing apart defences and sending the northern teams home humiliated and dazed. Oh, they had seen him on television and on their father's DVDs. Read a million words, heard the songs but now here he was. The man himself. Finally, the music ends and Diego was handed a microphone. Still they chanted his name until he began to talk, then a reverend hush fell across the Piazza.

'Nobody has ever loved me like you' he began. Diego spoke in detail about his love for the city and it's people. How proud he was to now be a citizen. The speech lasted for ten minutes and ended with the Argentinian declaring, 'Chi ama non dimentica.' 'He who loves does not forget.' Pure unadulterated madness broke out. A riotous display of acclaim for this man who had always been more Neapolitan than most Neapolitans. Now, he possessed a priceless piece of paper to prove it. Thirty-three years passing in the blink of an eye and how they still adored him so. Amore.

Past team-mates from the eighties glory days were called onto the stage one by one. Salvatore Bagni, Allesandro Renica, Bruno Giordano and Andrea Carnevale. Ciro Ferrara, who left Napoli for Juventus in 1994, was roundly jeered on appearing, despite Maradona beckoning for the crowd to stop. Ferrera smiled throughout. A son of Naples, he understood. With proceedings coming to a close there still remained time for a football to be hurled on stage from the crowd and the call went up for Diego to perform a few party tricks. Sadly, those expecting a grand display of ball-juggling were to be disappointed for a clearly close to tears Diego appeared in no mood. Instead, he just booted it back as a pile of hands leapt high to try and catch what would have been a perfect memento of the night Maradona came home. So, it ended, a last wave, one final half turn for a last singalong, then, gone. Vanishing from view. Five minutes later he was being whisked out of the square escorted with sirens blazing by a high-speed police cavalcade. Still the tifosi chasing into the Naples night determined to try and catch a last glimpse, for would they ever see him again?

A last stroll through Naples as this story finally ends. Past the shrine to Maradona at Bar Nilo, on Via San Biagio dei Librai, a short walk from City Hall, where the citizenship ceremony took place. In this a reliquary houses a lock of his hair. Another holds tears that it's claimed date back to 1991. The year it all went to hell. Maradona remains to be seen if not touched. Nowhere more than the giant mural of him painted on the end of a nine-storey housing block on the eastern outskirts of the city in Giovanni Teduccio. Known locally as the 'Bronx'. Painted by artist Jorit Agoch, the giant, head-and-shoulders work depicts a middle-aged Diego Maradona looking out across Naples. Beneath it the words 'Living God' scrawled. His beard heavily greying, eyes weathered, a life truly lived. Maradona, like the city whom have now officially adopted him lives for the moment, as tomorrow remains a distant dream. Today, Neapolitans still say their daily prayers to San Gennaro for Vesuvio to stay sleeping and 'El Diego' to keep safe. After all, he is one of them now. A love affair written in the stars and will be forever more.

Post Note:
On Sunday 22nd April 2018, Napoli won 1-0 in Turin against Juventus to go a point behind the Serie A leaders with just four games left to play. Mauro Sarri's brave, attacking, team had dominated throughout, but seemed to have run out of ideas and energy until the final minute when José Callejón's outswinging corner was met by the Senegal international, central-defender Kalidou Koulibaly, with a mighty header that left Gianluigi Buffon helpless. At the full-time whistle, Naples quite simply erupted in joy. Fireworks illuminated the bay. The streets and back-alley swiftly filled with jubilant Neapolitans as for the first time since the Maradona era they were in with a real chance of becoming champions. It's all set up to be a race to the finish. Prayers will be said, nerves shredded. Dare to dream? As this book goes to press the final scenario remains unknown. Whatever happens they had done their city proud this season. The only thing left to say is that within moments of the match finishing in Turin, Diego Maradona had logged onto his Facebook account and hammered in the phrase "Mamma miaaaa!!!" No finer way to end.

FINI

FIFTY QUOTES ON

DIEGO ARMANDO MARADONA

1: "People often ask me who was better, Maradona or Pele, but you can't compare the two. Pele scored goals, Maradona created them. Of course, Maradona scored goals as well but he created so many, not just with his passes, but by creating space for other players because the opposition would often put two or three players on him. His greatest moment came in the 1986 World Cup – people in England talk about the 'Hand of God' goal but his second was probably the best goal ever at a World Cup."
OSVALDO ARDILES

2: "When Diego scored that second goal against us, I felt like applauding. I'd never felt like that before, but it's true… and not just because it was such an important game. It was impossible to score such a beautiful goal. He's the greatest player of all time, by a long way. A genuine phenomenon."
GARY LINEKER

3: "The best of the lot, no question. In my generation, my era, he was simply the best. I saw Maradona do things that God himself would doubt were possible. He always had someone marking him, he always had someone hanging on to him, and yet he could still always conjure up wonderful pieces of magic. A genius." *ZICO*

4: "The best player I've seen in my life. He did things that didn't seem humanly possible. When he was on top of his

game, and even without training that much he was always in form, he was simply impossible to control. He decided matches alone, carrying average teams like Napoli, and Argentina in 1986, to glorious achievements. A genius."
MARCEL DESAILLY

5: On what the Gallaghers' were told by Maradona's interpreter at a party: "Maradona told me to tell you, if you leave with any of his bitches, he'll have you shot."
LIAM GALLAGHER

6: "I was very lucky to be his team-mate and get to play with him as well as watch him train every day. The things he did! He was and will always be unique. Off the pitch, I always liked his simplicity. He was Maradona, yet with the team, he seemed just like an ordinary lad like the rest of us. He didn't behave at all like a football star."
GIANFRANCO ZOLA

7: "With him on the ball, you didn't know where he finished and where the ball started."
JOSE MOURINHO

8: "If anyone inspired me, it was undoubtedly Maradona."
LIONEL MESSI

9: "Beyond everything else, no ball ever had a better experience than when it was at his left foot."
JORGE VALDANO

10: "Did he scare defenders? He scared absolutely everybody! You couldn't play against him."
JOHN BARNES

11: "The best player I've ever played against, miles ahead of anyone else. As you saw in the World Cup quarter-final in 1986, I just couldn't get near him – all I ever saw was his number 10! He had a low centre of gravity that shielded the ball, he had strength, pace and his passing was excellent. He also had a great leap for such a small man, as he showed with his Hand of God goal!"
TERRY BUTCHER

12: "In Argentinian football there is a before and after Maradona."
JULIO GRONDONA (President of Argentina FA)

13: "He was from another planet. He was different."
FRANCISCO CORNEJO (Maradona's youth coach)

14: "Maradona will always be the greatest."
ERIC CANTONA

15: "The greatest player ever. I played with him when he burst onto the international scene as a teenager but we'd all heard about him long before that. Phenomenally talented; just training with him was a joy."
RICKY VILLA

16: "Everyone has an opinion on Diego Armando Maradona, and that's been the case since his playing days. His magnificent performances and extraordinary goals at Mexico 86 will live forever in the memories of all football lovers, myself included. My most vivid recollection is of this incredibly gifted kid at the second FIFA U-20 World

Cup in Japan in 1979. He left everyone open-mouthed every time he got on the ball."
SEPP BLATTER

17: "Maradona left his mark on me, on my mind, especially in 1986 because he was sensational at that time. It's really at that moment that I became aware of the player he was, making differences as he did. He won games single-handedly. That's the extra thing he had over the other players. In 1986, he was on another level."
ZINIDANE ZIDANE

18: For Maradona to win a World Cup on his own, and let's face it, that's what he did as the rest of the team were ordinary, was an amazing achievement. He was the best player I've seen."
GLEN HODDLE

19: "I was always a big admirer of Diego Maradona. I think as a player he was an artist who had an incredible talent and for a long time he was the best player in the world."
JURGEN KLINSMANN

20: "The impressive thing about Maradona was his ability with the ball. He was very skilful and had great vision."
PELE

21: "The best player there has ever been, better than Pele. I watched him closely in Italy every week and he was at a different level to everyone else. Some of the things he did were unbelievable. He could control the ball without looking, which meant if the pass was on, he would take it."

RUUD GULLIT

22: "Diego Maradona was the best by far. For me he is the greatest player of all time."
RUDI VOLLER

23: "Maradona is the fastest player I've ever seen running with the ball, and he kept it perfectly under control. His pace was absolutely frightening, you just couldn't stop him. And he always got himself into positions where he could score."
SIR BOBBY CHARLTON

24: "Maradona was a fantastic player. Very fast, good dribbling, personality, good free kicks and high speed in the first 25 metres with the ball, not just without the ball, which is important."
LOTTHAR MATTHAUS

25: "Diego was capable of things no one else could match. The things I could do with a football, he could do with an orange."
MICHEL PLATINI

26: "For my generation, Maradona is the greatest player we've seen and I don't believe that will ever change."
PEP GUARDIOLA

27: "There's only one word for this man: genius. What he was able to do with a ball was not football, it was art. He was one of the best players ever seen. I also met him when he was only 21 and even then, I was shocked to see the level of the play he had."

GHEORGHE HAGI

28: "With Maradona you never knew exactly what you were going to get – quite simply one of the all-time greats. He was brilliant in whatever team he played for and could – and did – single-handedly turn games round. He was a born improviser."
EMMANUEL PETIT

29: "Maradona is a God to the people of Naples. Maradona changed history. In 80 years, we had always suffered, fighting against relegation, yet in seven seasons with him we won two leagues, a UEFA Cup, two Italian Cups. I'm a fan too and to live those years with Maradona was incredible. Being on the pitch when they won the Scudetto was amazing."
FABIO CANNAVARO

30: "Maradona is the best opponent I've ever played against in my career."
PAOLO MALDINI

31: "Maradona; when he was on form, there was almost no way of stopping him."
FRANCO BARESI

32: "I want to salute Diego Maradona because for me he has been, and always will be, football."
FRANCESCO TOTTI

33: Pele's my idol but I saw Maradona play. There's no question in my mind that he's the number one. He might have had his faults but he's shown on the pitch what real

football is all about. My dream is to play with him one day, if only for a few minutes. I learned a lot just by watching him play."
ROBERTO CARLOS

34: "A genius, a real artist, one of the greatest players in the world. He could win a match on his own. On his own."
SIR BOBBY ROBSON

35: "He's always been a street fighter, and I suppose that's the twist. Senna died very young, Amy died very young, and Diego is still going. You can't knock him down. When you knock him down, he bounces back. He keeps fighting."
ASIF KAPADIA (Film Director)

36: "Diego Maradona was special. I always enjoyed watching him, including everything he did even before the matches. He was the most playful; the one I liked the most in that sense of playing with the ball. Maradona could dribble at speed towards the goal. He had such a different technique from everyone else." *RONALDINHO*

37: "The best of all time, for me. Maradona was doing things that the rest were not able to do. Winning that World Cup in '86 was unique, the only time you can see a national team winning a World Cup practically because of one player."
GUS POYET

38: "In my eyes he is the best footballer ever. He is one of my heroes, if not the shining beacon when I was a kid. I

had all his videos. He was the player everyone wanted to be. He was the best. He was my idol and part of the reason why I started to play football. I can't hold him in higher esteem than that."
RIO FERDINAND

39: "It is arguable who is the best player in the world but without a doubt, he is in the best two or three."
SIR ALEX FERGUSON

40: "He's given us a lot of entertainment, to me personally and to everyone who loves good football. I'm a fan of Maradona's and I'll remain one till the end of time."
CARLOS VALDERRAMA

41: "The intellectuals criticised me- they said Napoli was a poor city and it was immoral. But it was my money, and I wanted to spend it that way. When I signed the contract in Barcelona, I went to a bar and ordered a whisky on the rocks. The waiter said to me 'Are you Italian? What a great deal we're getting out of this with Maradona, he's fat.' I didn't enjoy that drink at all." *PRESIDENT CORRADO FERLAINO*

42: "I've seen him play with the outside of his foot, instep, inner part of his foot, the backheel, the rabona, the bicycle kick. I've seen him do everything, every possible play imaginable, even the tunnel between the other player's legs."
CIRO FERRERA

43: "Maradona was the greatest player I ever played with."

MARIO KEMPES

44: "Maradona, turns like a little eel, he comes away from trouble, little squat man... comes inside Butcher and leaves him for dead, outside Fenwick and leaves him for dead, and puts the ball away... and that is why Maradona is the greatest player in the world!"
BRYAN BUTLER (BBC Radio)

45: "I asked myself, 'Who is this man? Who is this footballing magician, this Sex Pistol of international football, this cocaine victim who kicked the habit, looked like Falstaff and was as weak as spaghetti?' If Andy Warhol had still been alive, he would have definitely put Maradona alongside Marilyn Monroe and Mao Tse-Tung. I'm convinced that if he hadn't been a footballer, he would've become a revolutionary."
EMIR KUSTURICA (Film Director)

46: "And to think that before the World Cup people criticised me, saying Maradona wasn't qualified to be Captain and that he still had to prove himself. One month later he completely dominated the tournament. It was a huge step for him in terms of fame, and a great reward for his work."
CARLOS BILARDO

47: Before addressing a packed audience at the World Cup, South Africa 2010, Maradona clambered over reporters to bear-hug his friend and former Napoli team-mate Salvatore Bagni, who was working as a pundit at the tournament. 'Even knowing him as I have done all these years, Diego always does something to surprise you."

SALVATORE BAGNI

48: "Diego is great friend and very noble too. There's also no question he's a wonderful athlete and has maintained a friendship with Cuba to no material gain of his own."
FIDEL CASTRO

49: "He was my footballing hero. When I was young I tried to do the moves and score the goals he scored at Mexico 86. I've never admired any player as much as him."
RAUL GONZALEZ

50: "He's always been an idol. I wanted to emulate him when I started playing because of everything he did and conveyed out on the pitch. There's never been anyone better than him."
LUIS FIGO

Finally, one from the great man himself to finish.

"I worked hard all my life for this. Those who say I don't deserve anything, that it all came easy, can kiss my arse."
DIEGO ARMANDO MARADONA

Ciao Diego!

JOHN LUDDEN

@johnludds
www.johnludds@gmail.com

Made in the USA
Columbia, SC
19 May 2020